SHAKESPEARE SURVEY

ADVISORY BOARD

SHAKESPEARE SURVEY

AN ANNUAL SURVEY OF
SHAKESPEARIAN STUDY AND PRODUCTION

25

EDITED BY
KENNETH MUIR

CAMBRIDGE
AT THE UNIVERSITY PRESS
1972

Published by the Syndics of the Cambridge University Press
Bentley House, 200 Euston Road, London NW1 2DB
American Branch: 32 East 57th Street, New York, N.Y. 10022

© Cambridge University Press 1972

Library of Congress Catalogue Card Number: 49–1639

ISBN: 0 521 08528 4

Shakespeare Survey was first published in 1948. For the first eighteen volumes it was edited by Allardyce Nicoll under the sponsorship of the University of Birmingham, the University of Manchester, the Royal Shakespeare Theatre and the Shakespeare Birthplace Trust

Printed in Great Britain
at the University Printing House, Cambridge
(Brooke Crutchley, University Printer)

EDITOR'S NOTE

As previously announced, the central theme of *Shakespeare Survey 26* will be 'Shakespeare's Jacobean Tragedies'. This will include a retrospect by Clifford Leech, and the first of a series of articles on modern Shakespearian critics. The theme of Number 27 will be 'Shakespeare's Early Tragedies'. Contributions on that or on other subjects, which should not normally exceed 5,000 words, should reach the Editor (Department of English Literature, University of Liverpool, P.O. Box 147, Liverpool L69 3BX) by 1 September 1973. Contributors are asked to provide brief summaries of their articles and they should leave generous margins, use double-spacing, and follow the style and lay-out of articles in the current issue. A style-sheet is available on request.

K.M.

CONTRIBUTORS

NIGEL ALEXANDER, *Senior Lecturer in English Literature, University of Nottingham*

JOHN BARTON, *Producer, Royal Shakespeare Company, Stratford-upon-Avon*

MURRAY BIGGS, *Assistant Professor of Literature, Massachusetts Institute of Technology*

RICHARD DAVID, *Publisher, Cambridge University Press*

GARETH LLOYD EVANS, *Senior Lecturer and Staff Tutor in Literature, Extra-Mural Department, University of Birmingham*

MICHAEL JAMIESON, *Lecturer in English Literature, University of Sussex*

MARY M. NILAN, *Professor of English Literature, St John's University, New York*

DAVID ORMEROD, *Lecturer in English Literature, University of Western Australia*

ROGER PRIOR, *Lecturer in English Literature, Queen's University, Belfast*

RICHARD PROUDFOOT, *Lecturer in English Literature, King's College, University of London*

JEANNE ADDISON ROBERTS, *Professor of Literature, The American University, Washington, D.C.*

GĀMINI SALGĀDO, *Reader in English Literature, University of Sussex*

NORMAN SANDERS, *Professor of English Literature, University of Tennessee*

ANN PASTERNAK SLATER, *St Hugh's College, Oxford*

R. L. SMALLWOOD, *Fellow of the Shakespeare Institute, University of Birmingham*

SIDNEY THOMAS, *Professor of English Literature, Syracuse University*

SARAH C. VELZ, *Austin, Texas*

HERBERT S. WEIL, JR, *Professor of English Literature, University of Connecticut*

R. A. YODER, *Brookline, Massachusetts*

CONTENTS

PLATES

Plates I and II are reproduced by permission of the Theater Collection, New York Public Library; Plates III–VIII are reproduced by permission of the Governors of the Royal Shakespeare Theatre

THE PROBLEM PLAYS, 1920-1970:
A RETROSPECT

MICHAEL JAMIESON

A survey of attitudes since 1920 towards Shakespeare's Problem Plays or Dark Comedies, *Troilus and Cressida*, *All's Well That Ends Well* and *Measure for Measure*, invites two observations neither of which would be true of any other Shakespearian group. First, the plays – particularly *Measure for Measure* and *Troilus* – have undergone a revaluation so radical as to amount to a rediscovery, and this re-assessment itself reflects changes in literary and theatrical taste. Second, the aesthetic validity and critical usefulness of regarding these plays as a group has been increasingly questioned. A third point is that, while the study of texts and sources has advanced, research has unearthed no new fact about the original date of writing or the circumstances of first performance of any of the plays.

Today, when *Measure for Measure* and *Troilus and Cressida* are set books at 'A'-level, and when all three plays come up regularly, not just for a token staging, but for their full quota of performances in repertory at Stratford and elsewhere, it seems incredible that around 1870 William Poel (the first modern director ever to stage all three plays) was recommended by his tutor never to read *Measure for Measure* and *Troilus and Cressida*, as being improper; or that in 1906 townspeople in Oxford opposed an undergraduate performance of *Measure for Measure*; or that in 1913 F. R. Benson had such qualms about himself staging *Troilus* at Stratford that he preferred to invite Poel to revive his production for two performances

on a single day. *Measure for Measure* did, however, inspire Walter Pater's fine essay (1874) and Walter Raleigh's perceptive few pages in *Shakespeare*;[1] and in 1884 Bernard Shaw maintained before Furnivall's New Shakspere Society that in *Troilus and Cressida* Shakespeare 'treated the story as an iconoclast treats an idol'. Shaw later liked to suggest connections between his *Plays Unpleasant* and Shakespeare's: 'in such unpopular plays as All's Well, Measure for Measure, and Troilus and Cressida we find [Shakespeare] ready and willing to start at the twentieth century if the seventeenth would only let him'.[2]

The three plays were first grouped together by Edward Dowden in *Shakespere: his Mind and Art* and subsequent text-books as belonging to Shakespeare's 'third period: *In The Depths*'.[3]

---

[1] London, 1907.
[2] See Robert Speaight, *William Poel and the Elizabethan Revival* (London, 1954), p. 192; Harold Child, 'The Stage History', New Cambridge *Measure for Measure* (Cambridge, 1922), p. 165; J. C. Trewin, *Benson and the Bensonians* (London, 1960), pp. 197-8; R. F. Rattray, *Bernard Shaw* (Luton, 1951), p. 147; G. Bernard Shaw, Preface to *Plays Pleasant and Unpleasant*, 1 (London, 1898), xxi.
[3] In the first edition (London, 1875), Dowden found *All's Well* 'serious', *Measure for Measure* 'dark', and *Troilus* 'bitter' – and so puzzling that he deferred discussing it till later editions. The phrase 'In the Depths' does not occur in the 1875 text, and the embryonic theory of four periods was later expanded. S. Schoenbaum has stated: 'No biographical pattern imposed on Shakespeare . . . has made so profound an impact as Dowden's', *Shakespeare's Lives* (Oxford, 1970), p. 496.

F. S. Boas in *Shakspere and his Predecessors*[1] found links, some of them tenuous, between the three plays and *Hamlet* – 'we are left to interpret their enigmas as best we may' – and borrowed for them from the Ibsenist theatre the term 'problem play'. It did not win currency until recirculated by W. W. Lawrence in *Shakespeare's Problem Comedies*, a sane, slightly old-fashioned book,[2] dedicated to the octogenarian A. C. Bradley. Lawrence's was the first study of *All's Well, Measure for Measure* and *Troilus and Cressida* as a group. In each he perceived 'a perplexing and distressing complication in human life ... presented in a spirit of high seriousness' and the problem he defined as ethical in that 'complicated interrelations of character and action' are probed 'in a situation admitting of different ethical interpretations'. Lawrence argued that what is puzzling for modern readers would not have been so for the Elizabethan audience. E. M. W. Tillyard in *Shakespeare's Problem Plays*,[3] though not wedded to 'a highly unsatisfactory term', exploited its analogy with 'problem child' to discuss *All's Well* and *Measure for Measure* as 'radically schizophrenic' and *Hamlet* and *Troilus and Cressida* as dealing 'with interesting problems'. A. P. Rossiter in lectures given in the early fifties (posthumously published as *Angel with Horns*[4]) put forward a rationale for treating the three comedies as problem plays. Ernest Schanzer argued cogently against current uses of the term, himself giving a rigorous definition of 'problem play' which fitted only three of Shakespeare's plays, *Julius Caesar, Measure for Measure* and *Antony and Cleopatra*, which are the subject of his *The Problem Plays of Shakespeare*.[5] The term lingers on. Peter Ure, in his pamphlet *Shakespeare: the Problem Plays*,[6] continued to regard it as an accepted label for a group of plays, including *Timon of Athens*, which 'have some features in common'. In *Shakespeare's Problem Plays*[7] William B. Toole used the term only as 'a convenient tag for four plays', including *Hamlet*, in which he traced, with little profit to his readers, the same theological pattern that governs the structure and meaning of the *Divina commedia*.

Biographical assumptions that Shakespeare underwent a psychological crisis in 'the third period' for long coloured some critics' reading of the three plays. E. K. Chambers in three introductions to the Red Letter Shakespeare, 1906–8 (re-issued in *Shakespeare: a Survey*[8]) and in his much-read Shakespeare entry for the *Britannica*,[9] described them as 'unpleasant' and 'embittered' – 'the three bitter and cynical pseudo-comedies'. C. J. Sisson in his British Academy lecture 'The Mythical Sorrows of Shakespeare' (1934) demolished all such biographical fallacies, and his defence of *Measure for Measure*, 'one of Shakespeare's finest acting plays', contributed to that re-instatement of the problem plays which G. Wilson Knight had championed since 1929 in a changing climate of opinion. Bonamy Dobrée, reviewing *The Wheel of Fire* in *The Criterion*,[10] said that to his generation these plays and *Timon* did not seem 'incomprehensibly gritty; most of us prefer them to the romantic comedies'.

'All's Well That Ends Well'

G. K. Hunter lamented in 1959 that 'criticism of *All's Well* ... has failed to provide a context within which the genuine virtues of the play can be appreciated'. Certainly the New Cambridge edition[11] found *All's Well* the most neglected play in the canon by editors ('There

---

[1] London, 1896.
[2] London, 1931.   [3] London, 1950.
[4] London, 1961.   [5] London, 1963.
[6] London, 1961; revised 1964.
[7] The Hague, 1966.
[8] London, 1925.
[9] 11th edition (Cambridge, 1911).
[10] January 1931.
[11] Cambridge, 1929.

is no money in it, since it is never read in schools and very rarely in universities') and possibly in the theatre. Dover Wilson looked on the Folio text as a Jacobean revision 'by Shakespeare and a collaborator' of 'an Elizabethan play perhaps by Shakespeare but ... probably containing pre-Shakespearean elements', a view which induced neither editorial caution nor critical respect. Quiller-Couch dismissed the play as 'one of Shakespeare's worst', preferring Boccaccio's story as straighter and more dignified. He disliked 'the inept business with Parolles', thought Lafeu had 'no business in the play', that Lavache was 'nothing to any purpose' and Bertram ultimately 'a stage puppet'.

When 'Q' wrote his patronising introduction, G. P. Krapp's interesting article 'Parolles' had been published[1] and W. W. Lawrence's first thoughts on *All's Well* had appeared.[2] Lawrence traced two movements, centred on Helena and based on folk-themes: the Healing of the King and the Fulfilment of the Tasks. He showed that all the sources and analogues exalt the resourcefulness and devotion of the Clever Wench, and thus maintained that for the Elizabethans there was no impropriety in the bed-trick and Helena was wholly admirable. For Dr Tillyard *All's Well* was 'in some sort, a failure' – though probably not on the stage. He praised its construction, but followed Lawrence in stressing the rift between realistic characterisation and fairy-tale plot.

Three essays of the early fifties advanced the critical study of *All's Well*. M. C. Bradbrook in 'Virtue is the True Nobility'[3] surmised that 'the dramatist and the poet ... were pulling different ways': for her, the structure revealed a serious moral debate on 'the question of blood and descent versus native worth'. Clifford Leech, writing on 'The Themes of Ambition',[4] found 'the folk-tale stories and the Christian colouring ... strongly companioned

by other elements' – including satire. His reaction to the ambitious Helena was critical. Harold S. Wilson in 'Dramatic Emphasis in *All's Well That Ends Well*'[5] defended its deliberate artifice as a play on the wronged wife, and as stage entertainment rather than something that stands up to reflection.

In the spate of articles from the later fifties and the sixties there are three currents.[6] Many writers seek to establish the unity of the play by exploring the Age/Youth/Regeneration complex, or by teasing out the imagery (including the erotic), or by developing the view that our response to characters is more ambiguous than Lawrence imagined. The defence of Bertram has been accompanied by a blackening of Helena, shown up as having comic faults to match his, as aggressive where he is snobbish, or as sensual and predatory like the Venus of *Venus and Adonis*. Critics tend to quote in title or epigraph: 'The web of our life is of a mingled yarn, good and ill together ...' (IV, iii, 68–9). The vitality of Parolles, and his acceptance of life on any terms has also been related to the play's themes.

Dramaturgical analyses include discussion of *All's Well* as a 'prodigal son' piece, and Bertrand Evans's discussion in *Shakespeare's Comedies*[7] of Helena's manipulative control

[1] In *Shakespearian Studies*, ed. Brander Matthews (New York, 1916).
[2] *Publications of the Modern Language Association of America*, XXXVII (1922).
[3] *Review of English Studies*, XXVI (1950).
[4] *Journal of English Literary History*, XXI (1954).
[5] *Huntington Library Quarterly*, XIII (1949–50).
[6] See John Arthos, 'The Comedy of Generation', *Essays in Criticism*, V (1955); J. L. Calderwood, 'The Mingled Yarn of *All's Well*', *Journal of English and Germanic Philology*, LXII (1963) and 'Styles of Knowing in *All's Well*', *Modern Language Quarterly*, XXV (1964); Robert Hapgood, 'The Life of Shame', *Essays in Criticism*, XV (1965); and R. Y. Turner, 'Dramatic Conventions in *All's Well*', *PMLA*, LXXV (1960).
[7] Oxford, 1960.

over the action which finally 'borders on witchery'. By contrast a third approach has stressed religious, even mystical reverberations. 'The Third Eye', Wilson Knight's long suggestive essay in *The Sovereign Flower*[1] is in his own late manner. He discerned two antithetical concepts of honour, one masculine and military (Bertram), the other feminine (chaste love). The active Helena unites or transcends both; Shakespeare, with the creative bisexuality of genius, presented her as his supreme expression of feminine love, as 'miracle worker' and 'medium'. Robert Grams Hunter has written rewardingly and more soberly of the play as 'a secular comedy ... for a Christian audience' with Bertram as *humanum genus* in *Shakespeare and the Comedy of Forgiveness*.[2]

Different approaches sometimes yield contradictory conclusions. Richard David, reviewing in *Shakespeare Survey 8* (1955), a stage production which guyed the older generation, welcomed 'the lightening and depersonalizing of the story' which revealed the play's kinship with the last romances. C. J. Sisson in 'Shakespeare's Helena and Dr William Harvey'[3] presented material to prove that Helena's medical conduct and her status as a female practitioner would have struck the Elizabethans 'as consonant with the realities of contemporary life and not an element of fairy tale invention'.

The most accessible account of the play's source, text etc., is G. K. Hunter's excellent new Arden edition[4] which defines the play's 'strongly individual quality' as 'a quality of *strain*'. His tentative dating of the play is 1603–4, just before *Measure for Measure*, but Josephine Walters Bennet in 'New Techniques of Comedy in *All's Well That Ends Well*'[5] thinks that this 'wise, tolerant, and beautiful play' is both later and technically superior.

Joseph G. Price has dealt comprehensively with the theatrical and critical fortunes in *The Unfortunate Comedy*[6] and has shown that *All's Well* was adapted first as a farce about Parolles and then as a sentimental play about Helena. His own scene-by-scene defence of the play always keeps theatrical presentation in mind.

Barbara Everett in her edition[7] has defined the tone as 'mature, subtle, haunting', and 'sober' and 'elegiac rather than saturnalian'. A different view occurs in R. A. Foakes's recent *Shakespeare: from satire to celebration*:[8] 'What a stage performance reveals is the degree to which the tonality ... is governed by ... figures like Parolles and Lavache, who persuade us ... we are in a comic world.' Criticism has often taken *All's Well* too seriously and exaggerated its problems. After all, as Kenneth Muir has maintained, 'if the Clown were given better jokes and Bertram a better speech at the end, the play would leave us with feelings of greater satisfaction'.[9]

'Measure for Measure'

The bulk of criticism on *Measure for Measure* since 1930 almost rivals that on *Hamlet*. Much of it makes great claims for Shakespeare's achievement and some of it raises theoretical questions about the interpretation and evaluation of Renaissance plays. Writers fall into two categories: 'new critics' of different persuasions – there never was a 'School of Knight' – who regard the text as self-sufficient; and various 'historical critics' who assume that the meaning of the play, or important parts of it, can be elucidated only by recourse to prior knowledge about genres, Renaissance ethics,

[1] London, 1958.
[2] New York, 1956.
[3] *Essays and Studies*, n.s. XIII (1960).
[4] London, 1959.
[5] *Shakespeare Quarterly*, XVIII (1967).
[6] Liverpool, 1968.
[7] New Penguin Shakespeare (Harmondsworth, 1970).
[8] London, 1971.
[9] *Shakespeare's Sources*, 1 (London, 1957), p. 101.

medieval or Renaissance theology, or Elizabethan law.[1]

The New Cambridge edition no longer serves the general reader. Dover Wilson held that the Folio text incorporated theatrical revisions and was corrupt. 'Q' in his critique ('What is wrong with this play?') judged the characters by the criterion of psychological consistency. Some of his points were restated with greater ebullience and critical sophistication by William Empson in 1938 as a reaction against the idealisation or deification of the Duke, whom Empson saw as 'playing God'.[2]

Wilson Knight's by now classic essay, 'Measure for Measure and the Gospels',[3] approached the play as 'a parable' and 'a studied explication' of the theme 'Judge not, that ye be not judged'. Knight found that it tended 'towards allegory or symbolism', saw the Duke as 'the prophet of an enlightened ethic', and Isabella as a self-centred saint. W. W. Lawrence, however, postulated a stage Duke and a blameless Isabel. R. W. Chambers's forensic British Academy lecture, 'The Jacobean Shakespeare and Measure for Measure' (1937), represents, with C. J. Sisson's earlier one, the Establishment's rehabilitation of the play as a doctrinally Christian work of art. It defended Isabella.

Three separate studies appeared in Scrutiny during 1942. L. C. Knights, analysing words like 'scope', 'liberty', and 'restraint',[4] sensed in the play 'not paradox but genuine ambiguity', and was puzzled by both Claudio and Isabella, finding Angelo 'the admitted success of the play'. His qualified evaluation provoked from his co-editor, F. R. Leavis, an assertion of the play's value, 'The Greatness of Measure for Measure'.[5] Leavis maintained that there ought to be 'an element of the critical' in the way we regard Isabella, endorsed Wilson Knight's high view of the Duke 'the more-than-Prospero', and viewed Angelo sympathetically. In the third Scrutiny essay D. A. Traversi located a

poetic tension between Claudio's consciousness of the 'ravening' process of self-destruction and Lucio's 'great speech on Claudio's love'. In 'Measure for Measure: A Footnote to Recent Criticism',[6] J. C. Maxwell found no imperfection in Isabel 'beyond that involved in creaturely limitation'; the play seemed 'one of Shakespeare's most perfect works of art'.

Their views on Isabella split critics into camps. By Warren D. Smith's count in 1962 'fourteen critics praise her nobility in the prison scene and thirteen . . . charge her with inhumanity towards her brother'.[7] Some have developed the parallel between her and Angelo with differing emphases. While to one critic they were 'those senators of virtue', Philip Edwards has seen them as 'trapped by their own kind of ethical idealism'.[8] Angelo has been sensitively presented as a tragic protagonist by W. M. T. Dodds, now Mrs Nowottny,[9] and exposed as a Puritan by D. J. McGinn.[10] Ernest Schanzer discussed the five main

---

[1] See O. J. Campbell, 'Shakespeare and the "New" Critics', J. Q. Adams Memorial Studies (Washington, 1948); L. C. Knights, 'Historical Scholarship and the Criticism of Shakespeare', Further Explorations (London, 1965); Robert Ornstein, 'Historical Criticism and the Interpretation of Shakespeare', Shakespeare Quarterly, x (1959); J. M. Newton, 'Scrutiny's Failure with Shakespeare', Cambridge Quarterly, 1 (1966).

[2] The Structure of Complex Words (London, 1951).

[3] The Wheel of Fire (London, 1930).

[4] Ernest Leisi in his semanticist's 'old spelling and old meaning edition' (1964), lists as key-words: authority, scope, liberty, restraint, mercy, grace, weigh and seem.

[5] The Common Pursuit (London, 1952).

[6] Downside Review, LXV (1947).

[7] 'More Light on Measure for Measure', Modern Language Quarterly, XXIII (1962). Smith also claimed that Isabella's 'More than our brother is our chastity' is the only non-royal use of our save for Julius Caesar's. J. C. Maxwell noted earlier that the Folio printed it as a sententia.

[8] Shakespeare and the Confines of Art (London, 1968).

[9] Modern Language Review, XLI (1946).

[10] In J. Q. Adams Memorial Studies (Washington, 1948).

characters and their interplay, and revealed that German scholarship anticipated some American and British interpretations.

Miss Bradbrook in 'Authority, Truth, and Justice in *Measure for Measure*'[1] detected a medieval Morality structure: 'The Contention between Justice and Mercy, or False Authority unmasked by Truth and Humility.' A learned and extreme allegorical interpretation, with the Duke as the Incarnate Lord, by Roy W. Battenhouse in '*Measure for Measure* and Christian Doctrine of the Atonement'[2] has lately been faulted by the combative Roland Mushat Frye[3] on the grounds that Battenhouse drew on patristic and scholastic rather than Renaissance authorities. Elizabeth Marie Pope's paper, 'The Renaissance Background of *Measure for Measure*',[4] presented material from text-books and sermons of Shakespeare's day to suggest that the play is concerned with the duties of the Prince or Ruler and his privilege to use extraordinary means in tempering justice with mercy. This kind of approach produced a rejoinder from Clifford Leech 'The "Meaning" of *Measure for Measure*'[5] in which he argued against the narrow interpretation of plays as 'embodying theses' and demonstrated how complex this play is. More recently Marco Mincoff has denounced critical orthodoxies by declaring that as Providence the Duke 'is even less satisfactory than as ideal ruler'. In the closely argued '*Measure for Measure*: Quid pro Quo?' A. D. Nuttall showed that the Duke is a White Machiavel and that Angelo is morally 'worth four Dukes'. He also distinguished a different atonement pattern.[6]

Lawrence found law in Shakespeare 'a queer business'. Scholars have explained Claudio's 'offence' with Juliet and Angelo's betrothal to Mariana in the light of Elizabethan law, ecclesiastical and secular. Others have clarified Escalus's mid-way stance between Angelo (Justice) and the Duke (Mercy) by reference to Renaissance concepts of Equity.[7]

O. J. Campbell extended his theory about *Troilus and Cressida* to include *Measure for Measure* as a 'comicall satyre'.[8] R. G. Hunter discerned a pattern by which the main characters judge one another and are judged in 'a comedy of forgiveness'. Two dramaturgical analyses confirm Tillyard's view that the play 'changes its nature half way through'. Herbert Weil, Jr claims that Shakespeare deliberately terminated 'the dramatic intensity of his early acts' and that the play's 'descending action' ought to be played 'in a light comic, even farcical vein.'[9] Bernard Beckerman also sees the dramatic shift as deliberate but the play as a not entirely successful experiment in tragicomedy.[10]

Some critics have felt that Shakespeare never reconciled his vivid characterisation or his new learning with the pre-existing plot. The rela-

[1] *RES*, XVII (1941).

[2] *PMLA*, LXI (1946).

[3] *Shakespeare and Christian Doctrine* (Oxford, 1963), pp. 35–6. Frye attacked less scholarly men than Battenhouse for their union of subjective criticism with a naive understanding of theology. He also showed that Father William Sankey, the English Jesuit, excised the whole of *Measure for Measure* from the Folio, *c*. 1641–51, at the English College at Valladolid, Spain.

[4] *Shakespeare Survey 2* (Cambridge, 1949).

[5] *Shakespeare Survey 3* (Cambridge, 1950).

[6] *Shakespeare Studies*, II (1966) and IV (1968) respectively.

[7] See Davis P. Harding, 'Elizabethan Betrothals and *Measure for Measure*', *Journal of English and Germanic Philology*, XLIX (1950); Ernest Schanzer, 'The Marriage Contracts in *Measure for Measure*', *Shakespeare Survey 13* (Cambridge, 1960); S. Nazarjan, '*Measure for Measure* and Elizabethan Betrothals', *Shakespeare Quarterly*, XIV (1963); John Wasson, 'A Play of Incontinence', *ELH*, XXVII (1960); and J. W. Dickinson, 'Renaissance Equity and *Measure for Measure*' and Wilbur Dunkel, 'Law and Equity in *Measure for Measure*' – both in *Shakespeare Quarterly*, XIII (1962).

[8] *Shakespeare's Satire* (New York, 1943).

[9] 'Form and Contexts in *Measure for Measure*', *Critical Quarterly*, XII (1970).

[10] 'The Dramaturgy of *Measure for Measure*', *The Elizabethan Theatre*, II, ed. David Galloway (Toronto, 1970).

tion between *Measure for Measure* and various possible sources, discussed by L. Albrecht (1914) and W. W. Lawrence, has been further explored by Mary Lascelles, Madeleine Doran, Kenneth Muir, J. W. Lever, and Geoffrey Bullough, whose *Narrative and Dramatic Sources*,[1] includes the relevant materials. Mary Lascelles's humane and penetrating *Shakespeare's 'Measure for Measure'*[2] is responsive to the departures Shakespeare made, and to the distinctive role of the heroine, denied the self-revelation of soliloquy. J. W. Lever's compressed, informative introduction to the new Arden edition[3] copes with such folk-themes as 'the Disguised Duke', and with the play's ideas. He finds much less textual corruption than his predecessors and dates the play between May and August 1604, before its performance at Court on 26 December.

David Lloyd Stevenson in *The Achievement of 'Measure for Measure'*[4] gives an undoctrinaire, open, ahistorical account of a 'schematic' and 'disturbing' play about living people. Historically informed, he is ironic about 'neotheologians' and 'historical reconstructionists'. He relegates to an appendix, as irrelevant to our understanding the play, his revival of the theory that the Duke reflects King James.[5] Josephine Walters Bennet in *'Measure for Measure' as Royal Entertainment*[6] builds the many-tiered hypothesis that Shakespeare as author–actor–director complimented King James, who is shadowed in the Duke, whom Shakespeare played. Some of her insights were anticipated by Miss Lascelles and chime with suggestions by Anne Righter.[7] Acceptance of the theories would give us a light-toned, topical, witty comedy, centred on absurd situations 'like *The Mikado*'.

Writers have not agreed about the tone, meaning, or value of *Measure for Measure*. To Miss Lascelles it is 'this great, uneven play', to Dr Lever 'a flawed masterpiece', to Dr Leavis 'one of the very greatest of the plays'.

Its shrewdest critics believe that it possesses that *complexity* in which Miss Lascelles found 'the very proof of its integrity'.

'Troilus and Cressida'

Both *All's Well* and *Measure for Measure* have a two-part structure, source-materials in folklore and Italian literature, and comedic resolutions which involve the bed-trick. Virgil K. Whitaker has linked *Troilus and Cressida* with *Measure for Measure* ('radically faulty as drama, but ... the most explicitly learned plays that Shakespeare ever wrote'[8]), but J. C. Maxwell's view that *Troilus* is 'the most isolated of the Middle Plays' has won assent. To Sir Walter Greg it was 'a play of puzzles, in respect of its textual history, no less than its interpretation'.[9]

Bibliographical and theatrical speculations about Bonian's and Walley's Quarto and the play's ultimate position in the Folio have led to disagreement over the play's genre. Scholarship has now established that the first title-page of the Quarto was cancelled *before* publication and that the Folio printers originally intended *Troilus* to follow *Romeo and Juliet*. Thus two factions can each claim some Jacobean authority for regarding *Troilus* as comedy or as tragedy. Nevill Coghill's questioning of the credibility of the Bonian and Walley preface led to correspondence in *The Times Literary Supplement* in

---

[1] Vol. II (London, 1958).

[2] London, 1953.

[3] London, 1965.

[4] Ithaca, 1966.

[5] That the *Basilicon Doron* was a source had been suggested by George Chalmers (1779) and by L. Albrecht (1914) who did not convince W. W. Lawrence. Peter Alexander, who believed that 'Shakespeare did not neglect ... to show his knowledge of his sovereign's philosophy', found James often 'muddle-headed and inconsistent', *Shakespeare* (London, 1964), p. 152.

[6] New York, 1966.

[7] *Shakespeare and the Idea of the Play* (London, 1962).

[8] *Shakespeare's Use of Learning* (San Marino, 1953) p. 194.

[9] *The Shakespeare First Folio* (Oxford, 1955).

1967. E. K. Chambers in 1906 had speculated that *Troilus* might have been produced for an academic audience at Cambridge, and Peter Alexander, to explain the nature of the copy for the Quarto, conjectured that the play was commissioned for some Inns of Court festivity.[1] Alfred Harbage is adamant that there is 'no recorded instance . . . when a regular play was bought, rehearsed and acted by a professional company exclusively for a special audience'.[2] That the first audience could tell a true argument from a false remains an attractive hypothesis; that they could also distinguish between histrionics and sincerity is suggested by Patricia Thomson's essay 'Rant and Cant in *Troilus and Cressida*'.[3] A remarkable feature in the rediscovery of the play since 1920 has been its undergraduate appeal.

Unlike *Measure for Measure* this play seems to have had no early enthusiasts. Wilson Knight implicitly suggested its new importance in 'The Philosophy of *Troilus and Cressida*' in *The Wheel of Fire* where he elucidated its central idea – 'almost a "thesis"' – as the opposition between 'intuition' and 'emotion' (the Trojans) and 'intellect' and 'reason' (the Greeks). His coherent if over-simplified reading is imaginative and exciting alongside W. W. Lawrence's more cautious source-study of The Love-Story and The Quarrels of the Chieftains. William Empson's deeper perceptions about the operation of double plots[4] and Caroline F. E. Spurgeon's detailed charting of the iterative imagery of food and disease[5] also gave methodological leads. Theodore Spencer mentioned aspects of the play that were 'sympathetic to a generation that found expression in *Ulysses* and *The Waste Land*' in a long 'Commentary'[6] which he regarded as superseded by *Shakespeare and the Nature of Man*.[7] There he found in the case of Troilus 'a worse kind of tragedy than death . . . continued existence after everything that matters has been destroyed'. At the end of the war Una Ellis-Fermor wrote of her own revised view of *Troilus and Cressida* as a unity, and was reprimanded by Harley Granville-Barker for ceasing 'to distinguish between Shakespeare's better plays and his worse'.[8] Her essay, 'The Discord of the Spheres', suggested the paradox that, though the play's thought 'is an implacable assertion of chaos as the ultimate fact of being', its form testifies to order.[9]

The antithesis in content and in structure, and the play's preoccupation with Time, have led to other schematic and thematic readings along lines adumbrated by Wilson Knight. D. A. Traversi's analysis, written for *Scrutiny* in 1938, re-appeared without the limiting evaluation 'not, on any view, a successful play' in the enlarged editions of *An Approach to Shakespeare*.[10] He regarded the play as 'a dramatic statement of the emotional ambiguity whose resolution was to be the motive of the great tragedies'. L. C. Knights in 1951, taking Appearance and Reality as the theme, viewed the play as vital in the development of Shakespeare's thought.[11] In a subtle reading, '"Opinion" and "Value" in *Troilus and Cressida*', W. M. T. Nowottny saw between Ulysses and Troilus the 'great antithesis between two approaches to life, that of the statesman and that of the individual creative imagination'.[12] Frank Kermode replied in 1955 by suggesting a different antithesis, itself 'a simplification of something appallingly diffi-

---

[1] *The Library*, 4th series, IX (1929).
[2] *Shakespeare and the Rival Traditions* (New York, 1952), p. 116
[3] *Essays and Studies*, n.s. XXII (1969).
[4] *Some Versions of Pastoral* (London, 1935).
[5] *Shakespeare's Imagery and What it Tells us* (Cambridge, 1936).
[6] *Studies in English Literature* (Tokyo, 1936).
[7] New York, 1942.
[8] *RES*, XXII (1946).
[9] *The Frontiers of Drama* (London, 1945).
[10] New York, 1956; 2 volumes (London, 1969).
[11] *Some Shakespearean Themes* (London, 1959).
[12] *Essays in Criticism*, IV (1954).

cult'. A. S. Knowland[1] accused critics of over-simplifying and over-conceptualising the play and of over-stressing the Time theme, in his own effort to establish 'our total dramatic experience of the play'. R. J. Kaufmann's 'Ceremonies of Chaos: the Status of *Troilus and Cressida*'[2] shows that a thematic approach can still yield insight.

In *Comicall Satyre and Shakespeare's 'Troilus and Cressida'*[3] O. J. Campbell connected the play with the satirical plays of Jonson and Marston which flourished from 1599, but his response to the text, especially in *Shakespeare's Satire*,[4] was insensitively moralistic: the lovers' 'adventures ... exemplify lust' leading to 'deserved disaster'. That the play is a tragedy was argued by Brian Morris in 'The Tragic Structure of *Troilus and Cressida*'; he complained that the problem plays 'have been forcibly and unequally yoked together' and he regarded the 'monolithic design' of the generals' plot as the 'backcloth against which the lovers' tragedy is played out'.[5] Alice Walker in 1957 endorsed Campbell's view. R. A. Foakes, reconsidering the play, first in *The University of Toronto Quarterly*[6] and later in *Shakespeare: from satire to celebration*,[7] put the emphasis on the comical-satirical tone, on the play's 'three endings', and on the part played by the audience's prior knowledge of a familiar story. Bertrand Evans from a technical standpoint reported that 'our advantage over Troilus, Cressida, and Pandarus ... depends upon our extra-dramatic knowledge of outcomes', thus establishing a distinctive technique. Earlier G. F. Reynolds had proved that the play makes no elaborate stage-demands.[8]

The massive Variorum edition by H. N. Hillebrand and T. W. Baldwin[9] is replete with secondary materials. The New Cambridge editor, Alice Walker, admits a bias towards the Folio text; hers is the main critical edition.[10] Robert Kimbrough's *Shakespeare's 'Troilus and Cressida' and its Setting*[11] is a comprehensive

study and it relates *Troilus* to works in the repertory of public and coterie theatres. A wide range of sources, studied before 1920 by J. S. P. Tatlock and Hyder E. Rollins, has been reconsidered by, amongst others, R. K. Presson in *Shakespeare's 'Troilus and Cressida' and the Legends of Troy*[12] which stressed the Homeric influence through Chapman. Geoffrey Bullough, for reasons of space rather than genre, dealt with the sources in his volume on *Other 'Classical' Plays*.[13] Miss Bradbrook has suggested that 'What Shakespeare did to Chaucer's *Troilus and Criseyde*' included the 'lacerative destruction of Chaucer's whole vision'.[14] The 'play of puzzles' continues to be seen as comedy, 'comicall satyre', tragedy, and tragic satire.

Any outline of the critical fortunes of the three plays has to be selective, and much comment in books on the comedies and in wider studies has here been ignored. Writers on the separate plays or on three works 'which ingenious absurdity has thrown together' have no monopoly on critical insight; indeed anyone taking as his subject Shakespeare's word-play or his bawdy, his use of learning or of stage-convention, or his treatment of the Renaissance concept of honour, is bound, from that perspective, to see something distinctive in each of the three. Do we persist in seeing differences between these and other plays of Shakespeare's where his contemporaries saw none? Have critics in the Age

[1] *Shakespeare Quarterly*, X (1959).
[2] *ELH*, XXXII (1965).
[3] San Marino, 1938. [4] New York, 1943.
[5] *Shakespeare Quarterly*, X (1959).
[6] XXXII (1963).
[7] London, 1971.
[8] '*Troilus and Cressida* on the Elizabethan Stage', *J. Q. Adams Memorial Studies* (Washington, 1948).
[9] Philadelphia, 1953.
[10] Cambridge, 1957.
[11] Cambridge, Mass., 1964.
[12] Madison, 1953.
[13] London, 1966.
[14] *Shakespeare Quarterly*, IX (1958).

of Anxiety over-valued these three plays?[1] In 1944 T. S. Eliot remarked 'At a particular moment ... certain of the less popular plays may have a particular appeal'; and he went on to recall 'the limited but significant interest in *Troilus and Cressida* a few years ago'.[2] Interest in all three plays has not abated amongst critics and men of the theatre. It has increased. They are no longer Problem Plays, and no longer unpopular.

[1] See John Russell Brown, *Shakespeare Survey 8* (Cambridge, 1955), p. 13.

[2] Introduction to S. L. Bethell's *Shakespeare and the Popular Dramatic Tradition* (London, 1944).

© MICHAEL JAMIESON 1972

'SONS AND DAUGHTERS OF THE GAME': AN ESSAY ON SHAKESPEARE'S 'TROILUS AND CRESSIDA'

R. A. YODER

Of all Shakespeare, *Troilus and Cressida* is our play. It could be rediscovered only by a sensibility tuned to artistic discontinuity and preoccupied with the realities of love and war; and so it had to wait for cubism and atonality, for fascism and Freud. So given over to 'philosophy' and debate, it had to wait for Shaw to rescue this dramatic mode, and probably for the kind of painstaking analysis of texts apart from performance that modern criticism has indulged. In a narrower sense, it is our play because it makes sense to Americans in the 1970s. We know, albeit still in a remote and mostly vicarious way, the meaning of a protracted seven years' war. We know how the designs of war fail in their promised largeness and how the Greeks must have felt tented in a foreign land, so many hollow factions, with their great engine Achilles useless in seeming mockery of their very designs. Like the Trojans, too, we have heard endlessly the arguments for carrying on a war of doubtful justification, and we know what it really means to settle only for an 'honorable peace'. We have seen good men who spoke truth in council, even in public, suddenly capitulate to save the corporate image. Within the walls of our capital cities – or more accurately, in their gilded suburbs – we may observe an elegant and seething triviality to match the palace society of Troy. Last and worst, we know what this society and its war has done to our best youth – those not literally destroyed have suffered a degradation of spirit, and of those whose ideals are not fully corrupted, many have chosen a life of irreconcilable alienation. There is no doubt, *Troilus and Cressida* gives back our own world.

Not surprisingly, then, some of the most acute Shakespearian criticism of the past decade concerns this play, and these interpretations have been generally pessimistic: the play in some way ridicules or diminishes every character, and ultimately the human character, man himself; no one any longer seems to accept Ulysses's 'degree' speech as the established value of the play, yet for all the times I have read that Thersites is right about this or that incident, no one comfortably or categorically asserts that he speaks for Shakespeare. Instead, there is a tendency to philosophize about this philosophical drama, to gather it all up into one large design and stress the symmetry of parallels and contrasts between settings, persons, and arguments. Then 'multiplicity' rather than any one character's ideas governs the viewpoint of the play. And most of the traditional dichotomies – like Trojan/Greek, love/war, passion/reason, extrinsic/intrinsic theories of value, tragic/comic – are seen as 'complementary' and resolved in more encompassing generalizations.[1] Thus for Norman

---

[1] Contemporary notions about *Troilus and Cressida* go back certainly to Theodore Spencer, *Shakespeare and the Nature of Man*, first published in 1942, and to Una Ellis-Fermor's essay in *The Frontiers of Drama* (London, 1946). The trend toward 'complementarity' may have begun as a reaction against G. Wilson Knight's positive preference for Trojan intuition over

Rabkin the great issues of the play all point toward the realization that 'value is a function of time', and time a process growing of its own accord without regard to the desires of any man.[1] Or in Terence Eagleton's account *Troilus and Cressida* is epitomized in the inference Ulysses draws from his reading:

> ... No man is the lord of anything,
> Though in and of him there be much consisting,
> Till he communicate his parts to others
>
> (III, iii, 115–17)

The characteristic action of the play, describing or evaluating someone to someone else, and the imagery of merchants, mediators, and go-betweens show us that 'individual identity is a public creation', that we have no intrinsic identities apart from our relationships; thus Troilus who never objectifies himself in a public role or identity inevitably fails.[2] Particular man appears to dissolve in a discourse on the fallacy of simple location. For all the confusion on stage, the characters transcend the ordinary limitations of life – Troilus, Cressida, Pandarus would define themselves as mythical beings 'in the world to come' (III, ii, 171–203).[3]

This larger, philosophical view of *Troilus and Cressida* provides some relief from taxing ideological quarrels and from any lingering sense of aesthetic chaos. Yet its great virtue, I think, is to startle us with still another profound question, as all good philosophy does: Why in a play that so richly evokes an atmosphere, a sense of the here and now, are we asked to look so far beyond it, into the dim abstract, for answers? Why, in short, should we desert the world that is for 'the world to come'? A look at the actual world of Troy, and we may learn why its inhabitants – and following them, the audience – might refuge in a time outside of time and in a space that relieves them of an identity apart from public role.

I

What is going on at Troy is no secret. Some time ago the 'princes orgulous' came from Greece to meet the courteous Trojans in honorable battle, all over a point of honor in love. Now, 'after seven years' siege' (I, iii, 11) – 'after so many hours, lives, speeches spent', and 'honour, loss of time, travail, expense,/ Wounds, friends, and what else is dear that is consumed/ In hot digestion of this cormorant war' (II, ii, 1, 4–6) – they are still at it. Trojans

---

Greek cunning (*The Wheel of Fire*, 1st ed., London, 1930). Derek Traversi's treatment in *An Approach to Shakespeare* (1st ed., London 1938), Kenneth Muir's '*Troilus and Cressida*', *Shakespeare Survey 8* (Cambridge, 1955), pp. 28–39, and L. C. Knights's essay in *Some Shakespearean Themes* (London, 1959) are all in this vein. More recently, R. A. Foakes, '*Troilus and Cressida* Reconsidered', *University of Toronto Quarterly*, XXXII (1963), 142–54, Mary Ellen Rickey, '"'Twixt the Dangerous Shores": *Troilus and Cressida* Again', *Shakespeare Quarterly*, XV (1964), 3–13, make similar assumptions. The most philosophical exposition of complementarity is Norman Rabkin, *Shakespeare and the Common Understanding* (New York, 1967), pp. 31–57. Apart from this rather general point, these essays are not always similar. It should be clear that I have no quarrel with what I have called 'philosophical' criticism as a method; the only question is which philosophy to apply.

[1] Rabkin, *Shakespeare and the Common Understanding*, p. 53. His view does not take account of differences, particularly between the lovers' sense of time in III, ii, and Ulysses's in III, iii. Inevitably, Rabkin's stress on a philosophical theme resolved underplays the pessimistic tone of the whole play.

[2] *Shakespeare and Society* (New York, 1967), pp. 14–22, 34–7. My view of Troilus is almost the reverse of Eagleton's. Eagleton, in effect, shows how the dramatic techniques explored by Rudolph Stamm, 'The Glass of Pandar's Praise: The Word-Scenery, Mirror Passages, and Reported Scenes in Shakespeare's *Troilus and Cressida*', *Essays and Studies*, XVII (1964), pp. 55–77, can be interpreted as controlling the theme.

[3] Foakes, '*Troilus and Cressida* Reconsidered', pp. 149–54, argues that this passage shows the play is not de-bunking myth, but myth is modifying the play, directing us to the noble values that time has preserved from the somewhat ignoble action and diminished personages the play presents.

and Greeks are still playing the game according to the rules of knightly combat and the courtly lover's code. Yet nowhere in Shakespeare is the official standard of conduct more at odds with the action and language of the play.[1] Even Troilus, at the beginning, dissociates himself as a lover from this absurd war:

> Fools on both sides! Helen must needs be fair,
> When with your blood you daily paint her thus.
> I cannot fight upon this argument   (I, i, 92–4)

But he finds it easier to brush off this truth than to escape the war. Troilus, youngest son of Priam, a prince raised in the Trojan court, has inherited its code, though, to be sure, his courtly stance is still a bit awkward: he wallows – to use his own egregious verb – in a morass of conceits that invariably betray a less idealistic basis for love than Troilus realizes.[2] Not only do sensuous and financial images undercut his romantic protestations, but the strained pitch of his language leads him to absurd exaggerations – in the parting speeches, for example:

> Nay, we must use expostulation kindly,
> For it is parting from us.
> I speak not 'be thou true', as fearing thee,
> For I will throw my glove to Death himself
> That there's no maculation in thy heart;
> But 'be thou true' say I, to fashion in
> My sequent protestation: be thou true,
> And I will see thee.   (IV, iv, 60–7)

The challenge to death fits a code that joins love with honor in the field – that is why Troilus cannot escape the war. This extreme personification and the Latinized diction, which is a repeated device in the play,[3] suggest that Troilus has over-reacted to Cressida's twitting response. Were he able to know Cressida, Troilus would not need the merchant bark, 'this sailing Pandar' (I, i, 105) – and later in a grimly ironic figure 'my Charon' (III, ii, 10) – as a go-between. For the lovers the courtly role is inappropriate; somehow they have

been miscast, or misplaced. In the climax of the play, when he is faced with Cressida's infidelity, Troilus himself razes the structure of their love:

> The bonds of heaven are slipped, dissolved and
> loosed,
> And with another knot, five-finger-tied,
> The fractions of her faith, orts of her love,
> The fragments, scraps, the bits and greasy relics
> Of her o'ereaten faith are given to Diomed.
>
>   (V, ii, 156–60)

Here the subdued coarseness of Troilus's love poetry surfaces: the 'thing inseparable' is blasted to pieces, and her divine drapery shredded to scraps of fat for a Greek appetite.

In public the Greek and Trojan generals loyally act out their roles. Hector's challenge delivered by Aeneas exactly suits the conventions of the tiltyard, wholly ignoring the causes of strife while twining the themes of love and war in their formal courtly relation:

> If there be one among the fair'st of Greece,
> That holds his honour higher than his ease,
> That seeks his praise more than he fears his peril,
> That knows his valour and knows not his fear,
> That loves his mistress more than in confession
> With truant vows to her own lips he loves,
> And dare avow her beauty and her worth
> In other arms than hers – to him this challenge!
>
>   (I, iii, 265–72)[4]

---

[1] A paraphrase of Spencer, *Shakespeare and the Nature of Man* (New York, 1949), p. 111.

[2] Spencer, *ibid.*, pp. 115–17, rightly contrasts the imagery of Troilus and Romeo; but consciously Troilus is trying to imitate the high-flown courtly style. See also Traversi, *An Approach to Shakespeare* (New York, 1956), pp. 63–71, and more recently Raymond Southall, '*Troilus and Cressida* and the Spirit of Capitalism', in Arnold Kettle (ed.), *Shakespeare in a Changing World* (New York, 1964), pp. 222–31.

[3] See T. McAlindon, 'Language, Style, and Meaning in *Troilus and Cressida*', *PMLA*, LXXXIV (1969), 29–43.

[4] See the note on this passage in Alice Walker (ed.), *Troilus and Cressida* (Cambridge, 1963), p. 159. My references are to this edition.

After this prolixity and more posturing, when the duel finally comes off and Ajax, according to Ulysses's scheme, is representing the Greeks, Hector declines to continue the fight on the ground that he and Ajax are kin. With flourishing oratory (IV, v, 119–39)[1] he puts up his sword, the two contestants embrace, and the Trojan lords are invited to the Greek tents where Agamemnon's welcome aspires to Hector's own courtesy:

> Worthy of arms! as welcome as to one
> That would be rid of such an enemy –
> But that's no welcome; understand more clear,
> What's past and what's to come is strewed with husks
> And formless ruin of oblivion;
> But in this extant moment, faith and troth,
> Strained purely from all hollow bias-drawing,
> Bids thee, with most divine integrity,
> From heart of very heart, great Hector, welcome.
>
> (IV, v, 163–71)

This strained purity, akin to the lover's (cf. Troilus, IV, iv, 24), lifts the present moment out of time; it is the ceremony that holds off chaos. The public world of *Troilus and Cressida* teems with these ceremonial gestures of respect, friendship, and affection: Ulysses's deference to Agamemnon and Nestor in the Grecian camp (I, iii, 54–69); Agamemnon's greeting to Aeneas in the same scene (I, iii, 304–9), much like the later welcome to Hector; Hector's surprising reversal in deference to Troilus in the Trojan council (II, ii, 189–93, 205–13); the diplomacy surrounding the exchange of prisoners (IV, iv, 109–39), and the ceremonial salute, the kissing game, that welcomes Cressida to the Greek camp (IV, v, 16–53); and the profusion of oaths and prophecies, the insistent promises that mark almost every stage of the play (II, ii, 101–12, implicit in II, ii, 139–41, III, ii, *passim*, III, iii, 15, V, iii, 6–25).[2] All these gestures culminate in Hector's gallant refusal to take Achilles's life (V, vi, 13–21) – here, indeed, is the embodiment of the code, and Hector a

paragon of 'fair worth and single chivalry'. But the culmination is in fact merely a foil to the scenes that follow, where in shocking contrast the code is betrayed. Hector, suddenly stirred by an acquisitive and bloodthirsty lust, tracks down a Greek 'beast' and kills him for his 'sumptuous' armor (V, vi, 27–31; V, viii, 1–4).[3] Then, having disarmed, he is set upon by Achilles and the Myrmidons. A parallel is explicitly drawn when Hector cries, 'I am unarmed; forego this vantage, Greek' (V, viii, 9); but he is viciously cut down, and in Achilles's closure to the scene the omnipresent jaws of appetite return: 'My half-supped sword that frankly would have fed,/ Pleased with this dainty bait, thus goes to bed' (V, viii, 19–20).

The plots of love and war are obviously parallel: Hector's death carries us to the same conclusion as the disillusionment of Troilus, namely, that the ugly realities of this world are at cross-purposes with the codes of courtly love and honor that seem to govern it. Shakespeare's panorama of the Trojan war is an ela-

[1] McAlindon, 'Language, Style, and Meaning', p. 29, finds the diction incongruous and the speech mere bombast.

[2] Most of these are in Stamm's discussion of mirror passages ('The Glass of Pandar's Praise', pp. 62–8); see also McAlindon, 'Language, Style and Meaning', pp. 30–1, on gestures and vows.

[3] Cf. J. Oates Smith, 'Essence and Existence in Shakespeare's *Troilus and Cressida*', PQ, XLVI (1967), 172–3, and for a contrasting view on this point, R. J. Kaufmann, 'Ceremonies for Chaos: The Status of *Troilus and Cressida*', ELH, XXXII (1965), 151. I think that the two can be reconciled if we consider that an aristocratic code always distinguishes between the treatment of generals or heroes and of common soldiers like the nameless Greek. Thus Hector is playing the ceremonial game of war, as Kaufmann argues, but the incident shows up the intrinsic worth of the code. The next scene is a comment on its extrinsic value, its relevance to the way men actually behave. The essays by Smith and Kaufmann add a nihilistic and existential dimension to philosophical interpretations of the play. Smith's stress on infidelity and Kaufmann's view of ceremonies accord with my notion of evasion.

boration of his own famous epigram, 'Something is rotten in the state of Denmark' – or of the germ in a contemporary analyst's report of the Elizabethan scene: 'I do here grossly fashion our commonweal, sick or diseased.'[1] What is worse, as the disease progresses, cross-purposes do become complementary purposes. The sick world Shakespeare fashions is like the world of *Julius Caesar* or of *Hamlet*: its ceremonies and formal rhetoric disguise the actual condition of life; the truth, told in images of disease and devouring appetite and by the successive, unveiling actions of the play, is an unpleasant truth, and so to avoid seeing their world for what it is, Trojans and Greeks cling desperately to the superstructures they have erected to deny it.

Time itself serves this mechanism of evasion. Time is a complex notion, regarded with both fear and reverence. Everyone in the play holds a proper Elizabethan distrust for time conceived as mere process or in process; the process is too clearly one of decay. What they reverence is time considered teleologically – the process completed, somehow ended so that durable judgments can be made. Such a completed Time is allegorized in Hector's remark to Ulysses:

Hector.   The end crowns all;
  And that old common arbitrator, Time,
  Will one day end it.
Ulysses.   So to him we leave it.   (IV, v, 224–6)

There is an odor of empty circularity or tautology in the exchange, because time in this sense confers value upon objects and renders them meaningless – the end is all, but the end is also empty, nothing. It is like the 'formless oblivion' that comprises past and future for Agamemnon (IV, v, 167), whose prescription is to lift the 'extant moment' out of the process, elevating it with chivalry. Thus the code is called into service to combat decay. As in *Julius Caesar* the great defense is Roman constancy and

honor, illuminated by images of a soldier's polished metal. So Agamemnon harangued his council,

     Why then, you princes,
Do you with cheeks abashed behold our works,
And call them shames, which are indeed nought
                 else
But the protractive trials of great Jove
To find persistive constancy in men?
The fineness of which metal is not found
In fortune's love: for then the bold and coward,
The wise and fool, the artist and unread,
The hard and soft, seem all affined and kin;
But, in the wind and tempest of her frown,
Distinction with a broad and powerful fan,
Puffing at all, winnows the light away,
And what hath mass or matter, by itself
Lies rich in virtue and unmingled.   (I, iii, 17–30)

Here is the official, religiously orthodox view of temporal process – tending toward decay, but only as a means for God to weigh the fortitude of men. The hard, undiluted mass will stand the test. And so, in figures of hardened, shiny surfaces, does Ulysses explain to Achilles the nature of lasting virtue:

Nor doth he of himself know them [his virtues]
                 for aught
Till he behold them forméd in th'applause
Where they're extended; who, like an arch,
                reverberate
The voice again; or, like a gate of steel
Fronting the sun, receives and renders back
His figure and his heat.   (III, iii, 118–23)

Continuous deeds of heroism may outrun 'emulation' – 'Perseverance, dear my lord,/ Keeps honour bright' (III, iii, 150–1) – and similarly, in Ulysses's degree speech, only an order and authority constantly maintained can hope to withstand the downward spiral of time.

Time and timelessness are equally the concern of lovers. Both Troilus and Cressida

[1] From a report by Armigail Waad, 'The Distresses of the Commonwealth, With the Means to Remedy Them', quoted by Southall, '*Troilus and Cressida* and the Spirit of Capitalism', p. 229.

observe, in the early scenes, that love is a process working gradually toward its goal (Pandarus to Troilus, I, i, 15–30, Cressida in I, ii, 287–94), and in the maxim tossed off by Pandarus – 'Well, the gods are above; time must friend or end' (I, ii, 77–8) – lies the same sense of tautology and impotence in the face of time that is found later in the play. Impotence of this sort runs through the love plot: when Cressida says, 'Things won are done – joy's soul lies in the doing', she means that from a woman's viewpoint the stage of courtly wooing is more satisfactory than the consummation; and at the very point of union Troilus seems obsessed with the failure of achieved love to live up to its promise (III, ii, 18–29, 76–82). Like the generals they fear the ruinous process of decay, and so they too would look beyond to the end, or very nearly the end of time, when with assurance in their judgment 'True swains in love shall in the world to come/ Approve their truths by Troilus' (III, ii, 172–3). Then as myths and metaphors they will have no need to fear, and they will outrival all the hardened similes – steel, iron, the stones of Troy, the sun, and the very earth itself (III, ii, 176–8, 184–8) – as figures of constancy.

Time, then, is not a philosophical theme above the play, containing and unifying the dramatic action; nor are the speeches about time analytical rather than dramatic.[1] The characters of *Troilus and Cressida* share a special and heightened awareness of time, which is appropriate to the world they live in: who would not, after seven years of destruction, fear the procession of time passing before them? Their appeal to ultimate Time, the process ended, is a means of escape from the present.

II

If Time as the arbitrator of all value is tautological, at once all and nothing, and if the dramatic function of time is to serve as a means of evading the present, then what becomes of the debate over values in the play? The most common exposition of this problem has been to contrast the extrinsic theory proposed by Troilus, in which value is conferred by the evaluator, by the price he offers, with the intrinsic theory set out by Hector, which assigns value according to the inherent worth of the object. The first might also be called subjective, in that it requires no public reasons, and the second objective, since it is assumed to depend upon an impartial, reasoned judgment; hence the first is linked with will, the second with reason, reinforcing this larger dichotomy in the play. Moreover, the problem of value described in this way draws a parallel between the two camps: as Hector and Troilus represent opposite ways of evaluating Helen, so Ulysses and Achilles stand as extremes in judging the hero (the hero being Achilles himself, whom Achilles over-rates much as Troilus does Helen).[2] Valuable as this analysis is, it does disguise something of what happens. In the first place, this contrast has only limited importance in the debate over values because both parties in the Trojan camp shift their grounds, Hector most obviously and Troilus more subtly. Thus, although a rhetorical question like 'What's aught, but as 'tis valued?' (II, ii, 52) suggests that value is determined by 'particular will' (and Hector would gladly fix on Troilus this appearance of serving appetite), Troilus's argument is actually quite different. It does not really concern Helen at all, for Troilus

[1] Knight, *Wheel of Fire* (London, 1965), p. 51. While he points out the dramatic appropriateness of various speeches, Knight values the metaphysical inquiry for its own sake. Rabkin also tends to elevate the speculation about time above the drama, though his notion of time is diametrically opposed to Knight's: for Rabkin (*Shakespeare and the Common Understanding*, p. 53) time determines value, while for Knight (p. 65) time destroys values.

[2] Fully described by Rabkin, *Shakespeare and the Common Understanding*, p. 43.

is quite willing to accept Hector's theory and defend Helen's intrinsic merit: '– why, she is a pearl/ Whose price hath launched above a thousand ships/ And turned crowned kings to merchants' (II, ii, 81–3). Cressida, too, was a pearl (I, i, 102–6) and a desirable commodity. What really matters for Troilus, in questions of love and war, is not the woman involved but the 'manhood and honour' (II, ii, 47) at stake. Will may or may not fix value in Helen, that is irrelevant:

> – how may I avoid,
> Although my will distaste what it elected,
> The wife I chose? There can be no evasion
> To blench from this and to stand firm by honour.
> (II, ii, 65–8)

What is relevant is one's word, one's honor, and more, the fact that 'our several honours' are all engaged (II, ii, 124) in this enterprise. Hector, it seems to me, misrepresents Troilus and Paris when he contrasts their 'raging appetites' with the 'moral laws/ Of nature and of nations' (II, ii, 181–6), and perhaps because they are not so merely willful as he makes out, Hector finds it easier to go over to their side in the end.

> Yet, ne'ertheless,
> My sprightly brethren, I propend to you
> In resolution to keep Helen still;
> For 'tis a cause that hath no mean dependence
> Upon our joint and several dignities.
> (II, ii, 189–93)

Those are precisely Troilus's terms – 'our several honours' – and behind Hector's reversal may be a feeling he shares with his opponents: what they really want to keep is the 'well-ordered nation' Hector admires, and this state, they know, depends more on the consistency with which its honor is defended than on moral laws or abstract questions of value. Consistency, after all, is what Troilus and Paris have insisted upon; their argument is perhaps the Trojan counterpart to the Greek constancy

expressed in images of hardness and metals. After Hector has capitulated, Troilus shifts his focus from past to future; no longer needing the pearl as a standard of value, he paints Helen as a means to great possibilities:

> But, worthy Hector,
> She is a theme of honour and renown,
> A spur to valiant and magnanimous deeds,
> Whose present courage may beat down our foes,
> And fame in time to come canonize us;
> For I presume brave Hector would not lose
> So rich advantage of a promised glory
> As smiles upon the forehead of this action
> For the wide world's revenue.   (II, ii, 198–206)

We have already seen in other circumstances how Troilus's religiosity, this desire to be canonized, culminates in an appeal to the 'time to come' (cf. III, ii, 172–3), and how this appeal lures men away from things as they are.

Consistency, unity – in a word, 'order' in the nation is the underlying desideratum in the Trojan council, and the code of honor, as the concluding agreement indicates, is the means to that end. These assumptions about honor, shared implicitly by Troilus and Hector, are explicitly set forth by Ulysses among the Greeks. When his extraordinary portrait of cosmic order, the famous degree speech, finally boils down to the specific complaint, Ulysses attributes the failure of the campaign to social impropriety – the Greek soldiers haven't proper respect for their superiors:

> The general's disdained
> By him one step below, he by the next,
> That next by him beneath; so every step,
> Exampled by the first pace that is sick
> Of his superior, grows to an envious fever
> Of pale and bloodless emulation –
> And 'tis this fever that keeps Troy on foot . . .
> (I, iii, 129–35)

And like Hector, Ulysses tries to identify this situation in which 'degree is shaked' with 'appetite' (I, iii, 119–24), while his own concept of hierarchic order takes on the name of reason (I, iii, 210). But it is not reason, no more than Troilus's argument was purely appetite; rather it is a kind of reasoning that promotes order and unity, just as the code of honor, imposing deference upon inferiors and consistency upon superiors, cements the *status quo*. These appeals to 'reason' and to 'honor' are essentially nominal or arbitrary standards: Ulysses's social order originates in 'The primogeniture and due of birth,/ Prerogative of age, crowns, sceptres, laurels' (I, iii, 106–7) without reference to merit, and for Troilus honor demands constancy (II, ii, 84–92), as if to say that holding the course chosen is the best proof of a wise choice. Thus both depend upon the assumption of an infallible or omniscient authority, and that authority is stressed in the third important discussion of value, between Achilles and Ulysses. Achilles, bolstering his now unattended pride, would exempt himself from the run of men who are governed by a merely nominal concept of honor:

> And not a man, for being simply man,
> Hath any honour but honour for those honours
> That are without him – as place, riches, and
> > favour,
> Prizes of accident as oft as merit;
> ... But 'tis not so with me.   (III, iii, 80–3, 87)

But Ulysses cautions him that virtue, so far as men are concerned, lies in actual deeds, not in sheltered qualities; that laud goes to 'dust that is a little gilt' rather than to 'gilt o'er-dusted' (III, iii, 178–9) reminds us that 'Degree being vizarded,/ Th'unworthiest shows as fairly in the mask' (I, iii, 83–4). So Achilles puts aside this public world that seems to belong entirely to 'envious and calumniating Time', and pleads private reasons for his retirement. To this Ulysses answers, in effect, there is no private world:

> The providence that's in a watchful state
> Knows almost every grain of Pluto's gold,
> Finds bottom in th'uncomprehensive deeps,
> Keeps place with thought and almost like the gods

> Does thoughts unveil in their dumb cradles.
> There is a mystery, with whom relation
> Durst never meddle, in the soul of state,
> Which hath an operation more divine
> Than breath or pen can give expressure to.
> > (III, iii, 196–204)[1]

Nothing is unknown to the state, which is 'almost like the gods', and all authority, all honor and reputation, derive from it. What budding love there may have been in Achilles for Priam's daughter gives way to his pride which can be fed only by the official histories of Greece. In time to come – always this concern for an indefinable, 'eternal' future – 'When fame shall in our islands sound her trump' (III, iii, 210), Achilles's name must be inscribed as 'potent and heroical'. Patroclus, too, though he has 'little stomach to the war' (III, iii, 220), urges his lover Achilles to yield their privacy to the call of honor.

Ulysses's speech on the providence of the state, more sharply than any other, discovers the centripetal pull of all the philosophy and rhetoric in *Troilus and Cressida*. Beneath an apparent disparity, all the theories converge in a way that is more obvious if we consider the total action of the play: they all support, at the expense of privacy, a collective, public order which is absolute in its authority and which is geared to continuing the long, absurd war that stretches across the stage, infecting if not devouring the entire cast. Call it the state, or

[1] See W. R. Elton, 'Shakespeare's Ulysses and the Problem of Value', *Shakespeare Studies*, II (1966), 107, who explains with citations the medieval concept of monarchical sacred omniscience on which this speech is based. Elton argues that Ulysses's views are nominalistic and relativistic, significantly like the philosophy of Hobbes. Thus for Ulysses value is relative to human desires, a marketable quantity, and this is exactly the kind of relative or subjective evaluation Troilus makes in the debate over Helen. What Elton doesn't stress is implied in his discussion of the 'mystery of the state', namely, that the relativism of Ulysses, and of Troilus for that matter, is, like that of Hobbes, used as a defense of political absolutism.

call it the system, it is a subtle network that both 'reason' and 'honor' serve: it is what supposedly justifies the parleys and games between opposing generals in the midst of slaughter; it is the apology for awful sacrifices on the part of men forever hoping that Time will somehow redeem them; it is a part of the 'necessary form' of history, a Grand Mechanism rising above men, directing them to roles they are hardly conscious of – and not just the mechanism of political struggle, but the superior machinery of war that unifies society while squeezing out its very life. In *Julius Caesar*, and to an extent in the earlier history plays, the acts of successive political figures in their struggles for power begin to mirror each other as the mechanism gathers momentum.[1] In *Troilus and Cressida* the mechanism is superbly efficient: not only acts, but thoughts converge – as the action is all part of the game of war, so the arguments are all ceremonies of rededication to the code that maintains the war and dissolves all forms of personal expression.[2] What needs to be contrasted is not subtle variations among Greek and Trojan leaders, but rather the single dimension in all their reasoning set over against the prophetic cries of Cassandra and Thersites.

> Cry, Trojans, cry! lend me ten thousand eyes,
> And I will fill them with prophetic tears . . .
>
> (II, ii, 101–2)

> Farewell – yet soft! Hector, I take my leave;
> Thou dost thyself and all our Troy deceive.
>
> (V, iii, 89–90)

Weigh reason against prophecy in this play, and to borrow Thersites's incisive complaint, 'all the argument is a whore and a cuckold' – to the appetite of war.

III

The debate over value, like the descant on time, sustains the illusion fabricated by reason and honor. Bound by their heroic code, Greeks and Trojans march into oblivion; they are caught up in the machinery of a state at war; the only hope they know is that of a timeless, collective memory where reputation – what Cassio, another purveyor of the code, calls the 'immortal part' of man – will be sealed up long after their bodies have turned to dust. In such a world it is natural for Eros to be postponed or channelled to serve the state. And the story of the young lovers, the central characters from whom the play takes its name, reveals the full effect of the grand mechanism at work.

Love and war are traditionally parallel or complementary themes, and in the play the codes of the warrior and the lover are clearly made out to be symbiotic. The motifs are pervasively entwined: for example, when Aeneas delivers Hector's challenge, the beauty and worth of Greek opposed to Trojan women are at stake (I, iii, 268–76); in the witty exchanges between Pandarus and Cressida, love is treated as martial combat (I, ii, 260 ff.); Troilus also thinks of war in anticipating the taste of love – 'I shall lose distinction in my joys,/ As doth a battle, when they charge on heaps/ The enemy flying' (III, ii, 27–9); and in the duet that ends the scene the lovers battle to prove their constancy –

> Troilus.
> I am as true as truth's simplicity,
> And simpler than the infancy of truth!

[1] The 'Grand Mechanism' is introduced by Jan Kott, *Shakespeare Our Contemporary*, trans. Boleslaw Taborski (Garden City, 1966), especially pp. 6–11, 14. He does not mention it in connection with *Troilus and Cressida* though he does make the point that both feudal mystics and rationalists in the play attempt to justify the war (p. 79). I have used Kott's idea to interpret the other plays in 'History and the Histories in *Julius Caesar*', to be published in *Shakespeare Quarterly* in 1972.

[2] Kaufmann, 'Ceremonies for Chaos: the Status of *Troilus and Cressida*', pp. 139–59, stresses the inability of all characters to stand free of codes or concepts; by giving themselves to ceremonies that distort reality, they lose the integrity or selfhood that heroism requires.

Cressida.
In that I'll war with you.
Troilus.   O virtuous fight,
When right with right wars who shall be most
right!
(III, ii, 168–71)

War thrives on a kind of love – when knights defend their mistresses whose tokens they bear, and mistresses arm and disarm their knights. But privacy in love, as we have seen with Achilles, is dangerous to the field; it must be rooted out. So, in the moment of love's consummation, Shakespeare contrives that 'the time' should undermine the lovers. And this is not personified Time, but the actual moment, war-time, the here and now: Calchas is prompted by 'Th'advantage of the time' (III, iii, 2) to demand an exchange of Antenor for his daughter, and Paris sums up the plight of the lovers – 'There is no help;/ The bitter disposition of the time/ Will have it so' (IV, i, 49–51). In one of Shakespeare's characteristic dramatic actions, the public world comes knocking early at the private chamber. Troilus and Cressida have awakened, and in lines that recall a similar scene from *Romeo and Juliet* (III, v, 1–42) they lament night's brevity:

Troilus.
O Cressida! but that the busy day,
Waked by the lark, hath roused the ribald crows,
And dreaming night will hide our joys no longer,
I would not from thee.
Cressida.   Night hath been too brief.
Troilus.
Beshrew the witch! with venomous wights she
stays
As tediously as hell, but flies the grasps of love
With wings more momentary-swift than thought.
You will catch cold, and curse me.
Cressida.   Prithee, tarry.
You men will never tarry.
O foolish Cressid! I might have still held off,
And then you would have tarried.   (IV, ii, 8–18)

The young nobleman, who naively accepts the courtly code he has inherited, is frightened that the demands of sexual love will conflict with honor; he is afraid of being discovered and would flee with the night. Cressida pleads with him to 'tarry' – the essential of Pandar's recipe for love (I, i, 15) – for she realizes now in a fuller sense that love grows slowly, that it must struggle against the demands of the world, that men fear when it 'swells past hiding' in a sense more profound than her earlier witticism (I, ii, 270) entailed. This kind of love challenges the order, the mechanism.

But here love loses. Consider the response of Troilus, who was 'mad in Cressid's love' (I, i, 53), to the encroachment of the official world:

Aeneas.
My lord, I scarce have leisure to salute you,
My matter is so rash . . .
. . . within this hour,
We must give up to Diomedes' hand
The Lady Cressida.
Troilus.   Is it so concluded?
Aeneas.
By Priam and the general state of Troy.
They are at hand and ready to effect it.
Troilus.
How my achievements mock me!
I will go meet them; and, my Lord Aeneas,
We met by chance: you did not find me here.
(IV, ii, 59–60, 64–71)

This is far from madness – an off-hand question, a wistful comment, and Troilus departs with Aeneas to join the very council that has dealt the blow. 'The young prince will go mad', cries Pandarus (IV, ii, 75), but he reacts more passionately than Troilus. He is left to console Cressida whose grief, so unlike Troilus's, points toward tragic intensity:

Tear my bright hair and scratch my praiséd cheeks,
Crack my clear voice with sobs and break my heart
With sounding Troilus. I will not go from Troy.
(IV, ii, 106–8)

Thus there is, in this central incident of the play and moment of high passion, an obvious flattening in the character supposedly most susceptible to feeling. It is not an undramatic slip; surprisingly, perhaps, but with psychological precision, Shakespeare shows that Troilus is calmed, even relieved in returning to his public role – he belongs to 'the general state of Troy'.

The bargain that sends Cressida to the Greek camp is just another of the acts of shame war brings. It must therefore be disguised and treated as an elaborate public ceremony, like the ritualized assassination of Caesar or the murder of Desdemona. Like Othello, Troilus borrows imaginary priestly robes for his task:

> I'll bring her to the Grecian presently;
> And to his hand when I deliver her,
> Think it an altar, and thy brother Troilus
> A priest, there offering to it his own heart.
> (IV, iii, 6–9)

Cressida will be a sacrifice to the gods. Troilus invites religious sanction, and like Agamemnon who saw adversity as the trials of Jove, he explains this calamity as decreed by the gods:

> Cressid, I love thee in so strained a purity,
> That the blest gods, as angry with my fancy,
> More bright in zeal than the devotion which
> Cold lips blow to their deities, take thee from me.
> (IV, iv, 24–7)

Strained indeed, this purity and zeal that sloughs off responsibility on the authority of a world beyond: for we have seen such divine operations before, when the watchful state unveiled, 'almost like the gods', the privacy of lovers. Strained, too, are the phrases of his 'loose adieu', betrayed by the ubiquitous imagery of the market-place (IV, iv, 40) and by that other metaphysical scapegoat, 'injurious Time' (IV, iv, 42), whom Troilus blames for what clearly *the* time and *this* world have done ... and for what *he* is doing, almost in numbed default. Imagine Romeo or Hamlet in his place – would they be tamed to this hollow, passionless performance? But Troilus never sees beyond his part in the ceremony. It is a game he plays at quite seriously – she'll wear his sleeve, and with the special rights of the rich and noble, he'll go between the warring camps, bribing the Greek sentinels (IV, iv, 70–3). For the exchange proper Troilus flourishes with courtly demeanor:

> Welcome, Sir Diomed! Here is the lady
> Which for Antenor we deliver you.
> At the port, lord, I'll give her to thy hand,
> And by the way possess thee what she is.
> Entreat her fair; and, by my soul, fair Greek,
> If e'er thou stand at mercy of my sword,
> Name Cressid, and thy life shall be as safe
> As Priam is in Ilion. (IV, iv, 109–16)

Diomedes's refusal to join in the chivalrous pledges and his obvious attentions to Cressida puncture this gesture, leaving Troilus to complain about his lack of courtesy (IV, iv, 121). This rebuke foreshadows Hector's treatment at the hands of Achilles, which is also something less than courteous. It infuriates Troilus, stirring the obsessive fears he broached so insistently to Cressida. He does not realize yet how love has lost, but the extent to which eros has been subordinated to the state by his chivalrous, pseudo-religious act is conveyed in the final dialogue between Aeneas and Paris:

> *Aeneas.*　　How we have spent this morning!
> The prince [Hector] must think me tardy and
> 　　　　　　　　　　　　　　　　　　　　remiss,
> That swore to ride before him to the field.
> *Paris.*
> 'Tis Troilus' fault; come, come, to field with him.
>
> 　　　　　　　　· · · ·
>
> *Aeneas.*
> Yea, with a bridegroom's fresh alacrity,
> Let us address to tend on Hector's heels ...
> (IV, iv, 140–3, 145–6)

Troilus lingers only momentarily; in the end he is true to the world of his fellow courtiers – the bridegroom casts off his fleshly bride and renews his troth to the spectre of war.

And so Cressida, as perhaps all the words of love have foretold, is finally marketed and sold.

To see her as merely a shallow and experienced 'Trojan drab', as most critics now do, is to miss the significance of this act. Jan Kott's brief but vivid sketch is an appropriate antidote to Cressid's detractors:

This girl could have been eight, ten, or twelve years old when the war started. Maybe that is why war seems so normal and ordinary to her that she almost does not notice it and never talks about it . . . There is no place for love in this world. Love is poisoned from the outset. These wartime lovers have been given just one night . . . Pandarus has procured Cressida like some goods. Now, like goods, she will be exchanged with the Greeks for a captured Trojan general. She has to leave at once, the very morning after her first night. Cressida is seventeen. An experience like this is enough. Cressida will go to the Greeks. But it will be a different Cressida. Until now she has known love only in imagination. Now she has come to know it in reality. During one night. She is violently awakened. She realizes the world is too vile and cruel for anything to be worth defending. Even on her way to the Greek camp Diomedes makes brutal advances to her. Then she is kissed in turn by the generals and princes, old, great, and famous men: Nestor, Agamemnon, Ulysses. She has realized that beauty arouses desire. She can still mock. But she already knows she will become a tart. Only before that happens, she has to destroy everything, so that not even memory remains. She is consistent.[1]

Certainly there is no need to assume Cressida is sexually experienced because of her talk. Playful bawdry and sharp passion are commonly found in the speeches of Shakespeare's virginal heroines, Rosalind or Juliet, for example. Whatever she has done before, for Cressida this morning in Troy is unquestionably a rude awakening. Among the Greeks she is bound to be exposed and degraded; it is, in the cliché of courtly honor, a fate worse than death, and quite expectedly that is what we hear from Troilus: 'Hark! you are called. Some say the Genius so/ Cries "Come!" to him that instantly must die' (IV, iv, 50–1). The ceremony that welcomes her to the Greek camp is a brilliant contrivance – it is drapery that actually reveals her nakedness, and it should bring home the full meaning of her being turned over to the enemy. Despite the elaborate courtesy of begging kisses, the Greek generals are taking what Cressida, essentially a captive, has no real power to refuse. She plays their game with wit and spirit, for that is her best defense.

Rude as it is, Cressida is not shocked or distraught; there is in her less illusion than in Troilus and an adaptive, reserve strength. She is indeed a daughter of the game, but we must be sure what game is being played. Whether or not Cressida knows about sex, she knows about war; she has grown up with it, not as one who seeks its glory, for she disdains the heroic proportions of warriors –

> *Alexander.*
> They say he [Ajax] is a very man per se,
> And stands alone.
> *Cressida.* So do all men, unless they are drunk, sick, or have no legs. (I, ii, 15–18)

– but as an onlooker and victim who must learn to survive with it. That is why Cressida seems so worldly and why she plays so knowingly the courtly game of sweet withholding. Hers is the good training courtly standards provide, good for a war-torn world in which something must always be withheld or restrained. Love is degraded in this world, for the wisdom of survival reduces it to a series of one-night stands: tomorrow the lover is gone to battle, or the beloved is traded off to the other side. Thus what Cressida discovers on rudely awakening is what she has instinctively prepared for. If Troilus submerged his erotic self in honor, Cressida has consistently struggled to keep part of *her* self unengaged:

[1] Kott, *Shakespeare Our Contemporary*, pp. 80–1. The Cressida of the Loeb Theater production at Harvard in the summer of 1968 seemed to me very much like Kott's – young, fresh, attractive, alive to the pleasures of love and knowledgeable in a way that makes the question of her previous sexual experience really irrelevant.

I have a kind of self resides with you,
But an unkind self that itself will leave
To be another's fool. I would be gone.
(III, ii, 147–9)

She knows that secrecy and silence are 'cunning in dumbness' (III, ii, 131), estrangement is a means of self-preservation. She knows that wisdom, in her world, is incompatible with love: 'for to be wise and love/ Exceeds man's might; that dwells with gods above' (III, ii, 155–6).

Cressida surrenders to Diomedes a few hours after leaving Troy. The complex demands of her situation shroud her motives; she is shrewd and practices the wisdom of concealment. What we do know is that Cressida is still very much the divided self that she pictured earlier: dialogue and gestures – giving, taking back, and giving again the sleeve – mark her importunate uncertainty. When Diomedes has left, Cressida examines what she has done, speaking for the last time in the play.

Troilus, farewell! One eye yet looks on thee,
But with my heart the other eye doth see.
Ah, poor our sex! this fault in us I find,
The error of our eye directs our mind;
What error leads must err – O, then conclude
Minds swayed by eyes are full of turpitude.
(v, ii, 107–12)

If passing from one man to another is her role in the ceremony of war, she plays it; but unlike Troilus she holds something back, and in this withholding, this wandering or double vision, her critical faculty is sustained. By her own standards, and surely by the official standards of her world, she is condemned. Yet where minds are so readily corrupted and eyes so irresponsibly blind, it is self-righteous for her world to judge Cressida. After all, she is simply practicing the way of that world as envisioned by Troilus – 'My will enkindled by mine eyes and ears –/ Two traded pilots 'twixt the dangerous shores/ Of will and judgement' (II, ii, 63–4) – and by Ulysses – 'The present eye praises the present object' (III, iii, 180). Perhaps in the sensual pleasure of the here and now, however bittersweet it proves, Cressida has got hold of the only value her world affords. All that is left to her is a little touch of Troilus in the night – or of Diomedes, what does it matter? One or the other will be dead next evening.

IV

The betrayal of Troilus is an extraordinary scene which, together with the closing action of the play, points toward a number of motifs in *Othello*.[1] At the center is ocular proof of Cressid's infidelity. Troilus, whom Ulysses observes to be, like the noble Moor, 'both open and both free' (IV, v, 100), is shocked almost to silence. At first, he tries to stifle any response, his speech reduced to brief utterances –

by Jove, I will not speak a word.
. . . I will not be myself, nor have cognition
Of what I feel. I am all patience. (v, ii, 54, 65–6)

Then, so far from Cressida's reliance on her senses (v, ii, 107–12), he would simply deny what he sees:

But if I tell how these two did co-act,
Shall I not lie in publishing a truth?
Sith yet there is a credence in my heart,
An esperance so obstinately strong,
That doth invert th'attest of eyes and ears;
As if those organs had deceptious functions,
Created only to calumniate. (v, ii, 118–24)

[1] Stamm, 'The Glass of Pandar's Praise', p. 71, discusses technical aspects of this scene. Brian Morris, 'The Tragic Structure of *Troilus and Cressida*', *Shakespeare Quarterly*, X (1959), 488–9, calls the contrivance of the setting comic, but the development of the scene tragic. Both Morris (pp. 488, 491) and Kott (p. 82) suggest parallels with Othello. Othello naturally denies the 'evidence' of Desdemona's infidelity, but when he begins to believe it his speeches are shortened to perfunctory responses and his whole sense of order collapses. He, too, suffers the divided awareness that afflicts Troilus, and bolsters himself with rhetorical flourishes and the ceremonial sanctions of judge and priest.

For Troilus the 'esperance', a Latinate vision of what might be, has always been more comfortable than reality. Finally his whole world is split open and stood on end. Beginning his own degree speech, Troilus spells out the kind of spiritual hierarchy that reason imagines:

> If beauty have a soul, this is not she;
> If souls guide vows, if vows be sanctimonies,
> If sanctimony be the gods' delight,
> If there be rule in unity itself,
> This is not she.   (v, ii, 138–42)

And yet it is – so reason turns to madness and paradox makes sense. In the tradition of Shakespearian protagonists, not just Othello but Brutus and Macbeth and even Cressida herself, Troilus is a divided soul – the state of man, like a kingdom or a whole world, suffers an insurrection and chaos is come: 'a thing inseparate/ Divides more wider than the sky and earth'; 'The bonds of heaven are slipped, dissolved, and loosed' (v, ii, 148–9, 156). And the speech begun in celestial and Platonic order ends with the 'greasy relics' of appetite. Troilus cannot endure it; he cannot withhold or be 'but half attached' to his passion, as Ulysses counsels (v, ii, 161–2), so that the divisive loss of faith does not become for him, as it did for Cressida, a crippled wisdom accommodated to a corrupt world. Disillusionment paralyzes Troilus only for a moment, and then he begins to swell with hate; he steadies himself with what is most natural and accessible to him, the role of a faithful knight whose 'so eternal and so fixed a soul' swears to avenge its honor. Along with this role comes the rhetoric of *miles gloriosus*, dreadful bombast that should not be mistaken for Troilus coming to his senses:

> Not the dreadful spout
> Which shipmen do the hurricano call,
> Constringed in mass by the almighty sun,
> Shall dizzy with more clamour Neptune's ear
> In his descent, than shall my prompted sword
> Falling on Diomed.
> *Thersites.*   He'll tickle it for his concupy.
>   (v, ii, 171–7)

Troilus is posturing again, and his exercises carry over to the field where he redeems himself with 'Mad and fantastic execution', so careless of his own safety that his luck is to Ulysses the 'very spite of cunning' (v, v, 38, 41). The old 'dog-fox' Ulysses did his best, but in the distracted slaughter of this final movement there is no order, no 'degree', not even of cunning; policy 'is proved not worth a blackberry', and 'the Grecians begin to proclaim barbarism' (v, iv, 11, 15), evidently loosing the kind of savagery that lets Achilles murder Hector. Rising from this dust, Troilus speaks in concluding, funereal tones of Hector's death and the imminent destruction of Troy. 'Hector is dead; there is no more to say' – but Troilus is never at a loss for words –

> Stay yet. You vile abominable tents,
> Thus proudly pight upon our Phrygian plains,
> Let Titan rise as early as he dare,
> I'll through and through you! And thou
>   great-sized coward,
> No space of earth shall sunder our two hates;
> I'll haunt thee like a wicked conscience still,
> That mouldeth goblins swift as frenzy's thoughts.
> Strike a free march to Troy! with comfort go:
> Hope of revenge shall hide our inward woe.
>   (v, x, 23–31)

'Words, words, mere words', Troilus said of Cressida (v, iii, 108), but he cannot say it of himself. This speech is little more than a continuation of his spiteful threats in the betrayal scene and can hardly be construed as tragic recognition. Always what matters is what Troilus does not recognize: that 'after so many hours, lives, speeches spent', another oath of revenge is a terrible folly; that his late heroism and frenzied hatred for the enemy is one more instance of Eros harnessed to the purposes of the state, sublimated into the honorable outlet of duty – and Troilus is, in his own image, 'Mars his heart/ Inflamed with Venus' (v, ii, 164–5); that his world is not governed by the splendid systems and codes rehearsed throughout the play but is pretty much what Ulysses feared it might become:

> Then everything includes itself in power,
> Power into will, will into appetite;
> And appetite, an universal wolf,
> So doubly seconded with will and power,
> Must make perforce an universal prey,
> And last eat up himself. (I, iii, 119–24)

For the state at war 'everything includes itself in power' – all ceremonies, all speeches and all love, all secrets and all hope are drawn into the mechanism that must finally devour itself. The Troiluses, the Hectors, the Achilles and Ulysses of this world and ours, more or less unwittingly, are sons of the game. Thersites has told them the way things are: but will they ever learn?[1]

[1] For Morris ('Tragic Structure of *Troilus and Cressida*', p. 489) Troilus 'begins to find his true self' after his disillusionment at Calchas's tent and returns to the role of heroic warrior. McAlindon ('Language, Style, and Meaning', pp. 33–4) also sees Troilus recovering verbal and behavioral decorum. Stamm, on the other hand ('The Glass of Pandar's Praise', pp. 75–6), discredits such a recovery by calling Troilus's final speech a 'series of hyberbolic images'. Moreover, both rants by Troilus are undercut, first by Thersites's mockery (v, ii, 177) and then by the ending Pandarus gives to the play, especially the song that has much to do with the source of Troilus's wrath:

> Full merrily the humble-bee doth sing
> Till he hath lost his honey and his sting;
> And being once subdued in armed tail,
> Sweet honey and sweet notes together fail.
> (v, x, 41–4)

THE OPTIONS OF THE AUDIENCE:
THEORY AND PRACTICE IN
PETER BROOK'S 'MEASURE FOR MEASURE'

HERBERT S. WEIL, JR

Many years ago, after watching the Rosalind played by Edith Evans, an enthusiastic critic exclaimed, 'She made the audience one Orlando'. However imprecise this phrase may be, it captures some essential virtues of a superb portrayal: the ability to seduce us, to hypnotize, to convince us of charm and vigor – those qualities that come across immediately and fully in an excellent production. Like pace, rhythm, and humor, such virtues tend to elude us in our private studies and our chalky class-rooms. We all recognize that, unfortunately, the personal magnetism of an Edith Evans is not a universal option, but a rare one. The Rosalinds, for example, that I have been able to see, stopped far short of making me into an Orlando. They range from the actress, best left nameless, who played the role as if she were a rookie offensive guard for the New York Giants, to Ronald Pickup, the lead in the all-male Old Vic version of 1968. Pickup was a charming Rosalind, but far weaker than both a virile Orlando and a wryly witty Celia.

As You Like It can succeed whether its heroine is idealized or realistic, brilliant or subdued. But the charisma of a great Rosalind – Shakespeare's most effectively dominating comic heroine – would probably distort many other leading roles in his comedies. For recent audiences Valentine, Bassanio, and Claudio seem more credible if their unappealing selfishness receives some sporadic emphasis than if they are treated as nearly flawless conventional romance figures. Successful productions often induce diverging attitudes toward the same character or idea. The uneven high camp *As You Like It* of the Old Vic did release varying responses toward the traditionally overpowering heroine. In a comparable way, the 1968 production of *Much Ado About Nothing* by the Royal Shakespeare Company faced the problems which arise when Claudio behaves so outrageously after the church scene. At this time he must believe that Hero is dead as a result of his accusations. First he addresses her irate father and uncle in a cold formal way and then he goes on to bait Benedick and Don Pedro, attempting to exchange bawdy wise-cracks as if nothing serious had happened. Unlike many directors who have cut this puzzling scene, Trevor Nunn presented a clearly suffering Claudio. Horrified and tormented by what he had done, he cruelly badgered the others as a defense mechanism to avoid facing the truth of his own compassionless treatment of Hero.

Our awareness of multiple – or even conflicting – attitudes toward a character can almost always enrich our experience of an outstanding comedy. This is true especially for comedy because here character rarely determines action; seldom does a hero achieve *convincing* growth or moral responsibility. Why then need the spectator finally identify his evaluations with those of any one figure? Is a style which strives to break down our detachment appropriate for Shakespeare's comedies? Even the viewer who has momentarily become an Orlando must return home when the play is over.

27

There is a crucial difference between a production that overwhelms the spectator, thereby lulling his critical sensibilities, and one that opens up many new options for him. The first type tends to coerce the viewer. The latter may be able to liberate him. Recently such influential directors as Jan Kott, Jerzy Grotowski, Charles Marowitz, and Peter Brook have insisted upon the necessity of transforming theatrical classics. They argue that the contemporary spectator can respond in an honest, positive manner only if the director 'restructures' the text itself. Brook writes, 'To execute Shakespeare's intentions ... we need complete freedom, rich improvisation, no holding back, no false respect'.[1] But how often does such freedom permit a more direct communication with the intention of the author? Which approach really does liberate us? To understand the many possibilities of the play? Or to understand only the one vision of the director as *auteur*? The question unfortunately is loaded – as are any alternative phrasings I can imagine. I am only suggesting that freeing the play of historically accumulated debris may liberate the modern spectator – or it may not – that only the individual performance, not the theory, can validate the claim.

In order to consider how far theatrical excitement can lead to more full understanding, therefore, it will be most valuable to examine one production in detail. For this purpose, Peter Brook's *Measure for Measure* at Stratford-on-Avon in 1950 should be especially helpful. His staging of *Measure* has probably been the most influential and the most widely praised version of this increasingly popular problematic comedy. Lawrence Olivier has called it the most enlightening interpretation of any play that he has seen. Surprisingly, there has been little published history of *Measure* in the theatre. And most important for this argument, Brook's acting text was no extreme adaptation or experiment. Many reviewers, in fact, applauded its faithfulness to Shakespeare's conception and text.

The scholar can supplement the clear prompt-books in the Shakespeare Birthplace Library with Brook's statements on file there about his aims in 1950 and with his later thoughts in *The Empty Space* (1968). Furthermore, even should one disagree with the director's governing idea or some incidental touches, there can be little doubt that he planned carefully and intelligently. Brook stated that he was following the text closely and minimizing the extraneous frills – for which some of his earlier work had been attacked. He added no lines and relatively little unsupported stage business – with one modest exception. He did attempt to balance 'the brilliant succession of closet-scenes' or 'duets' with three teeming processions, one of which he invented: a full-stage scene moving through the central hall of the prison to bring 'its holes and corners into relation with each other'. As Richard David in *Shakespeare Survey 4* pointed out, Shakespeare's text gives only the slimmest pretext for this, in Pompey's enumeration of the old customers whom he has met again in his new employment.[2] But this addition seems rather modest when compared to those in other productions. Before the opening lines of the 1965 New York version in Central Park, an orgy of mimed copulation represented a Vienna badly in need of reform. And in the final act of the 1962 Stanford University staging, enthusiastic extras, representing the populace of Vienna, celebrated with signs and dances the alleged defeat of Puritanism and the restoration of the brothels.

Writing about his primary purpose in *The Empty Space*, published eighteen years after the production, Brook argues (p. 88):

[1] Peter Brook, *The Empty Space* (London, 1968), p. 88.
[2] 'Shakespeare's Comedies and the Modern Stage' (Cambridge, 1951), p. 136. Phrases in the preceding sentences are adapted from this excellent brief review.

Shakespeare succeeded where no one has succeeded before or since in writing plays that pass through many stages of consciousness. What enabled him technically to do so, the essence, in fact of his style, is a roughness of texture and a conscious mingling of opposites.

This seems to me very promising indeed. If a critic or a director can create for a reader or a spectator some experience of these 'stages of consciousness', he may have discovered the best path to an understanding, both deeper and more precise, of *Measure for Measure* – even of all comedies that achieve lasting literary significance. One of my primary concerns will be to explore as well as I can at this distance how far Brook could succeed in creating such stages of consciousness and to what extent his own governing view might have imposed severe limitations on them.

In *The Empty Space*, Brook finds co-existing side by side two opposites which he calls the Holy and the Rough. He then defines the latter (p. 88):

In *Measure for Measure*, we have a base world, a very real world in which the action is firmly rooted. This is the disgusting, stinking world of medieval Vienna. The darkness of this world is absolutely necessary for the meaning of the play . . . When so much is religious in thought, the loud humour of the brothel is important as a device, because it is alienating and humanizing. From the fanatical chastity of Isabella and the mystery of the Duke we are plunged back to Pompey and Barna[r]dine for douches of normality . . . We must animate all this stretch of the play, not as fantasy, but as the roughest comedy we can make.

These statements offer at the very least a direction that should prove fertile if one searches for the unity of the play. Too often, directors have used Lucio, Pompey, Elbow, and Barnardine only for moments of slap-stick or incidental amusement. Although I would prefer greater emphasis on the joyous vitality of the clowns than on the 'disgusting, stinking, and base', Brook – if he could establish the relevance of this 'rough' sub-plot group – would

certainly advance well beyond most published criticism and most performances of the play.

Reviews of his production show clearly that, for Brook, this rough base world finally is important not for itself, but because from it grows the Holy World – that of Isabella and the Duke. Except to praise Barbara Jefford for her emotional and moral simplicity, particularly in her scenes with John Gielgud's forceful Angelo, neither the director nor the reviewers had much to say about the significance of heroine or of deputy. In the reviews available, that by Richard David in the *Shakespeare Survey* was most thorough and seemed most reliable, particularly in demonstrating familiarity with the text. David summarized the central idea of the production (p. 137):

It is not Isabella, still less Angelo, that is the crux of the producer's problem, but the Duke. If the play is to mean anything, if it is to be more than a series of disjointed magnificences, we must accept the Duke's machinations as all to good purpose, and himself as entirely wise and just. Peter Brook presented Vincentio rather as Friar turned Duke than as Duke turned Friar . . . He found in Harry Andrews a Duke whose commanding presence could dominate the play, as the half-seen arches the stage, and whose charm of manner could convince us of his integrity and wisdom.

Like other reviewers, David was prepared to welcome the treatment of the Duke as an ideal ruler. Here Brook was not seeking originality or an atypical stance toward the play. Instead he followed the view probably most prominent in criticism published during the last forty years: that the Duke is far more than a simple controller or manipulator of the action; that he is both admirable in his deeds and reliable in his comments about himself and the other characters. This view comes from G. Wilson Knight and F. R. Leavis and has been developed more fully by David Stevenson, Josephine Waters Bennett, and many others. For most of these critics there are no significant flaws in the character or personality of the Duke. To them, any signs of weakness must be the result of anachronistic or irrelevant demands by the reader who foolishly expects naturalistic character traits where only those suitable for his Providential role should matter. Brook's production, then, conveniently provides a test for *both* the most influential critical position and for one of our most controversial directors.

For several years, I have wondered how well an uncut production could support this dominant view of the Duke – and with it, most arguments for the coherence of the play. Some dozen passages have seemed unplayable unless we are meant to laugh *at* the Duke and to find meaningful flaws in his personal private character as well as in his ability to rule. Partly because Shakespeare gave the Duke many more lines than any other character in the play, it seemed to me much more likely that the dramatist was experimenting with divergent ideas of his controlling figure than that he had left us a badly flawed or careless text.

Because of its reputed textual accuracy and because the director himself emphasized the significance of rough and holy elements, his production would seem to offer a superb test-case for a substantially uncut version based upon a charismatic holy Duke. But Brook's prompt-books surprise us by the number of significant passages that are deleted. Gone are a group of lines that suggest that the Duke is either confused or conniving. Brook omits Vincentio's explanation for his hasty departure when he assumes his disguise in the expository scene iii of act I, where he says that Angelo:

> may, in th'ambush of my name, strike home,
> And yet my nature never in the fight
> To do in slander.[1] (41–3)

For many scholars, these lines had presented the primary motive for the Duke's pretended absence. Also cut are Lucio's lines to Isabella in scene iv which complement Vincentio's tenuous explanation:

> His givings-out were of an infinite distance
> From his true-meant design. (54–5)

Brook sees fit to leave out much of the Duke's clumsy verbosity and the egotistical line with which he justifies his bed-trick to Isabella:

> To the love I have in doing good a remedy presents itself. (III, i, 195–6)

Gone, too, is the line climactic to the melodramatic plot-surface, one that invariably brings laughter in the theater;

> O, 'tis an accident that Heaven provides! (IV, iii, 73)

This line the Duke enthusiastically exclaims when the discovery of the dead pirate Ragozine miraculously provides him with a substitute head, a very convenient accident from Heaven when we remember that the last miraculously discovered prisoner, Barnardine, proved no docile substitute. In addition, Brook deleted large sections of the Duke–Friar's confusing instructions about his own return to Vienna and, as David noted, many sections of the long act V, which incidentally do not jibe neatly with the conception of an efficient Providential Duke. These include important parts of his instructions to Isabella just before the climax of the act that she should *not* sue for Angelo's life. Also gone is the only explicit reference to its title, which comes in a thoroughly ironic context when both Duke and audience know that Angelo has failed to execute Claudio. And absent are key phrases in the Duke's extremely awkward marriage proposal to Isabella and in his anticlimactic pardon of the still unrepentant Barnardine.

Besides making the Duke more efficient and less the manipulator, Brook deleted many specific moral references. Gone are strikingly

[1] Quotations are from *William Shakespeare, The Complete Works*, ed. Peter Alexander (London/Glasgow, 1951) except for my emendation of the Duke's couplet in response to Pompey.

atypical generalizations couched in unusual formal or archaic diction, such as that of Escalus, trying to judge between Pompey and Elbow the constable:

Which is the wiser here, Justice or Iniquity?

(II, i, 164–5)

Gone from act III is a passage of impersonal social comment by the bawd Pompey, an unusual echo of the much more extensive social criticism in the main source for *Measure*, Whetstone's *Promos and Cassandra*:

'Twas never merry world since, of two usuries, the merriest was put down, and the worser allow'd by order of law a furr'd gown to keep him warm.

(III, ii, 5–8)

Both of these comments could have been used to remind us how inseparable are the rough and the holy worlds of *Measure for Measure*. Brook then also proceeded to remove two important statements of the Duke in response to Pompey in act III: first, his bitter personal attack, so uncompassionate for a friar:

> Do thou but think
> What 'tis to cram a maw or clothe a back
> From such a filthy vice; . . .
> Canst thou believe thy living is a life
> So stinkingly depending? (III, ii, 18–24)

And then should come almost immediately the Duke's crabbed moralizing couplet:

> That we were all, as some would seem to be,
> [Free] from our faults, as faults from seeming, free.
> (35–6)

However difficult this couplet of eighteen monosyllables may be at first glance, it must have been inserted to make a clear moral statement – no doubt delivered with distinct measure to make sure that the audience would understand. It presents the Duke in a posture so very unusual for him in which he recognizes that the bawds (called 'faults') are free from seeming (or pretense) and that this very pretense plagues his fellow characters in the main plot – Angelo and Isabella.

Surely the spectator who is permitted to follow the original sequence of attitudes in these passages can reach a better sense of the 'brothel humor' and of why it is so fundamental in *Measure for Measure*. Particularly important are the encounters of the Duke with the 'Rough' world recurring through the second half of the play. His response to Pompey echoes that of Angelo. Neither ruler is effective in dealing with these comic figures. The Duke's vindictive tone to Pompey furthermore could well remind us of the brutality of Isabella's righteous outburst to Claudio:

> Mercy to thee would prove itself a bawd;
> 'Tis best thou diest quickly. (III, i, 151–2)

A production should be able to heighten our awareness of such resonances in successive scenes.

The rough world most disturbs Duke Vincentio when he meets Lucio. It is difficult to believe that any actor playing Vincentio could emerge from the dialogue with Lucio and still retain the charisma of an ideal ruler. It is therefore understandable that Brook cuts the lines of the furious Duke that provide the climax of their first encounter.

But a closer look at this dialogue will help us understand some of the dynamic interplay between the Rough and the Holy which Brook now calls Shakespeare's greatest accomplishment but often did not permit us to hear. When Lucio first meets the disguised Duke, he establishes the spirit of the scene with rapid rumors and questions, concluding with a vivid image of what the audience is watching:

It was a mad, fantastical trick of him to steal from the state and usurp the beggary he was never born to.

(III, ii, 86–8)

When Vincentio responds by defending his deputy Angelo for the harsh measures he has used in order to suppress fornication, 'He does well in 't . . . It is too general a vice, and severity must cure it', Lucio tries to adjust the argument to the level of common human weakness, 'Yes, . . . but it is impossible to extirp it quite, friar, till eating and drinking be put down'. But then, without a break, Lucio continues:

They say this Angelo was not made by man and woman after this downright way of creation. Is it true, think you? . . . Some report a sea-maid spawned him; some that he was begot between two stock-fishes. But it is *certain* that when he makes water his urine is congealed ice; that I *know* to be *true*.

(III, ii, 95–103)

In burlesquing Angelo's view which denies the natural in procreation, Lucio shifts his idiom easily from bluntly-phrased common sense to fantastic rumors and then to the pretense of certainty that the fantastic comic metaphor is fact. Equally incredible are the rumors he repeats and his claims to certain knowledge. Words like 'certain' and 'true' echo, mingle with the cavorting stock-fish, and mock the humorless Duke who is trapped in his disguise as a Friar.

The Duke next responds by revealing his submerged prejudices. Lucio means to compliment the Duke – both the ruler and the man – in contrast with the policies of the unnaturally cruel Angelo:

Why, what a ruthless thing is this in him, for the rebellion of a codpiece to take away the life of a man! Would the Duke that is absent have done this? Ere he would have hang'd a man for the getting a hundred bastards, he would have paid for the nursing a thousand. He had some feeling of the sport; he knew the service, and that instructed him to mercy.

(III, ii, 107–12)

Angered by the sexual allusion, the disguised Duke Vincentio ignores the compliments, praises himself, and forcefully rejects all of these claims. He thereby transforms both 'some feeling of the sport' and instructions 'to mercy' from carefree (apparently sincere) praise, so that they become ironic (apparently false) insults. By denying Lucio's statements,

the Duke leads his comic gad-fly on to exaggerate, in turn, his knowledge of the supposedly 'absent' Duke. After claiming that he cannot betray the Duke's secret motives for withdrawing, Lucio shifts subjects in a tantalizing, ambiguous manner (very much like that often employed by his listening ruler):

But this I can let you understand: the greater file of the subject held the Duke to be wise.   (III, ii, 127–8)

When Vincentio gracelessly insists upon commending himself still further:

Wise? Why, no question but what he was

(III, ii, 129)

Lucio – or perhaps Shakespeare – cannot resist the obvious target. Lucio now takes the opposite stance:

A very superficial, ignorant, unweighing fellow.

(III, ii, 130)

Losing all control of his temper, the angry Duke explodes:

Either this is envy in you, folly, or mistaking; the very stream of his life and the business he hath helmed, must, upon a warranted need, give him a better proclamation. Let him be but testimonied in his own bringings-forth, and he shall appear to the envious a scholar, a statesman, and a soldier.

Simply and effectively Lucio responds, 'Sir, I know him and I love him . . . Would he were return'd!'[1]

Brook's production has cut these final speeches in an effort to reshape the entire section so that Lucio will seem only a malicious and selfish gossip and – it seems – so that no lines

[1] For more development of the significance of the meeting between the Duke and Lucio, see H. Weil, 'Form and Contexts in *Measure for Measure*', *Critical Quarterly*, XII (1970), 55–72. Even the reader of that essay can hardly be expected to recall that the very passages emphasized in a discussion of literary criticism are those cut by Brook – and frequently by other directors.

will reflect unfavorably upon the Duke. But I find it difficult to believe that Shakespeare's audience was expected to treat Vincentio's self-praise as reliable characterization. Surely his last lines should be played to bring laughter. Lucio is not the only one blundering into a trap. Rather because the Duke holds all the best cards – with his power, his disguise, and his good intentions, at least in so far as he aims to prevent the execution of Claudio, the scene is much funnier if we laugh not only at the powerless Lucio but also at the Duke.

Lucio's needling and the rapid-paced dialogue create a flow that is rarely smooth. Subject-matter and mood fluctuate wildly – however rigid and defensive the Duke may be. The inconsistencies in detail of characterization, tone, and language – though not, I think, of underlying themes and perspectives – comprise part of the special mode of *Measure for Measure*. Here in a scene of jesting, banter, teasing insult, and intended compliment, any alert spectator can follow the darting fluctuations of Lucio as well as the stiff, humorless responses of the offended Duke. When we tease some one – however many half-truths we may suggest – we are quite likely to govern the flow of our conversation by picking up his responses and deflecting them. We do not determine our conscious or unconscious strategy through any logical quest for the absolute truth. From this perspective, at least, the passage, for all its wild fantasies and inventions, offers a kind of faithful, mimetic truth. Even more important than this mimetic truth, however, is the vision both of the world in the play and of its manipulator that the spectator is encouraged to create for himself.

We can explain Lucio's mercurial character, as well as the surprising accuracy of his jibes, by his expository function. Clearly the point is *not* what Lucio knows or what source he finds for his gossip; it is how the Duke reacts. Here, just as in responses to Pompey and Barnardine

and in his appeal to Isabella, the Friar reverts to egotistic justifications of his other persona, the 'absent' Duke. We can readily understand why a director, attempting to present for us a Providential or ideal Duke would cut so many of these lines. But they should accumulate to show a proud, awkward Duke – one who shares many qualities with his deputy, Angelo, and some with the Isabella he praises with hyperbole at her most cruel moment and to whom he later proposes. I think we have only two basic alternatives: either Shakespeare here wrote many clumsy, superfluous passages, thereby betraying his efforts to create a character we are supposedly to revere. Or – much more likely – the comic, ridiculous, pompous side of the Duke is an essential part in his rich, complex characterization.

We might almost say that Lucio recalls the Duke from his efforts to apply the virtues inherent in his role to his own personal character. Recognizing the Duke's function as near-omnipotent *deus ex machina* does not require us to accept his evaluations of other characters nor of himself. The discordance between a virtue claimed and the character whose actions we observe is one vital, recurring technique in *Measure for Measure*.

I have emphasized the foolish, self-centered side that the Duke reveals in order to help counter the highly influential praise for his character and his ideas as if they were to serve as near-flawless models. When we consider the whole play, the Duke's weaknesses become integral to its thematic unity. But we must remember that these unpleasant traits generally appear in comic contexts. However gratuitous may be the Duke's excessive reactions to Lucio or Pompey, he is still able to save the condemned victims. Once critics and directors do begin to pay more attention to the conflict between his technical or conventional role and his own personality, they can remain free to explore the large range of interpretations still possible within that conflict. If he is faithful to the text, a director will recognize that an idealized portrayal is not an option for Duke Vincentio as for Rosalind. But the individual director still may choose to emphasize in the Duke his bitter detestation for Pompey or his pride; he may decide to stress a pathetic ego in a powerful figure who requires so much flattery or even an appealing clumsiness in a well-meaning bumbler trapped in his own disguise.

Options of this sort can enrich a comedy. In contrast to the effect on an audience of a tragedy – or even a melodrama – that contracts toward an intensifying focus, any comedy that stimulates us intellectually will tend to open out into manifold possibilities. We often are encouraged to drawn conclusions that transcend those of any commentator within the play, and, in the process, make largely ironic the opinions of even the most reliable *raisonneur*.

Peter Brook's book, seeking unity and praising the opposition of Rough and Holy, becomes more faithful to the text of *Measure for Measure* than did his staging. In *Measure*, thematic unity is closely yoked to character, and the main characters share essential qualities. But it is only because of the 'Rough' world – Lucio, Pompey, Barnardine, and the responses they evoke – that we can be certain that we are *meant* to attend to the similar flaws in Angelo, Isabella, and the Duke. Any production which eliminates the many unflattering references to Duke Vincentio and his own self-revelations will coerce the spectator. Many of the best modern plays invite us to respond to apparent inconsistencies, shifting perspectives, and unreliable characters pretending to knowledge. Ironically, this very modern quality largely disappears from *Measure* when deletions attempt to create a completely admirable Duke.

If the last few pages have seemed to offer primarily negative criticism of a twenty-one-year-old production, the justification must come because the director seems able to offer us so much more. Brook's theoretical juxtaposing of Rough and Holy promises a brilliant modern interpretation, yet one that arguably has historical validity. But can we assume that Brook would apply his theory as I have suggested and thoroughly rethink his presentation of the play? One would like to think so, to assume that these suggestions would not offend. But we have only one clear fact: nowhere in his book does Brook declare that his ideas about *Measure for Measure* have changed – as he does about other plays. He includes no detailed description of the 1950 production, and the scholar who applied the principles of the book to imagine the staging would be very far off indeed. Even if he were fortunate enough to see it on stage, unless he has an alert and thorough memory, his main recourse must be to the prompt-books and to the sparse published comments. My main purpose has been to suggest some ways in which the theater and the study can complement each other. The scholar should be able to consider a record of the director's reasons *why* he made cuts he considered crucial and why he chose to emphasize certain lines or motifs. Otherwise research is often limited to the simple records of the prompt-books – and these, often of varying accuracy, usually become available only long after performances have ended. After all, when a critic proposes a meaning or theme, he operates in a way analogous to a director who stresses some lines and deletes others. But if the text is always there to check the scholar, this is true only in a very limited sense to test the production. I once thought that it would be ideal if one possessed total recall of the text to compare with the performance. But the very act of constantly comparing would eliminate the possibility of any full response to the production, which – at least *during* its playing – should convince us it captures the essence of the work. If they believe that Shakespeare's plays remain worthy of study and performance, the scholar and the director will not seek out

each other's shortcomings. All effective productions coerce the audience to some extent,
but the best ones also free our imagination to
follow any suggestions in the text. For me,
Brook's *Midsummer Night's Dream* of 1970–1
brilliantly evoked just such a *sense* of a liberated
imagination. Here – not in any striking *new*
insight into the meaning of the play, not in any
original additions or deletions to the text –
seems the very real achievement of this production. The critic and the director will both
seek to find interpretations that supplement and
fulfill our first responses in the theater when we
recall and reread the play.[1]

[1] An altered form of this paper was presented at the
World Shakespeare Congress at Vancouver, B.C. in
August 1971. The paper is closely related to a study of
Shakespeare's comedies which is being written with the
support of a grant from the University of Connecticut
Research Foundation.

MAN'S NEED AND GOD'S PLAN IN 'MEASURE FOR MEASURE' AND MARK IV

SARAH C. VELZ

Shakespeare might have taken the title of *Measure for Measure* from any one of the three synoptic gospels: 'For with what iudgement yee iudge, ye shall be iudged, and with what measure ye mete, it shall bee measured to you againe' (Matthew vii 2); 'With what measure ye mete, it shall bee measured vnto you' (Mark iv 24); 'For with what measure ye mete with the same shal men mete to you again' (Luke vi 38).[1] Few Shakespeare editions consider a source for the title and those that do generally give *3 Henry VI*[2] or Matthew vii without arguing the point, and apparently without having examined the contexts in the three gospels. A. D. Nuttall, however, has suggested that Shakespeare was probably thinking of Mark iv as he wrote because the Duke's lines, 'Heaven doth with us as we with torches do, / Not light them for themselves' (I, i, 32–3) are a restatement of Mark iv 21: 'Is the candle lighted to be put vnder a bushell, or vnder the table, and not to be put on a candlesticke?'[3] An examination of Mark iv reveals other striking analogues to the language of *Measure for Measure* and – beyond language – to the characterization and theme of the play; it can be argued that Mark iv was the focus of Shakespeare's biblical background for the play, though elements from all three evangelists are woven into its fabric.

Perhaps the most memorable verses in Mark iv are the parable of the sower and his seeds, in which Christ parallels the lives of good and bad men with the destinies of various seeds.

Situational and verbal similarities suggest that Shakespeare had these types in mind as he characterized Angelo, Claudio, Lucio, and Mariana. The first seed 'fell by the wayes side, and the foules of the heauen came and deuoured it vp' (v. 4). These are they, Christ explains later to his disciples, who hear the word of God, but 'Satan commeth immediately, and taketh away the worde that was sowen in their heartes' (v. 15). In act I Angelo is a man who has 'heard the word of God'; Escalus says of him,

> If any in Vienna be of worth
> To undergo such ample grace and honour
>   [as the Duke's commission],
> It is Lord Angelo.   (I, i, 22–4)

He regards himself as immune to temptation as he rigorously enforces the death penalty against Claudio:

> 'Tis one thing to be tempted, Escalus,
> Another thing to fall.   (II, i, 17–18)

---

[1] Quotations from the Geneva Bible (1586), contractions expanded. Richmond Noble observes that Shakespeare's biblical allusions in *M for M* are from the Geneva version (*Shakespeare's Biblical Knowledge*, London, 1935, pp. 68, 69); evidence to be offered in this paper will support this view.

[2] See II, vi, 52–5, where Warwick advocates the eye-for-an-eye ethic: 'Measure for measure must be answerèd.'

[3] A. D. Nuttall, '*Measure for Measure: Quid pro Quo*', *Shakespeare Studies*, IV (1968), 231–51 (237). Quotations from *M for M* in the present article are from R. C. Bald's edition in the 1969 one-volume Pelican.

Yet he succumbs in his first case of judgment; lamenting his fall he blames the 'cunning enemy' (II, ii, 180). Verbal evidence may also suggest that Shakespeare had the seeds that fell by the way in mind as he characterized Angelo; in act V, Isabella argues that since technically Angelo has not committed fornication he should be held innocent: his 'intent / ...perished by the way' (V, i, 448–9). Angelo himself perhaps echoes the parable when he vigorously defends the need for strict justice in Claudio's case and like Christ uses a metaphor of marauding birds: 'We must not make a scarecrow of the law, / Setting it up to fear the birds of prey' (II, i, 1–2). Giving in to temptation, which Angelo personifies as 'the birds of prey' and Christ personifies as 'the foules of the heauen', Angelo is to learn, is not prevented by strict justice.

The second seed in Christ's parable falls on stony ground, germinates immediately since the soil is not deep, but withers as soon as the sun is up because it has no root. Christ likens this type of seed to men who hear the word with gladness, but having no root 'when trouble and persecution ariseth' cannot endure, but fall from the word (vv. 5, 6, 16–17). When Claudio is first seen in the prison, he is hearing the word of God from the Duke, who disguised as Friar Lodowick is comforting him with a *contemptus mundi*: 'Be absolute for death' (III, i, 5). Claudio, like the seed on stony ground, hears the word gladly: 'I ... seeking death, find life: let it come on' (42–3)[1] and he soon insists to his sister,

> If I must die,
> I will encounter darkness like a bride,
> And hug it in mine arms.   (83–5)

Yet only a few lines later, when he learns that Angelo might reprieve him, he cannot bear the affliction of approaching death, falls from his resolution, and begs his sister to save him. His weakness is not his lust,[2] but his unmanly fear of death (III, i, 118–33) and his willingness to save himself through another's dishonor. Isabella has earlier had a premonition of this weakness in him: 'I quake, / Lest thou ... six or seven winters more respect / Than a perpetual honour' (III, i, 74–7).[3]

The third seed falls among thorns, the thorns choke it, and the seed bears no fruit. Such seed represents men who hear the word, but 'the cares of this world, and the deceitfulnes of riches, and the lustes of other things enter in, and choke the word, and it is unfruitfull' (vv. 7, 18–19). Lucio's concerns are patently riches and other lusts, and these concerns prevent him, metaphorically, from bearing fruit – literally from attending seriously to his friends when they turn to him in trouble. 'If I could speak so wisely under an arrest, I would send for certain of my creditors', he jests when Claudio speaks sadly to him of his offense (I, ii, 127–8). His response to Isabella after Claudio's supposed death is typical:

---

[1] The speech has seemed to some critics wholly pagan; yet the philosophy expressed is the traditional Christian view that life is a vale of tears one is best out of, and the word *absolute* at the beginning puns on the service of absolution. Likewise, Claudio's response, though not specifically Christian, expresses the Christian paradox that one finds life only through death.

[2] Only Angelo blames Claudio for fornication. Escalus pleads repeatedly for reprieve, and even upright Isabella would amend, not punish the fault ('O, let him marry her' I, iv, 49). The kindly Provost believes 'He hath but as offended in a dream' and he refers to Claudio as 'a young man / More fit to do another such offense / Than die for this' (II, ii, 4; II, iii, 13–15).

[3] Claudio's request that Isabella save his life must have marked him as doubly weak to a Renaissance audience. He loses his honor (reputation) by asking her to give up hers (chastity) – see Angelo's rationale, IV, iv, 26–30. Claudio also subverts the chain of being by effeminately asking a woman for protection. His inability to bear trouble is presaged in his decision not to tell Julietta's friends about his handfast marriage to her for fear they would not approve and would not provide a suitable dowry (I, ii, 144–8).

O pretty Isabella, I am pale at mine heart to see thine eyes so red; thou must be patient. I am fain to dine and sup with water and bran; I dare not for my head fill my belly; one fruitful meal would set me to't.

(IV, iii, 149–52)

Beginning with serious condolence, Lucio is soon diverted by random thought into an inappropriate joke. It is further significant that Lucio has forsworn responsibility for his child by Mistress Kate Keepdown (IV, iii, 165–9); the seeds choked by thorns bear no fruit. Finally, Lucio also uses ironically appropriate language from the gospel when he describes himself: 'Nay, friar, I am a kind of burr; I shall stick' (IV, iii, 173–4).

The last seeds fall on good ground and 'yeelde ... some thirtie folde, some sixtie folde, and some an hundreth folde'; they are those who hear the word of God and bring forth fruit (vv. 8, 20). This definition implies that to be meaningful goodness must produce good results. Appropriately, Julietta's pregnancy is described by Lucio as a fruition – the bountiful result of mutual love:

> ... as blossoming time
> That from the seedness the bare fallow brings
> To teeming foison, even so her plenteous womb
> Expresseth his full tilth and husbandry.
>
> (I, iv, 41–4; cf. II, iii, 24–5)

Mariana's goodness also acts with positive results. Her part in the Duke's plot preserves Isabella's chastity, helps to save Claudio and therefore Angelo as well, and eventually contributes to Isabella's understanding of mercy.[1]

The metaphor of fertility in Mark iv is not confined to the sower parable but is repeated later in two similes for the kingdom of heaven. Christ compares the kingdom to a man's casting seed into the ground. As the man goes about his work, the seed 'shoulde spring and growe vp, he not knowing howe. For the earth bringeth forth fruite of her selfe, first the blade, then the eares, after that, full corne in the eares'

(vv. 26–8). Christ continues in an almost identical simile: the kingdom of God, like a grain of mustard, is insignificant when sown, but when full-grown is the 'greatest of all herbes, and beareth great branches, so that the foules of heauen may builde vnder the shadowe of it' (vv. 30–2). The implication of the metaphor in the sower parable ('by their fruites yee shall knowe them'[2]) is different from the implication of the other two fruition similes in Mark iv (God's plan ripens quietly though man is not aware of it). But both meanings of fruition imagery unite in the providential theme of Mark iv. It will appear that in *Measure for Measure* Shakespeare makes use of both of these implications of fruition imagery, uniting them in the same providential theme he would have found in Mark iv.

The commonest use of seed and fertility imagery in *Measure for Measure* corresponds to the implication of the sower parable – that a man's worth is shown in his deeds. Lucio's reference to himself as a burr and his fear of even 'one fruitful meal', as well as his familiar

[1] G. Wilson Knight's essay, '*Measure for Measure* and the Gospels', in *The Wheel of Fire* (London, 1930/1949), pp. 73–96, proposes that Mariana contributes to Isabella's anagnorisis. (Knight does not include any of Mark's gospel or any detailed account of Matthew vii or Luke vi in this essay.) Vincentio's two dialogues with Mariana (V, i, 163–247, 412–50), coupled with the fact that he plans his plot at Mariana's house (IV, iii, 137–9), suggest that the Duke and Mariana are deliberately working together to educate both Isabella and Angelo.

[2] The phrase appears at Luke vi 44 and Matthew vii 20 (the wording here), not in Mark iv. Shakespeare seems to be alluding to it at I, i, 35–6: 'Spirits are not finely touched / But to fine issues.' This is one evidence – more will be discussed later – for Shakespeare's creative fusion of the three 'measure for measure' chapters in *M for M* (Kenneth Muir has called attention to Walter Whiter's observation in 1794 that this passage shares several words with Mark v 25–31 and notes that the passage is an allusion to the preceding chapter – see *Shakespeare's Sources* (London, 1957), p. 8).

lines about Julietta's pregnancy, have been cited. Angelo contrasts his own state, which 'as the carrion does . . . / Corrupt[s] with virtuous season', to Isabella's violet-like purity which blossoms in the sun (II, ii, 165–8). Disguised as the Friar, the Duke reminds Claudio that man is frail, existing 'on many a thousand grains / That issue out of dust' (III, i, 20–1). Before Isabella tells Claudio the condition Angelo has set for reprieve, she warns him that it is a condition which, if accepted, 'Would bark your honour from that trunk you bear, / And leave you naked' (III, i, 72–3).[1] After Claudio begs her to save him, she tells him that he must be illegitimately born, for 'such a warpèd slip of wilderness / Ne'er issued from his [her father's] blood' (III, i, 142–3). In his soliloquy at the end of act III, the Duke cries shame on Angelo for his willingness to 'weed' the vices of others while he lets his own 'grow' (253). And in act v the Duke, possibly echoing verse 19, tells Mariana that he has had Angelo marry her lest the scandal of fornication 'choke your good to come' (v, i, 418).[2]

In the Geneva Bible there is a marginal gloss explicating the two similes on the kingdom of heaven which throws light on the larger meaning of Mark iv and may serve as a guide in a reading of *Measure for Measure*: 'These two similitudes following proue, that although the kingdome of God seemeth to haue very litle appearance or beginning, yet God doeth increase it aboue mans reason.' Like the tiny grain of mustard which mysteriously grows into a large plant, God's plan for his people works out in ways they do not understand. As the Duke originally explains the bed-trick to Isabella it is a concise plot with well-defined ends:

... you may most uprightuously do a poor wronged lady a merited benefit, redeem your brother from the angry law, [and] do no stain to your own gracious person ...   (III, i, 196–9)

But he develops from it, above the understanding of any of the characters, the comic anagnorises of Angelo and Isabella, the marriage of Claudio and Julietta, the marriage of Lucio to his wronged doxy, and even the pardoning of Barnardine. Appropriately, the Duke uses a metaphor of planting and harvesting for this developing plot: 'Our corn 's to reap, for yet our tithe 's to sow' (IV, i, 75).

If the Duke's plan is an analogue to God's plan as glossed in Mark iv, the larger context of the chapter provides additional evidence that Shakespeare's conception of the Duke is at least in part that of a God-figure.[3] At the beginning of both Mark iv and *Measure for Measure* the 'God' separates himself from his people. So great a multitude gathered to hear Christ that he 'entred into a shippe, and sate in the sea, and al the people was by the sea side on the land' (v. 1); in I, i of *Measure for Measure* the Duke appoints Angelo and Escalus his secondaries and departs on a journey to an unnamed destination. Second, both leaders are aware of and in command of dangerous situations, although it seems to some that each is unaware, perhaps unconcerned. The closing verses of Mark iv are the familiar story of Christ's calming the waters; the disciples, terrified by a sudden storm at sea, awaken the sleeping Christ, crying 'Master, carest thou not that wee perish?' Christ calms the wind and sea with a rebuke and says to his disciples mildly, 'Why are ye so fearefull? howe is it that ye haue no faith?' (vv. 35–40). During Duke Vin-

---

[1] Here it appears that the image is from the marginalium to verse 11 in the Geneva version: those outside the kingdom of heaven 'are not of the number of the faithfull, neither atteine to the pith and substance, but onely stay in the outwarde rinde and barke'.

[2] Shakespeare parodies this thematic imagery in the comic plot. Pompey explains to Mistress Overdone the future of the city's bawdy houses: 'they shall stand for seed' (I, ii, 96).

[3] See Nevill Coghill's 'Comic Form in *Measure for Measure*', *Shakespeare Survey* 8 (Cambridge, 1955), pp. 14–27 for a reasoned argument that the Renaissance audience would have accepted the Duke as simultaneously figurative God and literal man.

centio's retirement, other characters assume that he is unaware of the trouble he has left behind him in Vienna and one accuses him of being frivolously unconcerned for his people. Isabella laments, 'But O, how much is the good Duke deceived in Angelo!' (III, i, 189); Lucio grumbles that 'It was a mad, fantastical trick of him to steal from the state, and usurp the beggary he was never born to' (III, ii, 87–8). Ironically enough, it is the Duke himself who listens to both plaints; he is not deceived in Angelo nor has he stolen from the state.

A third analogy between the departing Duke and the Christ of Mark iv is that both leaders test subordinates whom they have recently raised above the multitude.[1] As the Duke has made Angelo his deputy just before leaving on his journey, Christ exalts his disciples shortly before they depart in the boat by explaining to them alone the meaning of the parable of the sower which he has told the multitude (v. 11). Like the disciples, Angelo finds that being singled out does not make a man immune to frailty. In this theme of human frailty, common to the gospel and the play, the two meanings the evangelist and Shakespeare attach to fertility imagery unite. The worth of a man as seen in his deeds and the silently ripening providence of God unite in the central theme that all men, good or bad, are equally weak by comparison with deity and equally in need of God's providential mercy. Isabella states the theme as she pleads for her brother:

> Why, all the souls that were were forfeit once,
> And He that might the vantage best have took,
> Found out the remedy. How would you be,
> If He, which is the top of judgement, should
> But judge you as you are?
>
> (II, ii, 73–7)

The universality of human weakness is emphasized comically in the subplots. It is discussed with levity by Lucio and two other fantastic gentlemen in I, ii:

> *Lucio.* . . . Grace is grace despite of all controversy: as, for example, thou thyself art a wicked villain, despite of all grace.
>
> . . . . .
>
> *1 Gentleman.* I think I have done myself wrong, have I not?
> *2 Gentleman.* Yes, that thou hast, whether thou art tainted or free. (24–41)

Pompey, whose profession has made him well acquainted with human weakness, assures Escalus that 'If you head and hang all that offend that way but for ten year together, you'll be glad to give out a commission for more heads' (II, i, 224–6). Lucio's vision of man's nature is similar: 'it is impossible to extirp it [lechery] quite, friar, till eating and drinking be put down' (III, ii, 96–7). In some farcical choplogic, Abhorson the executioner manages to fit true men and thieves into the same clothing (IV, ii, 39–42). The low comedy of *Measure for Measure* underscores the lesson Angelo learns: though he is acknowledged virtuous and is the Duke's elect, he is as prone to error and therefore as much in need of God's forgiveness and grace as any Pompey or Claudio. Similarly, though they have been exalted over the ordinary people of Galilee, the disciples lose faith at the first test. The marginalium to the descrip-

---

[1] It is possible that Shakespeare's conception of the disguised Duke owes something to Mark iv. As Geoffrey Bullough points out, in none of the 'monstrous ransom' analogues to *M for M* does the ruler take as active a part in the plot as Vincentio does. Bullough suggests several 'ruler in disguise' analogues, but in all of them the ruler's purpose in disguising himself is to 'observe the condition of his court and people'. (See *Narrative and Dramatic Sources of Shakespeare*, vol. II (London, 1958), pp. 410–17.) Though Lucio may be based on the traditional courtier, spying on fantastics is not the purpose of the Duke's disguise. And Vincentio is under no illusion about the morality of his kingdom: '. . . Liberty plucks Justice by the nose; / The baby beats the nurse, and quite athwart / Goes all decorum' (I, iii, 29–31). Like Christ's in Mark iv, the Duke's purpose is to test his elect; finding Angelo less strong than the temptation he is under, the Duke, like Christ, quietly intervenes.

tion of Christ asleep in the boat during the storm could serve as an epigraph to *Measure for Measure*: 'Christ leaueth vs often-times to our-selues, both as well that we may learne to know our owne weaknesse, as his mightie power.'

Christ and Vincentio work by allowing man freedom enough to know his own weakness. The paradox is that their plans include, 'above man's reason', a method for man's salvation. Christ in the boat uses his power to calm the storm, and the Duke uses his power to prevent the execution of Claudio and thereby to save Angelo – but to fulfill their plans, Christ and the Duke must conceal the way out from their subjects until anagnorisis has been reached. As a result both God-figures may seem to be tormenting their subjects unnecessarily. It may seem merely cruel for Christ to allow his disciples to suffer while the storm rages; Vincentio has often been accused of torturing Angelo and especially Isabella by concealing the fact that Claudio is still alive. Yet it is only *de profundis* that man can realize his finiteness and thereby acknowledge his dependency on higher benevolence; this is the moral implication of both *Measure for Measure* act v and the closing episode in Mark iv. Isabella, at the moment of deepest grief and desire for revenge, is stirred to the generosity of forgiveness which had not been possible for her earlier when faced by Claudio's request. The Duke shows his hopes for Isabella when he says in soliloquy,

> ... I will keep her ignorant of her good,
> To make her heavenly comforts of despair
> When it is least expected.   (IV, iii, 106–8)

and still under the disguise of Friar Lodowick he writes her not to think it strange if he should speak against her, for ''tis a physic / That's bitter to sweet end' (IV, vi, 6–9).

This is an appropriate place to return to Professor Nuttall's suggestion that the torches at I, i, 32–3 are a paraphrase of the candle in Mark iv 21. The candle in Mark iv carries a primary meaning much the same as that in the parable of the sower: virtue must be active to be meaningful. The context in I, i makes it clear that Shakespeare places the same interpretation on his own 'torches'. The Duke comments on his simile,

> for if our virtues
> Did not go forth of us, 'twere all alike
> As if we had them not   (33–5)

and later he tells Isabella that 'Virtue is bold, and goodness never fearful' (III, i, 204). The dynamic of *Measure for Measure* supports this theme of active virtue; the play moves from seclusion to active participation. Though he has 'ever loved the life removèd' (I, iii, 8), even in retirement the Duke takes an active part in the disposition of affairs; Mariana leaves the seclusion of the moated grange to take her part in the Duke's plot; Isabella abandons the convent of St Clare to plead for her brother, takes part in the scheme to save him, and in the end remains in the world to marry the Duke; Claudio and Barnardine are both released from prison, the first to marry the woman he has wronged, the second to amend his life 'For better times to come' (V, i, 481).[1]

The reference to torches in I, i is the first of several lines in the play about light and darkness, an image pattern which enhances the main theme of the play. Christ gives a second meaning to the candle, 'For there is nothing hid, that shal not be opened: neither is there a secrete, but that it shall come to light' (V. 22). The marginal comment in the Geneva Bible elaborates: 'We may not take occasion to do euil vnder colour to hide our doings: for all shalbe disclosed at the length.' Lucio says of the Duke, unaware that the friar to whom he is speaking is the Duke in disguise, 'The Duke

---

[1] There is a serio-comic counterpoint to the move toward active virtue in the incarceration of the incorrigible Overdone, whom Escalus finally commits after 'Double and treble admonition, and still forfeit in the same kind' (III, ii, 181–2).

yet would have dark deeds darkly answered; he would never bring them to light' (III, ii, 165–7). Ironically, the Duke is in the process of bringing Angelo's dark deeds to light, and – further irony – Lucio is, unawares, betraying his own dark deeds, calumny and fornication, to the man who will be his judge. The ethical implication of light is comically inverted in Lucio's sexual innuendo in act v:

Lucio. . . . if you handled her [Isabella] privately, she would sooner confess; perchance publicly she'll be ashamed.
Escalus. I will go darkly to work with her.
Lucio. That's the way, for women are light at midnight.
(v, i, 274–7)

The idea that evil will out is essential to the theme that God's plan provides first for man's self-knowledge, then for his redemption. The purpose of the light-darkness imagery is closely related, therefore, to the purpose of the fertility imagery, and the two coalesce in Isabella's exclamation when the Duke pretends not to believe her accusation against Angelo:

Then, O you blessèd ministers above,
Keep me in patience, and with ripened time
Unfold the evil which is here wrapped up
In countenance.   (v, i, 115–18)

Given striking similarities in theme, language, and characterization between Mark iv and *Measure for Measure*, it is tempting to speculate about a similarity in tone as well. Both works are rich in dramatic irony. Christ as a parabolist is of necessity an ironist, since the stories he tells the crowd have only literal meaning to his listeners, while his chosen disciples are later shown a figurative and personal application. There is a further level of irony, as has been shown in comments above on the episode of the storm, since even those who hear the meaning of the parable are imperfect and in need of divine help. The Duke's disguise is, of course, the central ironic device in *Measure for Measure*; the disguise, like

Christ's parable, underlines the limits of human perception, and even when his real identity is revealed his subjects have not yet discovered the extent of his power to save Claudio or redeem Angelo.

The inclusion of a God-figure with redeeming power makes *Measure for Measure* comic in the same way that Christianity is comic. The tone of the Duke's speech which contains the title line does ring of retributive justice:

The very mercy of the law cries out
Most audible, even from his proper tongue,
'An Angelo for Claudio, death for death!'
Haste still pays haste, and leisure answers leisure,
Like doth quit like, and Measure still for Measure.
(v, i, 403–7)

He is, however, enunciating the old law of justice which must be replaced by a new dispensation of mercy. The prologue to the 'measure for measure' locus in Luke makes it clear that mercy is the reciprocity of Christianity:

But I say vnto you, . . . loue your enemies . . . pray for them which hurt you . . . and yee shalbe the children of the most High: for he is kind vnto the vnkind and to the euill. Be ye therefore mercifull, as your Father also is mercifull.   (vv. 27–36)

The triumph of mercy over the *lex talionis* as found in Luke vi is absolutely central to act v of *Measure for Measure*. Though it seems clear that Mark iv was the chapter that caught his imagination most, it is equally clear that Shakespeare drew on the 'measure for measure' chapters in all three evangelists, and cross-references in a Geneva Bible would have made it easy to do so. The triumph of mercy is the only element of the play which Shakespeare would not have found in the other two chapters. Luke vi and Matthew vii share two elements which Shakespeare makes use of. The importance to the play of the first of these elements, 'by their fruites yee shall knowe them' (Matthew vii 16–20; Luke vi 43–4), has been discussed above. The second element, the hypocrisy of the man who would cast the mote out of another's eye and ignore the beam in his own (Matthew vii 3–5; Luke vi 41–2), is obviously relevant to Angelo. Several casual allusions in the play suggest that verses from Matthew vii remained, perhaps subconsciously, in Shakespeare's memory, even though this chapter was not central to his conception of *Measure for Measure*, as Mark iv was.[1]

One final bit of evidence from the Geneva Bible supports the assumption that Mark iv was Shakespeare's principal biblical source for the play. The marginal cross-references in Mark iv are several of them to chapters of the New Testament in which Shakespeare would have recognized an analogy to *Promos and Cassandra*. The motif of a faithful servant, often contrasted with a faithless servant and sometimes connected with the parable of the talents, appears in Matthew xxv, Luke viii, Luke xix, Luke xii, and Matthew viii. The most interesting of these is preface to the parable of the talents in Luke xix. It describes a man, obviously to be equated with God, who is ruler of a large country, but who must leave it to undertake a journey. He appoints ten deputies, but 'his citizens hated him [the other nine deputies disappear in this context] and sent an ambassage after him,

saying, We will not haue this man to reigne ouer us' (vv. 12–14). How consciously Shakespeare made use of such biblical references it is impossible to say. It is, however, plausible to suppose that he had read Mark iv and the cross-referenced chapters carefully at some time, but that he relied on his memory as he wrote the play.[2] What is important to realize is that the Bible was a significant influence on his overall conception of the play, not merely the source for an occasional moral allusion.

[1] Verse 6 warns 'neither cast ye your pearles before swine, least they treade them vnder their feete …' – cf. Angelo's 'The jewel that we find, we stoop and take't / Because we see it; but what we do not see / We tread upon, and never think of it' (II, i, 23–6). In verse 9 Christ asks '. . . what man is there among you, which if his sonne aske him bread, woulde giue him a stone?' – describing his newly appointed deputy, the Duke says of Angelo that he 'scarce confesses / . . . that his appetite / Is more to bread than stone' (I, iii, 50–3). Pursuing a warning against hypocrites, in verse 15 Christ speaks of false prophets, men who pose as sheep, 'but inwardly they are rauening wolues' – Friar Lodowick exclaims to Mariana and Isabella in act v, 'But O, poor souls, / Come you to seek the lamb here of the fox?' (v, i, 295–6).

[2] Evidence of memorial reconstruction can perhaps be found in the second example given in footnote 1 above: the image of bread and stone remained vividly in Shakespeare's mind, though his ethical application of it is very different from the source's.

THE DESIGN OF
'ALL'S WELL THAT ENDS WELL'

R. L. SMALLWOOD

All's Well that Ends Well is not an entirely successful work. Its problems have been discussed at length and its shortcomings pointed out, sometimes with little compassion. From Dr Johnson, who could not reconcile his heart to Bertram,[1] to the late Poet Laureate, who found Helena 'a woman who practises a borrowed art, not for art's sake, nor for charity, but, woman fashion, for a selfish end',[2] its principal characters have seemed to critics inadequate or disturbing. Even the first editor of this journal found that the 'kindest thing' he could do with *All's Well that Ends Well* was to suggest that it was 'penned by Shakespeare in a time of illness or mental disturbance'.[3] And yet its two most recent Stratford productions have been surprisingly well received,[4] and it contains, in Helena, what Coleridge called Shakespeare's 'loveliest character',[5] and, in the Countess, Bernard Shaw's idea of 'the most beautiful old woman's part ever written'.[6] This mixture of undoubted success and apparent failure is familiar, of course, in that play with which *All's Well that Ends Well* is often linked, *Measure for Measure*. But while the problems of *Measure for Measure* seem, to some extent at least, to be imposed by Shakespeare himself – he it is who makes Isabella a novice, adds Mariana to the characters he inherited from Whetstone, and imports the bed-trick – those which remain in *All's Well that Ends Well* are fundamental to the story Shakespeare has chosen to dramatise.

All's Well that Ends Well has only one known source, the story of Giletta of Narbonne, the ninth story of the third day of Boccaccio's *Decameron* which Shakespeare found translated in William Painter's *The Palace of Pleasure* (1566 and 1575).[7] This short and sharply-focused tale concentrates exclusively on the ingenuity and determination of the heroine, Giletta, in her securing of the marriage to Beltramo which she desires, and then on her

[1] *The Yale Edition of the Works of Samuel Johnson*, vols. VII and VIII, *Johnson on Shakespeare*, edited by Arthur Sherbo (New Haven, Connecticut, 1968), VII, 404.

[2] John Masefield, *William Shakespeare* (London, 1911), p. 148.

[3] Allardyce Nicoll, *Shakespeare* (London, 1952), p. 116.

[4] It was produced at Stratford in 1959 by Sir Tyrone Guthrie, and in 1967 by John Barton. Joseph Price, the most comprehensive and sensitive critic of *All's Well that Ends Well*, records that the audience 'reacted with ... delight' to Guthrie's production, though admittedly the play was extensively cut (Lavatch disappeared altogether) and much comic business was added (*The Unfortunate Comedy: A Study of 'All's Well that Ends Well' and its Critics* (Liverpool, 1968), pp. 57ff.). I am indebted to Mr Price's excellent book at many points in this essay. He wrote too soon to deal with the Barton production; this offered a much fuller text (though one or two scenes were rearranged) and a more inclusive response to the play's varieties of mood. It was enthusiastically received throughout the season, and later televised.

[5] *Coleridge's Shakespeare Criticism*, edited by T. M. Raysor, 2 vols. (London, 1930), II, 113.

[6] *Shaw on Shakespeare*, edited by Edwin Wilson (London, 1961), p. 10.

[7] My quotations and references are from the text in *Narrative and Dramatic Sources of Shakespeare*, edited by Geoffrey Bullough, vol. II (London, 1958), pp. 389–96.

winning, through further resourcefulness and cunning, his recognition and acceptance of her as his wife. Its narrative speed and attack make it an amusing ten-minute read. But the details of its plot are responsible for many of Shakespeare's difficulties in the play. Indeed it is fair to say that some of the critics' complaints about *All's Well that Ends Well* are above all objections to the narrative material with which Shakespeare is working: Beltramo deserves Dr Johnson's censure for being noble without generosity more than Bertram does, and the vigorously determined selfishness of Giletta is throughout more worthy of the late Mr Masefield's rebukes than ever Helena is. A comparison of the play with its source reveals at every turn the dramatist's care to present the story and its principal characters in as mellow and engaging a light as possible, to give them a dramatic plausibility and a dignity which are entirely absent from the source, and, finally, to bring the story to a conclusion infinitely more moving and more human than that of Boccaccio's simple, vigorous tale. To these ends Shakespeare invents new characters, makes several telling modifications to the plot, greatly develops the hero and heroine, and turns the ending almost upside down. I want to examine these four general aspects of the play and their relationship to the source story, and to suggest some of the ways in which Shakespeare has wrested his successes from what may be rather intractable material for drama. The bones of the source remain at times perhaps too discernible, notably in some of the scenes in Florence in acts III and IV, and, it is sometimes suggested, in the rather abrupt dismissal from our contemplation at the end of the play of the newly reconciled hero and heroine. But Shakespeare's economy in these scenes is also based, I think, on the care he has taken with the adaptation of his source: the strength of characterisation and the dramatic impetus he has achieved in the surrounding parts of the play may be enough,

in performance, to enable the audience to accept scenes that provide little more than the essential development of the plot, but provide it rapidly and succinctly.

The new characters Shakespeare adds or develops in dramatising the story of Giletta of Narbonne form two groups: the older generation and the comics. There is no older generation in Boccaccio's story, except for some rather shadowy 'kinsfolk' of Giletta, and the King of France, whose function in the plot is simply mechanical – he exists to be cured of his fistula and to force Beltramo to marry Giletta. The patient, wise, and gentle trio of the Countess, Lafeu, and the King are entirely Shakespeare's invention. The context of mellow understanding and support which they provide for the awkwardness and sorrows of the youthful characters is a significant element in the overall effect. And their poignant reflectiveness creates also that feeling of autumnal calm which is so precious a part of the mood of *All's Well that Ends Well*. But more immediate to the question of Shakespeare's methods in adapting his source is that all these new and sympathetic characters (and I include the King as a 'new' character, for his role is so much fuller than in Painter) voice, movingly, their affection for Helena, support her in her quest, and direct the audience towards approval of her actions. At the same time they comment on the folly of Bertram's behaviour while still showing themselves ready to make allowances for the misdeeds of youth. The older generation provides the background of sympathy and understanding against which the problems and sufferings of youth can be explored and resolved.

The attitude of the older characters to Helena is consistently used by Shakespeare to guide the reactions of the audience. Helena, like Giletta, is the principal agent in the plot; but unlike Giletta, her actions are accompanied by a commentary of approving remarks and explanations from a group of characters which Shakespeare seems to have invented for just this purpose. The King discerns in her language the voice of 'some blessed spirit' and feels that she possesses 'Youth, beauty, wisdom, courage – all / That happiness and prime can happy call' (II, i, 180).[1] Lafeu, from feeling that her looks could 'breathe life into a stone, / Quicken a rock, and make you dance canary' (II, i, 72–3), goes on to warn us, from the evidence of what he sees of Helena, that the age of miracles is not past (II, iii, 1); and he is heard, towards the end of the play, wistfully describing her: ''Twas a good lady; 'twas a good lady. We may pick a thousand sallets ere we light on such another herb' (IV, v, 13–14). Above all through the gentle graciousness of the Countess, Shakespeare guides our sympathy and affection towards Helena. From her early tributes in the first scene – 'she derives her honesty and achieves her goodness' (l. 42) – to her carefully stated 'epitaph' before the denouement – 'the most virtuous gentlewoman that ever nature had praise for creating. If she had partaken of my flesh and cost me the dearest groans of a mother I could not have owed her a more rooted love' (IV, v, 9–12) – the Countess never ceases to focus our approval on Helena.

Shakespeare, then, through this group of older characters not provided by his source, seeks to create sympathy and affection for Helena, and approval of her quest. They have led some critics, however, to see the play in terms of a 'youth versus age' conflict. Clifford Leech, for example, writes that it 'shows us old and young characters juxtaposed, with the old rebuking the young and sighing at the present corruption of manners. On the one side the King, the Countess, Lafeu, the dead fathers of Bertram and Helena; on the other Bertram and Parolles.'[2] It is significant that the names he sets down in the scroll of youth are only two, the comic villain and his dupe. Yet Helena, with all the marks of ardent, hopeful youth upon

her, achieves throughout the play a remarkable harmony with the older characters. In the third scene of act 1, her interview with the Countess shows a touching sympathy of thought and purpose between them. 'Even so it was with me when I was young' (l. 123) is a remark from the old lady which suggests considerable understanding of the problems of youth. 'To be young again, if we could' she says to the clown a few scenes later (II, ii, 37), and goes on to demonstrate a delightful capacity to make the effort. In the scene of Bertram's arrival at the French Court (I, ii), one again sees the wholesome possibility of understanding between the generations. He is welcomed to court by the melancholy figure of the diseased King. Bertram is young, awkward, an 'unseason'd courtier', and he reminds the King of his father. The speech of reminiscence, of friendship in youth recollected in age and illness, is poignant and distressing. The King is surrounded by his lords; they begin the scene talking of the Italian war, and it would seem obvious to play these anonymous lords as the same individuals who later head south in search of military glory. Like Bertram they are full of the confidence of youth, but when the King's recollections bring on this melancholy mood, one of them is there with a moving reply. The King expresses the wish, since he brings home 'nor wax nor honey', that he might be 'dissolved from my hive, / To give some labourers room' (ll. 65–6). The anonymous lord's reply does

[1] My quotations and references are from the new Arden edition by G. K. Hunter (London, 1959).

[2] 'The Theme of Ambition in *All's Well that Ends Well*', *ELH*, 21 (1954), 17–29 (p. 20). There is in fact no real textual evidence of Parolles's youthfulness. Indeed his memories, or pretended memories, of previous service in the Italian wars (II, i, 40 ff.) and his presentation of himself to Diana as a man 'to mell with', in contrast to Bertram, a boy 'not to kiss' (IV, iii, 220), suggest that he should be played as visibly older than Bertram. Bertram's immaturity, of course, is crucial to the play's effect, as I suggest below.

not reason with him, or take up the argument in the terms in which he expresses it; it is a quiet statement: 'You're loved, sir.' It is simple but deeply understanding, and it should come, I feel sure, from a young actor.

Later in the play, the group of young French lords are in Florence, having just captured Parolles in order to expose him to Bertram. Shakespeare holds up the development of the plot for an extended dialogue between two of them (I, iii, 1–71) in which they comment on the behaviour of Bertram and Parolles. There is no question of this being the mean-spiritedness of crabbed age condemning the foibles of youth; these are young men, deliberately used by Shakespeare at this point to provide a commentary on the actions of misguided youth. And in so doing, these young men place themselves alongside the Countess, Lafeu, and the King, as well as Helena, in condemning Bertram's misdeeds while at the same time believing in his potential goodness. There is certainly a division of the play's characters into groups on the lines that Professor Leech and others have suggested, but the distinguishing marks of the parties are surely selfishness and generosity, or folly and goodness, rather than youth and age.

As the King leaves the stage at the end of the second scene, he requests the support of Bertram's arm for his old, frail body, worn out 'with several applications' (l. 74), and he welcomes him again: 'My son's no dearer.' The possibility of harmony and peace between the generations is here strongly felt. In the interview between Helena and the Countess in the scene that follows, we see it achieved. As Bertram and the King leave the stage, Bertram supporting his monarch, we may remember the King's earlier admonition as he remarked on Bertram's physical likeness to his father: 'Thy father's moral parts / Mayest thou inherit too!' (I, ii, 21–2). The capacity of Bertram to fulfil this wish takes the whole play to establish. With

the hope of its fulfilment provided at the end of the last scene comes the establishment of total harmony between the generations, comically picked up in the reconciliation of Parolles and his most vigorous mocker, Lafeu. The power of the young to give love and re-creation to the old is vividly seen in *All's Well that Ends Well*: the King is cured by Helena, the Countess responds wholeheartedly to the ardour of Helena's love, Lafeu's sympathy is awakened by the plight of Parolles. In his invention and development of this older group of characters Shakespeare has added a depth to the play far removed from anything in Painter's translation of Boccaccio's story.

As well as this group of older characters, Shakespeare has also added two comedians to his source material, Parolles and Lavatch. Parolles, in the years when *All's Well that Ends Well* was being staged in Garrick's version as a broad, farcical comedy, was the secret of the rather short-lived success it enjoyed.[1] King Charles I had earlier made clear his idea of the play's centre of interest by jotting 'Monsieur Parolles' as an alternative to the title in the royal copy of the Second Folio. Some more recent critics have been much sterner about Monsieur Parolles, who is seen as Bertram's wicked angel, as the counterweight to Helena in the morality scheme of the play. There is something of this pattern in the background no doubt, but to exaggerate it is to ignore the fact that Parolles is constantly and consistently funny. Without any of the loading that Garrick's text gave to the part, Clive Swift, in John Barton's 1967 Stratford production, made the audience laugh a great deal: one remembers especially his mimicry of Lafeu at the beginning of act II, scene iii – 'so say I too'; the mock duel that followed this; and, perhaps above all, the comic soliloquy of self-knowledge after his pretended valour has made him venture too far:

[1] See Price, *The Unfortunate Comedy*, pp. 3–22.

What the devil should move me to undertake the recovery of this drum, being not ignorant of the impossibility, and knowing I had no such purpose? I must give myself some hurts, and say I got them in exploit; yet slight ones will not carry it . . . And great ones I dare not give.   (IV, i, 34–40)

The interesting technique following this speech, in which the so-called asides of the listening lords are apparently heard by Parolles and used in his soliloquising, which reads rather oddly, worked brilliantly in the theatre.

Parolles, then, is genuinely comic. And Parolles, wicked angel so-called, is also accepted at the end by Lafeu his sternest critic, and takes a full share in the final forgiveness and joy. Shakespeare seems to have invented Parolles to provide a context for Bertram's follies, and a parallel to them on a baser level. He is an alternative to Helena, but not quite on the rigid morality level that has sometimes been urged. The joint plan of Bertram and Parolles to steal away to the Italian war after the King has refused them permission to go openly (II, i, 29–34) seems at first like little more than the escapade of naughty schoolboys. Parolles is certainly the 'tempter' here, though Bertram is quick on the uptake. Shakespeare carefully places the idea well before the enforced marriage to Helena, and before Bertram has any notion of the existence of such a possibility. This is a deliberate and important departure from the source story, in which Beltramo, after the marriage, 'praied licence to retourne to his countrye to consummate the mariage. And when he was on horsebacke hee went not thither but toke his journey into Tuscane' (p. 392). By thus bringing forward Bertram's decision to go to Italy, and making it dependent on his desire for honour and his envy of the freedom of his fellow courtiers, Shakespeare makes Bertram's behaviour less painful, and ultimately more forgivable. One sees him anxious not to lose face here, and Parolles, whose 'face' is of course his sole fortune, care-

fully encourages this attitude. From this partnership in high, if misguided, spirits, they drift into stupidity, unkindness, selfishness, and finally sin in the attempted seduction of Diana. Always Parolles's actions provide a reflection of Bertram's – even to the extent of his comic attempt, behind his master's back, to deflect the Florentine lady's interest towards himself. Parolles, and Bertram's attraction for him, are no more than the symptom of what is wrong with Bertram – his shallowness, his unthinking carelessness, and lack of thought for others. Shakespeare has paralleled their courses most deliberately in the exposure that each undergoes. That Parolles is not the wicked angel responsible for leading Bertram astray is vividly shown in the final scene where, long after he has been made to see his companion for what he is, Bertram goes on to show himself independently capable of his most objectionable behaviour, in that long demonstration of weakness, cowardice, and lying. There is a good deal of surface similarity in the two exposure scenes: both Bertram and Parolles are ruthlessly stripped of their covering of unmerited honour, and in their increasingly frantic efforts to avoid disaster, each shows himself capable of promising anything, however false or impossible. Parolles betrays his comrades to his comrades, Bertram betrays himself to his friends, his family, and above all to himself. Both of these scenes are carefully arranged and stage-managed, the first by the young lords, the second by Helena, working through Diana. There is one important difference between them, however, and it gives an indication of Shakespeare's purposes in his invention of the role of Parolles and the comic subplot. The exposure of Parolles is funny; the exposure of Bertram is painful. The reasons for this are indicated by those enormously useful anonymous lords.[1] Alone, looking for the

---

[1] Two of them are later (IV, iii, 171 ff.) named as the Dumaine brothers, and the complication of the speech

drum and 'not ignorant of the impossibility' of finding it, Parolles is overheard by his exposers. One of them comments succinctly: 'Is it possible he should know what he is, and be that he is?' (IV, i, 44). The answer of course is yes, as the exposure itself proves. Utterly humiliated in front of those he has sought throughout to impress, Parolles has a self-knowledge that makes him resilient:

> If my heart were great
> 'Twould burst at this. Captain I'll be no more,
> But I will eat and drink and sleep as soft
> As captain shall. Simply the thing I am
> Shall make me live . . .
> There's place and means for every man alive.
> I'll after them.   (IV, iii, 319–29)

And because this is a comedy and not a morality play, there is, as we see in the final reconciliation with Lafeu, 'place and means', 'drink and sleep', for him. During that blindfold scene of his exposure to Bertram, protected from any danger of over-seriousness by the frequent intrusion of the mumbo-jumbo of the 'choughs' language', Parolles piles outrageous disloyalty on to stupendous insult, from the comical precision of the military information he gives away, accompanied by the broad-minded offer to take the sacrament on it 'how and which way you will' (IV, iii, 133), to the vivid observation that Dumaine will steal 'an egg out of a cloister' (l. 241). It is a theatrical performance of great brilliance, one in which he 'hath out-villain'd villainy so far that the rarity redeems him' (l. 264) – which of course it does. Though Parolles *is* a fool and a knave, as Lafeu tells him again in the penultimate scene, we are content that he 'shall eat' and be on hand at the end to provide Lafeu with a 'handkercher', and with the prospect of making sport with him at home. Bertram's exposure, on the other hand, is the exposure of a man not fully knowing what he is, and with a heart capable, finally, of bursting. But I want to say more of this later.

About Shakespeare's other comic addition to his source in *All's Well that Ends Well*, one hardly knows what to think. R. H. Goldsmith finds Lavatch 'unlike Shakespeare's other fools in that his role bears no significant relationship to the theme of *All's Well*'.[1] This is a curious and difficult part certainly, but it is hard to believe that Shakespeare would deliberately invent a character who 'bears no significant relationship' to the rest of the play. Other critics, of course, have seen the bawdy cynicism of Lavatch as the key to Shakespeare's intention. To R. A. Foakes, this is a play in which 'the irrepressible Parolles, and the sardonic clown Lavache, set the tone. Indeed, Lavache has little other function in the play than this'.[2] Lavatch's harshness, his requests that he and 'Isbel the woman' be permitted to 'do as we may', because he is 'driven on by the flesh' (I, iii, 16ff.), and his suggestion of the impossibility of finding one good woman in ten, immediately precede Helena's revelation to the Countess of her love for Bertram. It has often been suggested that they therefore undercut the scene and make a mockery of it. But the critic who confuses the point of view of Lavatch with that of the dramatist surely reveals, as Joseph Price aptly observes (p. 147), 'his own cynicism, not Shakespeare's'. Price points out other plays in which a cynical or bawdy element is used along with a serious presentation of romantic love without devaluing it: *As You Like It* (Touchstone and Audrey), *Twelfth Night* (Feste), *Measure for Measure* (Lucio – though perhaps the problems

prefixes in the Folio (see Hunter edition, pp. xvff.) suggests that Shakespeare had particular actors in mind for these parts. But for their essential roles as manipulators of the plot and commentators on the action, anonymity is perfectly adequate.

[1] *Wise Fools in Shakespeare* (East Lansing, Michigan, 1955), p. 60.
[2] *Shakespeare: The Dark Comedies to the Last Plays: From Satire to Celebration* (London, 1971), p. 17.

here are too similar to those of *All's Well that Ends Well* for this to be a wholly convincing example). One might add the Nurse and Mercutio in *Romeo and Juliet* to his list of the comic, cynical 'safety valves', providing a necessary element of realism and worldliness to make a romantic situation credible, and to prevent it from cloying. Most of the characters listed, one also observes, are added, or developed, by Shakespeare to those he found in his source. Some such explanation of Lavatch's presence in the play is necessary, for it seems hard to imagine that anyone can have much hope of his proving worth employment as a potential source of mirth in the Rossillion household, in spite of R. H. Goldsmith's suggestion (p. 59) that his wit is 'modish, and to the very degree that it was stylish and smart in his day it has become flat and somewhat tedious to us'. Perhaps, with Kittredge,[1] we may think of him as a country clown, out of place in a courtly atmosphere. To contemplate Lavatch, though, is likely to create a feeling of sympathy with Lafeu, who remarks, at the end of a conversation with him, 'Go thy ways; I begin to be aweary of thee' (IV, v, 53). 'A shrewd knave and an unhappy' he calls him a few moments later, and on hearing from the Countess that he remains in the household because her dead husband was fond of him ('and indeed he has no pace, but runs where he will'), comments 'I like him well; 'tis not amiss', and changes the subject. The presence of the shrewd and unhappy Lavatch has its effect, certainly, on the general mood of the play, but to suggest, with Professor Foakes (p. 17), that the play is 'never free . . . from the vision of things as seen by Parolles and Lavache' seems to go against the evidence of Shakespeare's care in presenting the main plot to us. He is, of course, as Professor Bullough observes in his introduction to the source (p. 388), 'bringing into his comedy some of the knowledge of the darker sides of human nature which he has already revealed in

his Histories. But he is still the romantic dramatist who delights to show how far a good deed shines in a naughty world . . . and the proof of his continued assurance is Helena'. The presence of Lavatch in *All's Well that Ends Well* serves partly at least as a foil to Helena, to reveal her as a 'bright particular star' way above such earthly mortals as the poor clown, as well as to remind us of her common humanity with him. His touching tribute to her near the end of the play – 'she was the sweet-marjoram of the sallet, or, rather, the herb of grace' (IV, v, 15) – is a nice demonstration of the capacity of even the voice of bawdy cynicism to respond to Helena. In spite of R. H. Goldsmith's belief that Lavatch is a 'clever, urbane jester' (p. 59), it seems difficult to see him in the same company as Feste and Touchstone. In many ways he seems to have the simplicity and vulnerability of Lear's fool, though he lacks his capacity to penetrate to the heart of a situation. He is like Lear's fool too in the gentleness and compassion he calls forth in his patron. The Countess's patience and tolerance towards Lavatch, her protection of him within the security of the Rossillion household, allow this harsh and unlikeable knave to have his part in the scheme of forgiveness and tolerance at the end of the play. This bond of trust and understanding, quite superfluous to anything required by the plot, between two characters whom Shakespeare has added to those he found in Boccaccio's tale, is an epitome of the ways in which he has enriched the story from which he worked.

With two groups of new characters, the older generation and the comics, Shakespeare has, then, vastly altered the mood of Boccaccio's

[1] Referred to by Price, *The Unfortunate Comedy*, p. 153. John Barton's production seemed to be suggesting something of the sort when it presented Lavatch playing with a rabbit-skin – and, moreover, one which, to all appearances, had come from a not-long-dead rabbit.

story and provided a context for Helena and Bertram quite different from that against which they are seen in his source. Before examining the use they make of that context, it may be helpful to isolate some of the often telling modifications he makes in the plot of the story. At the beginning of the play, Shakespeare alters the heroine's circumstances. Giletta was 'diligently looked unto by her kinsfolke (because she was riche and fatherlesse)'; she also 'refused manye husbandes with whom her kinsfolke woulde have matched her' (pp. 389–90). Helena is poor, totally dependent on the kindness and generosity of the Countess, and has never been loved by or loved anyone but Bertram. This makes possible Shakespeare's presentation of her as the inexperienced, humble, timid, innocent girl we see in the first scene of the play, in her interview with the Countess, in her first scene with the King, and in her choosing of a husband after the cure of the King's disease. It is a timidity fired into resolve and strength by the power of her love, but it is a characteristic never shown by Giletta. Shakespeare's changes seem designed to make Helena more attractive to an audience. At the same time, however, the reduction of Helena's social status to that of a sort of servant in the Rossillion household makes Bertram's reaction to the idea of marrying her more understandable. His farewell to her in the first scene – 'Be comfortable to my mother, your mistress, and make much of her' (l. 73) – has all the nonchalance a young man might be expected to show to a girl of inferior station brought up in the family.

Helena's social inferiority and her dependence on the Countess are used to most telling effect in act I, scene iii. It is a scene carefully calculated to gain the sympathy of an audience as Helena, bashfully inarticulate after the initial half-comic awkwardness over the name of 'mother', is coaxed towards a moving declaration of her love by the kindness and understanding of the Countess, whose secret awareness of Helena's situation is shared by the audience. The interview between them concludes with the Countess's approval of Helena's project of going to Paris, which we have already learned of in her second soliloquy: 'Why, Helen, thou shalt have my leave and love ... I'll stay at home / And pray God's blessing into thy attempt' (ll. 246–9). Whether individual critics find it acceptable or not, Shakespeare has obviously tried, through this scene, to protect his heroine from those charges of predatoriness, of husband-hunting, which might legitimately be levelled at Boccaccio's Giletta. He has used our affection for the old lady, a character invented for this purpose, as a means to win our acceptance of Helena's plan. Seen in the light of the Countess's approval, it gains, or is surely supposed to gain, our approval too.

Helena's modesty and timidity are shown again when she reaches Paris. She is ready to withdraw (II, i, 124 ff.) at the King's first rebuff, and only continues when she has withdrawn her personality behind the disguise of her incantatory couplets (ll. 133 ff.). Helena shows the same humility in the great public scene at court, when she is again ready to withdraw at the revelation of Bertram's antipathy to the idea of marrying her: 'That you are well restor'd, my lord, I'm glad. / Let the rest go' (II, iii, 147–8). This is a very precise and deliberate alteration from Painter, and one to which Shakespeare's other changes contribute. When Giletta declared her choice of Beltramo, the King 'was very loth to graunt him unto her' and only did so because 'he had made a promise which he was loth to breake' (p. 391). There is no such reluctance about the King's 'Why, then, young Bertram, take her' (l. 105) in the play. Bertram's refusal comes as a painful jar in a jovial scene, and the King's insistence produces a speech which Professor Bradbrook sees as 'the germ of the play':[1]

[1] M. C. Bradbrook, *Shakespeare and Elizabethan Poetry* (London, 1951), p. 166.

> If she be
> All that is virtuous, save what thou dislik'st –
> A poor physician's daughter – thou dislik'st
> Of virtue for the name. But do not so . . .
>   Good alone
> Is good, without a name; vileness is so:
> The property by what it is should go,
> Not by the title. She is young, wise, fair;
> In these to nature she's immediate heir,
> And these breed honour; that is honour's scorn
> Which challenges itself as honour's born
> And is not like the sire. Honours thrive
> When rather from our acts we them derive
> Than our foregoers.   (II, iii, 121–37)

There is nothing like this in Boccaccio's story. The initial reduction of Helena's social status makes it possible in Shakespeare – by 1600 an aristocrat is unlikely to have thought marriage to a wealthy commoner as disgraceful as Beltramo appears to. And the King's willingness to ennoble Helena, a possibility of which there is no mention in the source, removes at a stroke the entire ground of Beltramo's objection and the ostensible ground of Bertram's. From this point on, the relationship between Helena and Bertram is forced on to the personal level of love and disdain, the disdain of familiarity and unawareness. Honour too is placed in perspective by the King: 'Honours thrive/When rather from our acts we them derive / Than our foregoers.' To those who can judge it best, Bertram's mother and the King, the poor physician's daughter proves herself worthy in honour of the hereditary nobleman, Bertram. In a sense Shakespeare has here, in act II, reached the point that Boccaccio reaches only at the end of his story: he has shown Helena worthy of her husband. The rest of the play is in fact to be about something with which the source is never concerned – Bertram's need of Helena.

The circumstances in which the hero and heroine go to Italy are also subtly changed by Shakespeare from the account he found in Painter. That Bertram reaches his decision to slip away to the south before he is forced into marriage has already been mentioned. This slight moderation of Beltramo's deliberate brutality goes some way towards softening the effect of Bertram's behaviour in the play. Helena's departure to the south is much more significantly modified. In Boccaccio's story, the constantly efficient Giletta spent some time putting Beltramo's estates into good running order before 'she toke her way, with her maide, and one of her kinsemen, in the habite of a pilgrime, well furnished with silver and precious Jewels: telling no man whither shee wente, and never rested till shee came to Florence' (p. 393). It is a purposeful and well thought-out step, and the pilgrim's guise is a deliberate attempt to mislead. Helena, on the other hand, leaves Rossillion with that wistful, tender soliloquy of fear for her husband's safety, entirely selfless in its devotion to Bertram and its despair at the danger to which she thinks she has exposed him. She says nothing of any intention to seek Bertram in Florence and in the letter which her mother-in-law receives two scenes later, announcing that she is 'Saint Jaques' pilgrim, thither gone' (III, iv, 4), the same mood of pity and love for Bertram is maintained. The next time we see Helena she is in Florence, 'somewhat out of the road', as Dr Johnson remarked, 'from Roussillon to Compostella'.[1] Though the suggestion has been made that by St Jaques Shakespeare intends not Compostella but San Giacomo d'Altopascio not far from Florence, and that the pilgrims' hostel at 'Saint Francis here beside the port' (III, v, 36) refers to San Francesco dei Vanchetoni in the neighbourhood of the Porta al Prato in Florence,[2] it is difficult to imagine how an audience could be persuaded to think in such precise geographical terms. Yet some critics of

[1] *Works of Samuel Johnson*, VII, 392.
[2] See Mario Praz, 'Shakespeare's Italy', *Shakespeare Survey 7* (Cambridge, 1954), pp. 96–7. The suggestion, which Praz dismisses, is G. Lambin's.

the play and of Helena's motives have examined the geography with remarkable scrupulosity. Bertrand Evans, for example, admits that the widow evinces no surprise at Helena's presence on pilgrimage in Florence, and even tells her (ll. 94–5) that 'There's four or five, to Great Saint Jaques bound, / Already at my house' (a detail, one notes, that Shakespeare has added to give plausibility to Helena's situation). But he goes on to demand, accusingly, 'was it coincidence that she chose a saint the road to whose shrine ran through Bertram's present location? Had she, at first, a real intention of going beyond Florence?'[1] Such an extraordinary search for motives with which Shakespeare does not concern himself seems to show a misunderstanding of the intention which the modification of the source here makes clear. Shakespeare sends Helena out of the play with a soliloquy of tenderness and love; he deliberately leaves her motives vague, relying on the goodwill he has established for her in the audience, through her behaviour and through the comments of characters he has invented for this purpose, to carry her through the necessary complications of the plot which will lead to the fulfilment of her hopes. Almost as soon as she has left the stage he brings on the Countess to reinforce our approval of Helena and to suggest that Bertram 'cannot thrive' unless Helena's prayers, which 'heaven delights to hear / And loves to grant, reprieve him from the wrath / Of greatest justice' (III, iv, 27–9). This is a remark which critics who see the play in terms of Christian allegory have seized on, and it is, indeed, their strongest evidence. More immediately, though, it is an example of Shakespeare's careful use of plot modification and invented characters to direct in advance the audience's reactions to what will be a slightly difficult phase in the development of the plot. The Countess's remark provides the necessary link between Helena's apparently purposeless exit at the end of act III, scene ii, and her appearance in

Florence in the scene that follows. After it we desire and expect that we should next see Helena near Bertram. A moment later (ll. 38–40) the Countess adds:

> Which of them both
> Is dearest to me I have no skill in sense
> To make distinction.

Shakespeare obviously wants the tenderness and love which this deeply sympathetic character feels for these two rather awkward young people to be reflected in the audience. His intention is clearly to put the audience into a frame of mind in which they are more likely to accept that chain of events which is to protect the Countess from any further necessity of making distinctions in her affections.

The plot modifications of the Florentine scenes of the play stem mainly from the fact that Shakespeare has to present a great deal of invented material relative to Parolles and Bertram. I have already said something about the significance of these scenes in relation to Parolles, and I shall return to them in considering Bertram. Their effect on the main plot, of course, is exactly what Shakespeare requires: they keep Helena in the background. If one sees the play dividing roughly into two at the departure of Helena from Rossillion at the end of act III, scene ii, an interesting pattern becomes apparent. Of the ten scenes up to and including III, ii, Helena appears in seven and speaks 320 of their 1,420 lines; of the thirteen scenes after III, ii, Helena appears in only five and speaks only 143 of their 1,375 lines. This is in sharp contrast to the situation in Painter, where Giletta, as the clever wench organising the means by which she is to answer Beltramo's riddle, is vigorous and busy right through this stage of the tale, her conversations with the widow (or her equivalent) reported at a length which seems disproportionate to the rest of the story. Shakespeare's intention is to carry

[1] *Shakespeare's Comedies* (Oxford, 1960), p. 154.

Helena through this second half of the play on the strength of the impression she has made in the first half. His main emphasis in this area goes on to his 'subplot' scenes as they prepare for the final revelation and the return to Rossillion, with the reappearance of Helena in the final scene. The plot-changes from the source are there more extreme than at any point in the play, but as that is the end, I should like to leave it till then.

To consider Helena and Bertram in relation to Giletta and Beltramo in this new setting of invented characters and modified plot reveals a number of interesting points. The basic aspect of the presentation of Helena has already emerged: that in her search for Bertram's love she has the support and sympathy of everyone in the play except Parolles – and even he betrays some little affection for her in his words of parting in the first scene: 'Little Helen, farewell. If I can remember thee I will think of thee at court' (ll. 184–5). Giletta's smooth efficiency and determination have gone, and our first close view of Helena is in that despairing, yearning soliloquy which reveals her consciousness of her own unworthiness, and her naive preoccupation with Bertram's beauty. She is revived from her despair by the strength of her love, by her fear for Bertram as she realises that 'the court's a learning-place' (l. 173), and by her awakening realisation of the power of virginity (to be understood both in spiritual and sensual terms) during the conversation with Parolles. Through the growing hope and resilience of the second soliloquy and the delightful interview with the Countess, she is prepared, and so is the audience, for her performance at Paris. Her modesty and willingness to withdraw at the beginning of the confrontation with the King lead into the strangely stylised couplets. The couplets recall her assertion at the end of the interview with the Countess that her medicine has something in it

'more than my father's skill' and is, in fact, 'sanctified / By th'luckiest stars in heaven' (I, iii, 237ff.). The King concludes that in her some 'blessed spirit' speaks (II, i, 174), and Lafeu regards her cure as a miracle. The idea is kept vague – the couplets themselves provide a screen of stylisation in the surrounding realism of presentation – and Helena remains throughout too vividly human to be categorised in schematic terms. She arrives at the choosing scene, however, secure in the approval of the Countess, Lafeu, the King, and, indirectly, of heaven – and so, one must also expect, of the audience. The effect of all this, followed by the modesty of her withdrawal at Bertram's unwillingness, and the ardour of the King's assertion of her 'honour', is to make Bertram's refusal of her seem utterly foolish, though not beyond understanding. She has been presented in the first half of the play on two fronts: as the means by which a miraculous cure comes to the King – 'A showing of a heavenly effect in an earthly actor' in the words of Lafeu (II, iii, 24); and as a physically attractive young woman in love – 'powerful to araise King Pippen' or 'give great Charlemain a pen in's hand', as Lafeu, again, somewhat broadly expresses it (II, i, 75). She is established by the middle of the play as sensitive, intelligent, and strong, and she leaves Rossillion with a soliloquy of selfless tenderness reinforced by the Countess's subsequent praise of her, and inability to say whether Helena or Bertram is dearer to her. This, and Helena's parting speech, are of great importance in directing our attitude to Bertram. That he is capable of foolishness and ingratitude we already know; he has recently demonstrated moral cowardice and, in the scene of his parting with Helena, an insensitiveness that amounts almost to cruelty; he is soon to show himself capable of falling more obviously into wickedness. Yet Helena's speech directs our attention to him as the object of her love; the soliloquy should catch us up with her emotions, keep Bertram and Helena together in our minds, and help us share the Countess's willingness to regard them with equal affection. It is on this that Shakespeare relies as he brings them towards the conclusion through the rather difficult intervening period of plot manipulation.

During the second half of the play we see only as much of Helena as is consistent with making the plot comprehensible. One scene in disguise as a pilgrim, two short scenes with the widow, and a brief scene as she is returning to France, are all that Shakespeare risks before Helena reappears thirty lines from the end of the play. For our impressions of her during the intervening period we have to rely on our memories, on the comments of the Countess in act III, scene iv, on the assessment of her by the young French lords as they comment on Bertram's behaviour – 'so good a wife and so sweet a lady' (IV, iii, 6), and on the remarks of Lafeu, the Countess, and even Lavatch as they deliver (IV, v, 9 ff.) what they think of as epitaphs. When Helena does reappear to accept the penitence of Bertram brought about by her *alter ego* Diana, Shakespeare intends, I feel sure, that the portrait of her established during the first three acts should remain untarnished by the necessary plot manipulation of act IV. One of the crucial questions of the play is whether he has succeeded in this rather daring bit of dramatic legerdemain, succeeded in getting through the somewhat awkward tale he inherited from Boccaccio without allowing our attention to focus too sharply on the mechanics of its plot. He has tried to use the realistic and sympathetic characterisation of Helena so strongly built up in the first part of the play to get her across this bridgeless little channel. And he has diverted our attention from the process of crossing by providing entertainment, with serious implications, through the unmasking of Parolles and its dependent scenes. The intention seems to be, as Joseph Price points out (p. 162), that the

bed-trick should be a symbol rather than a realistic plot device, a satisfaction of the demands of the story, and of the audience's expectations of happiness for Helena who has been so sympathetically presented to them. Provided that this sympathy for Helena has been strongly enough impressed by the end of act III – and Shakespeare has surely given an actress enough to make this possible – and that therefore during the rest of the play the audience is seeing Bertram through the glass of Helena's love for him, there is every possibility of success. This becomes clearer if one considers Bertram in the new context that Shakespeare has developed from that provided by Boccaccio for Beltramo.

If the essential point about Helena is the affection she inspires in other characters in the play, the essential point about Bertram is his immaturity, and the readiness of everyone to make allowances for it. The plot itself, of course, asserts Bertram's youth: he is a ward of court, too young to be left to manage the properties inherited from his father. In each of the first two scenes, characters whom we respect tell him that he looks like his father and that they hope he will learn to behave like him. The King's greeting on Bertram's arrival at Court has already been quoted; it follows hard upon his mother's farewell: 'Be thou bless'd, Bertram, and succeed thy father / In manners as in shape!' (I, i, 57–8). The hope is ultimately given promise of fulfilment, but it is his initial lack of moral shape that allows Bertram far too much room for manoeuvre. His youth is stressed throughout: it prevents his going to the Italian war with the legitimate permission of the King; to Lafeu he seems a young ass, but only one of that general group of asses who form the 'unbak'd and doughy youth' of the nation (IV, v, 3); even to Parolles Bertram is a 'foolish idle boy', a 'lascivious young boy' (IV, iii, 207, 290). This stress on Bertram's youth is important: none of the older, de-

pendable characters think his behaviour irre-
deemably vicious, nor do the young lords who
comment on it in act IV, scene iii. Even at the
end his misdeeds are, to his mother, 'Natural
rebellion done i' the blade of youth' (v, iii, 6).
Shakespeare presents him to us as a foolish and
misled boy, in need of rescue from the dangers
of his own folly. His last escapade in Florence
reveals the moral danger in which this folly
places him.

The affection which Bertram is capable of
inspiring in those around him is remarkable:
the Countess, even after his rejection of her
beloved Helena, cannot measure her love for
him; the King welcomes him to Court as his
own son; Lafeu is ready to marry his daughter
to him; the Duke of Florence appoints him
general of his horse; to Diana and the widow he
is 'a most gallant fellow' (III, v, 79). And above
all of course there is Helena, who keeps Bertram before our eyes as an object of love,
finding excuses for him, blaming herself,
constantly presenting him to us in the best
possible light. The most remarkable example of
this is the speech at the end of act III, scene ii,
when Helena, after Bertram's rejection of her,
talks only of the danger he is in, forcing the
audience to view him tolerantly when he
appears in the next scene at the height of his
military success. Helena's own comments on
her social inferiority, particularly in her first
soliloquy and in her conversation with the
Countess, also prepare the audience for Bertram's rejection of her on grounds of rank.
Joseph Price has even suggested that we are
to take the replies of the other lords in the
choosing scene (II, iii, 52 ff.) as elaborate but
insincere courtesy, rightly, *not* mistakenly,
interpreted by Lafeu.[1] Whether he is right or
not, there is no doubt that we are asked to
understand Bertram's unwillingness. His cry 'a
poor physician's daughter my wife' (l. 123)
would not, says Professor Bradbrook, 'sound
so outrageous to an Elizabethan ear as it does

today'.[2] It is essential that the audience should
acquiesce in the forgiveness of Bertram at the
end, and not go away, with Dr Johnson, unable
to reconcile their hearts to the fact that he is
dismissed to happiness. So the shape of his
career is carefully controlled by Shakespeare;
his relationship with Helena is suggested at the
beginning with economy and precision, so that
his horror at the marriage is understandable,
and the terms in which he expresses it, though
concealing personal reaction in social generali-
sation, not unexpected. Parolles is invented to
take much of the blame (from Lafeu, the Countess, and the young French lords) for Bertram's
youthful follies. Bertram is handsome and
young; everyone is prepared to like him and
give him the benefit of the doubt. He goes to the
war and wins glory; and the war exists only to
reflect honour on him – its rights and wrongs
are kept delightfully vague, with the French
King giving his courtiers permission to fight
on either side (I, ii, 15). Bertram achieves a
rank much higher than the command of 'a
certaine number of men' (p. 392) which is all
that Beltramo gets in Painter; the Duke of
Florence appoints him 'general of our horse'
(III, iii, 1). Even in the scene of Bertram's
parting from Helena (II, v) Shakespeare has
most carefully maintained the balance which
makes the final reconciliation possible. A real
showdown here would have a disastrous effect
on the play. Instead we have Helena's modest
request for a kiss, and Bertram's evasive refusal;
his dismissal of her protestations of loyalty
with the embarrassed 'Come, come; no more of

[1] Price's argument (*The Unfortunate Comedy*, pp.
155–6) is persuasive without, finally, being capable of
proof. He rightly points out, however, that Lafeu,
Shakespeare's invented commentator, is not wrong
elsewhere, and in predicting Bertram's refusal, is right
immediately afterwards; moreover, his being wrong
here would serve no particular dramatic purpose. But
if the lords' over-courteous replies betray reluctance,
Lafeu fulfils the useful function of giving expression
to, and sustaining, our feelings for Helena.

[2] *Shakespeare and Elizabethan Poetry*, p. 166.

that' (l. 73);[1] and, finally, his petulant shout 'Go thou toward home, where I will never come' (l. 90), carefully placed by Shakespeare *after* her departure from the stage. There is nothing in this, their final meeting on stage before the last scene of the play, to make their reconciliation there implausible.

That Bertram is young, headstrong, and foolish has, then, been made clear by the end of act III. During act IV we observe that his lack of moral shape is going to allow him to cross the boundary into unequivocal sinfulness. It has sometimes been suggested that Bertram's flirtation with Diana should be regarded only as the misdemeanour of a soldier abroad on active service. But that we are asked to see Bertram as here corrupting 'a well-derived nature' there seems little doubt. In the scenes of the attempted seduction, we should also remember that remark of the Countess which immediately precedes them: that Bertram 'cannot thrive' without the love, and guidance, of Helena. I have tried to suggest that the audience must, if the play is to work at all, be prepared to share in the forgiveness of Bertram at the end of the play; they must also be aware, if the last scene is to succeed, that he *needs* Helena. The two French lords, young men, are allowed to hold the stage for a considerable period at the beginning of act IV, scene iii, interrupting the Parolles episode in which the audience is much interested. They comment very pointedly on what Bertram is doing. They speak of his wife, whom they believe dead, 'so good a wife and so sweet a lady', and they describe his behaviour in unequivocal terms: 'He hath perverted a young gentlewoman here in Florence, of a most chaste renown, and this night he fleshes his will in the spoil of her honour; he hath given her his monumental ring, and thinks himself made in the unchaste composition.' And yet the immediacy of Bertram's sin is put into perspective as they go on to moralise, from Bertram's behaviour, about human con-

duct in general: 'As we are ourselves, what things we are ... Merely our own traitors.' Bertram in this action 'contrives against his own nobility' (l. 23), but in so doing he is not untypical of the human species. Some critics have used this idea to suggest a schematised pattern in the play,[2] with Bertram as a *humanum genus* figure, sinning and needing the forgiveness of divine grace, represented by Helena. The pattern is certainly in the background, though there is always such a vivid humanity about Bertram's misguided immaturity that it is difficult to schematise him into a 'symbol' of anything. The inference of the comments of the two young lords on Bertram's behaviour is, however, clear: that in contriving against his own nobility he rebels against his own better nature, and in giving away his monumental ring he epitomises the perversion of his honour as a nobleman, a son, and a husband. And all this is to satisfy what he himself calls his 'sick desires' (IV, ii, 35), his lust, capable, in Helena's words, of making use of 'what it loathes' (IV, iv, 25).

The trick played on Bertram to divert him from the consequences of the sin the young lords here accuse him of has been fully prepared for: in the earlier part of the play by the creation of the audience's affection for Helena; and, in the second half, by the establishment of Bertram's need of her. The revelation of the

[1] John Barton's 1967 production here carried a hint that Bertram was already, perhaps subconsciously, in love with Helena, but unwilling to admit it to Parolles, or himself, for fear of losing face. This did not seem an intrusive idea.

[2] The best essay on these lines is Robert Grams Hunter's chapter in his *Shakespeare and the Comedy of Forgiveness* (New York, 1965), pp. 106–31. Hunter does not push the schematisation too far, admitting at the end of his interesting discussion that the play 'is a secular comedy concerned with this world and with the relationships between men and women in this life' though it was written 'for a Christian audience and it draws naturally upon a Christian view of the world' (p. 131).

trick during the final scene will expose Bertram to himself, will bring home to him his self-treachery. It will, in those closing words of the conversation of the two lords (IV, iii, 68 ff.), prevent his virtues (which are latently there) from being proud, through the metaphoric whipping which the exposure of his faults will give him; and at the same time the presence and the love of Helena, cherishing those virtues, will prevent despair. These young lords, his peers, quite clearly condemn Bertram's behaviour; they are anxious (l. 43) that there should be no suspicion that they are involved with it. Yet they do not despair of him, and they see the exposure of Parolles as the first step on the road to his salvation. Parolles's search after the drum has something akin to Bertram's pursuit of Diana: neither succeeds, and both are brought to trial as a result of it. One of the lords, predicting Parolles's behaviour when caught, has already exactly predicted Bertram's also: he will 'in the highest compulsion of base fear, offer to betray you and deliver all the intelligence in his power against you, and that with the divine forfeit of his soul upon oath' (III, vi, 27–30). (For Parolles substitute Bertram, and for 'you' read 'yourself', and the lord might be predicting Bertram's behaviour in the last scene.) But while condemning Bertram's behaviour, the young lords see that he lacks self-knowledge, and that he must learn from the exposure of Parolles: 'I would gladly have him see his company anatomiz'd, that he might take a measure of his own judgments' (IV, iii, 30–2). While the exposure of Parolles is primarily a funny scene, it leaves Bertram deeply shocked, conscious of the folly and vulnerability of his own judgement, though for the time being still defiant, the 'ill' of his 'mingled yarn' temporarily overwhelming the 'good'. But the scene, the conversation of the lords, and the fate of Parolles, prepare for the end of the play; once more the material Shakespeare has added to his source clearly reveals his intentions.

The final scene of *All's Well that Ends Well* is enormously expanded, and its orientation much changed, from the last episode of Boccaccio's tale. In the source, Giletta, with the ring she has secured from Beltramo and the twin sons she has borne to him in secret in Florence, reports back to Rossillion to prove that she has successfully fulfilled her tasks. The story ends when Beltramo 'to kepe his promise made, and to please his subjectes, and the Ladies that made sute unto him to accept her ... imbraced and kissed her, acknowledging her againe for his lawefull wyfe ... and from that time forth hee loved and honoured her' (p. 396). Giletta has won Beltramo's bet, has proved herself worthy of him. As a favour to her and to his subjects, and, it seems, after a little hesitation, he takes her back. In the play, on the other hand, we have an elaborate stage spectacle which allows Bertram to expose his cowardice, lust, dishonesty, and fear to all those characters whom he most wishes to impress and who have all along been so willing to give him the benefit of the doubt. The curious role of Diana here, with her riddling remarks, works entirely to this end, infinitely more effective than those incredible twins in Boccaccio in shattering Bertram's self-confidence. His behaviour is arranged to allow him the fullest and most painful self-exposure. He enters full of confidence, fresh from his military triumphs in Italy, with an elaborately turned speech (v, iii, 44–55) of compliment to Lafeu's daughter which he also makes serve as an explanation of his own attitude to Helena. Though it may just be possible that Shakespeare is here suggesting a further excuse for Bertram's earlier behaviour, the tone of the speech seems more calculated to establish him in our eyes as a man with a sense of false security, and of self-importance, who needs to be lowered a little in his own estimation. During the remainder of the scene this is just what happens. Through that long series of twisting complications and increasingly frantic lies, we watch the bewildered young man behaving in a desperately human way, allowing fear and panic to push him further and further towards folly, dishonesty, sin. Our attitude is kept from contempt by our recognition of the normality of what Bertram's fear drives him to, by Shakespeare's carefully withheld surprise of the second ring, which helps us to share Bertram's initial bewilderment, and by our knowledge that the means of relief is at hand, waiting only until Diana's agency has created the right situation. When Bertram has been made to see himself as he was made to see Parolles, the process of recovery can begin and the high hopes expressed for him by his mother, the King, Lafeu, and the young French lords seem to have a possibility of fulfilment. Helena at last appears and the proud boy is brought, with the inarticulate half line, 'Both, both. Oh pardon', metaphorically at least, though surely physically also, to his knees. The moment is underwritten, as is the moment at the end of *Measure for Measure* when Isabella yields to Mariana's entreaties to kneel and beg for Angelo's life. But its theatrical potential, its simplicity and its capacity to catch and satisfy the mood of an audience at the end of the play, their hopes for Helena fulfilled, is, of course, enormous. The surface at last is penetrated, and the foolish, arrogant young man collapses before the woman he has spurned. Bertram's ability to collapse is his salvation; Parolles's heart, one remembers, was incapable of bursting. Bertram achieves this moment of exposure, of defencelessness, of self-giving, because his heart, ultimately, is 'great', or at least has the potential for greatness. And his realisation of his own failings, of his sin, comes before he understands, before the cause of the situation can be explained to him. His openness and generosity in begging Helena's forgiveness,

though on a smaller scale, is reminiscent of Isabella's begging for Angelo's life before she learns that Claudio is not dead, or Posthumus's forgiveness of his wife before he realises her innocence. It is in a minor key, certainly, but the spontaneity of Bertram's collapse has something of the same quality of imaginative human response. It produces, or should produce, a moment of high emotional tension in the theatre, reflected, and yet, appropriately at the end of a comedy, relaxed by Lafeu's confession that his 'eyes smell onions' (l. 314) and by his search for a handkerchief. If the scene has worked well, and the audience has been responsive, as happened on occasions at Stratford in 1967, Lafeu's search may already have been anticipated in the auditorium. The relaxation of tension continues with the King's offer to find Diana a husband – not, surely, the final cynical turn that some critics have suggested, but an appropriately light-hearted conclusion, a laughing reminiscence of all that has passed and ended well, not unlike, as Joseph Price suggests (p. 170), the effect of that momentary last confusion of identity in *The Comedy of Errors*.

All's Well that Ends Well concludes in gaiety and in hope for the future, though not in the triumphant joy of more unequivocally romantic comedy. Dr Johnson complained that Bertram is 'dismissed to happiness' after behaving very badly, and other critics have suggested that we see too little of Helena and Bertram after their reunion for their reconciliation to be convincing.[1] To the first objection, one must reply that the play ends, not in justice, but in mercy and forgiveness. Bertram is given another chance to reveal his better qualities, just as

[1] Clifford Leech, for example ('The Theme of Ambition', p. 23), writes that the end of the play is 'perfunctorily handled' and implies a contrast between Shakespeare's successful treatment of Parolles after his exposure, and the absence of any such portrayal of Bertram, whom we leave 'with no affection, no conviction'.

Angelo is in *Measure for Measure*; and even Parolles, though still, irretrievably, 'a fool and a knave', is to be cared for with the same absence of recrimination as the equally desertless Barnadine. To the second objection, one can only answer that the play ends, and is meant to end, not in fully achieved happiness, but in hope. In his reunion with Helena, Bertram has the chance to fulfil the wish expressed for him at the beginning of the play, that he will succeed his father 'in manners as in shape'. Shakespeare's complete reorganisation of the conclusion to Boccaccio's story has created a mood of hope and promise, satisfying our expectations and leaving us with a belief in the possibility of future joy. Here again the similarity to the conclusion of *Measure for Measure* suggests itself. The effect achieved at the end of *All's Well that Ends Well* is the culmination of Shakespeare's infinite care and subtlety in the handling of his narrative material. Given sympathetic theatrical realisation, it may vindicate his choice of a story that throughout has demanded the constant exercise of his dramatic ingenuity and imagination.

© R. L. SMALLWOOD 1972

DIRECTING PROBLEM PLAYS:
JOHN BARTON TALKS TO
GARETH LLOYD EVANS

G.L.E. John Barton, you are, I think, one of the few directors who have produced all of the so-called Problem Plays. Do you find this a useful label?

J.B. No, I don't really. I hate categorising plays, and find it difficult to say what is a tragedy, what is a comedy, what is a romance, etc. But if I did, I think I would link *All's Well That Ends Well* and *Measure for Measure* with *Twelfth Night*. I believe that they carried through something that was coming to the boil in *As You Like It* and *Twelfth Night*, i.e. Shakespeare's very conscious split between the 'happy-ever-after' world of romantic comedy and his sense of what life and people are really like. I see it in *As You Like It* to some extent, and even more so in *Twelfth Night* where what happens at the end to Malvolio and Belch and Maria is set against the conventional romantic ending given to Olivia, Orsino, Viola and Sebastian. That sense of reality breaking in on convention goes further in *All's Well* and *Measure for Measure*, where a wry sense of what life's really like and what people are really like is at odds with what the story-line dictates. I think that *Troilus* is a much profounder, more complex, and richer play. If I had to align it with any, I suppose I would do so, as other critics have done, with *2 Henry IV* and with *Hamlet*. I mention those two partly because of the common disease imagery in the three plays. I think that there is also a difference in Shakespeare's overall attitude in *Troilus*. I take it to be on the whole wry, tolerant and accepting in

Twelfth Night, *All's Well*, and *Measure for Measure*, and to be more disturbed and disillusioned about human beings and human life in *Troilus*, which seems to me to lead towards the extreme disillusion of *Timon*. So I personally would hesitate to group the 'problem plays' together, but I would also hesitate to put labels on them at all. When directing such plays, I do not think 'Are they tragedies or comedies?'. Such a question does not arise when I am trying to bring them to life in the theatre. Nevertheless, there are of course certain common features which the three plays share. They are magnificently summed up in *Angel with Horns*. A. P. Rossiter's summary of the peculiar quality of the plays is, for me, the most perceptive and helpful piece of critical writing yet made about them.

G.L.E. I understand what you are saying and, indeed, I agree with it. I'm interested that although you're not prepared to come down absolutely on one side or the other about this, you do, in effect, make a distinction between *Twelfth Night* – and I presume plays of that ilk – which you refer to as wry, tolerant and accepting, and *Troilus and Cressida* which you describe as disturbed and disillusioned. Do you think that it's quite fruitless to ask the question why this happened? In your heart of hearts, do you think that there is a personal reason inside Shakespeare for this, or has it something to do with the conditions of the theatre at the time, or what?

J.B. I think one should be very suspicious of

drawing autobiographical conclusions about Shakespeare. But, even so, I do have a picture of Shakespeare himself, which I mostly derive from his sonnets. These confirm what I feel about him in studying his plays. They show him responding to the common subject of love in so many different ways; sometimes he's humorous and frivolous, sometimes romantic and idealistic, sometimes sardonic to a degree, sometimes hurt, sometimes disillusioned, sometimes cynical and sometimes savage. Whatever the date span of the sonnets, I see him responding in them to love in such totally different ways, that I feel that his response to everything in life was shifting, unsettled, volatile and un-codified. I doubt if there was a simple historical and autobiographical development in him. I think that the subject matter of a given play rather dictated his attitude, but I also believe that there is some autobiographical content, not in terms of hidden biographical detail, but in overall mood and tone. I certainly believe that his sense of what life and men are really like increasingly made him break forms and conventions.

G.L.E.   Can I go back now to *Troilus and Cressida*? When the Old Vic revived *Troilus and Cressida* after the First World War, *The Times* said it was inevitably dull, and when Charles Laughton played Angelo to Flora Robson's Isabella, T. S. Eliot lamented in a letter to that paper, about the small audiences. How do you account for the lack of popularity of these plays till round about 1935?

J.B.   Well, I think the popularity of a particular play depends enormously on its being well done by a given group of actors and a director. But I think also something of the taste and climate of the age comes into it. For instance, the Victorians loved *Romeo and Juliet* and totally dismissed *Troilus*. Today, however, I think anyone would agree that to bring off a *Romeo and Juliet*, to make an audience sympathise with those two characters and that world, is far harder than to bring off a *Troilus*. I think that the sardonic, wry, realistic portraiture of human beings in the play is much more in tune with the taste of the last twenty or thirty years than it was in Victorian times. I think there's no doubt whatsoever – and it's something I've often discussed with my fellow directors – that a certain play can become more or less viable at a given time. I think, for instance, that it's very difficult to bring off *Richard II* today. I think that a self-pitying King, indeed the very subject of a King's fall, has far less import than it would have had for the Elizabethans. I think that modern taste, the modern response to life, immediately makes *Troilus* a popular play in a way it never was in the eighteenth and nineteenth centuries. I myself believe that it's one of his greatest plays, but that may be because of what I am, rather than of what the play is. I would hesitate to make an absolute judgement, but it's extraordinary to me that anybody could think of *Romeo and Juliet*, for instance, as being a better play than *Troilus and Cressida*.

G.L.E.   Would it be right then to say that the kind of society we've got today is more amenable to a rather darker-hued production of a play, even of a comedy, than, let us say, forty or fifty years ago; that it's easier to put on, let us say, even a *Comedy of Errors* or *Love's Labour's Lost*, or *Twelfth Night*, with a wryness in it, even possibly, a disillusion in it – that it's easier to do this kind of thing today than it was?

J.B.   Oh, I think it is, very definitely.

G.L.E.   In the 1930s there were protests at, of all places, Melton Mowbray, and indeed Buxton, about performances of *Measure for Measure*. Now the revival of interest, certainly for scholars and critics, in the play, was due to the work of Wilson Knight, R. W. Chambers, and Muriel Bradbrook. The Wilson Knight interpretation, most particularly, is of course very much a religious interpretation. In your 1970 production of *Measure for Measure*, in which

Ian Richardson played Angelo, and Sebastian Shaw played the Duke, were you reacting against such religious interpretations?

J.B. Not primarily. I read the critics, but basically what I try to bring out in a play is what I myself find in it. I think that, without doubt, one has to take religion into account in that the religious background is strong in the play, but – may be this is just a matter of personal taste – I don't like taking a symbolical or allegorical or philosophical or metaphysical view of the play, mainly because I'm a director working with actors. What I have to do is to answer their questions about the individual characters: what is his intention? what is he really doing or thinking, or feeling behind a given line? When a director explores a play he is bound, primarily, to be doing so in terms of character and psychology, even though he may – indeed must – remind the actors that this is not necessarily what Shakespeare always demands of them. The exploration of character is not the only objective of rehearsals, but it is at the heart of the acting tradition in England, and one has to work within that tradition. There are, for instance, two ways in which one can look at the Duke; one can take him as a symbolic figure, but it's very difficult for an actor to bring a symbolic figure to life. If one is rehearsing *Measure for Measure*, rather than just studying it, one has to answer questions about what the Duke's really like, and what's going on inside him, and that leads to finding out about a human being rather than defining an allegory.

In practice, I did not find any particular critic especially helpful about the play. Critical opinion is usually as diverse and divided as a series of productions of the same play by different directors would be. This is particularly true of *Measure for Measure*, where critics in the last thirty years have been totally divided on the question, for instance, of how we are meant to view the Duke. I find this division of opinion more significant about the play than any one particular view of it. I in fact made an abstract for the actors of the views of some ten critics, and suggested that the truth might lie somewhere in between. I urged that if they depended on one view only, e.g. Wilson Knight's, they would be taking too narrow a view.

One thing, however, did seem to emerge in rehearsal and performance. It has often been pointed out how, on reading the play, one finds it splitting down the middle. At the point Isabella leaves Claudio after her interview with him in prison, and is left alone with the Duke, the level of the writing changes. The Duke for the first time goes into prose, and into plotting the bed-trick; and the play, which has in the first half been poetically intense and psychologically subtle, is then worked out on a lower, almost fairy-tale level. The change is obvious enough in the study; but in the theatre, I think that the difference disappears. This is because the actors, if they have brought their characters to life in exploring the first half, can carry through that life into the play's more superficial resolution. I felt, in fact, that what seemed a problem in the study largely melted away in the theatre, when those characters were embodied by living actors.

G.L.E. Yes ... I don't know whether you quite realise (perhaps you do) what a great shock you gave quite a lot of people because, in your production, Isabella quite firmly did not agree to marry the Duke. I would be very interested to know why this was so – if indeed you intended it to be so. It seemed so deliberate that I must believe that it was an intention. Now, did she in fact not agree to marry the Duke because the Duke was older than usual (as indeed he certainly looked), or because she couldn't forgive him for pretending that Claudio was dead and was, as it were, indulging in a kind of feminine umbrage; or was it because Isabella found sex repugnant?

J.B.   Well, all those thoughts occurred to us in rehearsal, but that's not quite the way in which we tackled it. Again, what we did was to ask the question 'What would Isabella have done when the Duke made his proposal?' Shakespeare himself leaves it open-ended in the sense that he gives her no lines whatsoever in reply to the proposal. This is a situation which comes up again and again in rehearsal: Shakespeare doesn't provide a certain answer and one has to find one. One tends to do so by trying to deduce what a character's response would be from everything that we know about that character elsewhere in the play. What I actually intended was that Isabella's response should be open-ended. I suggested to Estelle Kohler, who was playing the part, that she was in no state at that moment to accept the proposal, and I asked her to reject it and yet think about it. The last thing that I presented on the stage, when everybody had gone off at the end of the play, was Isabella wondering, puzzling about what she should do.

G.L.E.   The evidence seems to be that in the past Parolles was regarded as one of the greatest comic characters, as indeed I believe Shylock was. Would you agree that audiences nowadays don't find him as funny as apparently they did in the past ... Parolles I mean, not Shylock?

J.B.   No, I wouldn't agree with that at all. I think that whether he is funny or not depends simply on how good the actor is who plays it. There are many parts in Shakespeare which may seem to be dreary if they are not brought alive by the individual talents of the actor. But provided that Parolles is well acted, I am sure he is still funny in the theatre today.

G.L.E.   I remember with a great deal of pleasure – I don't know whether you do – Guthrie's production of *All's Well*. I felt both affronted and delighted at the same time. I suppose it could be said, although I wouldn't necessarily say so myself, that Guthrie seemed to be implying, in the way he directed the play,

that it could not really appeal to a modern audience, so something pretty drastic had to be done; so, for example, he introduced an amount of farcical business, including a microphone. Some might say that this kind of behaviour clashed with, for example, great performances such as Edith Evans gave us as the Countess Rousillon. Do you think that *All's Well* is viable to a modern audience – without gimmicks?

J.B.   I certainly came to think so after doing the production. At first I was afraid of directing the play, and hadn't originally been going to do it. I had to take it over quickly because a director dropped out. I remember saying to the actors at the outset, 'Let's try and trust this play, explore it and find out how it works, and stage it simply without gimmicks.' We then found after a couple of frightened, doubtful weeks, that the play was coming alive. I believe, from that experience, that the play does work without jazzing-up, though I wasn't sure whether it did when I embarked on it. I ended by thinking the play much finer and more cohesive than I, or, indeed, most people had ever suspected. I think that what Guthrie did was brilliant; but he was always more a man of immense theatrical imagination, a giver of great delight, rather than someone who really tried to explore the content of a play. I think he overlaid plays with much creative invention but did not always try to realise their actual contents. As far as gimmicks are concerned, I think the question is whether an individual piece of business is an inventive overlay, or whether it's a truthful bodying-out of what's implicit in the text. But perhaps in the end it rather comes down to a question of taste.

G.L.E.   Would you agree that the difference between Guthrie's attempt to make *All's Well* speak to the twentieth century and your own (or indeed the Royal Shakespeare Company's attempt to make a play speak to the twentieth century), is between what you've described as

Guthrie's inventive overlay and what you would accept as a matter of principle? Does that make sense? In other words, whereas Guthrie seems to try to speak to the twentieth century by a kind of sensationalism, or theatrical effect, you personally, and the Royal Shakespeare Company, would attempt to make Shakespeare speak to the twentieth century on the basis of a certain attitude, a certain set of principles, a certain philosophy about the twentieth century, that you yourself or the Company have?

J.B.   I never personally think very much about the twentieth century. I simply read the play intensively in the study, and then work on it in the rehearsal room by responding to what the actors offer. My response is as often intuitive as it is analytic or rational. I say 'Wouldn't it be good if . . . ?' and then try to test a particular idea in terms of whether it tallies with what I take to be the play's meaning. I never consciously take a twentieth-century approach to the play. It's very difficult to define the process that goes on in the rehearsal room: instinct is a great matter – directors and actors work together on instinctive ideas which bubble up from day to day, which they then test with their reason. We sometimes cut things out because we think they are an overlay on the text, and sometimes leave them in, hoping and trusting that they are an embodiment of something implicit in the text. This process is certainly influenced by the fact that we are people living in the twentieth century. But as often as not we also try to modify our modern responses by asking 'What does Shakespeare *really* mean here? Are we distorting him by doing something which we *want* him to mean, because it appeals to us?'

G.L.E.   Do you regard the ending of *All's Well That Ends Well* as a cynical one, or do you think that Bertram has learnt from experience? Indeed, what has he learnt?

J.B.   I don't think Bertram's learnt very much; he's grown up a bit, he's learnt to value Helena more than he valued her at first, he's seen through Parolles, but he's still a pretty selfish and stupid man. I think that 'cynical' isn't quite the right word for the ending: the tone is more one of a worldly tolerance of people. There's no certainty that Bertram and Helena live happily ever after. Bertram ends with a couple of very spare lines which don't tell us much: 'If she, my lord, can make me know this clearly,/I'll love her dearly ever, ever dearly.' Their surface meaning is clear enough, but in the context of the whole scene, they also contain shame, awe of the King, and a resolve, at that moment, to make the best of things. Whether Bertram did in fact love her dearly ever is something which is surely made questionable by all we know of him from the play as a whole. And the end situation is well summed up in the text itself when the King says 'And if it end so meet/ The bitter past, more welcome is the sweet.'

G.L.E.   May I turn back again to *Troilus and Cressida*? Do you agree with Oscar Campbell and Alice Walker that it's a comical satire? Now, some of the satire in your production was brilliant, but it could be argued that it would be possible to produce it as a tragical satire – that is, with Hector and Troilus as tragic heroes. In your estimation, what kind of satire is it? Tragical or comical?

J.B.   I think there is satire in it, but I certainly don't think for one moment that the play is basically a comical satire. I think that people in it are too raw, too hurt, too bruised for it to be labelled on that superficial level. It is also comical, heroical, tragical, romantic – as a whole, it is a mixture of all these things. There is no play which I would less willingly tie down with a label. It continually invites a varying response. For much of it, it asks us to respond comedically, and at times one is drawn to say 'Ah, a "black comedy!"' But what happens, by the end, to Troilus and Cressida and Hector is not comic. The contrast, for instance, between what Hector professes and aspires to and what he does seems to me to be very sad. And I feel a great compassion for what becomes of Troilus and Cressida. If I had to give it a label, I would say it was closer to tragedy than to anything else, but I just don't believe those labels are useful. I've never understood myself what exactly it is that defines a tragedy; I don't think that way. *Troilus and Cressida* is unique and brilliant and resists labelling; one confines it terribly, and minimises its richness if one tries to categorise it.

G.L.E.   And yet, don't you think that Shakespeare himself would have had, in the Elizabethan way, a rather more formal notion of the kind of play he was writing? I agree with you that it is very difficult, and indeed probably for us not profitable, to think in these rather strict terms of Tragedy, Comedy, History, and so on, but is it not possible that Shakespeare himself would have been more inclined to than we are? If so, in what direction do you think his imagination would have been going in *Troilus and Cressida*? To make people laugh, or to make them feel bitter, or to make them, in fact, cry?

J.B.   I think he was trying to do all these things. I think there are bits of the play which are very comic, even farcical, bits that are very moving, bits that are horrifying, bits that are epic, and bits that are domestic and trivial. I think that he invites a much more mixed and complex response than other dramatists. One can categorise Jonson, for instance, far more easily than one can Shakespeare. I think that's true of Shakespeare throughout his career, but never more true than with *Troilus*. I think that it is one of his greatest plays precisely because of the way in which he invites in the course of a single play all the different kinds of response one can have in the theatre, which are normally isolated from one another. He invites tragic, comic, satiric, intellectual and compassionate responses almost at the same time. I believe that is how he himself responded to life. This shiftingness of view is also embodied in the play's presentation of character. There is a very remarkable difference between the declared intentions of the characters and the actual deeds done by them. Again and again a character enunciates certain intentions and beliefs which are confounded by his actions. Hector in the Trojan Council expresses a moral view of what the Trojans should think about the rape of Helen, but immediately after makes a volte-face for the slenderest of reasons. Cressida's declaration of faith and truth with Troilus is broken by what she does with Diomed. Ajax is presented as an oaf and a lout; and yet he is the one person who, in the Greek camp, utters a simple expression of grief and compassion for Hector's death, which is something one wouldn't have expected from what one sees earlier in the play. Again and again, a character who seems to be foolish or cruel or stupid turns up with something completely the opposite to one's first view of him; and that seems to me to be not a chaotic view of human nature, but a truthful and realistic one. It is something which Shakespeare tapped in a way that no writer before him had done, except fitfully.

G.L.E.   Do you mean something more than the old critical concept of appearance and reality? Is there a difference between your words 'declared intention' and 'action done' and this critical concept?

J.B.   I think there is a connection, though I haven't actually thought of it. I only want to make the simple point about the shiftingness of most of the characters. We see it around us all the time in life; we all say we believe something, and then in practice we do something quite different. This is of course a fact which most dramatists take into account to some extent, but I think no play exemplifies it so fully as *Troilus and Cressida* does.

G.L.E.   What about the later Jacobean dramatists – Massinger, Marston, and so on? Do you feel that they may have learnt something from

Shakespeare in this respect? I'm thinking of plays like *Women Beware Women*, which are rather later than the plays we are talking about now. Do you feel that these may have been influenced by Shakespeare in this particular context?

J.B.   Yes, I do think so.

G.L.E.   Despite the obvious theatrical differences which would tend to produce a different kind of play at a given time, I sometimes feel that, in fact, certain thematic pressures that Shakespeare has in this kind of play, do go forward. We tend to think of Shakespeare being wiped away by these later Jacobean dramatists, but I don't think he is, and I'm interested to know what you think.

J.B.   Yes, I think that's quite true. But I think also that when Shakespeare wrote his plays he often did things that no other dramatist had done and I think that this particular way of looking at people is both something new and something quite essential in his view of life. It is even more remarkable in one of the plays Shakespeare wrote soon after *Troilus*: in *Othello*, the Moor himself shifts from one point of view to another within the context of a single speech (For example, 'let her rot and perish and be damned tonight, for she shall not live; no, my heart is turned to stone; I strike it, and it hurts my hand. O, the world hath not a sweeter creature, she might lie by an emperor's side and command him tasks.' Or 'My relief/ Must be to loathe her' followed a few lines later by 'If she be false, O heaven mocks itself, / I'll not believe it'.) Of course, Shakespeare had done this earlier, as with the character of Richard II (in III, iii), but I have come to notice that it is often one of the most central facts about the way in which he presents character. I notice it particularly in the rehearsal room, where it often gives the actor great difficulty. The counsel I offer, 'Accept the inconsistencies without trying to iron them out' may be good; but it sets the actor great problems.

G.L.E.   Would you be prepared to agree that the kind of difference between *Troilus and Cressida* and the other two so-called 'problem plays', which you yourself are insistent upon, is indicated by the difference between Thersites and Lavache? Have you anything to say about those two characters? It seems to me that there is something of the Fool in Thersites, but he is 'not altogether fool'; he is much more and much less than Fool, and that this in itself indicates a difference.

J.B.   Maybe I would say that the difference in intensity in the two characters marks a difference in the two plays. They are both immensely disillusioned and sardonic. But Lavache doesn't probe very deeply, whereas Thersites is anguished by what he sees life to be – 'Still wars and lechery, nothing else holds fashion'. I think that Thersites's passion, and his whole response to life, is much more extreme, much more violent than it is in Lavache.

G.L.E.   As you know, the general tendency of modern criticism of Shakespeare has been to stress the options open to critics and directors. This emerged at the 1971 Shakespeare Vancouver Conference. Nevertheless, nearly all the critics and directors choose a particular interpretation when they are writing their criticism or directing their play, and therefore exclude all others. Do you think it is possible, or even desirable, for a director to present a play in such a way as to leave all the options open? Or is this just a pipe dream?

J.B.   I think it's certainly impossible, and I question whether it's desirable. It's impossible because, as I've said, you have to be specific with actors. Actors have got to know what effect they're trying to make with a given line, what they mean and what they feel. When one reads the play in the study one can say again and again of a given line, 'I'm not sure what Shakespeare intends here; it could be this or it could be that'. But, however unsure one may be, one can't leave things uncertain for the actor; he has to be specific. When there is a textual crux, where there are many editorial explanations, one's got to choose a specific reading for the actor to play. I think that what a given actor or director does with a play is very like what a given critic does when he is writing about it. He selects what seems to him the most important points, what seems to need bringing out the most, and in so doing he is very, very selective; he cannot write down everything. That is not even possible in a variorum edition. A given piece on a play is only the tip of an iceberg. And so it is in the theatre, especially with a dramatist as rich and complex as Shakespeare.

In practice, I think that the theatre's work is actually more open-ended than the critic's for a completely different reason. Whatever the actor and director decide that they are trying to do, they can't completely control the audience's response. I've often found that where an actor and myself have set out to define something, it has meant something quite different in performance to someone who was seeing it, and, indeed, something quite different to different members of the audience. To sum up, I think the only point at which the play can be said to be absolutely open-ended is when it exists as a mere text waiting to be performed or studied.

An example of an audience's response taking something in a different sense from what an actor and myself intended is the interpretation of Achilles which Alan Howard and I attempted in *Troilus*. We were attacked for presenting Achilles as an effeminate homosexual, which was something that had never entered our minds. We saw him as bisexual, a view which is surely embodied in Shakespeare's play and is also the view which an Elizabethan audience would have taken. Shakespeare shows him both with Patroclus and in love with Polyxena. What we did do was show him *playing* at effeminacy and homosexuality in order to mock and outrage the Greek generals. The real man we saw as

embodied in the aggression and destructiveness which surges from him when he confronts Hector ('In what part of his body shall I destroy him?') and when he finally appears on the battlefield. We hoped that we had made that plain enough, especially as Alan played most of the part with great vocal virility and power. But if it came over to members of the audience differently, then one must allow that what they thought they saw was perhaps of more weight than our intentions.

G.L.E. May I, as a final question, ask you to think yourself back into either the area of preparation for the production of a play, or, if you like, the period of rehearsal of the play, and ask you this question? As an academic and also as a distinguished theatre director, do you find that your academic knowledge of the plays, and indeed of the criticism about the plays, and *your* theatrical know-how, are in any sense at war? If you do, can you say what the nature of the war is? If you don't, what is happening in a rehearsal?

J.B. I think that they are deeply different. I think that, whatever one thinks about the play academically or privately, it becomes something completely different when one's working with the living actor. When I work on a play, I first of all read and think about it very hard. But when I go into rehearsal, my initial step is to say to the actors 'Do something; let's put the scene on its feet; you give me something and I will respond to it'. I find that when I do that, new thoughts come that have never occurred to me in the study; I call into question things that I had previously believed, or decide that they are wrong for a particular actor because his persona cannot embody it. Studying and directing a play are completely different experiences. I think the critic exists in an at times enviable isolation where there is just himself and the text and he can respond directly to it. Whereas a director is responding to individual human beings, to the invention and imagination and instincts of the individual actor, and that's the raw material he's got to deal with. He has to accept it, before he tries to mould it. And though his previous knowledge of the play helps him in defining it, in shaping it for the actor, the basic starting-point is not just a text. It's a text plus the creation and invention of the actors; which makes it a completely different experience.

A production of course gives a more impure, but possibly a richer and more complex reading of a play than a critic can provide. A book or an article consists of what the critic wants to say. A production, being a complex of design, music, movement, business, direction, and all that suggests itself in the voice and personae of the actors, is never one man's vision. It is a kind of anthology on the play made by all its participants. It is thus less precise than what the critic offers, and thus less easily pinned down. I always find after doing a production that it contains things which do not represent my preferred view of some detail in the play, but which are rather interpretations arrived at in rehearsal as the best solution to a particular problem for a particular actor. I don't regret this. A production finally belongs to the actors and not to the director, who is more a chairman than a dictator. All directors find their initial views modified by the independent interpretation powers of the actors they work with. I find I learn more from the actors than I could ever do by reading a variety of critical opinions.

© GARETH LLOYD EVANS 1972

THE QUEEN MAB SPEECH IN 'ROMEO AND JULIET'

SIDNEY THOMAS

Scholars are now generally agreed that Q1 of *Romeo and Juliet* (1597) is a bad Quarto which represents a memorial reconstruction of the play, and that Q2 (1599) is a good Quarto based at first or second hand on Shakespeare's foul papers.[1] If this is so, however, we must then recognize that 'the bad text seems a good deal better and the good text a good deal worse, than we are accustomed to find'.[2] The superiority of Q1 in many readings has been recognized by most editors since Pope, and not only such standard eclectic texts as the old Cambridge or Oxford, but even recent editions founded on strict bibliographical principles,[3] admit many words, even whole lines,[4] solely on its authority. Moreover, it is clear that the occasional surprising goodness of Q1 and surprising badness of Q2 cannot be explained simply by the varying competence or carefulness of the compositors of the two Quartos. There is unmistakeable evidence that the presumed Shakespearian manuscript which served as copy for Q2 was 'in a state of unusual disorder',[5] often virtually illegible and possibly lacking a continuous passage of almost one hundred lines.[6] And on the other hand, many

article on 'The New Way with Shakespeare's Texts: II. Recent Work on the Text of *Romeo and Juliet*', *Shakespeare Survey 8* (Cambridge, 1955), pp. 81–99; and in his Textual Notes for the New Cambridge edition of the play (1955). Wilson's position has, I think, been convincingly refuted in two recent articles: Paul L. Cantrell and George W. Williams, 'The Printing of the Second Quarto of *Romeo and Juliet*', *Studies in Bibliography*, X (1957), 107–28; and Richard Hosley, 'Quarto Copy for Q2 *Romeo and Juliet*', *ibid.*, pp. 129–41.

[2] W. W. Greg, *Principles of Emendation in Shakespeare* (British Academy Lecture, 1928), p. 23.

[3] For example, the Yale Shakespeare *Romeo and Juliet*, ed. Richard Hosley (1954). Though Hosley takes an extreme view of the corruption of Q1, he adopts (by his own count) about forty Q1 readings. Greg (*Principles of Emendation*, p. 21) estimates that the old Cambridge edition follows Q1 in 118 instances.

[4] I, iv, 7–8 (I use the Globe numbering) appears in all modern editions solely on the authority of Q1.

[5] Dover Wilson, 'Recent Work on *Romeo and Juliet*', p. 90.

[6] All recent students of the text agree that the section of the play from about I, ii, 57 to I, iii, 36 in Q2 is printed directly from Q1. I have argued in an earlier article, 'The Bibliographical Links Between the First Two Quartos of *Romeo and Juliet*', *RES*, XXV (1949), 110–14, that this section must either have been missing or completely illegible in the Q2 manuscript. G. I. Duthie, in his article on 'The Text of Shakespeare's *Romeo and Juliet*', *SB*, IV (1953), 3–29, dissents from this view and argues instead that 'Q2 leaves Q1 at I, iii, 36 not because the manuscript behind Q2 has suddenly become legible again, where before, for a considerable stretch, it has not been legible, but rather because before I, iii, 36 Q1 for a time gave a text in the main satisfactory, whereas after that it does not' (p. 7). If this is so, then we have the remarkable situation of sections of a bad Quarto being preferred as copy-text by the printer of a good Quarto, to Shakespeare's own manuscript.

[1] See, for example, E. K. Chambers, *William Shakespeare* (Oxford, 1930), I, 341–4; W. W. Greg, *The Shakespeare First Folio* (Oxford, 1955), pp. 225–31. The most thorough study of Q1 as a memorial reconstruction is Harry R. Hoppe's *The Bad Quarto of Romeo and Juliet* (Cornell University Press, 1948). The chief proponent of the theory that Q2 is based, not directly on Shakespeare's foul papers, but on a copy of Q1 corrected and supplemented by reference to the foul papers, has been J. Dover Wilson, in his

sections of Q1, especially in acts I and II, seem to be so remarkably accurate as to make it necessary that we assume either that the reporter was gifted with an extraordinary memory and an almost infallible metrical sense, or that he had some access to an authoritative manuscript.[1]

A recognition of the odd, often atypical qualities of Q1 and Q2 of *Romeo and Juliet*, and especially of the frequent dependence of Q2 on Q1, led one of the most recent editors of the play, G. I. Duthie, to the following conclusion:

The Q1 text is in the main a manifestly inferior text. But I submit that as one proceeds with the work [of editing] one must be prepared to consider the adoption of a Q1 reading in a given case, even though Q1 is a bad quarto. If one adopts a Q1 reading in preference to a Q2 reading, one must be prepared to state strong and cogent reasons for so doing. These reasons may in a given case be literary. I do not think that a textual critic can ignore literary considerations. But I repeat – the reasons must be strong and cogent. Yet if there are strong and cogent reasons, the modern editor should not ignore them on grounds of timidity.[2]

To few other passages in *Romeo and Juliet* is the approach suggested by Professor Duthie more relevant than it is to the Queen Mab speech (I, iv, 53–95). Every modern edition of the play bases its text of this speech upon Q2;[3] the Q1 version, as a matter of fact, is one of the principal items of evidence always adduced to prove that Q1 is a bad Quarto.[4] Yet a thorough and unprejudiced comparison of the two early Quarto versions of the speech will demonstrate, I think, the overall superiority of Q1's text of the speech. Since a discussion of this problem involves a line-by-line analysis, I give the Queen Mab speech as it stands in Q1 and in Q2:[5]

Q1

1 *Mer.* Ah then I see Queene Mab hath bin with you.
Ben. Queene Mab whats she?
She is the Fairies Midwife and doth come
In shape no bigger than an Aggat stone

5 On the forefinger of a Burgomaster,
Drawne with a teeme of little Atomi,
Athwart mens noses when they lie a sleepe.
Her waggon spokes are made of spinners webs,
The couer, of the winges of Grashoppers,
10 The traces are the Moone-shine watrie beames,
The collers crickets bones, the lash of filmes,
Her waggoner is a small gray coated flie,
Not halfe so big as is a little worme,
Pickt from the lasie finger of a maide,
15 And in this sort she gallops vp and downe
Through Louers braines, and then they dream of love:
O're Courtiers knees: who strait on cursies dreame
O're Ladies Lips, who dreame on kisses strait:
Which oft the angrie Mab with blisters plagues,
20 Because their breathes with sweetmeats tainted are:
Sometimes she gallops ore a Lawers lap,
And then dreames he of smelling out a sute,
And sometime comes she with a tithe pigs taile,
Tickling a Parsons nose that lies a sleepe,
25 And then dreames he of another benefice:
Sometime she gallops ore a souldiers nose,
And then dreames he of cutting forraine throats,
Of breaches ambuscados, countermines,
Of healthes fiue fadome deepe, and then anon
30 Drums in his eare: at which he startes and wakes,
And Sweares a Praier or two and sleepes againe.
This is that Mab that makes maids lie on their backes,

[1] See, for example, II, iv, especially the first 181 lines, for a Q1 text so excellent, especially in passages of swift-moving repartee, as to be beyond the powers of almost any conceivable reporter.

[2] Duthie, 'The Text of Shakespeare's *Romeo and Juliet*', p. 29.

[3] There may be exceptions, but I have not been able to find them. Most modern editions of the play are based, not directly on Q2, but on F1, which derives from Q3, which derives from Q2.

[4] P. A. Daniel, *Parallel Text Edition of the First Two Quartos of 'Romeo and Juliet'* (New Shakspere Society, London, 1874), p. vi; Alfred Hart, *Stolen and Surreptitious Copies* (Melbourne, 1942), pp. 185–6; and Hoppe, *The Bad Quarto of Romeo and Juliet*, p. 145 ('The entire Queen Mab speech ... is a welter of memorial errors').

[5] I have arbitrarily numbered the lines in these two passages for convenience of reference.

And proues them women of good cariage.
This is the verie Mab that plats the maines of
                            Horses in the night,
35 And plats the Elfelocks in foule sluttish haire,
Which once vntangled much misfortune breedes.

Q2

1 *Mercutio.* O then I see Queene Mab hath bin with
                                  you:
She is the Fairies midwife, and she comes in shape
no bigger thē an Agot stone, on the forefinger of
an Alderman, drawne with a teeme of little
5 ottamie, ouer mens noses as they lie asleep: her
waggō spokes made of lōg spinners legs: the
couer, of the wings of Grasshoppers, her traces of
the smallest spider web, her collors of the moonshines watry beams, her whip of Crickets bone,
10 the lash of Philome, her waggoner, a small grey
coated Gnat, not half so big as a round litle worme,
prickt from the lazie finger of a man. Her Charriot
is an emptie Hasel nut, Made by the Ioyner squirrel
or old Grub, time out amind, the Fairies Coatch-
15 makers: and in this state she gallops night by
night, throgh louers brains, and then they dreame
of loue. On Courtiers knees, that dreame on
Cursies strait, ore Lawyers fingers who strait
dreame on fees, ore Ladies lips who strait one
20 kisses dream, which oft the angrie Mab with
blisters plagues, because their breath with sweete
meates tainted are. Sometime she gallops ore a
Courtiers nose, and then dreames he of smelling
out a sute: and sometime comes she with a tith-
25 pigs tale, tickling a Persons nose as a lies asleepe,
then he dreams of an other Benefice. Sometime
she driueth ore a souldiers neck, and then dreames
he of cutting forrain throates, of breaches, ambuscados, spanish blades: Of healths fiue fadome
30 deepe, and then anon drums in his eare, at which he
starts and wakes, and being thus frighted, sweares
a praier or two & sleeps againe: this is that very
Mab that plats the manes of horses in the night:
and bakes the Elklocks in foule sluttish haires,
35 which once vntangled, much misfortune bodes.
This is the hag, when maides lie on their backs,
That presses them and learnes them first to beare,
Making them women of good carriage:
This is she.

If we examine these two passages carefully,
without preconceptions and without reference,

for the moment, to the general quality of the
Quartos in which they appear, it will be obvious
that it is the Q2 version, rather than the Q1,
which shows all the bibliographical marks of a
reported text. Most important and most immediately apparent is the fact that Q1 correctly
prints verse as verse while Q2 reduces it to
prose, except for l. 1 and ll. 36–9. There are,
of course, many good texts which confuse verse
and prose, but they usually do so in passages of
rapid transition between verse and prose, or in
short sections derived from verse lines written
marginally as prose. Long, continuous sections
of verse printed as prose are among the chief
hallmarks of reported texts. It seems improbable, to say the least, that Shakespeare could
have written so long a speech in the margins of
his manuscript. The argument that he revised
the original speech so heavily, in the margins
and interlineally, that the compositor could not
make out the line divisions,[1] is also hard to

---

[1] This argument forms one of the cornerstones of
the theory advanced by A. W. Pollard and J. Dover
Wilson ('Romeo and Juliet 1597', *TLS*, 14 August
1919) that Q1 was based on an abridged transcript of
an old play partially revised by Shakespeare, while Q2
represents a further stage in Shakespeare's revision.
This theory was later abandoned by Wilson and replaced by the theory that the Q2 prose lineation is the
work of a compositor baffled by copy consisting of the
Q1 page corrected and expanded by reference to
Shakespeare's manuscript ('Recent Work on *Romeo
and Juliet*', pp. 95–6). Greg (*The Shakespeare First
Folio*, pp. 233–4) puts forth a theory credited to a
suggestion by Wilson, that a dozen lines were omitted
from the text when the page was originally set up, and
that 'when the error was discovered an attempt was
made to crowd them in after the pages had been imposed', thus necessitating a prose setting. Wilson
himself argues against this theory, as involving too
many implausible assumptions ('Recent Work', p. 95)!
A different line of argument to support the theory that
the Q2 copy for the Queen Mab speech was in verse,
was developed by Leo Kirschbaum in his article,
'Shakespeare's Hypothetical Marginal Additions',
Modern Language Notes, LXI (1946), 44–9: 'That the
compositor had blank verse in his copy may be surmised, for in his prose he capitalized six words each
of which truly began a verse (67, 68, 72, 77, 82, 85).'

credit. In such a case, we would expect con-fusion in some lines, but not a total collapse of verse into prose.

The metrical irregularity of a number of lines in the Q2 version is also a more likely indication of a reporter than of a confused manuscript. Some of these lines can perhaps be defended as poetically effective, but it is difficult to believe that Shakespeare could ever have written so flat and incompetent a line as:

> then he dreams of an other Benefice.

The transposition of the second and third words of this line can, of course, be explained as the mistake of a bungling compositor; but taken in conjunction with other characteristics of the Q2 text of the speech, it would seem to reflect the faulty memory of a reporter.

Next to the printing of verse as prose, the most interesting bibliographical peculiarity of the Q2 passage is a group of misspellings almost certainly auditory in origin: 'ottamie', 'Philome', and 'tale'. The first of these (l. 5) may possibly rest upon an original misspelling by Shakespeare or a misreading by the com-positor, but it is much more likely to be a reporter's attempt to reproduce the sound of the unfamiliar word 'Atomi'.[1] About 'Philome' (l. 10) there can be hardly any doubt; Shakespeare could never have spelled 'film' in that way, nor could a compositor have so badly misread the word.[2] It can only be a reporter's version of a dissyllabic pronunciation of 'film'.[3] The capitalization is explained by the assumption, borne out by the punctuation, that the reporter associated the word with the following phrase, 'her waggoner', and therefore took it to be a proper name.[4] The spelling of 'taile' as 'tale' (l. 25) is also indicative of a reporter, setting down the sound of a word without troubling too much about its meaning.[5] The misspelling of 'Elflocks' as 'Elklocks' (l. 34) is just as likely to be a printer's error as a reporter's error, and I do not emphasize its significance.

The Q2 text of the Queen Mab speech con-tains a striking example of still another classic indication of a reported text: the misplacement of the three lines, 'Her Charriot . . . the Fairies Coatchmakers:' (ll. 12–15). All editors of the play are agreed that these lines should follow the phrase 'as they lie asleep:' (l. 5). Here again, it may be possible to explain the misplacement as due to a confusion in the manuscript, com-pounded perhaps by carelessness on the part of the compositor; but at least as likely an explana-tion is the faulty memory of a reporter.

The force of this observation is considerably weakened by the fact that four of these six capitalized words begin new sentences and would normally be capital-ized in prose; and Kirschbaum's own admission that Elizabethan dramatists and their scribes invariably wrote blank verse without capitalizing the first word.

[1] Greg (*Principles of Emendation*, p. 51) calls both 'Atomi' and 'ottamie' 'aberrant forms' and declares that 'it is very doubtful whether [they] are related'. But the *OED* shows that 'Atomi' was a correct sixteenth-century form for the plural of 'atomos'.

[2] It is, of course, true that ph– was often used in the sixteenth century where we would use f– today. In all the long history of 'film', however, from *c.* 1000 to the present, the Q2 spelling seems, according to the *OED*, to be the only example of a ph– spelling. Moreover, if we accept Hand D in *The Booke of Sir Thomas More* as Shakespeare's, then we have interesting evidence that he tended to use f– even in words where sixteenth-century usage would sanction ph–. At l. 84 of the *Additions* (see *Shakespeare Survey 2* (Cambridge, 1949), Plate XIV), we have the spelling 'fancies', whereas Hooker (as cited in the *OED*) uses the spelling 'phancies' in 1597.

[3] R. G. White, in his edition of Shakespeare (Boston, 1866), I, xxiv, called attention to 'Philome' as an auditory error, but explained it as the result of the compositor's setting by ear.

[4] Hart (*Stolen and Surreptitious Copies*, p. 185), if I understand him correctly, seems to think that 'Phi-lome' *is* meant to be the coachman's name.

[5] Bartlett's *Concordance* lists 18 uses of the word 'tail' by Shakespeare. I have checked every one of these in an early Quarto or First Folio text, and have found that except for this use of the word in Q2 of *Romeo and Juliet*, the spelling 'tale' is never used when 'tail' is meant. One of the uses listed by Bartlett (*Othello*, III, i, 8) is clearly meant to be 'tale,' used in a punning sense, and is so spelled.

We have, therefore, in the Q2 version three kinds of errors – breakdown of verse into prose, auditory misspellings, lines out of place – associated with reported texts. Each of these categories of error can be explained by some other hypothesis than that of a report. The coincidence of all three kinds, however, in a consecutive passage of 43 lines seems to me to give strong support to the presumption of memorial corruption.

If, now, we turn to the Q1 text of the speech, we find almost none of the bibliographical peculiarities just discussed. The verse is correctly lined; the punctuation, while not perfect, is generally effective, and far superior to that of Q2; and the spelling, especially of the learned and unfamiliar word 'Atomi,' is good. The only obviously faulty line is l. 34, which has three feet too many; but one overlong line in an otherwise perfectly lined speech is not enough to indicate the presence of a reporter. Nor does the absence of the speech-prefix *Mer.* at the beginning of l. 3 prove corruption of the text; if a reporter, particularly an actor–reporter, remembered nothing else about the play, he would recall that this speech belonged to Mercutio.

Any attempt to establish the superiority of the Q1 version of the speech, however, must be based on literary as well as bibliographical grounds, and must answer particularly the charge that ll. 8–11 of the Q1 speech are a demonstrable corruption of the corresponding lines in Q2. Few passages in any of the bad Quartos have received harsher criticism than these lines. Professor Hoppe speaks of 'Mercutio's nonsensical muddling of *spinners' webs* for *spinners' legs*',[1] and Dr van Dam calls these lines 'a badly corrupted text [in which] the sequence of the words is in the greatest disorder'.[2] The Q2 text is here held to be so markedly superior that it must be regarded as representing Shakespeare's manuscript.

Yet, when closely examined, these lines in

Q2, universally admired as they have been, reveal a certain carelessness in the writing and a peculiar inappropriateness of imagery. The use of spiders' legs for the wagon-spokes, and spider's web two lines later, for the traces, shows either an un-Shakespearian poverty of invention or great haste in composition. Even more puzzling and poetically inadequate is the representation of wagon-spokes by the long, jointed legs of the spider, of the straight reins by a spider's web, and of the tiny, presumably rigid collars by the long 'watery' beams of the moon.[3] Finally, the mention first of a whip, then of a lash, can be explained only if we make the dubious assumption that by 'whip' Shakespeare meant whip-handle: otherwise, the cricket's bones are patently absurd for the whip.[4]

All of these difficulties vanish when we turn to the Q1 version of these lines. There is no repetition of spiders' legs and spider's web, of whip and lash. The spider's web is much better as an image of the radiating wagon-spokes than are spiders' legs;[5] the moonbeams are

[1] Harry R. Hoppe, 'The First Quarto Version of *Romeo and Juliet*, II, vi, and IV, v, 43 ff.', *RES*, XIV (1938), 274.

[2] B. A. P. van Dam, 'Did Shakespeare Revise *Romeo and Juliet*?' *Anglia*, N. F. XXXIX (1927), 49.

[3] Alone among recent scholars, Duthie has recognized the poetic inadequacy of these lines. Though the New Cambridge edition gives the accepted Q2 text, an initialed note by Duthie on pp. 142–3 states: 'It is difficult to visualize moonbeams as collars round the necks of tiny coach-horses, but the framework of the common spider's-web might suggest the shape of a horse's collar. Thus the orig. Sh. Ms. may have run:

her traces of the moonshines watry beams,
her collors of the smallest spider web . . .

and, the comp. or collaborator, misled by "of the" in both lines, may have transposed the latter halves'.

[4] *OED* gives no instance of 'whip' used to mean 'whip-handle'.

[5] That a spider's-web is not only a possible but a natural image for wagon-spokes may be illustrated by the following from Caulfeild and Saward's *Dictionary of Needlework* (1882): 'arrange [these] like the spokes of a wheel or the chief threads of a spider's web'. I owe this citation to *OED* (under *spider, sb.,* 10).

eminently right for the long, infinitely thin traces; and the cricket's bones are clearly correct for the collars. It is not Q1 which corrupts Shakespeare's text here, but Q2. The poetic excellence of Q1 in these lines is so evident that it is difficult to understand why they have been so harshly condemned by so many able and responsible scholars.

The superiority of Q1 to Q2 is not confined to one group of lines; it is apparent at many points of the speech. Benvolio's interjection, 'Queene Mab whats she?' which is omitted in Q2, arrests the quick-moving word-play of the lines immediately preceding it, and focuses the audience's attention on the set speech which follows. 'Athwart' in l. 7 is so much better than Q2's 'ouer' that it has been adopted by almost all modern editors. Again 'maide' in l. 14 is unquestionably right and has been preferred by the editors to Q2's 'man'. The same is true of 'O're' for 'On' in l. 17. Though editors generally choose the Q2 sequence of 'breaches, ambuscados, spanish blades' (ll. 28–9), Q1's 'breaches, ambuscados, countermines' (l. 28) seems to me to be more coherent.

The effective, though somewhat mannered, chiasmus of ll. 17–18 in Q1 is considerably weakened in Q2 (ll. 17–20) by the insertion of an additional line, which turns a piece of verbal elegance into a wearisomely repetitious passage. The brilliantly staccato rhythm of ll. 30–1 in Q1 is ruined in Q2 (ll. 30–2) by the addition of the commonplace and unnecessary phrase, 'and being thus frighted'. The double reference to courtiers in Q2 (ll. 17, 23) has troubled a number of editors; but if we keep to the Q1 text, with a possible emendation of 'lap' to 'lip' in l. 21, this problem disappears.

Other differences between Q1 and Q2 are not as striking as these. Q1's 'vp/and downe' (l. 15) is not clearly superior to Q2's 'night by night' (l. 16); either 'Burgomaster' or 'Alderman' (Q1, 5; Q2, 4), 'pickt' or 'prickt' (Q1, 14; Q2, 12), 'breedes' or 'bodes' (Q1, 36; Q2, 35)

can be defended. But if we have established the principle that Q1 is the more reliable text for the Queen Mab speech, then it ought to be followed consistently throughout the speech. In only one respect is the Q2 version superior to Q1; it gives three lines (12–15) not found in Q1, though, as has been pointed out already, it obviously misplaces these lines.

The addition of these three lines in Q2, and some of the differences in wording noted above (e.g. 'Burgomaster/Alderman') have been used to support the theory that Q2 represents a revised version of the speech reported in Q1, that essentially what we have in the two Quartos are two stages of Shakespeare's workmanship.[1] This theory seems to me to be indefensible as a general explanation of the relationship between the two texts. Shakespeare could never have revised poetic sense into poetic nonsense. Even if we turn the theory upside down, and assume that Q1 represents the later version of the speech, it is still unacceptable: for the muddled imagery of the Q2 version could not have been created by Shakespeare even as a first draft.

If the reasons for preferring Q1 to Q2 for the Queen Mab speech are indeed 'strong and cogent', as I believe they are, we must explain how a thoroughly corrupt passage found its way into a good Quarto. For, it must be emphasized, I make no attempt to generalize about Q1 and Q2 on the basis of this one speech. There is not the slightest doubt that Q1, in the main, is a bad Quarto, and that Q2, in the main, is a good Quarto. On the other hand, there is nothing in the concept of good and bad Quartos which requires us to reject a priori the suggestion that a particular good Quarto may give us an unreliable text at a particular point. If we knew that a printed play represented a text authorized and prepared for publication by the writer himself (as we know this, for example, for the plays in the Ben Jonson 1616 Folio)

[1] See p. 75, n. 1.

then we would have to accept the authenticity of the text at every point, except for obvious misprints. But this is exactly what we do not know about Q2 of *Romeo and Juliet*. There is not the slightest bit of external evidence to show that the publication of Q2 was any more authorized by Shakespeare and his company than that of Q1 had been.[1] It is clear, from internal evidence, that Shakespeare's foul papers were available to whoever prepared the Q2 text for the printer; but it is also clear, from internal evidence, that Shakespeare himself could neither have prepared nor approved the Q2 text; not, that is, unless we are willing to convict him of the grossest indifference to the public transmission of his work. We cannot postulate that Shakespeare and his fellows deliberately sponsored the publication of Q2 in order to replace a 'stolen and surreptitious' text with an authoritative one, when Q2 is so disordered and careless a text itself.

I therefore suggest the following explanation for the corruptness of the Q2 text of the Queen Mab speech. Someone whom we may call Scribe E (to follow Duthie's terminology without agreeing with his theory as to Scribe E's method of operation) was responsible for preparing the text of Q2 for publication. Scribe E may have been connected with Shakespeare's company (as actor or bookkeeper) or he may have been an outsider; but he was familiar with the play, and he had available to him Shakespeare's foul papers. In the course of putting these papers into order for the printer, Scribe E discovered that the Queen Mab speech was missing. Since this speech was probably, in 1599 as today, one of the most popular and best-known things in the play, Scribe E added the speech to the manuscript either by writing it out himself from memory or getting one of the actors to dictate it to him or write it out for him. What resulted was verse put down as prose, with all the marks of auditory and memorial corruption already discussed.

Why was the Queen Mab speech missing from Shakespeare's foul papers? One possibility is that a leaf of the manuscript had been lost or stolen, but this is hardly likely, in view of the fact that only 27 lines of verse are involved, far fewer than would be contained on a manuscript page, and that the lines immediately surrounding this speech are clearly correct. A more likely possibility is that the play, as originally written by Shakespeare and as represented in his foul papers, did not contain the Queen Mab speech, except for the first line and the last three lines that are given as verse in Q2. Mercutio's lines at this point, one may guess, were as follows. (I give the lines immediately preceding and following Mercutio's, to supply the context):

Rom.   I dreampt a dreame to night.
Mer.   And so did I.
Ro.   Well what was yours?
Mer.   That dreamers often lie.
Ro.   In bed asleep while they do dream things truē
Mer.   O then I see Queen Mab hath bin with you:
  This is the hag, when maides lie on their backs,
  That presses them and learnes them first to beare,
  Making them women of good carriage:
  This is she.
Romeo.   Peace, peace, *Mercutio* peace,
  Thou talkst of nothing.

I submit that what happened was that at rehearsal or early performance it became clear

---

[1] I am aware that I am here going counter to the opinion of the great founder of the new bibliography, A. W. Pollard, who in his *Shakespeare Folios and Quartos* (London, 1909), p. 69, stated unequivocally: 'The second edition of *Romeo and Juliet*, printed in 1599 by Thomas Creed for Cuthbert Burby, was an authorized edition, printed with the goodwill of the players'. But I do not find, either in Pollard or elsewhere, any evidence to show that the players willingly cooperated in the publication of Q2. Many of the arguments and assumptions underlying the equation of good quartos with authorized quartos were, I think, effectively challenged by Leo Kirschbaum in *Shakespeare and the Stationers* (Ohio State University Press, 1955) though Kirschbaum himself believed that Q2 of *Romeo and Juliet* was an authorized publication.

that the character of Mercutio was an enormous success, and it was decided to build up the role further by giving him a set speech at this point, a kind of display aria, which was then added to the fair copy (together with Benvolio's interjection) but remained missing from the foul papers. Denied access to the prompt-book, as I believe, Scribe E could supply the missing speech only by recourse to his own or someone else's memory.

Another question inevitably arises at this point. Why didn't Scribe E simply use the Q1 version of the speech? We know, from indisputable evidence, that Q2 made use of Q1 again and again. Why not here? I believe that the answer to this question is to be found in the assumption that Scribe E made no use at all of Q1 in assembling the manuscript for Q2. It was only in the printing house that the compositor, faced with the problem of a difficult manuscript, adopted the practice of consulting Q1 from time to time, particularly in passages where he could see at a glance that there was remarkable agreement between Q1 and his manuscript copy.[1] But he would have had no reason for consulting Q1 for the Queen Mab speech; for this passage, he would have had a clearly and newly written text on a separate slip, differing moreover from Q1 in lineation and wording. In such a case, he would normally follow what he had every reason to believe was the more authoritative copy.

All this is only a guess; but I believe it is a reasonable guess, one that provides a plausible explanation of how a corrupt passage could have found its way into a good Quarto text. If we can agree that the Q2 version of the Queen Mab speech does show signs of memorial corruption, and if we can accept the possibility of such corruption in a good Quarto, then we are justified in insisting that future editors of *Romeo and Juliet* give serious consideration to the Q1 text of the Queen Mab speech as perhaps less corrupt and closer to Shakespeare's intentions than the Q2 text.

[1] This basically is Duthie's explanation ('The Text of Shakespeare's *Romeo and Juliet*') for the bibliographical links between Q1 and Q2.

'TIME'S DEFORMED HAND': SEQUENCE, CONSEQUENCE, AND INCONSEQUENCE IN 'THE COMEDY OF ERRORS'

GĀMINI SALGĀDO

Thirty years ago, the highlight of the Stratford-on-Avon Shakespeare season was Theodore Komisarjevsky's production of *The Comedy of Errors*. Between the house of Antipholus and *The Porpentine* a large clock-tower dominated the setting. 'To emphasize the note of farce', wrote the critic of the *Birmingham Gazette*, 'the clock in the tower between the two inns every now and again strikes an hour to which the hands of the clock are not pointing. And the hands gallop to overtake the time.' Other comments, including the producer's own, make it evident that Komisarjevsky considered the play itself to be a poor thing at best, and that therefore the more liberties taken with it the better. The business with the clock may be regarded as a typical instance, another being the weird mélange of costumes from all times and places, presumably to emphasise an Ephesus beyond the range of any time or place. It is therefore mildly ironical that these touches, especially that of the clock, intended as bold and original strokes of production (which indeed they were) should nevertheless be profoundly true to one of the chief concerns of the play, the movement of time and its apparent aberrations.

At about the same time as the production referred to above, G. R. Elliott published an essay on 'Weirdness in *The Comedy of Errors*'[1] in which he drew attention to the element of comic horror which is undeniably present in the play: 'Real horror attaches to the notion of the *complete* identity of two human beings.'

The author went on to trace the source of this horror to the fact that human beings set so much store by their individuality that resentment against, and resistance to, any threat to that individuality goes to the very depths of our being. But what *is* individuality, or rather, to be more metaphysically modest, how do I sense my identity, which is a necessary concomitant of my individuality? Is it not in my consciousness of inhabiting an ordered temporal dimension, in which, by exercising the functions of retrospect, observation and anticipation, I infer from the steady flow of future through present into past, the existence of the entity through which this flow passes? This is a portentous and schematic way of putting it, and most of us would not normally think of our individuality in these terms, but we take something like them for granted in our daily existence and our common speech. Part of the uneasiness which underlies our laughter in *The Comedy of Errors* is related to the tricks it plays, in form, language and action, with what we take to be a normal temporal sequence.

The duplication of identity in relation to time has two aspects relevant to the play. In a general sense, and from the standpoint of the audience, it is a way of distorting and distending time. As such it is for us a fulfilment of one of the functions of comedy, to transcend in some

[1] *University of Toronto Quarterly*, LX (1939), 95–106. Reprinted in *Shakespeare's Comedies, an Anthology of Modern Criticism*, edited by Laurence Lerner (London, 1967).

fashion the devouring power of human time, whose movement is always towards decay and death. The matter is not as simple as this however, because this movement, however sinister, is the natural 'given' movement of our world, and Shakespearian comedy, never content to rest in fantasy however much it values it and delights in it, always seeks to establish a viable relationship between the play-world and ours.

For the experiencing agents, on the other hand, duplication of identity which they themselves are unaware of is felt as a dislocation of the ordinary world and of the steady single direction of time as the medium of experience. Apart from observing the signs of decay in ourselves and the world about us, our sense of the flow of time and its direction is given to us by the observable sequence of cause and effect and the progressive accumulation of information. If either of these were disrupted, our sense of time would be deranged, as happens in a very mild way whenever we watch a film sequence run backwards, tapes of races which have just been run, or rather more disconcertingly in certain dreams. A good deal of the action of *The Comedy of Errors* can be fairly described as disruption of the sequence of causality and of the process of storing up information, from the point of view of those involved in it. I send a man off to find out what time the ship sails, and he brings me back a bag of gold. I ask him whether he has put my money away safely and he tells me the dinner is burning. I send for a rope and am brought news of a ship. A servant does what he is told and is beaten for his pains. And so it goes. What you have just seen or heard is denied a moment later. No information, however recently acquired, can be trusted. Of the 1,700 odd lines of the play well over 700 are taken up by characters giving their versions of what has just happened, and yet no one in the play is able to give a reliable account of the present or the immediate past.

If a developed sense of time and a sense of individuality are virtually two aspects of the same thing, this may account for the uncanny and more-than-farcical resonance of the play. When Shakespeare took *The Menaechmi* of Plautus and dovetailed it into his *Amphitruo* (the carpentry is painstakingly dismantled in chapters XXVIII and XXIX of Professor T. W. Baldwin's *William Shakespeare's Five-Act Structure*), he did more than multiply the possibilities of confusion. He introduced a new dimension where the protagonists could themselves make mistakes of identity. This was impossible for the citizen in *The Menaechmi* and while the real Amphitryon and Sosia do fall victim to this error in the other Latin play, the domestic setting keeps its repercussions narrowly confined. In *The Comedy of Errors*, as Professor Foakes notes in the new Arden edition,[1] the multiple confusions result in the disruption of family, social and personal relationships. But beyond this there is a kind of cosmic disruption caused by the dislocation of the time sequence. Not only does public time seem to have gone awry, but the inner time-sense of the protagonists, their notion of 'before', 'after' and 'now', has become seriously deranged.

The preoccupation with the movement of time in *The Comedy of Errors* with its direction, its pace, and its consequences, does not affect merely the content of the play. Since drama in performance is an art which exists in time, a play where the involutions and deviations of time are part of the theme may be expected to show this in its very structure; and certain quite distinctive effects are made possible by the fact that the actual unfolding of the drama must inevitably be in linear progression, while the ordering of events implicitly questions that very progression. *The Comedy of Errors* (like

[1] *The Comedy of Errors*, edited by R. A. Foakes, the (new) Arden Shakespeare (London, 1962). All references are to this edition.

The Tempest, with which it has notable affinities, not all of which can be adequately accounted for by a common range of sources) is one of the shortest of Shakespeare's plays. One of the effects of this brevity is to emphasise how much 'coiling' of time takes place in a bare two hours' traffic. In terms of 'clock-time', the entire action takes place within one day, formally marked out by Egeon's couplet

Yet this my comfort; when your words are done,
My woes end likewise with the evening sun
(I, i, 26–7)

at the beginning and by the Abbess's reference to 'this present hour' in the closing scene. In between, there are more references to the passing of clock-time than in any other comedy. Phrases such as 'within this hour', 'not half an hour since', 'but two hours old', 'some hour hence', 'at five o'clock', 'It was two ere I left him' and so on are scattered thickly throughout the dialogue. The joke is of course that it is quite impossible to fit all the various time divisions so precisely referred to in action within the limits defined by the opening and closing scenes.

The design of the play, *pace* Professor Baldwin, is not really based on a five-act structure on the Terentian model. Rather, its eleven scenes consist of an inner action contained within an outer one to which it is finally united. The structure of the action corresponds to two different aspects of time. The overarching framework, in spite of its threatening implications, is essentially benevolent. Against a ground of moving accidents by flood and field, it illustrates the normal workings of the temporal process in comedy, speaking of the great commonplaces of wedlock, childbirth, and familial piety and pointing the arrow of our expectation towards the fullness of time when all disorders are healed and all divisions settled. It is not fortuitous that this enveloping action comes to a close in a priory, a place where harmony and spiritual health both have extra-temporal sanctions.

Within this outer action, however, the main action takes place in a time gone crazy, twisted, looped, turning in on itself, not so much the medium of existence as a manifestation of its perplexities, even, at times, of its horror. G. R. Elliott describes the relationship between the opening scene and what follows in this way: 'An initial mood of swift and strange, almost weird romance is saturated, as the play proceeds, with fun that is swift, strange, weird. Thus the romance and the fun are congruent.'[1] As it stands, this can be misleading. To put the matter at its simplest, the opening exposition scene does not *feel* in the least like the action that follows. This is not merely because the matter in hand is more sombre than the later events. It is as much because the tempo and orderly unfolding of the past makes such a strong contrast with the chaos to come. There is all the difference between the measured tempo of sequential development, however distressing the incidents recounted, and the series of false starts, backtrackings, and collisions by means of which the main action is presented. The difference is precisely a difference in the way time unfolds. (Elliott himself seems to be aware of this, as he goes on to say that in the opening scene the note of 'weirdness or uncanniness' is not present explicitly enough.) In *The Shakespeare Inset*,[2] Francis Berry contrasts this scene with the expository opening of *The Tempest* and points out the relative flatness of the exposition in the earlier play. He attributes this flatness to the absence of variation of pace and tone, of vivid detail, of tense and grammatical construction and of the characters' position on the stage. In Mr Berry's own words 'though Egeon draws on the deep backward and abysm of time, as Prospero is to

[1] G. R. Elliott, 'Weirdness in *The Comedy of Errors*' (reprinted in *Shakespeare's Comedies*, ed. Lerner, p. 22).
[2] London, 1965, pp. 41–5.

do later, he does not once hale the "then" and "there" into the "here" and "now"".[1] Precisely. Tempo, tone, tense and stillness all conspire to place Egeon in a past whose rhythms are discontinuous with the tempo of the main action. An audience's sense of whether time is moving (and at what rate) or standing still while it is listening to the dialogue of a play is very largely a question of whether such dialogue is devoted to the business of the present movement (what is happening before its eyes), or to a character trying to understand what has just happened, or to retrospect. In the main action of the play the two latter functions are constantly juxtaposed; the overarching action is almost exclusively taken up with the former. The 'frozen' time of Egeon's tale contrasts briefly but markedly with the vigorous variety of tense in the Duke's closing words ('would', 'may', 'will', and the imperatives 'try', 'beg', 'borrow', 'live'). The real time of the play has begun to run with:

> I'll limit thee this day
> To seek thy health by beneficial help.
> (I, i, 150–1)

In the next scene, Egeon who has remained a character in a different past is briefly thrust into the play's present in the First Merchant's reference to him:

> This very day a Syracusian merchant
> Is apprehended for arrival here,   (I, ii, 3–4)

This is the only occasion, until the very end when all knots are untangled, that the confused present threatens to come into contact with the ordered past. If Egeon's shadowy identity in the present as 'a Syracusian merchant' were to be given any further definition, the action would have ended before it began. But it is not, and S. Antipholus looks confidently to the future, ignoring the past:

> Within this hour it will be dinner time;
> Till that I'll view the manners of the town,

> Peruse the traders, gaze upon the buildings,
> And then return and sleep within mine inn
> (I, ii, 11–14)

We are firmly within the moving moment. The time-bomb with the crazy clock has begun to tick. The First Merchant's parting words give us a hint that the inner and outer action will be completed at about the same time, recalling the Duke's 'I'll limit thee this day':

> soon at five o'clock,
> Please you, I'll meet with you upon the mart,
> And afterwards consort you till bed-time
> (I, ii, 26–8)

Ironically, the ominous implication of the Duke's words turns out to be providential, while the genial social promise of the Merchant's farewell conceals much trouble and confusion. 'I will go lose myself', says S. Antipholus, using the words in the first place in their colloquial sense of wandering aimlessly about the city. But their repetition a few lines later sharply points up the sense of loss of identity, linked as it is to the potent Shakespearian image of the water-drop.[2] The point is that both the literal and metaphorical senses of the phrase come to the same thing, as the action of the play demonstrates; it is by losing himself in the city that S. Antipholus loses his identity.

The notion of steady and regular time is briefly taken up in S. Antipholus's words to E. Dromio as he sees the latter approaching:

> Here comes the almanac of my true date
> (I, ii, 41)

but by the very next line, 'What now? How chance thou art returned so soon?' time's twistings and turnings have begun. The refer-

---

[1] *Ibid.*, p. 43.
[2] See H. F. Brooks, 'Themes and Structure in *The Comedy of Errors*', in *Early Shakespeare*, edited by J. R. Brown and Bernard Harris, Stratford-upon-Avon Studies 3 (London, 1961). Also Critical Introduction to New Arden edition.

ence to Dromio is unmistakably ironic, not only because of the audience's strong suspicion that the false Dromio is not the true date-keeper that S. Antipholus thinks him to be, but also in terms of the series of pictures of disrupted time which are the first words uttered by E. Dromio:

Return'd so soon? rather approach'd too late;
The capon burns, the pig falls from the spit;
The clock hath strucken twelve upon the bell;
My mistress made it one upon my cheek

(I, ii, 43–6)

Dromio's feeble pun, one of several quibbles on time which we shall encounter, goes to the heart of the matter. Clock-time and inward time have already begun to diverge and E. Dromio tells his supposed master as much: 'Methinks your man, like mine, should be your clock.'[1] The doggerel lines following the four I have quoted above, each leaning on the other, pile up with something of the hectic rhythm of a clock that will not stop striking.

The action of *The Comedy of Errors* takes the form of a series of broken appointments, circumscribed by one appointment that is scrupulously kept (the Duke's meeting at five o'clock with Egeon). The appointment most frequently mentioned throughout the play is that of dinner. (There are far more references to 'dinner' and its derivatives here than in any other Shakespearian play.) Dinner, as the principal Elizabethan meal, marked the chief event of the normal domestic day. Being usually taken around noon, it divided the day symmetrically in terms of clock-time. Dinner and the dinner hour may therefore aptly stand for routine, unhurried normality, when public and private time kept a congruent rhythm. It is not surprising that they should figure prominently in a story which deals with the breakdown of that congruence.

The causal sequence is disrupted when the money that we saw S. Antipholus hand to his servant a few moments ago becomes 'sixpence that I had o'Wednesday last'. The act ends with S. Antipholus reacting, not as one who is trapped in an unfamiliar dimension of time (which is a metaphysical luxury reserved for the audience) but, as is more natural, with a suspicion that he is in an enchanted place. (Ephesus already had this association for the Elizabethan mind. Many critics have pointed this out, but it has not been so often remarked that this is the tourists' view of the place; to those who live in it, the city is a centre of busy and ordered commercial transaction and of a fairly humdrum domestic life. Ephesus in *Pericles* is in sharp contrast.) The first two scenes of the play thus present us with a vivid contrast between the past and the present. For all its threat, the past is set in steady, natural time, while the present is wavering and distorted.

With Adriana's 'Sure, Luciana, it is two o'clock', the second act starts with the clock set right again, so to speak. The homiletic exchange between the two sisters on marital obedience, with its smooth and measured movement, is an oasis of calm soon to be disturbed by E. Dromio's arrival, and perhaps Luciana speaks wiser than she knows:

Time is their master, and when they see time,
They'll go or come.   (II, i, 8–9)

She means, of course, that men come and go as they please, but we are soon to see in full swing what the previous scene has already given us strong indications of – a more sinister way in which time dominates the principals in this play.

E. Dromio's recapitulation of the exchange between himself and his supposed master is entirely in terms of the latter's refusal to recognise the time for what it is – the dinner

[1] Pope's emendation (Folio's 'cooke' to 'clock') is almost certainly correct. See the new Arden editor's note, p. 16.

hour. For the audience, hearing the scene they had witnessed only a few moments earlier recreated in capsule form in E. Dromio's vivid snatches of phrase, there is the comic frisson of time telescoped and turned back:

> ''Tis dinner-time', quoth I; 'my gold', quoth he;
> 'Your meat will burn', quoth I; 'my gold', quoth
> he ...
> 'Where is the thousand marks I gave thee, villain?'
> 'The pig', quoth I, 'is burn'd'; 'my gold', quoth he;
> (II, i, 62–3, 65–6)

It is in his apparent failure to recognise the 'right time' that Antipholus's identity becomes a puzzle to his wife, and the servants, in their hithering and thithering and the 'strokes' they collect at either end become veritable travelling clocks being constantly reset. Perhaps E. Dromio's earlier pun ('The clock hath strucken twelve ... My mistress made it one upon my cheek'), feeble as it is, is slightly more pertinent than we had imagined.

> Hath homely age the alluring beauty took
> From my poor cheek? Then he hath wasted it.
> (II, i, 89–90)

Adriana's words not only make her intensely human. With their sudden poignant cutting back to normal processes of time they form a sharp contrast to the unnatural entanglings of the temporal process which we have witnessed and heard of. (The unusual word 'defeatures' which Adriana uses in speaking of her husband's responsibility for her present appearance is used nowhere else in all Shakespeare's plays except at the very end of *The Comedy of Errors*, where Egeon applies it to the inevitable workings of time (v, i, 300).)

The opening lines of the second scene of act II mark, in the new Arden editor's words, 'a point of rest in the play's mounting confusion'.[1] They attempt to impose order on the recent past and place S. Antipholus virtually back at the point where he had said: 'Here comes the almanac of my true date.' As far as he is concerned, the intervening time has been effectively cancelled. If S. Antipholus could resist the temptation for further recapitulation of the events of the half-hour that has gone awry, all would be well, but of course he cannot, and further time-trouble ensues. He accuses S. Dromio of making 'a common of my serious hours' and the conversation moves compulsively into a discussion of the 'right time', focused again upon the crucial event of dinner and lurching on to much quibbling on the power and attributes of Father Time himself. The twin themes of time and identity are completely interwoven in the comic exchange on time and hair. It may be an obligatory set-piece, but if it is, it is in just the right setting. The argument, let us recall, turns on the question of whether or not 'there is a time for all things'. The action of the play forces us to leave the question open, for there does indeed appear to be no 'time' for some of the things that happen in it.

Adriana's entrance and the accompanying change from jerky prose to blank verse harks back once more to an earlier 'natural' time – 'The time was once when thou unurg'd wouldst vow ... How comes it *now* ...' The figure in S. Antipholus's reply –

> ... I know you not.
> In Ephesus I am but two hours old,
> (II, ii, 147–8)

– is no doubt a commonplace but, supported as it is by all the other emphases on time, it plays some part in drawing our attention to a new identity related to a new beginning in time. From the moment of this confrontation, S. Antipholus and his servant abandon all attempts to balance their subjective sense of time against public clock-time. As in a similar situation in *Twelfth Night*,[2] the abandonment is

---

[1] P. 26n.

[2] Cf. Sebastian in *TN* IV, i, 59–62, 'If it be thus to dream, still let me sleep!' Also his later lines at IV, ii, 9–15: 'For though my soul disputes well with my sense', etc.

signalled in S. Antipholus's case by a conscious decision to enter the other time of dreams:

> What, was I married to her in my dream?
> Or sleep I now, and think I hear all this?
> What error drives our eyes and ears amiss?
> Until I know this sure uncertainty,
> I'll entertain the offer'd fallacy,   (II, ii, 182–6)

– while S. Dromio's 'This is the fairy land' puts us in mind of the most celebrated entry into dream-time in all Shakespeare. This readiness to yield to the promise of the future, a certain openness before the hazards of fortune, a willing belief in the essential benevolence of time, is not merely a precondition of the development of the comic plot, but also a characteristic of the Shakespearian comic hero and heroine, especially in disguise, where they always retain a certain freedom of comment on their assumed roles. Since comedy sees time ultimately in its aspect of fulfilment rather than of destruction, this faith is no more and no less than the acceptance by the protagonists of the world in which they live, move and have their being:

> Am I in earth, in heaven, or in hell?
> Sleeping or waking, mad or well advis'd?
> Known unto these, and to myself disguis'd,
> I'll say as they say, and persever so,
> And in this mist at all adventures go.
>   (II, ii, 212–16)

In performance, the words with which Adriana leaves the stage at the end of act II, 'Come, come, Antipholus, we dine too late', would still be in the audience's ears when E. Antipholus appears on the stage for the first time and identifies himself with the line 'My wife is shrewish when I keep not hours'. Here he starts out with the 'inner' and 'outer' clocks in perfect accord; they are never to be so again till the action is almost over. From the audience's standpoint, however, the public clock is turned back, because what E. Antipholus says is valid only on the assumption that the scene we have just witnessed (II, ii) has not in fact taken place. For E. Antipholus, his wife is still waiting for him to come home to dinner, as we see her waiting at the beginning of the second act; for us, she has already gone in to dinner with her husband.

The appearance of congruence between public and private time is appearance only. E. Dromio's insistence on what has been happening to him is already threatening his master's 'temporal' stability. If he inquired seriously into the slave's story, the comic world would disintegrate. Fortunately for us, he dismisses it with 'I think thou art an ass' (inevitably recalling his double's earlier comment to his servant) and there follows the debate between E. Antipholus and Balthazar on the comparative merits of good food and a warm welcome. H. F. Brooks has pointed out[1] (what we might have guessed from the banality of the language and the jog-trot of the rhymes) that this is not to be taken seriously in itself, being part of the social custom of discussing a set topic before dinner. The joke is of course that we have here the ritual without the reality which is to follow it and which is the *raison d'être* of the ritual. After the elaborate discussion as to whether food or welcome is better, 'Here is neither cheer, sir, nor welcome'. When the courtesy debate is reflected later in the distorting mirror of the slanging match between the two Dromios more is involved than the degeneration of ritual into chaos. Time, which had been, in a manner of speaking 'frozen' in the earlier discussion (as it is in much ritual), begins to run again. We are in the flowing present of the play, but it is a muddied and twisting stream.

A collision between the domestic and social worlds of the play appears inevitable at this point. It is averted only by Balthazar's appeal from the baffling disorders of the present to E. Antipholus's 'long experience' of marital

1 'Themes and Structure in *The Comedy of Errors*', p. 68. See also the new Arden editor's note, p. 41.

harmony. The verse moves from past through present into projected future – 'And about evening come yourself alone' – and once more settles into the smooth rhythms which are its ground bass. But some hint of the way the future itself will begin to twist and turn as it becomes the present is given in E. Antipholus's summing up of his intention: 'And in despite of mirth, mean to be merry'. His last words in this scene – 'this jest shall cost me some expense' has of course two very different meanings for himself and for the audience. Komisarjevsky's production very aptly used it as a kind of Gilbertian refrain repeated in chorus by everyone on stage.

In his stimulating essay on the play which I have cited earlier, H. F. Brooks refers to 'harmonic structure, the structure which by parallel, contrast, or cross-reference, independent perhaps of the cause and effect connections of the progressive action, makes us compare one passage or person of the play with another, and so find an enriched significance in both'.[1] In *The Comedy of Errors*, it is not so much that the two structures are independent, as that one is deliberately counterpointed against the other, and the counterpointing is part of the larger meaning of the play, since 'the cause and effect connections of the progressive action' are themselves called into question. In the scene that now follows (III, ii), for instance, the tone, the formal rhyming, and the subject matter recall the exchange between Adriana and her sister which opens the second act. There is even an explicit reference to the earlier conversation in 'Though others have the arm, show us the sleeve'. (Compare II, ii, 173.) It is, as far as Luciana is concerned, a shunting back in time, an attempt to get back again through retrospect on to the rails of normality. She invests Antipholus with a new identity on the basis of past and future hypocrisy. For his part, S. Antipholus is entirely willing to accept a new identity, but it is the transformation

wrought by love (an absolute, in spite of everything, in Shakespearian comedy), not by deranged time, which he craves:

> Teach me, dear creature, how to think and speak;
> Lay open to my earthy gross conceit,
> Smother'd in errors, feeble, shallow, weak,
> The folded meaning of your words' deceit.
> Against my soul's pure truth, why labour you
> To make it wander in an unknown field?
> Are you a god? would you create me new?
> Transform me then, and to your power I'll yield.
>
> (III, ii, 33–40)

The platonic overtones ('my earthy gross conceit', 'my soul's pure truth', etc.) are entirely appropriate; the affirmation S. Antipholus wishes to make, though exaggerated in its immediate context, is essentially beyond the vagaries of time. For him time begins again here, with love:

> Thee will I love, and with thee lead my life;
> Thou hast no husband yet, nor I no wife –
>
> (III, ii, 67–8)

Though under the influence of S. Dromio's sad tale of pursuit by Greasy Nell (which is of course a comic parallel of his own predicament) S. Antipholus decides to flee from the complications of the present ('Tis time I think to trudge, pack and be gone') we know that in the comic outcome his attempt will inevitably be thwarted. He accepts 'the offered fallacy' of the gold chain as he did Adriana's invitation to dinner and this acceptance once more deflects for him the straight course of time's arrow.

For a moment, but only for a moment, we are again in the sphere of public time at the beginning of the fourth act, in the world of debts due at Pentecost and five o'clock appointments. But with the entry of E. Antipholus and his servant the backward journey on the time machine begins again. 'Neither chain nor goldsmith came to me' – his words take us, with

[1] *Ibid.*, p. 56.

him, to a point before the two scenes we have just witnessed. This is not a world in which past or future have any coherence. Money disappears and so do tangible objects such as gold chains. The difference in the latter case is that more is involved than the trustworthiness or otherwise of a servant. The whole commercial existence of the community depends on the honouring of obligations voluntarily entered into in the past. That existence is now threatened when the immediate past seems to be present in two versions of equal authority but mutually contradictory. Private confusions have now spread into the public domain of Angelo, the Second Merchant and the arresting Officer. The vagaries of the past make future action impossible. Time has twisted itself into an inexplicable knot:

Angelo.
Then you will bring the chain to her yourself?
Antipholus of Ephesus.
No, bear it with you, lest I come not time enough.
Angelo.
Well sir, I will. Have you the chain about you?
Antipholus of Ephesus.
And if I have not, sir, I hope you have,
Or else you may return without your money.
Angelo.
Nay, come, I pray you, sir, give me the chain
(IV, i, 40–5)

The action literally cannot go forward but for the intervention of the Second Merchant, the only one of the speakers for whom public time still keeps a normal course: 'The hour steals on; I pray you sir, dispatch.' The whole scene of some seventy lines from which I have quoted above is, in terms of the use of performance time, a contrast to what Francis Berry has called 'the Shakespeare inset' as in the opening scene of the play. There a lengthy tract of the past is encompassed in a few moments of stage-time. Here, several minutes of stage-time are taken up by an action which, save as it keeps turning in on itself, is really no action at all.

S. Dromio's obsolete Elizabethan pun 'It was two ere I left him, and now the clock strikes on(e)' provokes in Adriana's comment the most explicit statement of the play's dramatic technique: 'The hours come back; that did I never hear.' The ensuing jesting on time as a debtor fleeing in fear of a sergeant is of a piece with the earlier set exchange on time and hair, but it is also bound to remind us of what we have just seen – the sergeant arresting E. Antipholus for debt – and thus effect a kind of identification of one of the protagonists (and his double?) with defaulting time. S. Dromio's cryptic line 'Time is a very bankrupt, and owes more than he's worth to season' has often been taken to mean 'There is never enough time to do all that occasion offers' but it could equally easily, and with perhaps greater relevance, be understood as saying that time has so exhausted itself that it's more trouble than it's worth to set it straight ('season' neatly combining the two usual senses of 'bring to maturity' and 'make palatable or agreeable'). Alternatively, if we are not too snobbish to credit the lower orders with quasi-metaphysical intuitions, S. Dromio may be saying that time in itself is empty and owes all its powers and more to 'season', the harmonious cyclical regularity of the natural world. In either case the involved and often – admittedly – tedious fooling does have an important bearing on the play's theme and structure.

When S. Dromio meets his master (IV, iii) their two clocks collide, so to speak – 'Why, sir, I brought you word an hour since, that the bark *Expedition* puts forth tonight' – and that way madness lies. The courtesan's speech which ends this scene not only prepares us for the madness to come, but gives us, as it were, a progress report on the action so far, as it is recorded in terms of public duration and behaviour. At the very end of the fourth act, what had before been simple if confusing contradictions in the experiences of different persons becomes vastly more involved. We see that there is not so much flat contradiction as overlapping combined with divergence in the various accounts of the events of the recent past given by Adriana, E. Antipholus and E. Dromio. Some of what Antipholus says is corroborated by Dromio, some of what Dromio says corroborated by Adriana. Even the presumed madness of Antipholus is insufficient as an explanation of what is going on. In the end, the onlookers are compelled to consider whether it is not they themselves who are mad, when what they have just witnessed (the binding of Antipholus) appears not to have happened: 'God for thy mercy they are loose again!' The audience itself is involved in a sensation of *déjà vu* when the same action (Antipholus with drawn sword) is repeated a few moments later in the encounter with Angelo.

When the last act begins, S. Antipholus is still at the end of act III (where Angelo had just given him the chain) and Angelo at the beginning of act IV, where E. Antipholus had denied receiving the chain from him. Our final reminder of public time ('By this I think the dial points at five') comes after Adriana's abortive effort to rescue her husband from the priory (the play is full of such false starts); and it foreshadows the union of the main action of the play, where time has been going crazy, with the over-arching action, where the clock has been ticking steadily away to the hour of doom. The Duke's words to Adriana – 'Long since thy husband served me in my wars' – looks back to a stable past, a centre of normality beyond the confused events of the play. Similarly, Egeon's apostrophe evokes both in its sense and in the measured dignity of its rhythm, the progression of natural time as it is found in ordinary human experience. The imagery of music, light and the seasons evokes a world in which objective time is in harmony with human time, and Egeon's experience, however

severe and testing, is seen as inevitable and therefore natural and liberating:

> O time's extremity,
> Hast thou so crack'd and splitted my poor tongue
> In seven short years, that here my only son
> Knows not my feeble key of untun'd cares?
> Though now this grained face of mine be hid
> In sap-consuming winter's drizzled snow,
> And all the conduits of my blood froze up,
> Yet hath my night of life some memory;
> My wasting lamps some fading glimmer left;
> My dull deaf ears a little use to hear –
> All these old witnesses, I cannot err,
> Tell me thou art my son Antipholus.
>
> (v, i, 307–18)

In the Duke's words, 'Why, here begins his morning story right:' natural time starts flowing again. It is left to the Abbess to bring the immediate past into alignment with the ordered perspective of true temporal experience in an image whose capacity to move is partly due, I think, to the fact that it has, hovering about it, the resonance of the phrase 'the fullness of time':

> Thirty three years have I but gone in travail
> Of you, my sons, and till this present hour
> My heavy burden ne'er delivered.   (v, i, 400–2)

'After so long grief, such felicity.' If the twists and turns of time in *The Comedy of Errors* do no more than tease us, it is because we have been put in a position where *our* time-sense is not threatened. As Bertrand Evans points out,[1] we are let into the only secret early on in the play, a secret of which all the characters involved are equally ignorant. There is no *character* who plays tricks on the others, so that he knows what they do not know. Only the outcome of the over-arching action – the real identity of the Abbess and the family reunion – are withheld from us too so that at

[1] *Shakespeare's Comedies* (London, 1960). I am very grateful for the comments of my colleague A. D. Nuttall on an earlier version of this essay.

the very end of the play we too begin to feel the movement of time. For the rest, our superior awareness prevents us from identifying with any of the characters involved, except indirectly. The play remains a farce where Shakespeare takes us backstage, as it were, to show us what tricks can be worked with time without, for the most part, playing such 'tricks' on us, as he does in *The Winter's Tale* and *The Tempest*. For the moment, we are protected from the puzzlements of time dismembered.

© GĀMINI SALGĀDO 1972

FAITH AND FASHION IN 'MUCH ADO ABOUT NOTHING'

DAVID ORMEROD

Most critics who have written on the subject of *Much Ado about Nothing* seem agreed that the play must take its pace in Shakespeare's incessant debate about the conflict between appearance and reality, and the difficulties which beset an individual when he attempts to make a right choice, particularly in love, between superficial seeming and inner truth. Few readers, I imagine, would quarrel with the following verdict:

Shakespeare's ideas about love's truth – the imaginative acting of a lover and the need for our imaginative response to it, the compulsion, individuality, and complexity of a lover's realization of beauty, and *the distinctions between inward and outward beauty, appearance and reality, and fancy and true affection* – all are represented in *Much Ado about Nothing*; they inform its structure, its contrasts, relationships, and final resolution; they control many of the details of its action, characterization, humour, and dialogue. Indeed, in fashioning these elements into a lively, dramatic whole, Shakespeare achieved his most concerted and considered judgment upon love's truth.[1]

I agree with this reading, and would like to attempt to amplify it by using a methodology pioneered by Miss Dorothy Hockey.[2] Taking her stand upon Helge Kökeritz's treatment of Richard Grant White's suggestion that the play's title may contain a pun upon 'Nothing' and 'noting',[3] Miss Hockey reads the play as an extended treatment of the implications of this pun, and examines in detail all the occasions during the play when attention to the act of 'noting', of eavesdropping and observing,

enhances our understanding of the play's structure and morality.[4] I do not wish to quarrel with Miss Hockey's conclusions.[5] Rather, I would like to draw attention to an occasion in the play when Shakespeare makes an explicit identification of the word 'Nothing', and then to follow the appearances of 'Nothing's' alias throughout the play. Here, in a scene of central importance for the resolution of the story, and at almost the exact centre of the play's extent in time, we hear Conrade and Borachio in earnest discussion. They are talking about the conspiracy directed against Hero and Claudio; they are also choosing to talk about it, very incongruously, in terms of fashion.

Borachio. . . . Thou knowest that the fashion of a doublet, or a hat, or a cloak, is nothing to a man.
Conrade. Yes, it is apparel.
Borachio. I mean the fashion.
Conrade. Yes, the fashion is the fashion.
Borachio. Tush, I may as well say the fool's the fool. But seest thou not what a deformed thief this fashion is?

[1] John Russell Brown, *Shakespeare and his Comedies* (London, 1957), p. 109 [my italics].
[2] Dorothy Hockey, 'Notes, notes, forsooth . . .' *Shakespeare Quarterly*, VIII (1957), 353–8.
[3] Helge Kökeritz, *Shakespeare's Pronunciation* (New Haven, 1953), pp. 132, 233, 320.
[4] For a detailed examination of the 'Nothing' of the play's title, see P. A. Jorgensen, *Redeeming Shakespeare's Words* (Berkeley, 1962), pp. 22–42.
[5] Her verdict that 'The play . . . is a dramatization of mis-noting – a sort of dramatized, rather than verbal, pun' ('Notes, notes, forsooth . . .', p. 354), seems to me impeccable.

(*2 Watchman*. I know that Deformed, a' has been a vile thief this seven year, a' goes up and down like a gentleman: I remember his name . . .

Borachio. Seest thou not, I say, what a deformed thief this fashion is? how giddily a' turns about all the hot-bloods between fourteen and five-and-thirty? sometimes fashioning them like Pharaoh's soldiers in the reechy painting, sometime like god Bel's priests in the old church window, sometime like the shaven Hercules in the smirched worm-eaten tapestry, where his codpiece seems as massy as his club?

Conrade. All this I see, and I see that the fashion wears out more apparel than the man . . . But art not thou thyself giddy with the fashion too, that thou hast shifted out of thy tale into telling me of the fashion?

Borachio. Not so neither . . .   (III, iii, 114–39)[1]

Several facts strike us. Borachio insists that the plot against Hero is intimately linked with the idea of fashion, and firmly repudiates Conrade's suggestion that, by invoking the machinations of fashion, he is digressing. We note, in passing, that fashion is associated with the decline of Hercules (see below, pp. 96–7, 99–100, 104–5). And, again, the Watch, in its own fumbling way, immediately recognises the villainous role which fashion plays in society, and elevates it to the stature of some Spenserian allegorical figure. An attentive reading of the play fully confirms Borachio and the Watch in the importance they attach to fashion. This essay contends that fashion, in its guise of Deformed, the vile thief, is the real villain of the play, and that its destructive function is recognised to a greater or lesser extent by many of the play's characters.

According to Bartlett, Spevack, and the Oxford Concordance, the word 'fashion' occurs nineteen times in *Much Ado About Nothing*; 'fashions', 'fashioned', and 'fashioning' each occur once. The only other plays in which the word figures at all prominently are *Hamlet* and *Julius Caesar*, with seven occurrences each. In *Much Ado*, Shakespeare has used the word in a number of senses, all of which are pejorative, and which seem to

encompass the following meanings, as given by the *OED*.

As a noun –

1. The action or process of making. Hence, the 'making' or workmanship as an element in the value of plate or jewellery.

2. Make, build, shape. Hence, in wider sense, visible characteristics, appearance.

7. Conventional usage in dress, mode of life, etc., *esp.* as observed in the upper circles of society; conformity to this usage. Often personified, or quasi-personified.

10. *The fashion:* a. The mode of dress, etiquette, furniture, style of speech, etc., adopted in a society for the time being.

And, in a verbal sense –

3b. To counterfeit, pervert. [*OED* here cites *Much Ado*, I, iii, 27]

Just as Othello's Venice (and Shylock's Venice, too) provides us with an icon of a society totally given up to gross commercial criteria, a society which assesses human beings in terms of money, jewels, and outward appearance, so Messina is ruled by fashion, and the individual must learn to distinguish between externals, which are misleading and often downright vicious, and the internal truth. So, Beatrice, in her search for a husband, is in a dilemma – how is she to see through the fashionable exterior in order to attain a true assessment of the real man beneath? In antithesis to 'fashion', which must be recognised and shunned as a corrupting force, the play establishes the opposing entity of 'faith'.[2] This

---

[1] Sir Arthur Quiller-Couch and John Dover Wilson (eds.), *Much Ado about Nothing* (Cambridge, 1923, repr. 1953), to which edition all subsequent citations refer. Quotations from the other plays are from Charles Jasper Sisson (ed.), *William Shakespeare: The Complete Works* (London, 1953).

[2] This semantic antithesis, upon which the remaining analysis of the play rests, was pointed out to me more than ten years ago by Mr E. L. Jones, of Magdalen College, Oxford, and I most gratefully acknowledge my debt to him. I would also like to thank Professor Jay L. Halio and Mr John Ingledew, who have read the manuscript with friendly severity.

is, of course, but one aspect of Shakespeare's perennial love-ethic, which relies closely on the faculty of independent choice.

Things base and vile, holding no quantity
Love can transpose to form and dignity.
Love looks not with the eyes, but with the mind . . .

(*MND*, I, i, 232–4)

In *Much Ado*, faith and mind seem to be synonymous, in contrast to appearance, which deceives. This motif is too well recognised to need elaborate development, but we will immediately think of Desdemona's unselfish and virtuous love (she 'saw Othello's visage in his mind' (I, iii, 253)), of Cressida's lament upon the fickleness of women, easily led astray by the evidence of their eyes,[1] and of the aphoristic treatment of the doctrine in *The Merchant of Venice* –

So may the outward show be least ourselves
The world is still deceived with ornament.

(III, ii, 73–4)

Faith is judgement and eyesight supplemented by imagination, so that we can 'apprehend / More than cool reason ever comprehends' (v, i, 5–6). The opposite, romantic love,[2] is ultimately bestial: Venus urges Adonis to adopt the ethic of his horse, and Titania becomes a sort of Pasiphae – in the midst of a labyrinthine wood (there is even a character called Theseus) we encounter a monster with a human body and an animal's head.

So, 'the fashion of a doublet . . . is nothing to a man' – appearances don't count. The man, not his clothes, is what matters. But Claudio is deceived by Margaret's disguise, for fashion, which deforms, is a thief, and Margaret disguises herself to steal Hero's honour. As Hero is deceived by Don Pedro's disguise, Claudio is deceived by the disguises which the ladies adopt at the end of the play.[3] Don John, in accordance with his role of 'plain-dealing villain', is not fooled by disguise, but rather, he employs disguise – hence he pretends to be

duped by Claudio's disguise at the masked ball, in order to confide a secret to him. Fashion is a sinister conspiracy. Don Pedro's plot to bring Beatrice and Benedick together – 'I would fain have it a match – and doubt not but to fashion it' (II, i, 344–5) – counterpoints Borachio's plot to alienate Claudio and Hero – '. . . I shall so fashion the matter, that Hero shall be absent, and there shall appear such seeming truth of Hero's disloyalty, that jealousy shall be called assurance, and all the preparation overthrown' (II, ii, 43–6). The sinister aspect of the word is amply conveyed by Don John, for '. . . it better fits my blood to be disdained of all than to fashion a carriage to rob love from any . . .' (I, iii, 27–8) – yet, in a sense, this is just what he does.

To step outside the criteria of the fashionable world is to invite its censure. So, for instance, Hero speaks critically of Beatrice's contempt for her foppish suitors –

Ursula.
Sure, sure, such carping is not commendable.
Hero.
No, nor to be so odd and from all fashions,
As Beatrice is, cannot be commendable.

(III, i, 71–3)

It is most appropriate that the bride Hero should condemn the unfashionable Beatrice in such jargon, for, to the frivolous characters of the play, marriage is equated with a fashionable

[1] Ah poor our sex, this fault in us I find,
The error of our eye directs our mind.
What error leads, must err. O then conclude
Minds swayed by eyes are full of turpitude.

(v, ii, 109–12)

[2] I employ the term as it is understood, passim, by Denis de Rougemont in *Love in the Western World* (New York, 1956).

[3] There is a slight parallel with *The Winter's Tale*. Hermione and Hero feign death in order to awaken shame in the lovers who suspected them unjustly; Leontes and Claudio find reborn love and greater self-knowledge when they have supposedly learnt their lesson, and the awakening of Hermione's statue parallels the removal of Hero's mask.

garment. Leonato wishes to see Beatrice 'one day fitted with a husband', which, if we discount the lewd joke, is tantamount to saying that a man is no more than the clothes he wears. Beatrice peremptorily dismisses this attitude when she rejects Don Pedro's jocular offer of marriage – 'your grace is too costly to wear every day' (II, i, 307–8). This discussion is paralleled quite soon by the discussion which Hero and her attendants have on the subject of her approaching marriage, for their attention is concentrated, not upon the institution itself, but upon an external –

Margaret. I like the new tire within excellently if the hair were a thought browner: and your gown's a most rare fashion i'faith. I saw the Duchess of Milan's gown that they praise so –
Hero. O, that exceeds, they say.
Margaret. By my troth's but a night-gown in respect of yours – cloth o'gold and cuts, and laced with silver, set with pearls down sleeves, side sleeves, and skirts, round underborne with a bluish tinsel – but for a fine quaint graceful and excellent fashion, yours is worth ten on't.   (III, iv, 12–22)

Hero's wedding preparations ('. . . I'll show thee some attires, and have thy counsel / Which is the best to furnish me tomorrow' (III, i, 102–3)) should prepare us for the tragic and violent outcome of the wedding day, as should the words of Don Pedro to Claudio when the latter offers to escort him to Aragon immediately after the ceremony, for Pedro, too, speaks of marriage as a garment: 'Nay, that would be as great a soil in the gloss of your marriage, as to show a child his new coat and forbid him to wear it' (III, ii, 5–7). Claudio and Hero are entirely creatures of the eye, not of the mind. Claudio can mistake Margaret for Hero because the latter is only a dressed-up nothing, identifiable only by her clothes. Hero's name (which does not occur in any of the sources)[1] is pathetic – the devoted Leander is contrasted with the fickle Claudio. As we might expect,

Claudio is a slave to fashion, and Benedick elaborates on this:

. . . I have known when he would have walked ten miles afoot, to see a good armour, and now will he lie ten nights awake carving the fashion of a new doublet: he was wont to speak plain, and to the purpose (like an honest man and a soldier) and now he is turned orthography – his words are a very fantastical banquet, just so many strange dishes.   (II, iii, 12–21)

In the terminology of the play, this is very strong condemnation indeed, and serves to lead us to a discussion of a minor but insistent motif – the function of the frequent allusions to Hercules and Blind Cupid, whom I take to be the tutelary deities associated with faith and fashion respectively. Hercules is, of course, synonymous with courage, manliness, and honesty, and Beatrice laments that the society of Messina will not tolerate the Herculean virtues, but speedily corrupts them. The virtuous Hercules was, of course, an iconological figure which was instantly recognisable to Shakespeare's audience. 'In the Renaissance Hercules was one of the two or three best-known mythological personages, the subject of paintings, tapestries, engravings, drawings, sculptures, plays, poems, learned treatises, emblems, adages, schoolboy essays, and countless incidental allusions.'[2] The immediate significance of the Hercules allusions is obvious, and springs from his association with the Twelve Labours.[3] So, when the characters of

[1] See Geoffrey Bullough (ed.), *Narrative and Dramatic Sources of Shakespeare* (London, 1958), II, 61–139.
[2] Richard Knowles, 'Myth and Type in *As You Like It*', E.L.H., XXXIII (1966), 3.
[3] 'In the Renaissance Hercules' physical power came to symbolize any other kind of heroic strength, whether moral, religious, or intellectual. This wide range of symbolic meanings had grown within the medieval tradition of allegorical commentary on pagan myths that culminated in the encyclopedic *Ovide Moralisé* and Pierre Bersuire's *Ovidius Moralizatus*. In the Renaissance, Ovidian commentaries by Raphael

Much Ado point out that Hercules is an unpopular deity in Messina, they are also indicating that the values associated with him are in desuetude. Borachio has pointed out that in Messina the cod-piece of 'shaven Hercules' takes precedence over his club, but it is Beatrice who indicates the reason for this decline.

Princes and counties! Surely a princely testimony, a goodly count, Count Comfect – a sweet gallant surely. O that I were a man for his sake! or that I had any friend would be a man for my sake! But manhood is melted into curtsies, valour into complement, and men are only turned into tongue, and trim ones too: he is now as valiant as Hercules, that only tells a lie and swears it ... (IV, i, 314–21)

The speech is crucial. Perhaps, as Benedick indicates, Claudio was once a Hercules – at the beginning of the play, after all, we hear of him 'doing in the figure of a lamb the feats of a lion' (I, i, 14–15) – but Messina has proved his Omphale. Dressed in elegant, fashionable clothes, the young men of Messina have been metaphorically castrated, their former valour metamorphosed into trivial social accomplishments; fashion, the thief, has deformed them. As Omphale clad Hercules in feminine garments and set him to spin amongst her women, so has Messina unmanned her warriors, and Beatrice in search of a husband finds herself surrounded by effeminate boys.[2] Such a one is of no use to her – 'What should I do with him? dress him in my apparel and make him my waiting gentlewoman?' (II, i, 31–2). She has no desire herself to play Omphale,[3] for 'he who has no beard is less than a man,' and such a one is Claudio. Benedick so taunts him to his face – 'My Lord Lackbeard' (IV, i, 187). We note that when the plan, conceived by Pedro and Claudio, to bring Beatrice and Benedick into 'a mountain of affection' seems to be succeeding, the conspirators discuss Benedick's alleged symptoms in terms of appearance, clothes, fashion, disguises, and the shaving off of beards (III, ii, 29–45).

But effeminacy and fashionableness are not just trivial lapses from grace – they are heinous sins, and from the fashionable syndrome can come bloody events. In the play, this is conveyed partly by the antagonism between generations. While Leonato and Antonio share in the general moral decline, there is yet a sense in which they are not as far gone in triviality as is Claudio himself; it is the younger generation which has most completely succumbed to the temptation to pursue the fashionable, which is, by definition, ephemeral and mutable. Leonato, for instance, sees himself, however waywardly, as embodying older, simpler, and more virtuous modes of conduct. Hence, when he

Regius and Georgius Sabinus, mythographical compendia by Alexander ab Alexandro, Lilio Giraldo, Natalis Comes, Vincenzo Cartari, and Cesare Ripa, and treatises like Coluccio Salutati's *De Laboribus Herculis* and Giraldo's *Herculis Vita*, not to mention the countless artistic treatments that these helped engender, represented Hercules as the supreme exemplar of moral fortitude ... and of virtuous works, as typified by his twelve or more Labors' (*ibid.*, pp. 14–15).

[1] In Ovid's Ninth Heroic Epistle, Deianira upbraids Hercules for allowing Omphale to steal his arms and masquerade as a man. 'To her passes the full measure of your exploits – yield up what you possess; your mistress is heir to your praise. O shame, that the rough skin stripped from the flanks of the shaggy lion has covered a woman's delicate side!' (Ovid, *Heroides and Amores*, trans. Grant Showerman [Harvard, 1921], p. 117.)

[2] 'Largely because of Ovid's Ninth Heroic Epistle, well known in George Turberville's translation, Hercules brought from club to distaff ... had become the proverbial example of the power and folly of love' (Knowles, 'Myth and Type', p. 8).

[3] Unlike Cleopatra, who clothed Antony in her own garments at one juncture (II, v, 17–21). Antony, of course, is closely identified with Hercules (I, iii, 84; IV, iii, 16; IV, xii, 43–4). See Eugene M. Waith, *The Herculean Hero* (London, 1962), pp. 113–21. However, Benedick at one point fears that Beatrice, because of her shrewishness, may prove a very dynamic Omphale: 'She would have made Hercules have turned spit, yea, and have cleft his club to make the fire too ... You shall find her the infernal Ate in good apparel' (II, i, 235–8).

challenges Claudio to a duel, and derides his 'nice fence', he is not only being contemptuous of the new-fangled rapier (a young man's weapon), but is taking the two contrasting styles of fencing to embody a moral antithesis. Antonio develops this line of thought:

> *Leonato.*
> If thou kill'st me, boy, thou shalt kill a man.
> *Antonio.*
> He shall kill two of us, and men indeed –
> ... Win me and wear me! Let him answer me.
> Come follow me, boy, come sir boy, come follow
> me.
> Sir boy, I'll whip you from your foining fence ...
> Content yourself, God knows I loved my niece,
> And she is dead, slandered to death by villains,
> That dare as well answer a man indeed
> As I dare take a serpent by the tongue.
> Boys, apes, braggarts, Jacks, milksops! ...
> Hold you content. What, man! I know them, yea,
> And what they weigh, even to the utmost scruple –
> Scambling, out-facing, fashion-monging boys,
> That lie, and cog, and flout, deprave and slander,
> Go anticly, and show outward hideousness,
> How they might hurt their enemies, if they durst,
> And this is all.   (v, i, 79–99)

It is significant that Antonio identifies Claudio's treachery directly with his subservience to fashion; he is capable of slandering a woman to death in this cowardly way, but loth to fight real men, precisely *because* he is a 'fashion-monging boy'. The same phrase is used to identify moral turpitude with fashion among the young when Mercutio denounces Tybalt in *Romeo and Juliet*:

> The pox of such antic lisping affecting fantasticoes, these new tuners of accent! By Jesu a very good blade – a very tall man – a very good whore! Why, is not this a lamentable thing, grandsire, that we should thus be afflicted with these strange flies, these fashion-mongers, these pardon-me's, who stand so much on the new form that they cannot sit at ease on the old bench?
>   (II, iv, 28–35)

And the fashionable fantasticoes are ubiquitous – Claudio has many of their accom-

plishments. Challenged to a duel by Benedick, Claudio paraphrases his acceptance in a peculiar jargon '... he hath bid me to a calf's-head and a capon, the which if I do not carve most curiously, say my knife's nought' (v, i, 151–3) – for presumably he prides himself on his ability to carve intricately at table, another fashionable accomplishment. The orchard, in which so much of the eavesdropping and conspiring takes place, is 'pleached', recalling the Spenserian and Shakespearian commonplace of the moral antagonism embodied in the nature *versus* art antithesis, almost as if we can see, in the pleached branches, a faint analogy to the Bower of Bliss, with its rejection of nature for artifice; to the artificial court of Leontes rejecting the pastoral simplicity of Bohemia, and so on. Don Pedro says something in much the same vein when he commends Leonato for his hospitality, for '... the fashion of the world is to avoid cost, and you encounter it' (I, i, 92–3), and the fashion of the world (presumably at least in part the dictates of contemporary social mores) is opposed to hospitality and solicitousness. Don Pedro continues to harp on the difference between seeming and being when he asserts his belief in the sincerity of Leonato's wish that something should occur to prolong the visit to Messina – 'I dare say he is no hypocrite, but prays from his heart' (I, i, 144–5).

Yet the play provides a polar opposite to the vices of shallowness, triviality, pettiness, volatility, and wrong choice embodied by fashion. This antithesis is contained in the word 'faith'. To distinguish between faith and fashion is the task which Beatrice has imposed upon herself, and her initial inquiries about Benedick indicate that she is seriously concerned to discover whether he is a man of fashion or a man of faith, for, if he is the latter, he is worthy of her regard and her love. The deep commitment with which she undertakes this dialectical search contrasts dramatically with the opportunistic and trivial questions with which Claudio initiates his own courtship. Thus she questions the Messenger concerning Benedick in the following way: '. . . I pray you, how many hath he killed and eaten in these wars? But how many hath he killed? for indeed I promised to eat all of his killing . . . He is a very valiant trencherman, he hath an excellent stomach' (I, i, 36–49). She wishes to know if Benedick is a braggart soldier, a fashionable fop who only pretends to be manly. How is one to know the real man from his words? She goes on to accuse Benedick of fickleness in friendship, and introduces the fashion image in one of its most important guises by making it synonymous with inconstancy:

Beatrice. . . . Who is his companion now? he hath every month a new sworn brother.
Messenger. Is't possible?
Beatrice. Very easily possible. He wears his faith but as the fashion of his hat, it ever changes with the next block.   (I, i, 67–72)

This is obviously an important passage. Benedick, she alleges, equates faith and fashion. This he should not do. In the play's moral framework, it is a very grave offence. A man of faith is a moral Hercules; so, when Benedick professes his friendship for Beatrice after the church scene, she is quick to turn the conversation into the channel already discussed:

Benedick. Is there any way to show such friendship?
Beatrice. A very even way, but no such friend.
Benedick. May a man do it?
Beatrice. It is a man's office, but not yours.
                  (IV, i, 262–5)

For manhood is melted into curtsies; by her gibes, Beatrice attempts to spur Benedick into manly action – to prove he is no Count Comfect. Benedick himself seems to realise the import of Beatrice's order to 'Kill Claudio', for when events absolve him of his promise to fight Claudio, he regards the challenge, in retrospect, as a very basic test:

Antonio.
Well, I am glad that all things sort so well.
Benedick.
And so am I, being else by faith enforced
To call young Claudio to a reckoning for it.
                  (V, iv, 7–9)

Fashion implies wrong choice; faith implies the ability to thread one's way through the moral labyrinth and to attain to right choice. The process, though, is a difficult one. It is hence doubly appropriate that the party of faith should owe allegiance to Hercules, for, although Hercules was important to the Renaissance as a result of the moral glosses traditionally applied to the Twelve Labours, his main importance stems from the story of Hercules's Choice (The Hero at the Fork in the Road).[1] The tale was a commonplace in Shakespeare's day; Cicero's popular *De Officiis* contains a reference to Xenophon's version of the Choice (I, 118),[2] and was a widespread school Latin text. Nicholas Grimald's translation was printed nine times between 1553 and 1600.[3] Geoffrey Whitney's *A Choice of Emblems* represents Hercules's dilemma graphically,[4] and 'The plainness of Lady Virtue and the gaudiness of Lady Vice led to allegorical interpretations of the two figures beyond their obvious significances'.[5] The story was originally derived from Hesiod's *Works and Days*,[6] which adumbrates the idea of two roads in life. The addition of making the roads cross, placing the hero at their intersection, and providing each road with its advocate, was effected by the sophist Prodicus, and Socrates's account in Xenophon's *Memora-*

[1] See Richard Knowles, 'Myth and Type', passim, and Hallett Smith, *Elizabethan Poetry* (Harvard, 1952), pp. 295–7.
[2] Cicero, *De Officiis*, trans. Walter Miller (London, 1913), p. 121.
[3] Smith, *Elizabethan Poetry*, p. 295.
[4] See Henry Green's reprint (London, 1866) of the Plantyn edition of 1586, p. 40.
[5] Smith, *Elizabethan Poetry*, p. 297.
[6] See Richard Hooper's edition of George Chapman's translation (London, 1888), I, ll. 449–63.

bilia presents Vice and Virtue in contrasting robes.[1] Athenaeus goes so far as to elevate the choice of Hercules to the level of the most famous of such dilemmas.[2] But the most appropriate version of the story for our purposes, emphasising the garb of Hercules's suppliants, is provided in the third century by Philostratus. 'You have seen in picture-books the representation of Hercules by Prodicus; in it Hercules is represented as a youth, who has not yet chosen the life he will lead; and vice and virtue stand on each side of him plucking his garments and trying to draw him to themselves. Vice is adorned with gold and necklaces and with purple raiment, and her cheeks are painted and her hair delicately plaited and her eyes underlined with henna; and she also wears golden slippers, for she is pictured strutting about in these; but virtue in the picture resembles a woman worn out with toil, with a pinched look; and she has chosen for her adornment rough squalor, and she goes without shoes and in the plainest of raiment, and she would have appeared naked if she had not too much regard for feminine decency.'[3] Ben Jonson, in *Pleasure Reconciled to Virtue*, presents the demi-god's choice simply and didactically –

First, figure out the doubtfull way,
    at which, a while all youth shold stay,
    where she [i.e., Pleasure] and Vertue did contend,
    which should haue Hercules to frend.[4]

The issue of making a correct choice in such complex matters is hence central to the play's morality; Beatrice, for instance, initiates her courtship by denigrating Benedick with the object of finding out what inner qualities he possesses. Claudio opens his courtship of Hero by inquiring after, and remarking upon, her external qualities. For instance, he has 'noted' the daughter of Leonato. Benedick 'noted her not, but I looked on her' (I, i, 155–6) – a reproach, which he amplifies in answer to

Claudio's further queries: 'Would you buy her, that you inquire after her' (I, i, 171). Claudio significantly betrays his materialism in his reply, 'Can the world buy such a jewel?' (I, i, 172). He goes on to praise Hero in sinister language – 'In mine eye, she is the sweetest lady that ever I looked on' (I, i, 178–9) – an outrageous remark in Shakespeare's world, where love should look not with the eyes but with the mind. Since Claudio is the acme of fashion, which, by definition, stands for all that is ephemeral, then his love will be subject to Time's ravages, and he confesses as much – 'If my passion change not shortly' (I, i, 207). Again, in the same vein, Claudio announces 'That I love her I feel' (I, i, 216), but this is inadequate. He should know, not feel. Don Pedro replies 'That she is worthy I know' (I, i, 217), but Benedick reproves them both when he implicitly points out that neither is as yet in any position to make such sweeping statements; 'That I neither feel how she should be loved, nor know how she should be worthy, is an opinion that fire cannot melt out of me – I will die in it at the stake' (I, i, 218–20). In other

[1] See Xenophon, *Memorabilia and Oecomicus*, trans. E. C. Marchant (London, 1923), p. 95: 'And there appeared two women of great stature making towards him. The one was fair to see and of high bearing; and her limbs were adorned with purity, her eyes with modesty; sober was her figure, and her robe was white. The other was plump and soft, with high feeding. Her face was made up to heighten its natural white and pink, her figure to exaggerate her height. Open-eyed was she; and dressed so as to disclose all her charms.'

[2] See Athenaeus, *The Deipnosophists*, trans. C. B. Gulick (Harvard, 1933), V, 295: 'And I for one affirm also that the Judgement of Paris, as told in poetry by the writers of an older time, is really a trial of pleasure against virtue ... I think, too, that our noble Xenophon invented the story of Heracles and Virtue with the same motive.'

[3] Philostratus, *The Life of Apollonius of Tyana*, trans. F. C. Conybeare (London, 1912), II, 33–5.

[4] C. H. Herford and Percy and Evelyn Simpson (eds.), *Works of Ben Jonson* (Oxford, 1941), VII, 488, ll. 257–60.

words this opinion is, metaphorically, an article of faith for which he is prepared to suffer martyrdom. Claudio, Leonato, and Don Pedro all lack faith in Hero, and can therefore believe her to be unfaithful to Claudio. Beatrice and the Friar, on the contrary, are paragons of faith, and adhere to a belief in Hero's innocence when the evidence points to the opposite. Claudio, too, easily loses faith in his leader over the business of the courtship, for he is a creature who knows only the outward appearances of things. He can talk of Hero's '*show of truth*' – 'you *seemed* to me as Dian . . .' or 'If half the *outward* graces had been placed . . .' Claudio often mixes semblance and reality. Hero was fair and virtuous 'in my semblance'; from this she can speedily degenerate to 'but the sign and semblance of her honour'. Claudio's remark to the effect that 'I love her I feel' is a great self-indictment. A man who makes such a remark asks others to confirm his judgement and to act for him; appropriate in view of the man of fashion's subservience to the dictates of society. He provides a great contrast to Benedick, who requires no official imprimatur from society to sanctify his intentions:

. . . since I do purpose to marry, I will think nothing to any purpose that the world can say against it.

(v, iv, 103–5)

Again this sturdy pronouncement we might set Claudio's vacillatory and crab-wise approach to the same truth:

Let every *eye* negotiate for itself,
And trust no agent: for *beauty* is a witch
Against whose charms *faith* melteth into blood

(II, i, 165–7)

culminating in his eventual determination to honour his vow to marry an unknown bride: 'I'll hold my *mind*, were she an Ethiope' (v, iv, 38 – my italics).

The Shakespearian virtues do not reside in princes' courts. Guiderius and Arviragus grow up in naive but robust innocence in the harsh pastoral of the Welsh hills; the exiled Duke of *As You Like It* finds the winter pastoral of Arden more conducive to virtue than the court he has lost, and Sicily, the traditional home of pastoral, is blighted by the suspicions of Leontes and becomes a wasteland, only to be renewed by the Bohemian pastoral figures of Perdita and Florizel. There is no pastoral scene in *Much Ado* to provide an antidote to the sterile and fashionable court, no setting for the *vita contemplativa* to which the characters can retire in order to understand themselves better. Instead, we have the laughable but laudable simplicity of the Watch. These people may be unlettered, but their unfashionable uncouthness, their upside-down euphuism, ensures that they keep the basic virtues intact. As Borachio realises bitterly: 'What your wisdoms could not discover, these shallow fools have brought to light' (v, i, 226–9). Fashionable people are less perspicacious than the Watch, who are fully informed of the machinations of Deformed, the fashionable thief, and who are introduced at the first line of their appearance by Dogberry's question, 'Are you good men and true?' and by Verges's affirmative 'Yea' (III, iii, 1–2). Their simplicity is echoed by the Friar, who is a visual icon of faith, refusing to be deceived by appearances. In his home-spun raiment, the Friar provides a simple visible exemplum of the abjuration of fashion, and his religious faith parallels the more secular faith of Beatrice. We think of the Duke-as-Friar of *Measure for Measure*, repairing Angelo's broken faith with Mariana. The Friar and Claudio, faith and fashion, stand over the prostrate Hero like some emblem graphically representing sagacity and credulity. The whole image is a fitting culmination to the plot which Borachio concocted, a plot held together by the recurring words 'appear . . . paint . . . show . . . seem . . . seeming truth'. The very language of the play embodies this urgent dichotomy.

'The body of your discourse is sometime guarded with fragments ...' (I, i, 268–9), for truth is disguised with elegant rhetorical fol-de-rols, just as Claudio is 'turned orthography'. Hence the often noticed contrast between the masculine strength of the play's prose, and the strained, feeble nature of the verse.

We have constantly attempted to identify faith and its attendant values with the mythological figure of Hercules. Fashion also has its patron deity, and it is hardly surprising for the student of Renaissance iconology that this should be Blind Cupid. Don Pedro and Claudio at one point taunt Benedick that he will one day be in love, despite his protests. But they predicate of love all the symptoms of the Petrarchan madness: 'I shall see thee, ere I die, look pale with love' (I, i, 233). Benedick retorts that if ever he is in such a state, then 'hang me up at the door of a brothel house for the sign of Blind Cupid', for to him the passion they champion is associated with brothels and Blind Cupid. 'According to the standards of traditional iconography ... the blindness of Cupid puts him definitely on the wrong side of the moral world.'[1] The love which Claudio and Don Pedro recommend must therefore be accorded its place in the whole Renaissance pageant of illicit love for which Blind Cupid is the patron, and which is most vividly represented by Spenser's 'Masque of Cupid'. The debate is a constant one in Shakespeare; Claudio and Don Pedro are the allies of one of the poet's earliest creations, the Venus who attempts to convert the chaste Adonis to her metaphysic of lust. Don Pedro even seems to give a grudging approval to Benedick's stand: '... if ever thou dost fall from this faith, thou wilt prove a notable argument' (I, i, 240–1). It is appropriate that Claudio should ask if Leonato has a son. He is told that Hero is Leonato's only heir, and indulges in words reminiscent of Gloucester (who was literally deformed) at the beginning of *Richard III*: 'War thoughts / Have left their places vacant ... in their rooms / Come thronging soft and delicate desires, / All prompting me how fair young Hero is ...' (I, i, 279–89). We do not hear the lascivious pleasings of a lute, but Claudio has unconsciously elaborated on Benedick's gentle denunciation. He lusts after Hero's body, and will marry her for her fortune – lust and money, Blind Cupid and brothels. Soon Claudio is the embodiment of the state which has been maliciously predicted for Benedick, and in his Petrarchan attitudinising he remarks that Don Pedro is one of those 'that know love's grief by his complexion!' (I, i, 296). And Don Pedro is as blind as his protégé. 'If Cupid have not spent all his quiver in Venice, thou wilt quake for this shortly' (I, i, 255–6), he threatens Benedick, locating his deity firmly in the city of commerce and courtesans. Don Pedro's matchmaking is a fashionable pastime – Blind Cupid's love-in-idleness, to borrow an attitude from *Venus and Adonis* – and he wishes to bring Beatrice and Benedick into 'a mountain of affection' (II, i, 343), just as Claudio 'affects' Hero. Indeed, Don Pedro goes so far as to hope that he surpasses his deity – 'If we can do this, Cupid is no longer an archer ... for we are the only love gods' (II, i, 361–3).

Claudio's headlong and precipitate rush into a fashionable marriage is the sort of conduct we would expect from a devotee of Blind Cupid:

> And therefore is wing'd Cupid painted blind
> Nor hath love's mind of any judgment taste;
> Wings and no eyes figure unheedy haste:
> And therefore is love said to be a child,
> Because in choice he is so oft beguil'd ...
>
> (*MND*, I, i, 235–9)

Cupid is traditionally *alatus et caecus*, and Claudio and Benedick must be associated with

[1] Erwin Panofsky, *Studies in Iconology* (Oxford, 1939, rev. ed. New York, 1962), p. 109. See esp. ch. IV, 'Blind Cupid', pp. 95–128. For a list of Shakespeare's allusions to this deity, see p. 112, n. 55.

'blind' and 'clear-sighted' love respectively, with Eros and Anteros.[1]

Yet Eros and Anteros are aspects of the same personality. Panofsky cites a representation (by Lucius Cranach the Elder) of Blind Cupid removing his own blindfold – passing from moral blindness to enlightenment. In this representation, Cupid is standing, very significantly, upon a large volume labelled *Platonis Opera*.[2]

Platonic thought was familiar with the concept of two loves, one base, the other admirable, and in the *Symposium* Plato, through the words of Pausanias, describes these under the guise of two Venuses. 'The elder one, having no mother, who is called the heavenly Aphrodite – she is the daughter of Uranus; the younger, who is the daughter of Zeus and Dione – her we call common, and the love who is her fellow-worker is rightly named common, as the other love is called heavenly.'[3] Iconologically, there was a precedent for depicting the higher goddess as nude, to denote not eroticism, but freedom from vanity.[4] The lower goddess could be depicted as clothed in opulent, fashionable garments, to denote her involvement with the passing vanities of this world. '. . . the clothed Venus is the *Venere vulgare* or *Aphrodite Pandemos*, whom Plato and the Platonists opposed to the *Aphrodite Urania* (*Venere celeste*) . . .'[5] Yet the two goddesses are not polar opposites. Rather, man can ascend to the higher love through the agency of the lower. Being distracted by the beauty of garments is itself a Platonic metaphor denoting preoccupation with the body (the soul's garment) at the expense of the soul. Hence Claudio, who must rise above considerations of flesh and fashion, pursues within the confines of the play a process of initiation commonplace in Platonic thought, and most accessibly described in Castiglione's *The Courtier* or Spenser's *Platonic Hymns*. The aspiring lover must learn to spurn *amore bestiale*, transcend

amore umano, and attain the heights of *amore celeste* (to borrow the terminology of Pico della Mirandola). So, the first two steps up the Platonic ladder, as described by Bembo, constitute a transition from the purely physical craving for the beloved object, to a realisation of the beloved's image in the mind's eye:

To avoid therefore the torment of his absence, and to enjoy beautie without passion, the Courtier by the helpe of reason must full and wholy call backe againe the coveting of the bodie to beautie alone, and (in what he can) beholde it in it selfe simple and pure, and frame it within in his imagination sundred from all matter, and so make it friendly and loving to his soule, and there enjoy it, and having it with him day and night, in every time and place, without mistrust ever to lose it: keeping alwaies fast in minde, that the bodie is a most diverse thing from beautie, and not onely not encreaseth, but diminisheth the perfection of it . . . And beside, through the vertue of imagination, hee shall fashion with himselfe that beautie much more faire than it is in deede.[6]

[1] Panofsky, *Studies in Iconology*, pp. 126–7.
[2] *Ibid.*, p. 128.
[3] Irwin Edman (ed.), *The Works of Plato* (New York, 1956), pp. 343–4.
[4] Cf. Panofsky, *Studies in Iconology*, p. 155: '*Nuda virtus* is the real virtue appreciated in the good old days when wealth and social distinction did not count, and Horace speaks already of *nuda Veritas*, though the Greek writers, characteristically enough, rather imagined Truth as dressed in simple garments.'
[5] Edgar Wind, *Pagan Mysteries in the Renaissance* (London, 1958), p. 118.
[6] Baldassare Castiglione, *The Book of the Courtier*, trans. Sir Thomas Hoby (London, 1928), p. 317. Hoby's translation first appeared in 1561, and was reissued during Shakespeare's lifetime in the editions of 1577 and 1588, of which the latter edition is trilingual in Italian, French, and English. It has, incidentally, been suggested (somewhat implausibly) that Benedick and Beatrice are modelled on two of Castiglione's characters, the Lord Gaspare Pallavicino and the Lady Emilia Pia. See Mary Augusta Scott, 'The Book of the Courtier: a Possible Source of Benedick and Beatrice', *PMLA*, XVI (1901), 475–502. Since the initial composition of this current essay, however, an important and convincing article on the relationship between *The Courtier* and *Much Ado* has appeared in the form of B. K. Lewalski's 'Love, Appearance and Reality:

Hence, the Friar's plan takes on a new significance:

> When he [i.e. Claudio] shall hear she died upon his words,
> Th'idea of her life shall sweetly creep
> Into his study of imagination,
> And every lovely organ of her life
> Shall come apparelled in more precious habit,
> More moving-delicate and full of life,
> Into the eye and prospect of his soul,
> Than when she lived indeed . . .
> Let this be so, and doubt not but success
> Will fashion the event in better shape . . .
>
> (IV, i, 222–34)

Thus the play's scheme proposes that out of the evil of fashion should be brought forth the good of a higher faith, and the two entities whose antagonism we have scrutinised eventually meet to work in conjunction. We reached this synthesis through an examination of the forces accumulating around the figure of Blind Cupid, but we could perhaps equally well have done so by examining the Hercules-motif in greater detail, for as Wind observes,

Voluptas is appointed to tempt the hero with her specious allurements, while Virtue acquaints him in all her austerity with the arduous prospect of heroic labours: and it may be expected of a reliable Hercules that he will not remain suspended between them. The choice is clear because the two opposites, having been introduced in a complete disjunction, obey the logical principle of the excluded middle: *tertium non datur.* It is the absence of any transcendent alternative which renders the moral so respectable; but although the humanists used it profusely in their exoteric instruction, they left no doubt that, for a Platonic initiate, it was but the crust, and not the marrow . . . In Ben Jonson's *Pleasure Reconciled to Virtue*, a sequence of 'knots' is introduced by the dancing master Daedalus, who interweaves the two opposites in a perfect maze; and his labyrinthian designs are accompanied by a warning that while the 'first figure' should suggest the contrast of Virtue and Pleasure as in the Choice of Hercules, it is the purpose of the dance to 'entwine' Pleasure and Virtue beyond recognition:

> Come on, come on! and where you go,
> So interweave the curious knot,
> As ev'n the observer scarce may know
> Which lines are Pleasure's, and which not.[1]

I am not necessarily trying to contend that *Much Ado* is a neo-Platonic homily. I would simply like to suggest that the play may be profitably examined against the background of such modes of thought. In this way the faith-fashion antithesis may be seen as one aspect of the age's preoccupation with the conflict Much Ado about Something' (*Studies in English Literature*, VIII (1968), 235–51). Lewalski's conclusions substantially parallel (and, in my opinion, vindicate) my own, although she arrives at them by a different route. Noting the ostensible absence of the pastoral element in the play, Lewalski locates it in the higher area of consciousness described by Bembo in Book VI of *The Courtier*, and not, as I do, in the Watch, for whose activities she invokes I Cor. i 27 ('God hath chosen the foolish things of the world to confound the wise'). Lewalski identifies Claudio with Bembo's 'young lover' misled in love-judgments by 'judgement of sense' (p. 240), one who 'acts primarily in terms of sense knowledge rather than reason, and is moved by desire and passion rather than the higher love' (p. 246). Hero's epic death-and-rebirth pattern is seen as an image of Christ's passion and resurrection – 'the archetype of sacrificial love for the restoration of others' (p. 251), and the neo-Platonism is almost explicitly Christianised in the well-observed words of the Friar: 'But on this travail look for greater birth' and 'Come, lady, die to live' (*idem*). Lewalski's conclusion seems to me wholly admirable: 'Only because of these new terms – love as redemptive sacrifice and knowledge as faith – is the Platonic ascent possible for such as Claudio.'

[1] Wind, *Pagan Mysteries in the Renaissance*, pp. 168–9. For our own purposes, an alternative passage from Jonson's masque (Herford and Simpson, *Works of Ben Jonson*, VII, 486–7, ll. 200–13) might be even more appropriate:

> Pleasure, for his [i.e. Hesperus'] delight
> is reconcild to Vertue: and this Night
> Vertue brings forth twelve Princes haue byn bred
> in this rough Mountaine . . .
> Theis now she trusts with Pleasure, and to theis
> she gives an entraunce to the Hesperides,
> faire Beuties gardens: Neither can she feare
> they should grow soft, or wax effeminat here,
> Since in hir sight, and by hir charge all's don,
> Pleasure the Servant, Vertue looking on.

between eternity and mutability, and with the right resolution of this conflict, a resolution which Spenser has mapped in detail in *Epithalamion*, the 'Garden of Adonis', and the 'Mutability Cantos'. This solution argues that, by loving chastely and wisely, man can conquer time, flux and mutability, and transcend them to attain a state wherein he will be, like Spenser's Adonis, 'eterne in mutability'. Shakespeare's Ulysses, of course, has asserted that the arch-villain of the age, time, the Saturnian *edax rerum*, is 'like a fashionable host', but our investigation can perhaps be most suitably concluded by Hallett Smith's oddly apt assertion that, in the heroic poetry of the Renaissance, 'the guiding and predominating motive was that of Virtue, pictured symbolically as the lady whose path Hercules chose to follow, as a kind of Venus–Beatrice of a neo-Platonic scheme'.[1]

[1] Smith, *Elizabethan Poetry*, p. 324. Don Pedro, the play's most ambivalent character, speaks with unconscious irony when he pronounces what might serve us as an alternative epigraph: 'What a pretty thing man is, when he goes in his doublet and hose and leaves off his wit' (v, i, 194–5).

© DAVID ORMEROD 1972

'THE MERRY WIVES OF WINDSOR'
AS A HALLOWE'EN PLAY

JEANNE ADDISON ROBERTS

In trying to define the mood and the artistic movement of Shakespeare's *The Merry Wives of Windsor*, it is provocative to imagine what the season of the setting ought to be. Since much of the action takes place out of doors, the season is important to the realist; and if any symbolic or ritual progress is to be discerned, the season is significant in establishing the tone and in possibly indicating the occasion.

The text of the play itself is not very helpful. 'Birding' is a sport which can be indulged in at any season; and laundry might conceivably be sent to the Thames any time, though certainly spring, summer, and fall are more likely than winter. The reference by Simple (I, i, 211)[1] to the use of a *Book of Riddles* on 'Allhallowmas last' is interesting but inconclusive. And Mistress Page's reference to the fact that Herne the hunter wanders in the winter forest (I, iv, 30) does not necessarily set the season for the current action.

Traditionally *The Merry Wives* has been thought of as a summer play. William Mark Clark, for example, in 1835 spoke lyrically of the 'sylvan splendour of its enchanting scenes' with special reference to Herne's Oak, immortalized 'fresh and green' for succeeding generations.[2] Charles Cowden Clarke in 1863 refers similarly to the visions conjured up in the play of 'leafy nooks' on the Thames, with 'barges lapsing on its tranquil tide'.[3] John Middleton Murry finds the play 'redolent of early summer', with 'the air ... full of May or June'.[4] And

Northrop Frye suggests spring, mentioning the play as an 'elaborate ritual of the defeat of winter'.[5]

All these associations of spring and summer perpetuate in our minds the notion of *The Merry Wives* as a harmless farce or a light-hearted insignificant comedy, whereas, in fact, I believe the action is, though uproariously funny, crucial to the development of our image of Falstaff, and disturbingly shadowed in its conclusion.

Two modern approaches to the seasonal background of the play cast sharp new light on its mood and, I think correctly, illuminate its purpose. By extension, this new view of the play makes possible new speculation about its date of composition and about how it properly relates to *1 Henry IV* and *2 Henry IV*.

Anne Righter in *Shakespeare and The Idea of the Play* refers without elaboration to the 'wintry darkness' of Windsor Park with its 'huge leafless oak'.[6] Possibly following up her suggestion, the Royal Shakespeare Company production of *The Merry Wives* in 1968–70 specifically associated it with Hallowe'en. The program is done in orange and black, and an early set of descriptions of Hallowe'en rites is

---

[1] Line-references are to the Globe Shakespeare.
[2] Ed. *Plays of Shakespeare* (London, 1835), v, 7.
[3] *Shakespeare's Characters* (London, 1863), p. 142.
[4] 'The Creation of Falstaff', *Discoveries* (London, 1924), p. 251.
[5] 'The Argument of Comedy', *English Institute Essays 1948* (New York, 1949), p. 69.
[6] London, 1962, pp. 146, 147.

included in the background materials.[1] The careful student's response to this interpretation is an overwhelming assent. Yes, *The Merry Wives* is a Hallowe'en play. In saying this I do not mean to insist that Shakespeare had Hallowe'en deliberately in mind as the time of the action, although such an interpretation would help account for all those elves and fairies cavorting in the forest, and for Falstaff's disguise. I mean rather to argue that a Hallowe'en setting strikes the right note for the mood of the play.

Hallowe'en, 31 October, is the night before the Christian festival of All Hallows or All Saints Day. But it is also clearly a relic of pagan times. J. G. Frazer in *The Golden Bough* associates the celebration with a Celtic festival of the beginning of the New Year, marking the 'transition from autumn to winter'. It was, he says, a night on which witches, fairies, and hobgoblins were thought to roam freely.[2] *The Merry Wives* is a play about the final fling of mischievous, sometimes dangerous spirits before the dawning of a pious and orderly All Saints' Day. It is also, to use the more primitive implications of the feast, a play about fertility, about the end of one harvest season and the preparation for the next. And it is, for Falstaff at least, a play about the beginning of winter. It is in a very genuine sense a festive comedy,[3] releasing, clarifying, and at the same time poignantly foreshadowing worse days to come.

The mischievous spirit of the play – ranging from mild to malevolent – is abundantly evident. Mistress Ford and Mistress Page trick Falstaff; Mistress Quickly tricks the suitors of Anne Page; Falstaff tricks Ford, who is attempting to trick his wife. Master and Mistress Page attempt to trick each other in arranging Anne's marriage, but Anne succeeds in tricking them both. The Host tricks Sir Hugh. Slender and Caius are tricked by the Pages, and so on. The great majority of the trickery is directly related to sex and marriage; and thus the pranks of the Hallowe'en spirit relate to the more ancient fertility celebration.

Elsewhere[4] I have discussed in some detail the four cardinal enemies of good marriage which are explored in this play: greed, jealousy, stupidity, and lust. All these problems are related in the play to sex and marriage, and all are, at least temporarily recognized, contained, and rendered harmless at the end. With more mercy than justice, the chief offenders, except Falstaff, in each category escape punishment and are forgiven in the final harmonious celebration. The process sounds very much like that described by C. L. Barber as the ritual associated with the scapegoat,[5] where the evils potential in society are recognized and enjoyed (Falstaff shares in all except jealousy) and then driven out.

Barber does not mention this process, however, in regard to this play. He regards *The Merry Wives* simply as a later play (1598–1602) where Shakespeare's creative powers were not 'fully engaged'.[6] The scapegoat ritual is associated by him with the Falstaff of only *1 Henry IV* and *2 Henry IV*. And yet Barber's own description of what happens in *2 Henry IV* sounds much more precisely like a description of *The Merry Wives*:

[1] The production of the play at Stratford, Connecticut, in the summer of 1971, began with townsmen carrying jack o'lanterns and followed through with a Hallowe'en motif in the costume of the 'fairies' in the forest.

[2] London, 1919, Part vii, i, 224–6.

[3] I am using the term as described by C. L. Barber, *Shakespeare's Festive Comedy* (Princeton, 1959), p. 4.

[4] In a forthcoming article, 'The Merry Wives of Windsor: Suitably Shallow but Neither Simple Nor Slender', *Shakespeare Studies*, VI (1971).

[5] *Shakespeare's Festive Comedy*, p. 168. Northrop Frye refers to Falstaff as a scapegoat in *The Anatomy of Criticism* (Princeton, 1957), p. 45. In his paper, 'Falstaff and the Merry Wives' delivered at the Modern Language Association meeting in New York on 29 December 1970, J. A. Bryant further developed the scapegoat associations of the character in this play.

[6] *Ibid.*, p. 222.

To put Carnival on trial, run him out of town, and burn or bury him is in folk custom a way of limiting, by ritual, the attitudes and impulses set loose by ritual. Such a trial, though conducted with gay hoots and jeers, serves to swing the mind round to a new vantage. . . .

From this new vantage, says Barber, misrule is seen not as 'benign release', but as a source of destruction to society.[1] This is exactly what happens in *The Merry Wives*. Inevitably, and a little sadly, the virtuous forces of fidelity and matrimonial love triumph over disruption. Law and order are restored.

The process is not primarily a rational one. Falstaff acts from beginning to end as butt and scapegoat, attracting and personifying the threats to the community. Motivated himself by greed in the beginning, he draws to himself and further incites the jealous Ford, displays considerable stupidity, and finally presents himself as the embodiment of lust, horned and eager for sexual encounters in the forest. Assembled society acts with one accord to disarm him. He is burned, pinched, 'dishorned', deflated, and rendered impotent, literally and figuratively; and then, once he is harmless, invited home for dinner. Having had their fling, the goblins and elves are prepared to be saints on the morrow. Falstaff's 'sacrifice' restores Ford's harmonious potency with his wife, provides the occasion for Anne's successful union with her lover, and restores harmony to the community. On one level the old fertility god is sacrificed; order is restored to marriage; and posterity is assured. On another, rather uglier, level, social forces have focussed their hostilities on a convenient butt, and having vented their explosive power, subside into calm normality.

The situation at the end of *The Merry Wives* is rather like that in *The Merchant of Venice*. In each case the community has chosen an outsider as scapegoat, in each case thoroughly defeated him, and then in each case offered him token membership in the community. The chief difference is that Shylock is a 'kill joy', opposed to the 'holiday' qualities enumerated by Barber,[2] whereas Falstaff is the very embodiment of 'holiday' – drinker, lover, and riotous liver. His defeat in *The Merry Wives* is the inevitable sequel to the defeat of Shylock in *The Merchant of Venice*. Holiday may triumph momentarily; but, as Barber says, misrule must be defeated when it seeks to become an everyday racket.[3] Defeated it is in Windsor forest. If the three Falstaff plays are read in proper order, we see that this scene in the forest foreshadows Falstaff's rejection by Hal at the conclusion of *2 Henry IV*. But I will come back to the question of the proper order.

The process of 'scapegoating', however skillfully portrayed, is a disquieting one to watch. Banding together against an outsider does indeed unite a community, and driving him out does create a temporary sense of unanimity. But it is perhaps the least rational of all means of achieving concord and the most short-lived. It is significant that both these scapegoating plays (*The Merry Wives* and *The Merchant*), in spite of the surface serenity of their endings, leave their audiences with a lingering uneasiness. And it is also significant that when Shakespeare uses the pattern one final time in *Twelfth Night*, he reduces it to a minor position in the resolution of the actions and confines it to lower-class characters. Even so, it is disturbing.

Any attempt to describe the tone, technique, and spirit of *The Merry Wives* must take into account the much-vexed question of its date. Obviously there is no new objective evidence here. But if my estimate of the play's mood and progress is correct, there is artistic argument for the 1597 date proposed by Leslie Hotson,[4] William Green[5] and others.

[1] *Ibid.*, p. 213. [2] *Ibid.*, p. 7. [3] *Ibid.*, p. 14.
[4] *Shakespeare Versus Shallow* (Boston, 1931), p. 111.
[5] *Shakespeare's 'Merry Wives of Windsor'* (Princeton, 1962), p. 192.

Bertrand Evans in his detailed structural analysis[1] has shown how *The Merry Wives* relates in complexity and sophistication of manipulation of audience expectation to *Much Ado About Nothing* and *As You Like It*. Such evidence militates strongly against the early (1592–3) date for the hypothetical 'original' version of the play which has been sporadically suggested by such critics as Charles Knight,[2] Frederick Fleay,[3] and Allan Gilbert.[4] More firmly entrenched among dating theorists is a later date (after 1598). E. K. Chambers proposes 1600–1 as the probable time, after *Henry V* and *Hamlet*;[5] and this date is accepted by W. W. Greg,[6] Barber, J. M. Nosworthy[7] and others. James G. McManaway admits the possibility of an earlier date, or of continuous change from 1597 to 1601 but concludes that certain questions remain unanswerable.[8] Considerable circumstantial evidence for a 1597 date has been amassed by Leslie Hotson, and most recently by William Green. The play's affinity with *The Merchant of Venice* adds some weight to the hypothesis of a 1597 date. It is notable that both comedies relegate the young lovers to sub-plots; both deal with clashes between the mercantile middle-class and the lower aristocracy; in both plays the young girl is courted by three suitors, each with some mercenary interest. Both contain some alternation between town and country. Both are concerned, one explicitly and one implicitly, with the relationship between justice and mercy. And, most important, both deal with the action of society in relation to a scapegoat.

Much more significant in dating than ties with *The Merchant of Venice*, however, is the problem of the relationship between *The Merry Wives* and the two parts of *Henry IV*. The question is one which has been hotly debated by a long line of scholars, and there is no need to rehearse the whole argument here. Nearly everyone agrees that the *Henry IV* plays belong to the period between 1596 and 1598, and that

Falstaff was originally named Sir John Oldcastle, with the name being changed because of a complaint from the Cobham family, whose ancestor was the historical Oldcastle. Reasons for dating *The Merry Wives* later than the *Henry IV* plays have depended as late as Chambers and Greg chiefly on three points: (1) the absence of the play from Meres's list in 1598 in *Palladis Tamia*; (2) the appearance in *The Merry Wives* of *Corporal* Nym, thought necessarily to postdate his appearance in *Henry V* in 1599; and (3) the appearance in *The Merry Wives* Quarto of what Chambers calls a line quoted from *Hamlet*. All three reasons now seem inconclusive. Green has shown in considerable detail in his book that the first two reasons for a late date need not be decisive. As for the repeated line, it is the very undistinctive 'What is the reason that you use me thus?'; and its appearance in the reported 1602 Quarto of *Hamlet* has no necessary relation to its date of composition.

Once we relinquish the idea of the late date, we return to what seems to be the most likely possibility of all – that the Windsor play belongs to the same period of composition as the other plays about Falstaff. Green's circumstantial case for *The Merry Wives* as Shakespeare's Garter play, written at the Queen's command, possibly in two weeks, for the Garter Installation of the spring of 1597, seems to me convincing, though probably not

[1] *Shakespeare's Comedies* (Oxford, 1960), chapter 3.
[2] Ed. *Works of Shakespeare* (London, 1846), II, 149.
[3] *A Chronicle of the Life and Work of William Shakespeare* (London, 1886), p. 212.
[4] *The Principles and Practice of Criticism* (Detroit, 1959), pp. 73–5.
[5] *William Shakespeare* (Oxford, 1951), I, 434.
[6] Greg favors a date after *Henry V*, possibly not after *Hamlet*, in *The Shakespeare First Folio* (Oxford, 1955), p. 337.
[7] *Shakespeare's Occasional Plays* (London, 1965), p. 88.
[8] 'Recent Studies in Shakespeare's Chronology', *Shakespeare Survey 3* (Cambridge, 1950), p. 29.

capable of final proof. I do not share his conviction that the Garter celebration was the actual setting of the action, but the date of composition fits well with what happens to Falstaff in the play.

Many, many nineteenth- and twentieth-century critics have expressed distress over the treatment of Falstaff in *2 Henry IV*. In our own century notably A. C. Bradley,[1] Murry[2] and Barber[3] have analyzed at length their sense that the play is emotionally unsatisfying. But if we suppose that *The Merry Wives* – the action and the composition – precedes the final scenes of *2 Henry IV*, the problem disappears. H. N. Paul suggested that Shakespeare was interrupted in the composition of *2 Henry IV*, after IV, iii, to write the play showing Falstaff in love,[4] and I think his idea is right, though I do not insist on such precise specificity. Following the story this way, we see that the 'festive' rejection and then social inclusion of Falstaff, which Barber finds missing in *2 Henry IV*, are clearly contained in the Windsor play. Only the political rejection, necessary for Prince Hal, remains for the history to act out. It is interesting that during the seventeenth and eighteenth centuries, when the three Falstaff plays were commonly played together, there were no complaints about the rejection of Falstaff. It is a custom to which we should probably return: reading or seeing *The Merry Wives*, as Edmond Malone once suggested,[5] between the two parts of *Henry IV*.

One other point for interesting speculation remains. At what point in the composition of the three plays did Oldcastle become Falstaff? We know that the speech-heading '*Old.*' appears at I, ii, 137 in the 1600 Quarto of *2 Henry IV*, and this may lend some weight to the supposition that the change was made during the writing of that play. Paul supposes that the name Falstaff was a modification of Fastolfe, and that the name was chosen while Shakespeare was writing the Garter play because Sir

John Fastolfe was deprived of his Garter in *1 Henry VI*. But why the change from Fastolfe to Falstaff? We know that 1597 was a time of popularity of humours characters, and Falstaff's retinue is notable for humours appellations: Pistol, Nym, Quickly, Tearsheet, Mouldy, Shallow. It seems reasonable to guess that his own name was selected for humours overtones. Harry Levin says that, like *Shake spear*, *Fall staff* suggests cowardice.[6] But it also suggests impotence – a quality that seems singularly inappropriate to the man of most of *Henry IV*. Falstaff is old but not exhausted. As late as II, iv of *2 Henry IV* he is apparently still diverting Doll Tearsheet. And his heavily erotic soliloquy when he appears horned in Windsor Forest leaves no doubt of his potency at that point. His name only becomes suitable after the pinching scene in *The Merry Wives*.[7] It is extremely tempting, therefore, to suppose that it was at this point, or with this point in mind, that the choice of the new name was made.

It is at least possible that the objector to the

---

[1] 'The Rejection of Falstaff', *Oxford Lectures on Poetry* (London, 1909), pp. 245–75. Bradley almost suggests a similar conclusion to my own but dismisses it: 'If, as the Second Part of *Henry IV* advanced, he had clouded over Falstaff's humour so heavily that the man of genius turned into the Falstaff of the *Merry Wives*, we should have witnessed his rejection without a pang' (p. 272).

[2] 'The Creation of Falstaff', pp. 227–62.

[3] Barber, *Shakespeare's Festive Comedy*, chapter 8.

[4] In a letter dated 10 January 1935. Quoted by Samuel B. Hemingway in *A New Variorum Henry IV, Part I* (Philadelphia, 1936), p. 355. The two references to Windsor in IV, iv provide some support for this hypothesis.

[5] In *Supplement* (London, 1780), to *Plays of Shakespeare*, ed. Samuel Johnson and George Steevens, I, I, 89. Malone later changed his mind and dated the play after *Henry V*, in his edition of *Poems and Plays of Shakespeare* (London, 1790), I, I, 328.

[6] 'Shakespeare's Nomenclature', *Essays on Shakespeare*, ed. Gerald W. Chapman (Princeton, 1965), p. 87.

[7] For more extended discussion of sexual imagery, see my forthcoming article in *Shakespeare Studies*, VI.

Oldcastle was the younger Lord Cobham, successor to his father who had died 6 March 1596–7, and that the objection came during the composition or even rehearsal of *The Merry Wives*.[1] Such an explanation would account not only for the 'humour' of Falstaff, but also for the original choice of 'Brook(e)' (the family name of the Cobhams) as a pseudonym for Ford in the play – a choice which would almost certainly not have been made if Cobham had already expressed his sensitivity on the subject of names.

Whether or not we assent to this theory of the naming of Falstaff, we need to take *The Merry Wives* more seriously than it has been taken in recent years. It is a vital part of Falstaff's story. In spite of the seeming inconsistencies of settings, discrepancies in biographical details of characters, and the disturbingly reduced stature of the great wit, this play

belongs with the histories. It is not a light-hearted midsummer romp, or a springtime celebration, but rather a record of the transition from fall to winter – an effort to put the house in order, to become reconciled to the passing of fertility from the old to the young. Just beyond the frivolity of the play's pranks and the 'innocent' revenge of its night-wandering spirits lie the gravity and earnestness of a sober New Year. All Hallow's Eve must give way to the Feast of All Saints.

[1] H. J. Oliver in the New Arden edition of *The Merry Wives* (London, 1971) characterizes Green's suggestion in *Shakespeare's 'Merry Wives of Windsor'* (pp. 116–17) that the Brook(e)-Broome name change was made *during rehearsal* as 'surely desperate' (p. lvi*n*). In my own view the idea is attractive; and it surely seems more economical to imagine the two related name changes to have been made at the same time than to suppose they were made on different occasions.

'THE TEMPEST'
AT THE TURN OF THE CENTURY:
CROSS-CURRENTS IN PRODUCTION

MARY M. NILAN

The history of *The Tempest* on the English-speaking stage from the Restoration era through mid nineteenth century is mainly a story of highly theatrical adaptations and alterations or of spectacular 'illustrations' of Shakespeare's play.[1] While, by the close of the nineteenth century, Shakespeare's original text was the basis of presentations, many minor producers were still imitating the theatrical innovations of Samuel Phelps's 1847 revival and major ones, such as Augustin Daly and Herbert Beerbohm Tree, were attempting to surpass the lavish illustrations of Charles Kean's 1857 extravaganza.[2]

But, at the same time, a new trend was evident, one which conflicted with the highly theatrical theory of staging and indicated a new direction for *Tempest* revivals in the twentieth century. For, at the turn of the century, some professional producers were intentionally attempting to pare down the traditionally superimposed spectacles rather than condensing the text to make room for them, and others, because of financial limitations, chose to present a simpler theatrical version rather than none at all. A study of this era is then particularly interesting because two conflicting theories of *Tempest* staging were being tested, providing reviewers and critics with an opportunity for comparison.

I

In America by the end of the nineteenth century, *The Tempest* was no longer a play for the audiences of the Eastern metropolises alone. On 23 June 1889, it was presented by Mr McVicker at his theater in Chicago. *The Chicago Times* reported that the play had 'never been tried in this country west of New York'.[3] According to the same paper, while McVicker did present the original Shakespearian text, he did some 're-arranging':

The order of the scenes at the opening is reversed and the whole is condensed into four acts, with 'cutting', of course, distributed throughout, but nothing material is omitted and nothing is added but music and bits of dances, if they can be said to be additions.

The 'additions' included, in the words of the *Chicago News*, 'music that is ascribed to the version of Davenant and Dryden'. The paper did not specify exactly how much was added, but according to the *Chicago Evening Journal* 'the singing is done by Ariel and the Philharmonic and Schumann Lady Quartettes, the latter being invisible to the audience'.

Although in the McVicker production I, i followed I, ii, and there was some added music from the Restoration version, the beginning

[1] There were of course exceptions, notably David Garrick's 1757 revival of Shakespeare's text which de-emphasized theatricality.

[2] The history of earlier as well as later productions is recounted in my unpublished doctoral dissertation, '*The Tempest*: A Question of Theatricality' (Evanston, Illinois, 1967).

[3] Unless otherwise specified all theatrical reviews in this study are from '*The Tempest* Scrapbook: Clipping, 1777–1936', in possession of the Theater Collection of the New York Public Library. Reviews of McVicker's production are all for 24 June 1889.

of a new trend or a new philosophy in staging may be detected in that six Chicago reviewers concurred with the observation of the *Chicago Tribune*: 'More pretentious and sensuous spectacles have been offered; but here, not only the eye was flattered but the imagination was stimulated by the poetry which swept all realms of thought, from fairyland to high philosophy'. And the *Chicago Inter-Ocean* reported: 'The stage pictures ... are pleasing without attracting attention, to the sacrifice of the ideals of the poet.' Apparently the theatricality of McVicker's production did not obscure Shakespeare's text.

The producer relied on two spectacles. The first which caused comment among the reviewers was the storm scene, transposed to the close of act 1. As described by the *Chicago Inter-Ocean* it appears to have been as elaborate as Kean's rendition of 1857:

The swift-passing clouds, penetrated ever and anon by vivid flashes of lightning, the beating waves, ominous in the darkness, and the huge ship that comes plunging into view, its decks crowded with people, and is finally driven upon the rocks as a lightning stroke shivers its mast, makes a remarkably realistic picture.

The second major visual display occurs in the masque where, according to the *Chicago Globe*, 'the cars of Juno and Ceres, drawn respectively by the sacred peacock, and glittering butterflies, enter amid filmy clouds and, in a forest scene, mermaids float dreamily through running waters'. The masque then focusses on a series of dances. The one which excited the most admiration was executed, according to the same reviewer, by 'a throng of brightly costumed children and girls'. The goddesses leave their cars and 'dance in company with the sprites' and Ariel then executes 'a pleasing dance solo'.

Apparently, however, the storm scene and the masque were the only extravaganzas in the show. While the reviewers praised the various scenes of 'caves and landscapes', no other elaborate scenic displays are mentioned. Moreover, according to the *Chicago News*, instead of presenting a series of separate production numbers, McVicker attempted to merge one scene into the next by the skillful use of stage lighting. He also attempted to merge one act into the next by using a series of special 'act curtains', each depicting a scene from the play which blended with the previous one. The main curtain was never used 'to break the illusion' and the time between each act was 'only a short space'.

Since McVicker's production featured a storm sequence as elaborate in its own way as Kean's and a masque with numerous scenic delights, a large corps of dancing girls and children, and an invisible chorus composed of the Philharmonic and Schumann Ladies Quartettes, it is likely that the Chicago producer could have rivaled Kean's lavish presentation spectacle for spectacle. It is significant, however, that with the exception of two major displays the American producer chose not to do so, but instead devoted his attention to merging smoothly scenes and acts, letting Shakespeare's poetry speak for itself without being smothered by the numerous theatrical distractions prevalent in most productions of the period.

II

Two years later, Frank Benson's troupe, which had been playing in the English provinces, was performing at the Stratford Memorial Theater. In the summer of 1891 Benson offered *The Tempest* at the Stratford Festival. He portrayed Caliban and made a starring role of the part. His conception of the monster was based on Daniel Wilson's *Caliban: The Missing Link* (1873). Here it was asserted that Shakespeare had imaginatively created in Caliban, the creature which fills a gap between the highest ape and the lowest savage:

There was obviously something marine or fishlike in the aspect of the island monster. 'In the dim obscurity of the past', says Darwin, 'we can see that the early progenitor of all the vertebrates must have been an acquatic animal' . . . In Caliban there was undesignedly embodied, seemingly, an ideal of the latest stages of such an evolution. (p. 73)

Following this suggestion, Benson played Caliban on all fours with costume and makeup suggestive of an ape.[1] He would scurry up a corrugated palm trunk, hang from a branch head-downward and then swing through the branches of the tree. He always entered with a large and very real fish clenched between his jaws.

Because of his limited budget, Benson attempted to give a somewhat simpler theatrical version of *The Tempest*. In some ways, however, he did try to imitate the lavish stagings of Phelps and Kean. Since he could not hope to match the magnificent storm and shipwreck prologue of his predecessors, he simply cut the scene. The play commences then with Miranda and Prospero discovered 'on a sea-marge, sterile and rocky hard'. The main setting depicts the luxury of a tropical island with rocky ledges surrounding a gorge of fern and palm. The 'yellow sands' are reminiscent of Kean's production as is the masque with its 'rainbow arch, Juno descending through the clouds in a shaft of light in a peacock-drawn car, and the naiads floating in a lily-pond below'. For the finale Benson again imitated Kean by showing a tableau of Ariel and attendant spirits in flight; however, he was not able to follow his predecessor in presenting a practical ship to bear Prospero away from the island. But Benson did add some innovations of his own including a number of lavish ballets and an elaborate entrance for Ferdinand who comes on stage 'drawn by a silver thread, held by two tiny Cupids whose costumes' are 'chiefly wings'.[2] This somewhat simpler theatrical revival of *The Tempest* met with success and was to be repeated in ensuing years at Stratford as well as the Lyceum Theater.

III

Despite the fact that McVicker had made some attempt to simplify theatricality in his presentation, the idea seemed to persist in America that, as the theater critic for the *New World* (7 April 1897) suggested: '*The Tempest* is by no means a comedy that could be presented with curtains for scenery and imagination for effects.' Writing on the same date, William H. Fleming contended in the *Looker-On*: 'From the nature of the play, it is not possible to give a presentation of it which is very powerful and dramatic. It appeals not so much to the thoughts and emotions of the spectator as to his aesthetic nature.'

Assuming apparently that the play would not appeal to 'the thoughts and emotions of the spectator', Augustin Daly felt free to cut liberally Shakespeare's text and this he did for his New York revival which opened on 6 April 1897. On 7 April the *New York Herald* observed that 'of the 2,064 lines . . . surely 1,000 are missing, too great a condensation'. A study of Daly's production prompt-book confirms the estimate.[3] For example, in act IV, which coincided with act V in Shakespeare's printed text, 156 out of 318 lines are omitted. Daly not only made numerous cuts in the text but he also transposed speeches freely. Daly's act III is a peculiar mélange which Marvin Felheim, in

---

[1] Except when otherwise specified information on Benson's production is taken from J. C. Trewin, *Benson and the Bensonians* (London, 1960), pp. 71–4.
[2] See Lady Constance Benson, *Mainly Players* (London, 1926), p. 94.
[3] Unless otherwise specified citations concerning Daly's production are from the 1897 prompt-book (Shattuck, 33) in possession of the Theater Collection of the New York Public Library. For a more detailed account of this and other source material, see Charles H. Shattuck's descriptive catalogue, *The Shakespeare Promptbooks* (Urbana, Illinois, 1965), pp. 453–4. (Shattuck assigns a number to the listed source material and, when applicable, these numbers are cited in this study.)

The Theatre of Augustin Daly,[1] constructs from the Shakespearian text as follows:

> III, iii
> IV, i, 164–92
> III, ii, 48–73
> IV, i, 194–5, 221–35
> III, ii, 76–132
> IV, i, 1–59, 118–24, 146–57 (p. 265)

According to the prompt-book, during the masque Prospero is directed to 'recite slowly' the speech beginning 'Our revels now are ended', as a sort of background to the vision itself. Besides obscuring the speech, the direction also seems pointless as the 'revels' are beginning, not ending.

Rather than magical effects, the production emphasizes songs, dances, and striking stage pictures; each act ends with a climactic tableau, featuring song and dance. For example, act I closes with the entrance of Ferdinand and the directions read:

> Ariel, floating in the air, attended by Nymphs and Spirits, playing and singing 'Full Fathom Five'. Other Spirits enter and dance round Ferdinand as if to distract him from Miranda. Ariel sings 'Come Unto These Yellow Sands' as the act ends.

Act II concludes with the second scene between Miranda and Ferdinand and, at the close, Ariel arrives to sing 'Where the bee sucks' (transposed from act v) and attendant spirits dance again. Act III closes with the spectacle of the masque which follows the now traditional concept of a triptych of goddesses, surrounded by a rainbow arch. And, reminiscent of Kean, act IV terminates with a scenic epilogue:

> Ariel appears in the air at the back of the stage. The walls of the Cave dissolve. The sea appears beyond, and a ship approaches the shore – Prospero's Spirits guiding the ship (as the curtain falls) singing 'Merrily, Merrily'.

Daly added more music to *The Tempest*. Ariel renders 'Oh, bid thy faithful Ariel fly' and Miranda and Ferdinand are given a duet at the close of act II. While the producer used the compositions of both Arne and Purcell to accompany the airs, he also used an additional score, Taubert's 'Tempest', written for the Munich Court Theater. A musical background is provided for each scene. As Felheim concluded: 'Music and scenery together apparently seemed to Daly the quintessence of poetic drama' (p. 265).

The critic for the *New York Herald* objected to this emphasis on theatricality, stressing that in *The Tempest* the text was more important than any scenic or pantomimic representation:

> The ship scene as Shakespeare wrote it, word for word, properly acted, and without a rag of scenery, would be a thousand times more impressive and more stimulating to the imagination in a theatre than the finest scenic representation of a wreck, as would the beautiful 'cloud-capp'd towers' speech, a bit of poet's frenzy, which is torn out of its proper place and recited slowly as the accompaniment to an actual vision of gorgeous palaces and solemn temples on a 'back cloth'.

Essentially, then, the *New York Herald* critic was contesting the *New York World*'s contention that '*The Tempest* is by no means a comedy that could be presented with curtains for scenery and imagination for effects'.

IV

While the *New York Herald* reviewer might be in the minority in America, the concept which he espoused was being tried out, and defended by at least one notable critic in England. In the same year that Daly's elaborate production held the boards in New York, William Poel's semi-professional London group, the Elizabethan Stage Society, was presenting *The Tempest* without any elaborate scenery on a stage re-created to resemble the Society's conception of the original Elizabethan one. It will be recalled that in Chicago, almost ten years earlier, McVicker had concentrated on

[1] Cambridge, Mass., 1956.

devices for merging one scene into another and one act into another. In 1897 Poel's group overcame the problem by eliminating scene shifts altogether.[1] Moreover, the large and often augmented orchestra, which had been an accepted part of professional productions, was omitted. Instead of elaborate music scored for wood-wind and percussion, Mr Dolmetsch's background music made use of simple instruments of pipe and tabor. The only element in the production which might be termed 'elaborate' was the costuming, an area in which the Society had made a reputation for itself. But essentially Poel intended that the audience listen to Shakespeare's verbal imagery and then create for itself the magical effects and the vision of Prospero's island.

This concept was applauded by one of the more notable reviewers of the day. In his capacity as theater critic for the *Saturday Review*, George Bernard Shaw discussed the production of 13 November 1897.[2] Approving the basic philosophy behind the Society's presentation, Shaw compared it to the kind of production accorded the play for the last fifty years in both England and America:

The poetry of *The Tempest* is so magical that it would make the scenery of modern theatre ridiculous. The methods of the Elizabethan Stage Society . . . leave to the poet, the work of conjuring up the isle 'full of noises, sounds and sweet airs'. And I do not see how this plan can be beaten. If Sir Henry Irving were to put the play on at the Lyceum next season . . . what could he do but multiply the expenditure enormously, and spoil the illusion? He would give us the screaming violin instead of the harmonious viol . . . an expensive and absurd stage ship; and some windless, airless, changeless, soundless, electric-lit, wooden-floored mockeries of the haunts of Ariel. They would cost more but would they be an improvement on the Mansion House arrangement?

Despite the absence of scene changes, the production was not taken at the rapid-fire pace which typifies most revivals done 'in the manner of the Elizabethan stage' in our day.

The costumes were somewhat restrictive, allowing for interesting stage pictures but not for freedom of movement. On this point Shaw observed:

The whole performance had to be taken in a somewhat low key and slow tempo, with a minimum of movement. If any attempt had been made at the impetuosity and liveliness for which the English experts of the sixteenth-century were famous throughout Europe, it would not only have failed, but prevented the performers from attaining what they did attain.

But despite the shortcomings Poel's revival was a landmark, heralding a new era for future productions of *The Tempest*.

V

The Elizabethan Stage Society's revival did not immediately influence the style of *Tempest* presentations in the next decade. Benson's simplified imitation of earlier lavish revivals was repeated at Stratford in the same year as Poel's production and it was to be revived at the Lyceum in 1900 and again at the Memorial Theater in 1904, 1908, and 1911.

In 1903 the western half of America was treated to a touring production of *The Tempest*. Originating at the Columbia Theater in San Francisco, the revival by Frederick Warde (who played Prospero) and Louis James (who played Caliban as a 'missing link') visited, among other theaters, the McVicker's in Chicago and English's in Indianapolis. Ignoring all the obvious hazards of touring a highly technical production, the Warde–James presentation came complete with a realistic storm and shipwreck sequence and a bag of elaborate 'supernatural' stage tricks. The *San Francisco Chronicle* for 27 January 1903 exclaimed: 'Why there have been so few attempts to stage it

[1] See Robert Speaight, *William Poel and the Elizabethan Revival* (London, 1943), pp. 89–92.
[2] Reprint of this review available in *Shaw on Shakespeare*, ed. Edwin Wilson (New York, 1961), pp. 191–3.

stands explained when one sees how much of scenic and other effects it needs!' From the *Indianapolis Journal* for 11 April 1903 we learn that 'in places the text of Shakespeare had been departed from so as to allow the interpolation of love songs or ballet measures and much incidental music'. One of these interpolated songs, rendered by Ferdinand, consisted of words from one of Shakespeare's sonnets set to 'suitable music'. (The precise sonnet is not mentioned.)

Now, however, theater critics were becoming more outspoken in questioning the value of such a highly theatrical *Tempest*. Thus, when the tour reached Chicago, reviewers had an opportunity to compare the elaborate Warde–James revival with McVicker's comparatively simple one fourteen years earlier. On this point the *Chicago Tribune* (23 March 1903) commented: 'The production here in 1889 by the late J. H. McVicker had about it more of the atmosphere of poetry and fantasy than does the present one.' One specific difference which the *Tribune* noted was the fact that McVicker had employed a series of gauze drops while Warde–James relied on heavy, painted flats. But more significantly, some reviewers questioned the philosophy behind the touring revival. Should Shakespeare's poetry be lost amidst theatrical displays? *The Chicago Daily News* critic echoed the thoughts of his colleagues when, on 23 March 1903, he observed:

Disillusionment is perhaps the inevitable result of a stage presentation of *The Tempest* and a real lover of the poetic fairy fantasy must forgo the sight of his favorite fairies embodied in the flesh, if he would retain the elusive delight of their being which the lines of Shakespeare conjure up. This is true even with all the elaboration of scenic investiture which characterizes the production at McVickers.

Indeed it would seem that 'scenic investiture' had not aided the illusion but had created 'disillusionment'.

VI

In the same year that the Warde–James tour was performing *The Tempest* in America, a London revival by J. H. Leigh at the small Royal Court Theater ran for between seventy and eighty performances – certainly an excellent record at that time for a Shakespearian production at a minor theater where the actors were not well known. The question naturally arises: What was it that attracted the audiences? It was undoubtedly a combination of the good acting of the performers and, even more, the simplicity of the presentation. There was no attempt to imitate the lavish extravaganzas of the major theaters; while some semblance of settings and theatrical additions were employed, these were held to a minimum. For this reason, as the critic of the *Illustrated Sporting and Dramatic News* (5 December 1903) observed, Shakespeare's poetry was projected with unusual clarity:

The fact that although the scenery and accessories were sympathetic, they were neither costly nor overwhelming, was an important feature of the production. I could not help asking myself why my attention had been engaged by interest in the poetry of the play and whether half-hours of elaborate sets and gorgeous processions, with which it seems at present the fashion to adorn the bard – or subordinate him – are really and truly after all worth five minutes of actual Shakespearean acting.

VII

Sir Henry Irving, who managed the Lyceum from 1878 until 1901, never produced *The Tempest* although he allowed Frank R. Benson to stage his version there in 1900. But a year after the elaborate Warde–James tour in America and the relatively simple Royal Court Theater presentation, Herbert Beerbohm Tree added *The Tempest* to his repertoire of Shakespearian revivals at His Majesty's Theater, London. Staged first on 14 September 1904 with William Haviland as Prospero, Tree himself as Caliban, his daughter Viola Tree as Ariel, and Louis Calvert as Stephano, the production became a staple at His Majesty's and was revived there in succeeding seasons from 1904/5 through 1907/8.

Tree used Shakespeare's text but made some changes. He transposed the second Caliban–Trinculo–Stephano scene (III, ii), placing it between the banquet scene (III, iii) and the masque (IV, i).[1] He cut Shakespeare's epilogue and concluded the play instead with Prospero's speech beginning 'Ye elves of hills, brooks, standing lakes, and groves' (v, i, 33–57). While there were a number of deletions throughout the text, the principal ones occur in act v; the act was reduced to about one-half its former length.

By 1904 stage mechanism had progressed to such a point that the prompt-book for Tree's production speaks of almost all scene changes being of a 1½-minute interval. (In the mid nineteenth century, if we are to judge from William Burton's 1854 prompt-book, 4- to 8-minute waits were common.[2]) Tree did not, however, use the additional time to retain more of Shakespeare's dialogue but instead inserted additional pieces of 'business'.

Where his predecessors had concentrated on devising spectacles and effects to be achieved through scenery and machinery, he concentrated on creating pantomimes to interpret Shakespeare's text and to enlarge on the Folio stage directions. In an apology attached to the souvenir program for the fiftieth representation of his *Tempest* revival, he attempted to justify all his pantomimic innovations as merely an elaboration of Shakespeare's implicit or explicit directions: 'What in this production was not actually contained in the letter of Shakespeare's text, sprang from the spirit which animated it.'[3] Moreover, he assumed that such pantomimes were a part of the original presentation and that, had Shakespeare had turn-of-the-century stagecraft at his command, the playwright would have made ample use of it to achieve effects similar

to Tree's own: 'Of all Shakespeare's works *The Tempest* is probably the one which most demands the aids of modern stagecraft.'

As has been noted, there was a growing feeling among critics against 'scenic Shakespeare' and it is significant of course that Tree's innovations involved business rather than scenery. While he had as many individual settings (twelve) as Kean had had fifty years earlier, still, with the exception of the opening shipwreck sequence, there was a decided difference about the type of setting employed. The turn-of-the-century producer relied on small set-pieces such as rocks and water rows working in combination with gauze drops and subtle changes in color and intensity of stage lighting. Kean had relied chiefly on heavy painted scenery, using gauze and special lighting only for certain specific magical effects. Tree's prompt-book, on the other hand, shows more concern for 'light changes' than 'scene changes'. For example, near the close of act I, by changing the dominant lighting from amber to purple he was able to change the yellow sands into 'a misty vision', described as 'the light that never was on land or sea'.

Tree may have sensed the direction modern stagecraft would take with emphasis on lighting rather than scenery in presentations of poetic drama in general and Shakespearian drama in particular. In his book of memoirs, *Thoughts and Afterthoughts* (1913), he noted under 'Afterthought' regarding *The Tempest*: 'The art of stage presentations has progressed – and I think rightly progressed – in the direction of greater simplicity of treatment. This progress

[1] Citations concerning Tree's production are from a transcription of the final prompt-book by Fred Grove, in possession of Folger Shakespeare Library (Shattuck, 39).

[2] Burton's 1854 prompt-book in possession of Folger Shakespeare Library (Shattuck, 15).

[3] '*The Tempest:* Souvenir Programme', in possession of the Theater Collection of the New York Public Library.

is chiefly due to the increased facilities for economy in the lighting of scenery. Suggestion is often stronger than actuality where purely fantastic and imaginative works are concerned' (p. 224). But in 1904 Tree's three-act version of *The Tempest* was anything but 'simple' or purely 'suggestive'.

Act I opens with the inevitable storm and shipwreck sequence done in a manner to rival Kean's realistic illustration, but there is one interesting innovation: four small boys dressed as mariners are on the replica of the Neapolitan vessel; they pretend to speak the lines of the scene which are, in reality, spoken by offstage actors. Thus, gauged in relation to the size of its mariners, the vessel appears to be full-scale. Apparently Tree was striving for as much realism as possible here. The same is true of the exposition sequence which takes place in Prospero's cell. The setting is fitted out with books, which the magician is reading at the opening; a couch, upon which Miranda sleeps in the course of the scene; and a table, on which Ariel perches for part of the dialogue with Prospero.

Suddenly, prior to the entrance of Caliban, a far more imaginative and fanciful picture is presented, one of Tree's many added pantomimes:

As Ariel exits from Prospero's cell, there is a blackout. The curtain and gauze comes down. 'Come Unto These Yellow Sands' is sung by the offstage chorus. As the chorus starts, the curtain goes up in the dark and lights gradually come up to purple, disclosing Nymphs playing on the waters and on the sands. Four Nymphs on wires are behind the first water row. On the last lines of the song, lights gradually check down. Nymphs go off slowly behind rocks R and L and lights gradually come up amber, revealing the yellow sands.

Now with his magic wand Prospero strikes the forbidding rock inhabited by Caliban; it opens disclosing the monster, who 'crawls out with a fish in his mouth'. His dress consists of fur and sea-weed and around his neck he wears a string of pearls, shells, amber, and coral. Dropping the fish, he announces: 'I must eat my dinner.' As he proceeds to search the beach for more shells to add to his necklace, Prospero exits. Caliban, left alone, starts after his master in a threatening manner but is stopped by the strains of prelude music; he listens, looks up and attempts to dance before finally exiting over some rocks. (Throughout the production Tree insisted on Caliban's quick responsiveness to the 'sounds and sweet airs' of the island.) Another pantomime then follows in which six nymphs assist Ariel in a dressing routine. Properties for the sequence are a shell, comb, headdress, necklace and cloak. Once the sprite is attired, the nymphs, with Ariel between them, 'form a circle centre, dancing.' They are interrupted by a note in the orchestra. 'The Prelude to "Yellow Sands" is sung offstage and they steal away by various exits.' Ariel, singing the Shakespearian air, disappears only to reappear a moment later, waving Ferdinand on. Nymphs are directed to peep at him 'over the rocks and in the waves'. Ariel toys with a large sea-shell while singing 'Full fathom five'.

The stage is set for the meeting between the Prince and Miranda. Tree added more physical business between the two lovers than had any previous producer. At the close of their first scene, 'they advance slowly toward each other in the wonderment of first love'. During the course of Prospero's long aside, 'Ferdinand touches Miranda and kneels at her feet'; Miranda presents the Prince with a shell which she finds on the shore. The scene closes with some pantomimic business in which Caliban enters carrying wood and regarding the lovers with hatred. As the monster raises a log to strike the Prince, he is charmed by Prospero and skulks back to his rock. Since Ferdinand is the last to leave the stage, the act ends with a tableau of Caliban 'crouching in his cell and looking at Ferdinand' as the Prince looks offstage after Miranda.

Act II begins with the first scene involving

the shipwrecked nobles, but prior to the scene there is another pantomime in which Ariel is discovered in a bower made by surrounding trees 'from which wild honeysuckle stands in profusion'. The sprite sings 'Where the bee sucks' and the song is echoed by a chorus of children offstage. Lowered to the stage, Ariel sings the refrain and then dances before exiting. The nobles arrive and the scene proper begins. Ariel, hidden behind a gauze set-piece, suddenly is revealed to waken the sleeping courtiers. There is a pantomime here too: at the end of the song, Antonio and Sebastian make a sudden rush at Alonso and Gonzalo; Antonio is above Alonso, with sword drawn, and Sebastian is above Gonzalo, with a dagger; the music swells and stops dead. After the nobles retire, Ariel is taken up in the swing and from the honeysuckle bower sings a chorus of 'Merrily, merrily'.

Caliban, Stephano, and Trinculo appear for their first scene together. This is followed by the second sequence between Miranda and Ferdinand. Again there is more physical business as, at the close: 'The lovers kiss for the first time. They walk slowly up and look out at the sea. A silence falls. The lights begin to fade. Miranda's head falls on Ferdinand's shoulder and sweet music is heard as the scene fades out.' The act concludes with the banquet scene. The 'strange shapes' are dispensed with and a pantomime involving tumbling acrobats is substituted. To the sound of thunder the table rises through a stage trap and the lights are brought up to reveal the banquet. Two boys enter and, presenting a spoon and fork to each of the principals, invite them to eat. They then exit by tumbling offstage to the accompaniment of rolling thunder. There is a blackout and a crash of thunder. During the brief distraction, 'Ariel is helped up on the table by the principals and then switches on the lights in headdress'. The nobles kneel around the table and are directed to stab at the harpy but Ariel 'laughs and it is re-echoed off-stage by children'. The

speech ended, there is another blackout during which Ariel leaves and the table sinks.

Act III opens with the second Caliban–Trinculo–Stephano scene (Shakespeare's III, ii). At the beginning 'Caliban is discovered seated on the shore listening to sweet music in the air, weaving a wreath of flowers wherewith to crown his new-found master. Placing the wreath on his head, he looks at his reflection in the pool'. There are numerous pieces of business to indicate Caliban's admiration for Stephano. He presents his master with the garland, strokes, pats and fans him. Throughout the episode the 'invisible' Ariel flits about the stage with a long lily which is used to tickle the other three participants in the scene; they, thinking it is a fly, attempt to catch it. At the end 'Ariel leads them about like a will-o'-the-wisp, then flies above them, still playing in the air'. Caliban listens to the music and attempts to dance and sing; Stephano and Trinculo 'watch him with curiosity'.

The masque follows as the second scene of act III. The three goddesses each appear in turn in a spectacle reminiscent of Kean's presentation. Juno and Ceres sing and then disappear in a blackout. In the darkness Iris takes up a position on a platform in the center and naiads take up their positions behind water rows. As blue lights come up gradually Ferdinand starts to speak but Prospero silences him and, according to the cue, 'when the blues are full up, the Nymphs are seen playing in the water'. Obedient to Iris's command, the naiads leave the water and come to dance on the land. A pantomimic ballet follows, so involved that Tree explained it in his souvenir program:

The sudden appearance of the boy Cupid interrupts their revels – the Naiads modestly immerse themselves in the water. Cupid, ever a matchmaker, brings in his train of sunburnt sicklemen who, leaving their lonely furrow, are enjoined by Iris to make holiday with the nymphs 'in country footing'. The reapers attempt to embrace the nymphs but their advances are repulsed, the maidens pointing to their ringless wedding-fingers, it being illegal (in fairyland) to exchange kisses without a marriage certificate. Thus rebuffed, the reapers continue their dance alone. Suddenly Cupid re-appears on the scene and shoots a dart in the heart of each coy maiden – at once they relent; they sue to the reapers, but the reapers are now obdurate. They laugh, the maidens weep. Cupid now shoots an arrow into the heart of each of the reapers, who seeing their little friends weep, now sue to them pointing to their wedding-fingers. Cupid re-appears and an impromptu wedding is arranged. To the wedding song of 'Honour, riches, marriage blessings', the nymphs assume the marriage veils which they gather from the mist of the lake, and having received a ring and a blessing at the hands of Rev. Master Cupid, they dance off in quest of everlasting happiness.

The ballet finished, Prospero delivers his speech beginning 'our revels now have ended'.

The time has come for Prospero to punish Caliban and his associates, and again there is a special pantomime for this anti-masque. The conspirators are seen creeping stealthily into the monstrous cave of Prospero. Suddenly Ariel enters clashing cymbals and dashes across the stage; there is an accompanying crash of thunder and then darkness. When the blue lights return the three discover themselves in a cave filled with strange and monstrous animals. The directions, at the beginning of Tree's III, iii, continue:

Caliban, in pantomine, shows a way of escape and all three make for it, holding on to each others' coat tails. Just as they reach the entrance, a horrible thing appears with long neck and bows to them in silence. The three back off in terror and are met by three other animals. They cross from R to L and are met by two more who drive them upstage where they are met by a six-legged horse and more animals. At this moment, a wild yell is heard and noames enter from all sides, some down over the rocks. Illuminated heads appear and disappear quickly on the back cloth and on rock pieces. Acrobats enter quickly from behind rock row and climb a tree from behind so that when Caliban, Stephano and Trinculo climb it, the acrobats come tumbling to the ground. Caliban, Stephano and Trinculo then rush downstage where four goblins drop in front of them

from an overhanging bridge. The three attempt to battle with them and the curtain descends.

In Tree's words, 'the comic Inferno dissolves and we are once again in Prospero's cave'.

The final scene is a highly condensed version of Shakespeare's act v. The ship sails away, carrying Prospero and the others as the nymphs sing a reprise of 'Come unto these yellow sands' and the 'homing-song' of the sailors is heard in the distance. Creeping from his cave, Caliban watches the departing ship. Ariel appears singing a reprise of 'Where the bee sucks'. 'Taking flight at the words "merrily, merrily," the sprite's voice rises higher and higher until it merges into the song of the lark – Ariel is now free as a bird.' At the end the curtain rises for a final tableau showing Caliban stretching out his arms towards the departing ship in mute despair. 'The night falls and Caliban is left on the lonely rock. He is king once more.' Thus Tree's version concludes with Caliban both literally as well as figuratively 'in the limelight'.

London critics now had an opportunity to contrast this elaborate revival with Benson's simpler one and with Poel's even more simple version. The critic of the *Daily Chronicle* (15 September 1904) yearned for less ornate music, such as that used by Poel: 'Roze's or Sullivan's music would have been well replaced by a note or two of Purcell's simple old "Come unto these yellow sands" for which one listened in vain'. Regarding Tree's realistic shipwreck sequence, the same reviewer contended that it 'failed to prove even so appealing as the device resorted to by the Elizabethan Stage Society who . . . allowed their mariners to pretend to be wrecked on a simple balcony above the stage – with a result that was curiously effective'. Contrasting Tree's revival with Benson's, the critic remarked: 'It is to be doubted if the spirit of the production was anything like as true to the play as was Mr. Benson's far less splendid effort at the Lyceum.'

The London *Times* (15 September 1904) compared the presentation with the original Jacobean one, and Tree's again came off second best for the reviewer emphasized that Shakespeare had achieved his effects by words, not illustration:

Above all Prospero is a man of words. Ariel is a sprite of words. And Caliban is a monster of words. Shakespeare got his atmosphere mainly through the utterances of his personages. They made their set speeches, and sang their songs, and the imagination of the audience had to do the rest. This cannot be so today. It is the manager and his stage managers who had to do the rest. And the 'rest' is now the chief part. All the sensorial elements of drama become prominent and the words take second place ... The atmosphere of enchantment has no longer to be suggested; it has to be realized.

The most pronounced indictment, however, was published in *Blackwood's Magazine* for October 1904. This particular criticism elicited Tree's 'Personal Explanation', first published in the souvenir program of the fiftieth representation of the play and later reprinted in *Thoughts and Afterthoughts* (pp. 211–24). The *Blackwood* critic was disturbed by the use of an ornate musical background rendered by a full orchestra: 'As the cast always speaks to musical accompaniment, generally slow, it is surprising that they make a single speech intelligible.' And, more than this, the reviewer observed:

Tree has so betricked and bemused the author's text that, were it not for the purple passages which now and then silence the orchestra, hidden beneath a mass of vegetables, you would not have the smallest suspicion that you are assisting at a performance of Shakespeare's comedy. ... Shakespeare's plays afford no decent opportunity for elaborate scenery. Shakespeare has kept his hold upon the world's admiration by the splendour and beauty of his poetry which require no embellishment ... Imagination and fancy cannot be expressed by the stage carpenter.

The *Blackwood* critic thus joined his colleagues on The *Times* and the *London Chronicle* in condemning Tree's version and in yearning for less highly theatrical revivals of *The Tempest*, ones which would free Shakespeare's poetry.

Tree's production can be viewed not only in chronological terms as a turn-of-the-century revival but also, in terms of stage history, it can be seen as the turning point for a new era. Apparently Tree at least had intimations that twentieth-century producers would move in the direction of substituting business for machinery and would emphasize lighting rather than settings in Shakespearian productions. But his presentation also climaxed an era which emphasized spectacles and magical effects over the text. Tree, like major producers before him, offered the spectator a series of illustrations, pantomimic or scenic, accompanied by a full orchestrational and choral background. However, in 1897, Poel had demonstrated that simple music and simple staging could be more effective, if not most effective, where this play was concerned; Tree's lavish revival of 1904 thus inspired many critics to address themselves to this problem of simplicity versus elaborateness with respect to theatricality and *The Tempest*. By the turn of the century most critics had almost completely abandoned the position of their mid-century colleagues as they hailed the producers of less highly theatrical revivals as the true 'innovators', concurring that simplicity was a virtue devoutly to be wished. And this consensus was to influence the staging of *Tempest* revivals in the first half of the twentieth century.[1]

---

[1] Since 1945 a number of professional productions of the play have been presented in England, the United States and Canada. While at this time it is impossible to determine with any historical perspective the relative importance of these revivals, a certain trend can be seen insofar as the majority of revivals tended to return to the concept of emphasizing aural and visual potentialities. While *The Tempest* has continued to be performed on the platform stage suggested by Poel and popularized in the early years of this century; nevertheless, more magical effects, more combinations of music and various sounds, and more scenic displays have been added.

VARIATIONS WITHIN A SOURCE:
FROM ISAIAH XXIX TO 'THE TEMPEST'

ANN PASTERNAK SLATER

'And whom among the learned do ye deceive? Reckoning up those – forty is it? – your plays you've misbegot, there's not six which have not plots as common as Moorditch.'

'Ye're out, Ben. There's not one. My *Love's Labour* (how I came to write it, I know not) is nearest to lawfull issue. My *Tempest* (how I came to write *that*, I know) is, in some part, my own stuff.'

Rudyard Kipling, *Proofs of Holy Writ*[1]

The words Kipling gave to his Shakespeare were true. *The Tempest* interweaves a variety of details from the Bermuda pamphlets with fragmentary echoes of Vergil; one speech draws on Montaigne, and another on Golding's Ovid, but no origin has been found for its central theme. Yet by an odd coincidence Kipling almost stumbled against a hitherto neglected source for the play, in the *jeu d'esprit* from which the quotation above is taken. For here he imagined Shakespeare in his Stratford orchard, whiling away a summer afternoon with Ben Jonson, translating some verses of the Bible, which had been surreptitiously entrusted to him by a neighbouring Oxford divine in difficulties with his part of the translation for the new, Authorised Version. And the verses Kipling happened to choose, for their Shakespearian splendour of phrase, come from the book of Isaiah. 'How I came to write *that*, I know', Shakespeare says mysteriously of *The Tempest*, mocking the author who made him speak:[2] one of the sources for *The Tempest* is, very probably, Isaiah xxix.

Isaiah xxix has had a disappointing history in the study of sources for *The Tempest*. Its opening verse has admittedly been recognised as a possible source for the name of Ariel, ever since the time of Malone, but even in this function it is usually mentioned only in order to be dismissed. So, in *Shakespeare's Biblical Knowledge*, Richmond Noble quoted the reference with marginal interest, since, apart from the name, Shakespeare's Ariel 'is independent of any Biblical model'; for him, 'Scriptural interest is small' in *The Tempest*, and he listed only a few passages of tenuous relevance from other parts of the Bible.[3] Frank Kermode, in his Arden edition of the play, quoted Noble with approval in an appendix on Ariel,[4] and brushed the Isaiah passage aside in slighting

[1] First published in *The Strand Magazine*, April 1934. I am most grateful to Miss K. M. Lea for bringing this to my attention, and for her help and criticism with the rest of this article.

[2] Kipling had evidently been intrigued by the source of *The Tempest* for many years. In fact, this cryptic remark of Shakespeare's is probably an arcane reference Kipling inserted for his own pleasure, to an article he had written thirty years before, on the Bermuda background to the play. On his own travels Kipling had seen a beach near Hamilton, Bermuda, that struck him as being scenically so close to the setting described in *The Tempest*, that he imagined Shakespeare had actually met a survivor of the wreck, and milked him for details preserved in the play, which make its actual location still recognisable. The piece was originally printed as a letter to *The Spectator*, 2 July 1898, and can be found in the Sussex edition of his complete works (London, 1938), xxx, Uncollected Prose II, 53–60. *Proofs of Holy Writ* can be found in the same volume, pp. 337–56.

[3] Richmond Noble, *Shakespeare's Biblical Knowledge* (London, 1935), p. 251.

[4] *The Tempest* (London, 1954), pp. 142–5.

terms: the name Ariel 'occurs in the Bible, notably in an obscure passage in Isaiah xxix', but 'the source of the name is probably in the magical tradition'. In this view Kermode was following the suggestion of A. Koszul, and others, whose chief purpose was to find different, more satisfying sources for Shakespeare's creation of Ariel. So Koszul too dismissed 'that impressive, if somewhat incoherent and obscure, lamentation of the prophet over Jerusalem', and turned instead to Cornelius Agrippa's *De Occultu Philosophia*, in which Ariel makes a fleeting appearance as one of the angels of the four elements, but, in the confusion of the chapter in which he appears, seems to correspond rather to the earth than the air.[1] As the search for Ariel's original home turned elsewhere, all subsequent interest in Isaiah xxix seems to have waned. It was finally and completely extinguished by Robert Graves, who was the first to pick on the entire chapter, with a poet's unerring instinct, and to point out the striking similarity between it and *The Tempest*. But Graves then went on to discover such improbable allegories of personal history linking what he understood of Shakespeare's private life from the Sonnets, with this chapter of Isaiah and *The Tempest*, that the initial sense of his observation was dissipated.[2] He is firmly dismissed in a footnote by the Arden editor.

Robert Graves's elaborate and implausible interpretation may have dissuaded recent criticism from giving the whole chapter serious attention;[3] the initial and longstanding lack of interest in the chapter was probably due firstly to its being considered only as a source for the figure of Ariel, in which capacity it has indeed little to offer, and secondly, to its being consulted by good Shakespearians in the translation of the Geneva Bible, supposedly the one used by Shakespeare. Here the passage certainly begins obscurely: 'Ah, altar, altar of the citie where Dauid dwelt', which is explained in a marginal note: 'The Ebrew word Ariel

signifieth the Lyon of God, and signifieth the Altar, because the Altar seemed to deuoure the sacrifice that was offered to God.' This is the quotation wearily given by Noble, Koszul and Kermode. One would agree, here, with Koszul, that Shakespeare was probably drawn to the name for its sound alone, and, 'not caring overmuch about the origin of it "in Ebrew", he just trusted to what may be called its unavoidable paretymology'. The reference in the Geneva Bible is both obscure and unmusical; it would be easy to dismiss it as irrelevant, and to read no further.

It is another matter when the chapter is read in any other of the major translations current at the beginning of the seventeenth century, all of which have variations on the Great Bible's 'Woe vnto thee, O Ariel, Ariel'.[4] It is much easier to imagine Shakespeare being struck with the sound of this, heard in a church reading, for instance, than to envisage him digging the name out of a marginal note (which would not be read out in church and which he could therefore find only by reading). It is certainly possible that Shakespeare may have come across the chapter in church, since it is stipulated as the first lesson for morning service for 8 December in the Church Lectionary of the time.[5] There is even a possible echo of the Psalm listed for this morning's service (to be illustrated later), though not of

[1] A. Koszul, 'Ariel', in *English Studies*, xxix (1937), 202–4.

[2] Robert Graves: 'The Sources of *The Tempest*' (1925), reprinted in *The Common Asphodel* (London, 1949), pp. 27–49.

[3] Professor Muir quotes Graves's reference, and supports him with further parallels from the adjacent chapters of Isaiah, and from James iv 14, in his and Sean O'Loughlin's *Voyage to Illyria* (London, 1937, reprinted 1970), pp. 222–3. I am very grateful to Professor Muir for correcting my mistakes in the present article.

[4] Bishop's Bible: 'Woe vnto thee, O Ariel, Ariel.'

[5] The Lectionary had been slightly revised in 1561, and was next modified only in the nineteenth century, but the readings have hardly changed since 1559. See

the second lesson (Acts viii). In favour of this hypothesis is the general agreement that Shakespeare would have attended church regularly, as the law demanded,[1] and the supposition that he would be more likely to attend morning service, since Evensong took place between two and three in the afternoon and would clash with the theatre's performances.[2] December 8 falls at a propitious time in the probable composition of *The Tempest*, coinciding with the months in which the Bermuda pamphlets first became public and could reasonably be guessed to be occupying Shakespeare's imagination,[3] but the probability of Shakespeare's having heard Isaiah xxix in church on this particular day is diminished by the fact that 8 December fell on a Wednesday in 1610. He may equally well have heard or read it on an earlier occasion, the memory of it lying dormant till it was re-created in this play, maybe only some years later. We can only speculate on the date and circumstances of Shakespeare's acquaintance with Isaiah xxix; neither are of ultimate importance, since on internal evidence alone this play shows many significant links with the chapter, and it is these that concern us.

Before embarking on a comparison of Isaiah xxix and *The Tempest*, something should be said about the nature of a source. Clearly a source is not always as obvious and direct a host as, for instance, Brook's *Tragicall Historye of Romeus and Iuliet* was for *Romeo and Juliet*, or Plutarch's *Lives* were for *Julius Caesar* and *Coriolanus*, but can be, and often is, tangential and apparently irrelevant. It is an experience familiar to anyone attempting even the most trivial creative writing of his own, that images and ideas from other writers can creep into his own work without his having any intention of imitation or significant dependence; his reading and his day-to-day experiences, tumbled and metamorphosed, will emerge in his work, wholly or half digested, often unbidden and even unnoticed by the writer himself. Walter

Whiter's *Specimen of a Commentary* (1794) was the first quasi-psychological study to draw attention to the haphazard workings of unconscious association in the conglomeration of Shakespeare's images with references to contemporary life; Livingston Lowes's study of the *Ancient Mariner* was able to go much further in the identification of 'the hooked atoms that dance along the road to Xanadu', since he had Coleridge's notebooks and a knowledge of his reading at his disposal. He was able amply to illustrate how Coleridge's imagination had stored fragments from the most diverse sources, and then thrown them up in widely differing states, sometimes as they were originally found, sometimes transformed and coalesced in the new creation. The same process is evident in the relationship of Isaiah xxix to *The Tempest*. Here, as in much of Livingston Lowes's work, the relevance of the parallel can best be seen

F. Proctor and W. H. Frere, *A New History of the Book of Common Prayer* (London, 1902), pp. 109–10, 222; and Noble, *Shakespeare's Biblical Knowledge*, p. 14.

[1] 'The laws insisting upon attendance at church were persistently enforced by the authorities ... and it is not likely that a member of the Lord Chamberlain's company of players which occupied so conspicuous a position and enjoyed such distinguished patronage would compromise himself and his company by refusing to conform to the law of the land', The Rev. Ronald Bayne, 'Religion', in *Shakespeare's England* (Oxford, 1916), I, 75.

[2] 'He could hardly have attended Evensong when in London during the theatrical season, for the performances took place on Sunday afternoons ... If it is concluded that Shakespeare normally attended on Sunday mornings, then, in our list of Biblical books, the portions of the Old Testament occurring as Sunday morning proper lessons are very important', Noble, *Shakespeare's Biblical Knowledge*, p. 39.

[3] The ballad *News from Virginia* is dated 1 October 1610, and the first full description of island life, Sylvester Jourdain's *A Discovery of the Barmudas* (1610), has a dedicatory epistle dated 13 October. Strachey's account, to which Shakespeare owes most, is not known to have been printed before 1625; it seems he must have seen it in manuscript at the same time as the other reports.

retrospectively: knowing *The Tempest*, we can then recognise a jumble of elements already familiar to us from the play, unexpectedly co-existing in a single chapter of the Bible. It is the striking number of parallels within such a small area, and the many variations between them in the different kinds of relation they bear to *The Tempest*, which strongly suggest that this chapter had some influence, maybe unconscious, on the creation of the play. For the two texts agree in their shared thematic movement from sin, to punishment involving a trance-like state, to the final coming of understanding, justice and joy; yet in details the links can run counter to this over-all concord. So names and phrases can recur out of context and without the same implications (Ariel's name is the most obvious example); similarly, at certain moments, it seems that the Biblical phrase, whose purpose is merely illustrative, reappears in Shakespeare in its untranslated form, the image robbed of its meaning and occurring merely as an incident (passages 5 and 7 below are possible instances of this); details, also, from two different sources can fuse in the final work, rather in the manner of Lucretius's explanation of the creation of composite fabulous creatures like the centaur or the mermaid, where the image-film of two natural forms are superimposed and fuse together in the mind of the perceiver. This process, in the realm of literary influence, is constantly illustrated by Lowes, and at least two examples present themselves here, where details from Isaiah marry with an echo of Vergil (in passage 5), and with a description from Strachey's *True Reportory* (in passage 3 – a detail later to be appropriated by Coleridge also). But at the same time a single phrase can set off a note that reverberates through the whole play, elusive and yet unmistakable (such is the unearthly voice of passage 2); finally several verses from Isaiah strike at the heart of the play, presenting in a concise form the motto for the play's action

and its import: such are the passages on the trance-sleep (passage 6), the futility of subterfuge (passage 8), the natural dependence of the order of creation on the creator (passage 9), and the coming of understanding (passage 10). The final impression of cumulative relevance is remarkable: while at first the play merely echoes incidents and phrases from the opening verses in an obvious and mechanical fashion, by the second half of chapter and play the relationship becomes more fundamental, until it seems that the themes of Isaiah's prophecy take on a dramatic form in the play, so that the last act of the play could with no distortion have as its text the last verses of Isaiah. It is almost as though Isaiah xxix were the lesson, and *The Tempest* a dramatic sermon embodying its theme.

It seems unlikely that such a close relationship between text and play should be consciously intended or undertaken by Shakespeare. The impression is certainly not that of a sought-out source, but rather of the Isaiah chapter providing a yeast-like impulse to the growth of the play, an influence hardly recognised, perhaps, by the author. Such influence is, of course, not exceptional; for instance, there are similar examples in other plays where part of the Bible has evidently worked in Shakespeare's mind and affected the play's whole outlook. The most striking of these is *Antony and Cleopatra*, where the imagery that draws on the Book of Revelations (first pointed out by Ethel Seaton[1]) is one of the elements that enlarge this play from the purely mundane history related by Plutarch, to an extramundane tragedy in which Antony and Cleopatra defy the narrow limits of the Roman world, and find their triumph in a greater universe. The apocalyptic vision of the Book of Revelations is their key-note, proclaimed by them at the beginning of the play:

[1] Ethel Seaton '*Antony and Cleopatra* and the Revelation of John the Divine', *Review of English Studies*, XXII (1946), 219–24.

I   A scene in act III of J. H. Leigh's production of *The Tempest* at the Royal Court Theatre in 1903

II   Studies of Herbert Beerbohm Tree in the role of Caliban, originally published
in *The Sketch*, 12 October 1904

III *Much Ado about Nothing*, Royal Shakespeare Theatre, 1971. Directed by Ronald Eyre, designed by Voytek, with music by Carl Davis. Elizabeth Spriggs as Beatrice and Derek Godfrey as Benedick

IV *Much Ado about Nothing*, with (l. to r.) Miles Anderson and Ted Valentine as Watchmen,
Peter Woodthorpe as Dogberry, Sydney Bromley as Verges, and Anthony Langdon and
David Calder as Watchmen

V *Othello*, Royal Shakespeare Theatre, 1971. Directed by John Barton, designed by Julia Trevelyan Oman, with music by Guy Woolfenden. Emrys Jones, as Iago, takes a photograph of (front row, l. to r.) David Calder as Cassio, Lisa Harrison as Desdemona, Brewster Mason as Othello, Bernard Lloyd and Miles Anderson as Soldiers and (back row, l. to r.) Anthony Langdon as Montano, Elizabeth Spriggs as Emilia, and Matthew Robertson as a Soldier

VI *Richard II*, Royal Shakespeare Theatre, 1971. Directed by John Barton, designed by
Ann Curtis, with music by Guy Woolfenden. Richard Pasco as Richard II

VII *The Merchant of Venice*, Royal Shakespeare Theatre, 1971. Directed by Terry Hands, designed by Timothy O'Brien, with music by Guy Woolfenden. Bassanio chooses the lead casket, with (in foreground) Judi Dench as Portia and Michael Williams as Bassanio

VIII *The Duchess of Malfi*, Royal Shakespeare Theatre, 1971. Directed by Clifford Williams, designed by Farrah, with music by Marc Wilkinson. Richard Pasco as Antonio and Judi Dench as the Duchess

Cleopatra.

Ile set a bourne how farre to be belou'd.

Antony.

Then must thou needes finde out new Heauen,
new Earth.

(I, i, 848: 23–4)[1]

(Revelations xx 1: 'And I sawe a new heauen, and a new earth.') Their language continues to echo this source of imagery at moments of tension throughout the play.[2] It is partly by use of this language that Shakespeare transforms Plutarch's narrative into a drama of triumph and scorn for earthly grandeur. Yet to call the Book of Revelations a 'source' for *Antony and Cleopatra* might imply a dependence too consciously sought out and maintained. Certainly it set up imaginative currents in Shakespeare's mind, which have profoundly affected the play. The relationship between Isaiah xxix and *The Tempest* is equally subtle and significant.

In the following discussion, for the sake of clarity, a factual outline only of the parallels between the two is given. In order for these to be seen distinctly, I quote the Isaiah chapter in its entirety, italicising and numbering those passages that have special relevance to *The Tempest*. These are then briefly illustrated in turn, but the whole chapter should be remembered as their setting. The translation used is that of the Bishop's Bible.[3]

[1] Quotations from Shakespeare give act and scene and page and line number from Charlton Hinman's Norton Facsimile of the First Folio (New York, 1968). The Revelations quotations are taken from the Geneva Bible, which, in this case, appears to have been the translation known to Shakespeare (see Seaton, '*Antony and Cleopatra* and Revelation', p. 223, footnote 2).

[2] A clear instance of Shakespeare's fusion of his two sources, in which the echo of Revelations immediately expands the dryness of Plutarch's narrative into universal disaster, occurs at Antony's outburst when he finds Thidias kissing Cleopatra's hand. Antony's speech runs as follows:

Get thee backe to Caesar,

Tell him thy entertainment: looke thou say

He makes me angry with him. For he seemes
Proud and disdainfull, harping on what I am,
Not what he knew I was. He makes me angry,
And at this time most easie 'tis to doo't:
When my good Starres, that were my former guides
Haue empty left their Orbes, and shot their Fires
Into th'Abisme of hell. If he mislike
My speech, and what is done, tell him he has
Hiparchus, my enfranched Bondman, whom
He may at pleasure whip, or hang, or torture,
As he shall like to quit me.

(III, xiii, 866: 2, 319 ff.)

Apart from the addition of the three italicised lines, Shakespeare has versified Plutarch almost exactly:

'Whereupon Antonius caused him to be taken and well favouredly whipped, and so sent him unto Caesar: and bad him tell him that he made him angry with him, because he showed him selfe prowde and disdainfull towards him, and now specially when he was easie to be angered, by reason of his present miserie. To be short, if this mislike thee said he, thou hast Hipparchus one of my enfranchised bondmen with thee: hang him if thou wilt, or whippe him at thy pleasure, that we may cry quittaunce.'

The three alien lines that replace Plutarch's 'by reason of his present miserie' echo Revelations ix 1–2:

'And the fift Angel blewe the trumpet, and I sawe a starre which was fallen from heauen vnto the earth, and to him was giuen the key of the bottomlesse pit.

And he opened the bottomlesse pit, and there arose the smoke of the pit, as the smoke of a great fornace; and the Sunne, and the aire were darkened by the smoke of the pit.'

[3] The Bishops' Bible was authorised by the episcopate for church reading, and this is the most likely claimant to Shakespeare's attention, if he heard the chapter rather than read it. The Authorised Version was only published in 1611. The differences between the Geneva and Bishops' Bibles are slight, after the first verse; the most significant departures in the Geneva Bible are listed below:

1 'Ah, altar, altar of the citie where Dauid dwelt.'
2 'Thy voyce also shall bee out of the ground like him that hath a spirit of diuination.'
4 'as a dreame *or* vision by night.'
6 'they are blinde, & make *you* blinde.'
7 'and the vnderstanding of their prudent men shalbe hid.'
9 'Your turning *of deuises* shal it not be esteemed as the potters clay?'
10 'Then they that erred in spirite, shall haue vnderstanding, and they that murmured, shall learne doctrine.'

Esay xxix

1   *Woe vnto thee, O Ariel, Ariel,* thou citie that Dauid dwelt in: Goe on from yeere to yeere, and let the lambes be slaine.

I wil lay siege vnto Ariel, so that there shall bee heauinesse and sorow in it: and it shalbe vnto me euen an altar of slaughter.

I will besiege thee round about, and will fight against thee thorow a bulwarke, and will reare vp ditches against thee.

2   *Thou shalt bee brought downe, and shalt speake out of the ground, and thy speech shal goe lowe out of the dust:*

Thy voice also shall come vp out of the ground, like the voice of a witch, and thy talking shall whisper out of the dust.

Moreouer, the noise of the strange enemies shall be like thin dust, and the multitude of tyrants shall be as drie strawe that cannot tarie: euen suddenly and in haste shal their blast goe.

3   *Thou shalt be visited of the Lord of hosts, with thunder, earthquake, and with a great noise, with storme and tempest, and with the flame of a consuming fire.*

4   *And the multitude* of all nations that fight against Ariel, *shall be as a dreame seen by night:* euen so shall they be that make warre against it, and strong holds to ouercome it, and that lay any siege vnto it.

5   In conclusion, *it shalbe euen as when an hungrie man dreameth that hee is eating, and when he awaketh, his soule is empty, or as when a thirstie man dreameth that hee is drinking, when he awaketh, he is yet faint, and his soule hath appetite:* euen so shall the multitude of all nations be that fight against mount Sion.

6   Ponder these things once in your minds, and wonder: *Blinded are they themselues, and the blind guides of other, they are drunken, but not with wine: they are vnstable, but not through strong drinke:*

For the Lord hath couered you with a slumbring spirit, and hath closed your eyes: your prophets also and rulers that should see, them hath he couered. And the vision of all the prophets, is become vnto you as the wordes of a booke that is sealed vp, which men deliuer to one that is learned, saying, Reade thou in it: and he saith, I can not, for it is sealed.

And the booke is giuen to him that is not learned, saying, Reade thou in it: and he saith, I am not learned.

Therefore thus hath the Lord said, For as much as this people, when they be in trouble, do honour me with their mouth, and with their lips, but their heart is farre from mee, and the feare which they haue vnto mee, proceedeth of a commandement that is taught of men.[1]

7   Therefore I will doe a marueiles among this people, euen marueilous things I say and a wonder: for *the wisedome of their wise men shall perish, and the vnderstanding of their witty men shall hide it selfe.*

8   *Woe vnto them that keepe secret their thoughts, to hide their counsell from the Lord, and to do their workes in darkenesse, saying, Who seeth vs? and who knoweth vs?*

9   *Doubtlesse your destruction is in reputation as the Potters clay: and doeth the worke say of him that made it, He made not mee? And doeth an earthen vessel say of him that fashioned it, He had no vnderstanding?*

Is it not hard at hand that Libanus shall bee turned into a lowe fielde, and that the lowe field shalbe taken as the wood?

10   And in that day shall deafe men heare the wordes of the booke, and *the eyes of the blinde shal see euen out of the cloude, and out of darkenesse. The meeke spirited also shalbe merie in the Lord, and the poore among them that bee lowly shall reioice* in the holy one of Israel:

For hee that did violence is brought to nought, and the scorneful man is consumed, and they rooted out that made haste early to vnrighteousnesse, Making a man to sinne in the word, and that tooke him in a snare, which reproued them in the open place, *and they that haue turned the cause of the righteous to nought.*

Therefore thus saith the Lord to the house of Iacob, euen thus sayth hee that redeemed Abraham, Iacob shal not now be confounded, nor his face pale. *But when he seeth his children the worke of my hands in the mids of him, they shal sanctifie my name,* and praise the holy one of Iacob, and feare the God of Israel.

They also that haue bene of an erronious spirit, shal come to vnderstanding, and they that haue bene scorneful shal learne doctrine.

1   *Woe vnto thee, O Ariel, Ariel*

The name is transferred directly to Ariel the spirit.

---

[1] Noble points out that this verse is twice echoed in two successive scenes in *Measure for Measure*, II, iii, 87:986 ff. and II, iv, 87:1,006 ff.

2 *Thou shalt bee brought downe, and shalt speake out of the ground, and thy speech shal goe lowe out of the dust*

The play is full of unearthly sounds. First there is Prospero's description of Ariel's groans, when trapped by Sycorax in the pine (and 'like the voice of a witch' may have a step-relationship with the 'damn'd Witch Sycorax' of the same passage):

> she did confine thee . . .
> Into a clouen Pyne, within which rift
> Imprison'd, thou didst painefully remaine
> A dozen yeeres . . .
>   where thou didst vent thy groanes
> As fast as Mill-wheeles strike. (I, ii, 22:401 ff.)

The whole play re-echoes with Ariel's invisible voice, but, like his name, his voice quickly expands and refines on its source, losing the sad and subterranean quality of the voice of Jerusalem. When Ferdinand first hears Ariel singing, he says: 'Where shold this Musick be? I'th aire, or th'earth?', but by his next speech he has realised: 'This is no mortall busines, nor no sound That the earth owes: I heare it now aboue me' (I, ii, 23:530, 549–50), and so it remains throughout the play. The island is suffused with sound, as Caliban reminds us again:

> the Isle is full of noyses,
> Sounds, and sweet aires, that giue delight and hurt
>   not:
> Sometimes a thousand twangling Instruments
> Will hum about mine eares; and sometime voices.
>   (III, ii, 30:1,492 ff.)

And finally, Alonso describes the low voice of the conscience troubling him; this sound is the nearest in mood to that described by Isaiah:

> O, it is monstrous: monstrous:
> Me thought the billowes spoke, and told me of it,
> The windes did sing it to me: and the Thunder
> (That deepe and dreadfull Organ-Pipe) pronounc'd
> The name of Prosper: it did base my Trespasse.
>   (III, iii, 31:1,632 ff.)

3 *Thou shalt be visited of the Lord of hosts, with thunder . . . and with a great noise, with storme and tempest, and with the flame of a consuming fire*

The sudden destruction of Jerusalem recurs in the swift and noisy catastrophe of the storm in the opening scene, and Isaiah's *flame of a consuming fire* is personified by Ariel, who gleefully describes the part he plays as this fire, dancing over the sinking ship:

> I boorded the Kings ship: now on the Beake,
> Now in the Waste, the Decke, in euery Cabyn,
> I *flam'd* amazement, sometime I'ld diuide
> And burne in many places; on the Top-mast,
> The Yards and Bore-spritt, would I *flame* distinctly,
> Then meete, and ioyne. (I, ii, 21:308 ff.)

These lines also draw on Strachey's description of St Elmo's fire.[1]

4 *as a dreame seen by night*

The phrase itself, and its implications, are re-echoed in Prospero's speech: 'we are such stuffe As dreames are made on; and our little life Is rounded with a sleepe' (IV, i, 33:1,827 ff.). In Isaiah the enemies of Jerusalem will vanish like a dream; in *The Tempest* the insubstantiality of the marriage-masque created by Prospero is a miniature of the play's own transience, and both are an image of the dream-like evanescence of all life.

5 *it shalbe euen as when an hungrie man dreameth that hee is eating, and when he awaketh, his soule is empty*

Shakespeare seems to ignore the narrow

[1] 'Upon the thursday night Sir George Summers being upon the watch, had an apparition of a little round light, like a faint Starre, trembling, and streaming along with a sparkeling blaze, halfe the height upon the Maine Mast, and shooting sometimes from Shroud to Shroud . . . running sometimes along the Maine-yard to the very end, and then returning.' Livingston Lowes points out Coleridge's probable confusion of this with the 'death-fires' described as dancing round the ship of the Ancient Mariner, in *The Road to Xanadu* (1933), p. 85.

sense apparently given to this image in Isaiah, where it refers merely to the disappointment of the impotent enemies of Jerusalem; he enlarges its implications and transforms it to his own use in the striking scene where Prospero's spirits present the weary and despairing Alonso and his entourage with a banquet, and then snatch it away just as they are about to eat:

Solemne and strange Musicke: and Prosper on the top (inuisible:) Enter seuerall strange shapes, bringing in a Banket; and dance about it with gentle actions of salutations, and inuiting the King, &c. to eate, they depart.

. . . . .

Alonso. I will stand to, and feede,
  Although my last, no matter, since I feele
  The best is past: brother: my Lord, the Duke,
  Stand too, and doe as we.

Thunder and Lightning. Enter Ariell (like a Harpey) claps his wings vpon the Table, and with a quient deuice the Banquet vanishes. (III, iii, 31:1, 535–85)

For it is not food or drink that can nourish and strengthen malefactors such as Alonso, while they are yet unabsolved of their crime; illusory sustenance such as this, the food of rebellious despair, evades their touch.

Shakespeare has further elaborated the scene by dressing Ariel as a Harpy, and so imitating the descent of the Harpies in the *Aeneid*, III, 225–8.

Robert Graves has also pointed out the similarity between this image from Isaiah, and Caliban's famous speech from the preceding scene (already quoted in part in paragraph 2):

Sometimes a thousand twangling Instruments
Will hum about mine eares; and sometime voices,
That if I then had wak'd after long sleepe,
Will make me sleepe againe, and then in dreaming,
The clouds methought would open, and shew riches
Ready to drop vpon me, that when I wak'd
I cri'de to dreame againe. (III, ii, 30:1,494–500)

6 *Blinded are they themselues, and the blind guides of other, they are drunken, but not with wine: they are vnstable, but not through strong*

drinke: For the Lord hath couered you with a slumbring spirit, and hath closed your eyes

This is fundamental to the play. Here every human except Prospero is sunk into a trance state at a point significant to their own development. Miranda falls into a deep sleep after her father's story (I, ii, 21:296), and wakes to find Ferdinand and life in her new world. The mariners are laid asleep under the hatches after the storm, and wake to find their shattered boat whole, and the drowned company resurrected, reassembled, and ready to sail (in the last act). Ferdinand, about to attack Prospero, is suspended by him in a trance (Ferdinand: 'My spirits, as in a dreame, are all bound vp:' I, ii, 24:652), '*is charmed from mouing*' (the stage direction), and then released into a position of humbleness and servitude, which wins him his reward. All but Sebastian and Anthonio fall asleep till Ariel wakes them and saves them from assassination (II, i), but more significant is their second trance, cast on them by Ariel when he snatches the banquet away: they are left in a daze (Ariel: 'Your swords are now too massie for your strengths, And will not be vplifted'; Prospero: 'my high charmes work, And these (mine enemies) are all knit vp In their distractions: they now are in my powre', III, iii, 31:1,600, 1,624), and they remain in such a state till Prospero draws them into his magic circle, disenchants them, and their understanding returns. The drunkenness of Caliban, Stephano and Trinculo is Shakespeare's characteristic transference of this state into a cruder form for those characters that belong to a lower plane; they seem indeed to be drunken and unstable with wine and strong drink, but this is simply the downgrading demanded by decorum, of the state of suspended consciousness suffered by all the humans under Prospero's redeeming care. And again we have the blind leading the blind; Caliban is repeatedly acclaimed as leader by Stephano, and Stephano leads Trinculo, in his turn (Stephano: 'O braue

Monster; lead the way' for their exit at II, ii, 28:1,233; and Stephano: 'Leade Monster, Wee'l follow..' Trinculo: 'Wilt come? Ile follow Stephano' for their exit at III, ii, 30:1,508 ff.).

7 *the wisedome of their wise men shall perish, and the vnderstanding of their witty men shall hide it selfe*

This immediately suggests Prospero's abjuration of his magic, burnt, buried and drowned, just as wisdom here shall perish and be hid:

> I'le breake my staffe,
> Bury it certaine fadomes in the earth,
> And deeper then did euer Plummet sound
> Ile drowne my booke.   (v, i, 34:2,005 ff.)

As in the vanishing banquet of passage 5, if Shakespeare's idea of Prospero's abjuration of his magic owes anything to this source, then he has both enlarged on it, and changed its frame of reference, since in Isaiah the phrase amplifies the preceding passage and refers to impending popular ignorance. In this sense it should strictly be connected with the distraction of Alonso, Sebastian and Anthonio after the enchantment just discussed above. But this parallel, though logically the more correct, is imaginatively the less convincing, and the imagination is not logical.

8 *Woe vnto them that keepe secret their thoughts, to hide their counsell from the Lord, and to do their workes in darkenesse, saying, Who seeth vs? and who knoweth vs?*

This is illustrated three times, emphatically. In the upper rank of characters, Anthonio and Sebastian plot to kill Alonso and Gonzalo, who with the courtiers have fallen into an enchanted sleep; the opportunity would be ideal, if Prospero were not all-seeing, as Ariel informs us: 'My Master through his Art foresees the danger That you (his friend) are in' (II, i, 26:1,000), and he wakes the sleepers in time to rescue them. In the lower plane is the ludicrous insurrection raised by Caliban; the sight of this grotesque trio creeping across the stage to murder Prospero in the supposed oblivion of his afternoon nap (Prospero, the only non-sleeper of the play!) is a beautiful caricature of the thinking condemned by Isaiah. The audience already knows the futility of Caliban's elaborate care for silence ('Pray you tread softly, that the blinde Mole may not heare a foot fall ... speake softly ... be quiet ... no noise' IV, i, 33:1,870 ff.). The third and main illustration is of course the starting point of the play: Anthonio's treacherous deposition of his brother does not go unpunished.

9 *doeth the worke say of him that made it, He made not mee? And doeth an earthen vessel say of him that fashioned it, He had no vnderstanding?*

The due dependence and order of created things is stressed by Prospero in his rule over Ariel and Caliban; his emphatic reminder to Ariel of what he once was, before Prospero rescued him, is a rhetorical reiteration of the question, *doeth the worke say of him that made it, he made not mee?* 'Do'st thou forget From what a torment I did free thee? ... hast thou forgot The fowle Witch Sycorax ... hast thou forgot her? Thou hast ... I must Once in a moneth recount what thou hast bin, Which thou forgetst' (I, ii, 22:375 ff.). And Caliban is just such a one who, with the vessel's ignorance, says *of him that fashioned it, He had no vnderstanding.* Caliban was 'a thing most brutish' till taught by Prospero and Miranda, who gave him speech (I, ii), but he says of Prospero, without his magic books 'Hee's but a Sot, as I am' (III, ii, 30: 1,447), and is confident of supremacy, once the instruments of Prospero's art, and the unfair advantage they bestow, have been destroyed. The vessel finally recognises its creator, however; in the last act, on seeing

Prospero in normal dress, Caliban exclaims: 'How fine my Master is? what a thrice double Asse Was I to take this drunkard for a god? And worship this dull foole?' (v, i, 36:2,255, 2,292 ff.).

10   *the eyes of the blinde shal see euen out of the cloude, and out of darkenesse*

    The closing passage of Isaiah xxix sums up the end of *The Tempest*: as Prospero's charms begin to work and understanding dawns on Alonso and his company, Prospero echoes these words:

> The charme dissolues apace,
> And as the morning steales vpon the night
> (Melting the darkenesse) so their rising sences
> Begin to chace the ignorant fumes that mantle
> Their cleerer reason.   (v, i, 34:2,020–4)

The meeke spirited also shalbe merie . . . and the poore among them that bee lowly shall reioice

    These find their representative in Ferdinand, whom Prospero had subjected to servitude and indignity, 'least too light winning Make the prize light' (I, ii, 23:605). But the meek and poor Ferdinand learnt his lesson early, realising that 'Some kindes of basenesse Are nobly vndergon; and most poore matters Point to rich ends' (III, i, 28:1,237 ff.); now, at the end of the play, he finds the increase of his joy.

hee that did violence is brought to nought . . . the scorneful man is consumed . . . and they that haue turned the cause of the righteous to nought

    The harsh retribution of the wicked is characteristically spared by Shakespeare. Although Anthonio and Sebastian had amply shown their capacities for being *the scorneful man*, and those *that haue turned the cause of the righteous to nought*, in their mockery of Gonzalo (in I, ii), and as those *that did violence* and *made haste early to vnrighteousnesse*, in their attempted murder of Alonso and Gonzalo in the same scene, as well as by their earlier misdeeds, yet Prospero is merciful. Shake-

speare's justice is not that of Isaiah; from his earliest plays he taught the principle that 'the rarer Action is In vertue, then in vengeance' (v, i, 34:1,977).

when he seeth his children the worke of my hands in the mids of him, they shal sanctifie my name

    This is triumphantly dramatised by Prospero, who discloses the children Ferdinand and Miranda – in their unity truly the work of his hands – in his cave, oblivious of the company around them, absorbed in their game of chess; *they shal sanctifie my name* is realised in the exalted tone of Gonzalo's thanksgiving: 'O reioyce Beyond a common ioy, and set it downe With gold on lasting Pillers . . .' (v, i, 36:2,188 ff.).

    And what more apposite last motto could there be for *The Tempest*, than the closing words of this chapter?

They also that haue bene of an erronious spirit, shal come to vnderstanding, and they that haue bene scorneful shal learne doctrine

    This is the very illumination worked by Prospero, and his own words echo Isaiah once again, as Alonso, Sebastian and Anthonio emerge from their trance:

> Their vnderstanding
> Begins to swell, and the approching tide
> Will shortly fill the reasonable shore
> That now ly foule, and muddy.
>
>   (v, i, 35:2,035)

The scornful find their voice in Caliban, who leads Stephano and Trinculo offstage, proclaiming the doctrine he has learnt at last:

> Ile be wise hereafter,
> And seeke for grace.   (v, i, 36:2,291–2)

    Finally, there is the psalm specified for morning service on 8 December. This is Psalm viii, already repudiated by Shakespeare in an earlier, more troubled period:

For I will consider the heauens, euen the works of thy fingers: the moone and the starres which thou hast ordained.

What is man that thou art mindfull of him: and the sonne of man that thou visitest him?

Thou madest him lower then the Angels: to crowne him with glory and worship.

Thou makest him to haue dominion ouer the works of thy handes: and thou hast put all things 'in subiection vnder his feete.

All sheepe & oxen: yea and the beasts of the field.

The foules of the aire, & the fishes of the sea: and whatsoeuer walketh thorow the paths of the seas.

O Lord our gouernour: how excellent is thy Name in all the world?[1]

What a piece of worke is a man! how Noble in Reason? how infinite in faculty? in forme and mouing how expresse and admirable? in Action, how like an Angel? in apprehension, how like a God? the beauty of the world, the Parragon of Animals; and yet to me, what is this Quintessence of Dust? Man delights not me ...   (*Hamlet*, II, ii, 770: 1,350 ff.)

But now, in the serener certainty of this last play, the psalmist's praise is reaffirmed by Miranda, and her enlightened and innocent vision is the starting-point with which this play closes:

O wonder!
How many goodly creatures are there heere?
How beauteous mankinde is? O braue new world
That has such people in't.   (V, i, 35: 2,157 ff.)

[1] Quoted from a 1606 edition of the Book of Common Prayer.

© ANN PASTERNAK SLATER 1972

THE LIFE OF GEORGE WILKINS

ROGER PRIOR

Very little has hitherto been known about the minor dramatist and pamphleteer, George Wilkins. From all the available evidence, it seems likely that he wrote the first two acts of *Pericles Prince of Tyre*, and that Shakespeare wrote the last three, apart from the Gower choruses.[1] Several of his works survive, but he is not mentioned by his contemporaries, and hardly any facts about him have come to light. This is the more to be regretted because *Pericles* is an important experiment. It was the turning-point which led to the other late Romance plays. It is interesting that Shakespeare should have derived half his play, and possibly the original conception,[2] from a minor dramatist like Wilkins. In these circumstances, any information about Wilkins is of particular value.

It is therefore extremely fortunate that a great quantity of such information has been preserved among the records of the seventeenth-century Middlesex Sessions in the Greater London Record Office (Middlesex Section).[3] Professor Mark Eccles seems to be the first and only scholar ever to have pointed this out, in his *Christopher Marlowe in London*.[4] He writes there that he intends to describe the records in full elsewhere, but, if he did so, it has eluded me and all other writers on Wilkins that I have come across. The Sessions records reveal much about Wilkins that is new, and positively confirm what had already been inferred from other evidence. They show that his life and his literary works have some strange characteristics in common. Lastly, they provide at least one new link

between Wilkins and *Pericles*. Before describing this new material, I shall summarise what is known about Wilkins from other sources.

All or most of his work seems to have been published between the years 1606 and 1608, a comparatively short period of time. Besides the conjectural first two acts of *Pericles*, he certainly wrote the novel *The Painfull Aduentures of Pericles Prince of Tyre* (1608) which is based on the play. His other extant works are a translation, *The Historie of Iustine* (1606), most of which is copied from an earlier version by Arthur Golding; a play, *The Miseries of Inforst Marriage* (1607); a pamphlet, *Three Miseries of Barbary*, probably published in 1606 or 1607;[5]

---

[1] The Arden *Pericles*, ed. F. D. Hoeniger (London, 1969), conveniently summarises the evidence (Introd., pp. lix–lxii).

[2] Several critics have suggested that *Pericles* was originally written in full or drafted by Wilkins and that Shakespeare then re-wrote the second half. See, for example, Dugdale Sykes, *Sidelights on Shakespeare* (Stratford-upon-Avon, 1919), pp. 188–203.

[3] For this discovery I am indebted to Mr W. J. Smith, Deputy Head Archivist to the Greater London Council, who first pointed out to me the references to Wilkins and their mention by Eccles. I am deeply grateful to him and to his staff for this and much other help. Mrs Susan Avery gave invaluable help with deciphering the entries. All the original documents here referred to are in the Greater London Record Office (Middlesex Section), 1 Queen Anne's Gate Buildings, Dartmouth Street, London, S.W.1.

[4] Cambridge, Mass., 1934, p. 104.

[5] See G. S. Greene, 'A New Date for George Wilkins's *Three Miseries of Barbary*', *Modern Language Notes*, XXXIX (1924), 285–91. He shows that it must have been published between 1606 and 1610.

and parts of at least two other works. We know that he wrote parts of *Iests to Make you Merrie* (1607) with Dekker, and some scenes of *The Travailes of Three English Brothers* (1607), a play written in collaboration with Day and Rowley. Parts of other plays have been attributed to him.[1]

Who was this minor author? The almost complete lack of external evidence has made identification difficult. He cannot have been the 'George Wilkins, the Poet' who was buried in Shoreditch on 19 August 1603, according to the burial register of St Leonard's Church. But he could have been that man's son, and the Sessions records tend to confirm this long-standing theory. George Wilkins the elder lived in Halliwell Street; he probably died of the plague, which was widespread in 1603. It has been suggested that the Wilkinses, if they were father and son, may have been the 'G. W. Senior' and 'G. W. I' (presumably for Iunior) who wrote the two sonnets prefixed to Spenser's *Amoretti*, 1595. This is certainly possible.[2]

The first real clue to Wilkins's identity was found by C. W. Wallace when he came across the documents of the Belott–Mountjoy Suit of 1612.[3] Stephen Belott sued his father-in-law and employer, Christopher Mountjoy, for non-payment of the dowry which he had promised to give his daughter Mary on her marriage to Stephen. The two men were French Protestants and makers of wigs. Both Shakespeare and George Wilkins gave depositions. Shakespeare had lived in Mountjoy's house, and testified that he had known Belott and Mountjoy for ten years 'or thereabouts'. Wilkins had known them for seven years. He is described as of 'the parishe of S^{ct}· Sepulchers London Victuler of the Age of thirtye Syxe yeres or th^{r}aboutes'. Shakespeare was then forty-eight. Part of Wilkins's deposition is as follows:

To the vth Interr this deponent sayth that after the plt was married wth Marye the deftes daughter he the

plaintiff and his wyffe came to dwell in this deponntes house in one of his Chambers. And brought wth them A fewe goodes or houshould stuffe wch by Reporte the defendt her fath^r gaue them, ffor wch this deponent would not haue geuen Aboue ffyve poundes yf he had bene to haue bought the same./ And more he cannott depose touching the same Interr:/

George Wilkins

From the description of Wilkins as a victualler and the mention of 'one of his chambers', Wallace inferred that Wilkins kept an inn. This inference was, it turns out, quite correct.

Both Shakespeare and Wilkins were obviously close friends of the Mountjoy family, and must have known each other. The conclusion is irresistible that this is George Wilkins the dramatist. Although the evidence is circumstantial, the coincidences of name, age, and association with Shakespeare altogether make a strong case.

The only other piece of evidence hitherto discovered[4] allows us to identify the dramatist for certain, but unfortunately tells us next to nothing about him. The records of the church of St Sepulchre's were destroyed in the Great Fire of 1666, but Wilkins appears in the records of a nearby parish, St Giles's, Cripplegate, which adjoined the parish of St Sepulchre's on its north-east, beyond the Charterhouse. In the St Giles's register, on 11 February 1605, is recorded the christening of Thomas, son of

[1] By Sykes and others. Sykes, *Sidelights on Shakespeare*, pp. 77–98, 145. See p. 149, n. 1.

[2] F. I. Carpenter in *Modern Philology*, XXII (1924), 67–8, argued for the Wilkinses; R. Gottfried put forward Geoffrey Whitney and his father (*Modern Language Quarterly*, III, 1942, 543–6). Gottfried's case is ingenious but unconvincing. Elsewhere I hope to show other reasons for supporting the Wilkinses.

[3] C. W. Wallace, 'Shakespeare and his London Associates as Revealed in Recently Discovered Documents', *The University Studies of the University of Nebraska*, X (1910), 261–360. The quotations are from p. 289.

[4] By Mary R. McManaway: see 'Poets in the Parish of St. Giles, Cripplegate', *Shakespeare Quarterly*, IX (1958), 561–2.

'George Wilkens, Poett'. Of all the surviving records, only this one describes Wilkins as a poet. Clearly this man could also be the Wilkins of the Belott suit, and son of the George Wilkins, poet, who died in 1603.

If Belott's friend was not the dramatist, then who else could have been? No other convincing candidate has been found. A search for George Wilkins was carried out by Mr George B. Dickson who, for reasons of his own, rejected the man found by Wallace.[1] He turned up three other men bearing this name in this period. One lived in Surrey and can be excluded for that reason. The other two lived in London, and deserve more consideration. One was buried on 4 February 1639, at the age of fifty, in the parish of St Botolph's, Bishopsgate.[2] In 1605, when, if he was the dramatist (and father), he must have been hard at his creative work, this Wilkins was only sixteen. By 1608, with all his work published, he was nineteen. On the lucky remaining candidate, if he is to be the dramatist, must be bestowed the gift of a very long life. He was buried on 5 April 1675, from St Paul's Church, Covent Garden.[3] If we allow him to publish his works between the ages of twenty-one and twenty-three, he died at the advanced, though possible, age of ninety. On grounds of age alone the George Wilkins, victualler, of the Belott–Mountjoy suit is the man most likely to have been the writer. The Sessions records confirm this identification.

The original sixteenth- and early seventeenth-century records of the Middlesex Sessions of the Peace are copious, but far from complete. Some are missing: the Rolls, in particular, of the reign of Elizabeth have in most cases become separated into their constituent documents, many of which have inevitably been lost. In the cases which concern Wilkins, for example, the actual indictments have rarely survived. But after January 1608, the records are more complete; moreover, at this date begin the Sessions Registers and the

Gaol Delivery Registers. The records which mention Wilkins are of three kinds: Sessions Rolls, Sessions Registers, and Gaol Delivery Registers. The Sessions Rolls, in their complete form, comprised all the formal documents of the court, such as indictments, recognizances and lists of jurors. Almost all mentions of Wilkins in the Rolls occur in recognizances, which were bonds, attested by a Justice of the Peace, to secure a person's appearance at the next Sessions, or to require him to keep the peace. The recognizances and the other formal documents are written in an extremely abbreviated legal Latin and are not always easy to read. Annotations, in English, usually a description of the charge, are often added. The Sessions Register is a formal record, kept in a large book and usually well written, of the actual proceedings of the Middlesex court. It records the appearance of witnesses and accused, and the details of some indictments, verdicts, and sentences. It is partly in Latin and partly in English. The Gaol Delivery Register is a similar record of the Sessions held in the Old Bailey for the delivery of Newgate Gaol. These Sessions were separate from the Middlesex Sessions of the Peace, which were held in Clerkenwell, but of course they often dealt with the same offenders. The Middlesex court sat in the Castle Inn, St John Street, and after 1612, in Hicks's Hall in the same street. All the entries in these records up to March 1618, are catalogued in three series of modern calendars, compiled under the supervision of Mr John Cordy Jeaffreson, Mr W. J. Hardy, and Mr William Le Hardy. For the period from March 1618 to April 1619 some entries are available in handwritten transcripts in the Greater London

[1] 'The Identity of George Wilkins', *Shakespeare Association Bull.*, XIV (1939), 195–208.

[2] A. W. C. Hallen, *The Registers of St. Botolph, Bishopsgate* (Alloa, 1889–95), II, 51.

[3] *The Registers of St. Paul's Church, Covent Garden*, ed. W. H. Hunt (London, 1908), IV, 69 (Publications of the Harleian Society, Registers, vol. XXXVI).

Record Office, and most entries are card-indexed. The first series of calendars[1] and the last,[2] in chronological order of entries, have been published and are available in libraries. The middle series[3] consists of ten volumes of mimeographed typescript and is available in the Greater London Record Office (Middlesex Section), the British Museum, and the Public Record Office. The calendars conveniently gather together all the entries which relate to a particular case and reproduce the sense of the originals in full, omitting duplicate information, legal formulae, and such details as the amount of bail. All details of the charge and sentence are given, usually word for word, in modernised spelling. Latin is translated. The account which follows is derived from both the calendars and from the original documents, which in every case I have consulted. Quotations reproduce the words of the original, except where for convenience I quote the calendar's translation of the original Latin. I have expanded abbreviations.

The references to George Wilkins in the Sessions records are extraordinarily numerous. The first certain reference to him is in April 1610, and from that date until October 1618, when he appears for the last time, he is mentioned in connection with eighteen separate cases. In the original records he appears in no fewer than thirty-eight entries. (A single indictment may of course involve several separate entries in the records.) The question immediately arises: do all these entries refer to the same man? Or do some refer to another George Wilkins, perhaps one of the two discovered by Mr Dickson? The answer to the second question is almost certainly no. It can be established with some certainty that in the period between 1600 and 1619 only one George Wilkins appears in the Sessions records. The abundance of information allows a confident identification. The very large number of entries makes cross-reference possible, and

provides easy and reliable checks on identity. Wilkins can even be identified on the two occasions when he is called George Wilkinson, or Wilkeson, despite the fact that this name was borne by other men mentioned in the records. The portrait of Wilkins which emerges from the records is a consistent and distinctive one. But before discussing the man in detail, I shall establish the case for his identity. In my analysis of names and descriptions I have compared those used in each court case rather than those from each separate entry, since the former procedure has more relation to the needs of the court. If a description varied from case to case it would hardly matter to the officers of the court, whereas in the entries which referred to a single case it would obviously be in their interest to maintain consistency. On the whole they were consistent in this respect; the only two exceptions will be indicated. For ease of reference, and to save innumerable footnotes, I have numbered the cases, in chronological order, from 1 to 18, and tabulated the details of identity which they contain in an appendix. References to the calendars and to the original records are also gathered together there under each case.

Of the eighteen separate cases in which George Wilkins appears, sixteen give the name in that form, one gives it as George Wilkinson, and one as George Wilkeson. The name George Wilkinson occurs on three other occasions in the records, but in each case, as I shall show, it is unlikely to refer to the dramatist. For the moment I shall leave all the Wilkinson entries out of account. In the sixteen remaining cases Wilkins is eleven times described as living in Cow Cross, a street just to the north of Smithfield. He is most frequently said to be 'of Cow

[1] *Middlesex County Records*, ed. J. C. Jeaffreson, vols. I–IV (London, 1886–92).
[2] *Middlesex Sessions Records*, New Series, ed. W. Le Hardy, vols. I–IV (London, 1935–41).
[3] *Calendar to Middlesex Records*, vols. I–X.

Cross, yeoman' (6 times), but he is three times called a victualler and twice a gentleman, of Cow Cross. Twice he is said to be of Turnmill Street, once as a yeoman and once without his trade or status being named. Once he is described as a victualler, of St James's, Clerkenwell, and in two cases his name alone is given.

There can be little doubt that all these entries refer to the same man, and that this man is identical with the George Wilkins, victualler of St Sepulchre's, who gave evidence for Stephen Belott. The discrepancies in the descriptions of dwelling-place and social status are easily accounted for. To begin with, there is no discrepancy between the statements that he lived in both Turnmill Street and Cow Cross. Cow Cross ran (and still runs) east–west, and the southern end of Turnmill Street joined it at its west end, being in effect a continuation of it to the northward. Wilkins's house may have been on a corner of the two streets, or possibly the two streets were sometimes thought of as being one. The area was notorious as the haunt of whores and thieves, a reputation which the Sessions records amply confirm. Turnmill Street itself was particularly infamous, and is constantly mentioned by contemporary writers, under the alternative names of Turnball, Turnbull and Tunbold Street.[1] The Wilkins who knew Stephen Belott could well have been living in this area, for both Cow Cross and the southern end of Turnmill Street which runs into it were within the parish of St Sepulchre's. In one case (no. 3) Wilkins appears, under the variant name of Wilkeson, as a victualler of St Sepulchre's. In every respect – name, dwelling-place, trade, and date – the George Wilkins of the Sessions records corresponds with the deponent of the Belott–Mountjoy suit.

The remaining calendar entry (case no. 5), which assigns him to the parish of St James's, Clerkenwell, is easily explained. In fact more than one explanation is possible. St James's was the parish immediately north of St Sepulchre's.

It included the northern part of Turnmill Street, and its southern boundary ran close to Cow Cross. So the discrepancy may have been due to parochial confusion or carelessness. But a more likely explanation is that, as the Middlesex Sessions were held in Clerkenwell, it was not uncommon for the accused to be described as being from Clerkenwell, when in fact he lived elsewhere. Another reason is suggested by the charge, added to the recognizance: 'The said George Wilkins bound over for abusing m^{r} Barnes Constable of Clerkenwell in the execucion of his office.'[2] Quite possibly, therefore, the offence was committed in Clerkenwell, and Wilkins was assigned to the parish for that reason. But, whatever the explanation, we can be sure that the description of residence is not to be taken literally, for the following reason. Wilkins had one guarantor of bail in the case, Geoffrey Eames, a gardener, who is also said to be of St James's, Clerkenwell. But only two days earlier this man appears with Wilkins in another case (no. 6, where he is called Geoffrey Emms, gardener), and on this occasion both men are said to be of Cow Cross. All variations in place of residence can thus be accounted for.

Nor do the three different descriptions of status present any difficulty. We might reasonably suppose the victualler and the yeoman to be one and the same man, but luckily positive proof of this exists. For the George Wilkins whom one entry describes as a yeoman of Cow Cross is in the same entry 'enioyned by this Courte not to victell without lycense'.[3] A similar ban was imposed on the yeoman of Turnmill Street (case no. 11). And in one case (no. 16), which has an unusually large number of entries, Wilkins is a yeoman in two entries and a victualler in two entries. This is one of

---

[1] E.g. 2 *Henry IV*, iii, ii, 300 (Arden edn, ed. A. R. Humphreys; London, 1966). There are several references in *The Black Book* of Thomas Middleton.

[2] Sessions Roll 506/215.

[3] Sessions Register 1/247. Case no. 1.

two instances where different descriptions of status occur in the same case. In the other case (no. 18), four entries describe Wilkins as a yeoman, but one as a labourer.

That the yeoman victualler sometimes went under the title of gentleman cannot be proved, but is highly probable. Otherwise we would have to believe that two men, both bearing the same name and living in the same street at the same time, both came to trial for the same kind of offences, and that the court distinguished between them by their status alone. It is more reasonable to suppose that Wilkins was a 'new man', or one whose social status was ambiguous. He lived in a poor district, but his writings show him to have had an education, though not a very sound one. His own description of himself agrees with the evidence of the Sessions records, for in the dedication to *The Painfull Aduentures*, he writes

I see Sir, that a good coate with rich trappings gets a gay Asse entraunce in at a great Gate (and within a may stalke freely) when a ragged philosopher with more witte shall be shutte foorth of doores: notwithstanding this I know Sir that Vertue wants no bases to vpholde her, but her owne kinne.[1]

The Sessions records certainly confirm that Wilkins was 'ragged', though they make his claim to virtue sound rather strange. The passage implies a bitter disappointment at his lack of success and a deep resentment of his low station in life. This is illuminating, for the records show Wilkins to have lived in the lowest quarter of London, under circumstances which an ambitious man might well resent. Moreover, if any shadow of a personality emerges from the cases, it is that of a man wretched and at odds with his life.

Two cases remain, in which we are given no more details of identity than the name, George Wilkins. Even here, however, identification is reasonably certain; it must be remembered that no other George Wilkins can be distinguished in the Sessions records of this period. In one

case (no. 12) Wilkins and his wife were assaulted by a resident of Cow Cross. No other identifying information is given. As Cow Cross is the only location mentioned in the case, it is reasonable to assume that all those concerned were from that area. In the second case (no. 9), there are more clues. A gentleman of Chancery Lane was accused of 'comitting a notorious outrage in the house of George Wilkins and for abusing one Bonner at the same time'.[2] The charge suggests that Wilkins's house was a victualling house where such 'outrages' would be common (see case no. 17). 'One Bonner' is likely to be John Bonner, a factor of Cow Cross, who seems to have been an associate of our Wilkins in another, rather shady case (no. 5). All the evidence suggests that the Wilkins of case no. 9 is identical with the man who kept a tavern in Cow Cross.

While the name Wilkins is comparatively rare in the Sessions records, Wilkinson is extremely common. The name George Wilkinson occurs in five cases between 1600 and 1619. In three of these it probably does not refer to George Wilkins the victualler. We can quickly eliminate two: one man is described as an armourer, of Christ Church.[3] The other is a tanner, of St James's, Clerkenwell (he was ordered to answer the constable of Clerkenwell).[4] The third case is more doubtful, partly because this Wilkinson is a yeoman and partly because the case is dated more than two years earlier than the first Wilkins entry, at a time when he may not have been living in Cow Cross. On 19 January 1608, 'George Wilkinson, yoman, Jane Wilkinson, widow... late of St. Andrew's in Holborn co. Midd.', together with

---

[1] *The Painfull Aduentures of Pericles Prince of Tyre*, ed. Kenneth Muir (Liverpool, 1967), p. 1. The resentment implied here is expressed more strongly in the 'Cock Wat' passage in *Iests to Make you Merrie*. This part of the work has several verbal echoes of Wilkins.

[2] Sessions Roll 508a/72.

[3] *Calendar to Middlesex Records*, IV, 6.

[4] *Ibid.*, X, 51.

more than a score of others were convicted of 'not going to church, chapel or any usual place of Common Prayer during three months beginning on 1 Sept., 5 James 1' (1607).[1] Such entries are frequent, and indicate that the accused were Catholic recusants. But Wilkins's writings give us no reason to think that he was a Catholic. Moreover the Belott suit suggests that he was living in Cow Cross soon after Belott's marriage in 1604. I am therefore inclined to reject this Wilkinson. A Wilkinson whose Latinised Christian name ended in 's' (the rest is missing) occurs in an entry of October 1618 as a victualler of High Holborn.[2] Circumstances make it unlikely that he was our Wilkins (see case no. 18); but he may have been the recusant.

The remaining two cases are comparatively free from doubt. In one (no. 3), Wilkins is George Wilkeson, a victualler of St Sepulchre's; in the other (no. 7), he is George Wilkinson of Cow Cross, victualler. Identification is certain in the latter case as it must be connected, on internal evidence, with another where he bears his usual name of Wilkins (no. 6). The relationship between the two cases is described below (p. 146). Wilkins, then, was sometimes known as Wilkinson. If he was in fact the son of the other George Wilkins, poet, this would have been an appropriate surname.

His use of this name raises a final question of identity. We know that Wilkins was married (see case no. 12). We also learn from the Sessions records that in 1612 and 1617–18 there was living in Turnmill Street a woman who called herself both Alice Wilkins and Alice Wilkinson. She was the injured party in two cases.[3] The coincidence of dwelling-place, coupled with the comparative rarity of the name Wilkins, might lead us to suppose that she was George Wilkins's wife. But this cannot have been the case, for in January 1618, when George Wilkins was still alive, Alice Wilkins

was described as a widow. Her former husband was almost certainly one Bartholomew Wilkins, who figures prominently in the Sessions records. No Sessions record links him with Alice, but the register of St James's, Clerkenwell, records the marriage of Bartholomew Wilkins and Alice Tanner, on 4 February 1599.[4] According to the Sessions records he lived in Pistol's manor of Pickt-Hatch, an area not far from Turnmill Street and equally notorious. In December 1609, he was convicted of clipping the King's coin. For this act of treason he was sentenced to be hanged, disembowelled, and burned while still living.[5] Although Alice was not married to George Wilkins, there remains the possibility that she lived in his house. He and Bartholomew may have been related, in which case it would be natural for him to have supported the widow after her husband's death. This theory derives support from the odd coincidence that Alice and George Wilkins were both involved in brawls with local women at about the same time. She was attacked by two women; he attacked another (case no. 10). A causal connection seems possible here. Wilkins's wife may well have been the Katherin Fowler (or Fowles) whose marriage to a George Wilkins is recorded in the register of St

[1] *Middlesex County Records*, II, 27–8, 33. The entries are taken from the Gaol Delivery Roll.

[2] See the Process Register Book of Indictments, II, 35 and the index. The card-index records this entry.

[3] (a) 27 March, 1612. Two women to keep peace towards Alice Wilkins. *Calendar to Middlesex Records*, IX, 183. Sessions Roll 512/149, 150. Sessions Register 1/504, 511; G.D. Register 1/196. (b) 14 or 15 January, 1618. Theft of linen from Alice Wilkins. *Middlesex Sessions Records*, New Series, IV, 326. Sessions Roll 562/104, 174; G.D. Register 2/137 *dorso*.

[4] *A True Register of all the Christeninges, Mariages, and Burialles in the Parishe of St. James, Clarkenwell*, ed. R. Hovenden (London, 1887) III, 23. (Publications of the Harleian Society, Registers, vol. XIII.)

[5] *Calendar to Middlesex Records*, III, 93, 114, 122, 221. Sessions Roll 479/100, 104, 484/9, etc., G.D. Register 1/101 *dorso*.

Lawrence Jewry.[1] The date was 13 February 1601, when Wilkins was about twenty-five. His son Thomas was christened almost exactly four years after this marriage, on 11 February 1605.

In the account of Wilkins's life which follows it must be remembered that our evidence consists mostly of recognizances and the records of their discharge in the Sessions Register, with whatever annotations may have been added to them. Hence we usually know the charge, but less often the verdict and penalty. According to the records, Wilkins first appeared before the Middlesex bench in April 1610. No firm conclusion can be drawn from this date, as the records are so far from complete before January 1608. But in view of his constant later troubles it may be significant that there is no record of him coming to court during the time when he was writing and publishing his work, and for two years afterwards. On 4 April 1610, William Mendham, a 'girdler' of St Peter's, West-cheap, and Michael Hayworth, husbandman, of Cow Cross, on penalty of £10 each (the usual amount of bail) undertook that Wilkins would appear at the next sessions and meanwhile keep the peace towards Anne Plesington, or Pleasington (case no. 1). The Sessions began five days later on 9 April. The court's decision is not recorded, except that Wilkins was banned from victualling, presumably temporarily. We can tell something of Anne Plesington from an entry for 31 March 1612. There she was indicted for being 'a noted queane herself, and also a comon harborer of lewd persons'.[2]

Wilkins faced no more charges in 1610, but he gave recognizances of £10 in two cases. The first occasion (case no. 2) was on 22 April, not long after his own appearance. He and Miles Ayer, a Holborn vintner, were guarantors for the appearance of John Fisher, a cordwainer of St Brides'. Fisher had 'unlawfullye begotten one Grace Saville with childe'. At the sessions of 23 May Wilkins again stood bail for Fisher,

who was directed 'to repair in the meane tyme to Sir Robert Leighe & Mr. Vaghan to be ordered touching the keepinge of the Basterd'. Sir Robert Leigh and Mr Vaughan (as his name is spelt elsewhere) were both Justices; Leigh's signature appears particularly often in the records. Another magistrate on the bench at these Sessions was a Mr Henry Fermor. This fact is of interest, for two years earlier Wilkins had dedicated his novel *The Painfull Aduentures of Pericles Prince of Tyre* 'To the Right Worshipfull and most woorthy Gentleman Maister Henry Fermor, one of his Maiesties Iustices of Peace for the Countie of Middlesex'.[3] Wilkins's friend Dekker had dedicated *The Seven Deadly Sinnes of London* to him in 1606. Fermor's signature is on many recognizances, although never on an entry which concerns Wilkins. But it is clear that in the case of John Fisher's bastard child, writer and patron may have faced each other in court, and in the next case in which Wilkins came to trial (no. 4) his patron may have tried and even sentenced him.

The second recognizance that Wilkins gave in this year was on 23 September under the name of George Wilkeson (case no. 3). He and William Bennytt, a coachman, gave surety for a butcher with the appropriate name of Thomas Cutts. Cutts was bound over 'for woundinge one John Ball in the head with a welshe hooke'.

In March of the next year, 1611, Wilkins was again in trouble (case no. 4), before a bench which included Henry Fermor. The charge is noted at the foot of a recognizance, dated 3 March. He was accused of 'abusinge one Randall Borkes and kikkinge a woman on the Belly which was then greate with childe'. We do not know if he was convicted. Quite apart

[1] *The Register of St. Lawrence Jewry*, transcribed and ed. A. W. Hughes Clarke (London, 1940), I, 88 (Publications of the Harleian Society, Registers, vol. LXX).
[2] Sessions Roll 512/62. *Calendar to Middlesex Records*, IX, 165.
[3] *The Painfull Aduentures*, p. 1.

from the extraordinary suggestiveness of the charge, this recognizance has the most literary interest of all the Sessions records. It provides additional and much needed evidence that George Wilkins, victualler, was also a writer, and it further strengthens the already strong links between Wilkins and *Pericles*. For some reason, neither of Wilkins's two guarantors in the case was, as they usually were, from the area round Cow Cross. Each, as usual, was liable for £10. The first was Richard Daniell, of St Benedict, Shoreditch, described both as a barber-surgeon and as a silk-weaver. He is often mentioned in the Sessions records as one who stood bail in unimportant cases[1] and is almost always described as a weaver. The other guarantor was Henry Gosson, of St Lawrence Poultney, gentleman. He is well known as a publisher of extant ballads and sensational pamphlets. He was also the publisher of *Pericles*. He had brought out another work by Wilkins, the short pamphlet *Three Miseries of Barbary*, probably in 1606 or 1607, although it could have been as late as 1610. The recognizance shows that in March 1611 Gosson was a friend of Wilkins, or indebted to him, or both. Their friendship may have had origins of which we know nothing. But it cannot have been entirely separate from their common interests as writer and publisher, and the facts that we know suggest an obvious hypothesis. The writing of a short pamphlet would by itself hardly account for Gosson's friendship. But *Pericles* was a valuable property – far more so than *The Three Miseries*. It was twice reprinted, once in 1609 and again in 1611, the very year in which Gosson stood bail for Wilkins. If it was through Wilkins's help that Gosson had got hold of a copy of *Pericles*, a play still in print and making money, what could be more natural than that Wilkins should ask him to stand bail and that he should agree to do so?

The suggestion that Wilkins had a hand in the possibly surreptitious publication of *Pericles* has of course been made before. E. A. J. Honigmann pointed out that the title-page of *Pericles* in its wording resembles the title-pages of his two other known plays:[2] all three take care to emphasise that the plays in question are either currently being performed or have been recently. Wilkins, he suggests, liked to bring out his plays in print while they were still fresh in the public mind. The evidence is slight, but the theory fits all that we know of Wilkins. From the strange variety of his published work, some trivial, some copied from existing books, we might guess that he was unusually eager to appear in print. We can see a similar eagerness in his hasty adaptation of *Pericles* as a novel, during or soon after its success on the stage. The passage quoted above from the novel's dedication shows his need for recognition and success as an author. Such a man might well try to publish a play for which he was partly responsible, even under another man's name. Here is the principal objection to the theory that Wilkins obtained *Pericles* for Gosson. If he did so, why did he not add his own name to the title-page? Gosson may have thought the play more likely to sell under Shakespeare's name alone. Or perhaps it was a gesture to appease Shakespeare's company, the King's Men, who owned the play. There are many possible explanations. Another serious difficulty, however, is that when Wilkins based his novel on *Pericles* in 1607–8, he does not seem to have possessed a copy of the play. For the novel, on internal evidence, almost certainly relies on memory of the play rather than on a manuscript.[3] If so, Wilkins must have acquired a copy in the few months between the writing of his novel and the publication of the play.

[1] For example, *Calendar to Middlesex Records*, I, 1–2.

[2] E. A. J. Honigmann, *The Stability of Shakespeare's Text* (London, 1965), pp. 178–9.

[3] See S. Spiker, 'George Wilkins and the authorship of *Pericles*', *Studies in Philology*, XXX (1933), 551–70. I entirely agree with Miss Spiker on this point.

Here supposition reaches a dead end. Whatever the truth of the matter, we can say that the recognizance goes a long way to identify Wilkins the victualler positively as the dramatist, and that the whole case strangely brings together his publisher and his patron.

The next case throws some fascinating light on Wilkins's connection with the underworld. A recognizance dated 2 September 1611, records that George Wilkinson of Cow Cross, victualler, was 'Bound over to answere his makinge of a composition in a matter of fellony & convayinge away of Mawline Sames who committed the fellonye' (case no. 7). Two butchers of Cow Cross stood bail for Wilkinson. The sum was unusually large: £20 each. Two other recognizances (case no. 6) tell us what the felony was and prove that this George Wilkinson is identical with George Wilkins. The first is a surety for Mawline Sames. This, in its many variant spellings, was her maiden name, which she was usually given, although she was married to Thomas Morris, a glover of St Giles-in-the-Fields. Earlier this year she had been to gaol for living incontinently with one William Hodgson.[1] Added to the formal Latin bond are the words 'Condicion is yᵗ Magdalen Morris also Samwaise shall appeare at the gaole delivery uppon suspicion for the filonius stealinge of 50ˢ from one william usurer'. Magdalen's guarantors were the two men from Cow Cross whom I mentioned earlier as being friends of Wilkins: Geoffrey Emms, or Eames, the gardener, and John Bonner, factor. The date was 18 September. Four days later, on the 22nd, George *Wilkins*, not *Wilkinson*, undertook on his own recognizance to give evidence at the next Sessions of Gaol Delivery in the case of 'Maudalen Morris also Samwaiese'. Wilkins and Wilkinson are therefore in this instance identical. A footnote adds that his evidence was needed for preferring the charge. But two days before this, in a bond dated 20 September, he had undertaken to appear at the next General Sessions of the Peace on another indictment (case no. 5): 'for abusinge mʳ· Barnes Constable of Clarkenwell in the execucion of his office'. His sole guarantor was Geoffrey Eames. It seems quite possible that this offence, so close in time to the Mawline Sames case, was also causally connected with it. One can reconstruct the sequence of events as follows. Mawline was wanted on suspicion of theft, but could not be found. Wilkins was arrested for helping her to escape and compounding the felony. She and he may have been well-known as associates. Wilkins was released on bail, which was heavy, since the crime was a serious one. Mawline was caught, and it may have been in an attempt to obstruct the search or arrest that Wilkins abused the constable. He may have felt able to do so with impunity because clear evidence of her guilt seems to have been lacking. One can infer this from the fact that she was allowed bail, from the words 'uppon suspicion' in her bond, and from the fact that the obviously unreliable testimony of Wilkins was necessary to bring the charge. No one else is known to have given evidence in the case. The records show that both Mawline and Wilkins (under the name Wilkinson) came to the next sessions of Gaol Delivery held at the Old Bailey on 4 October. Wilkins also appeared three times at the General Sessions of the Peace which were held in Westminster and began on 3 October. On the first occasion he gave evidence; on the second he discharged his undertaking to appear for abusing the constable. It seems likely that the charge of felony either failed or was never brought. If Mawline had been found guilty of stealing fifty shillings she would probably have been hanged. Yet in October 1613 she was charged with picking a purse, and in June 1614 with being a whore.[2] It would be interesting to

[1] *Calendar to Middlesex Records*, VI, 110.

[2] *Middlesex Sessions Records*, New Series, II, 283 (Sessions Roll 526/12, 208; G.D. Register 2/6); and p. 453 (Sessions Register 2/70).

know more about Wilkins's relationship with her. The fact that he protected her suggests that he may have kept a brothel. Did he also get her to steal for him? Such relationships are described in detail in the Dekker parts of *Iests to Make You Merrie*.

Wilkins's third appearance at the Sessions of 3 October (case no. 8) was to stand surety of £5 for Francis Stone of Turnmill Street, a victualler seeking a licence to tipple: 'pro tiplacone', as the clerk's latin has it in the margin of the Sessions Register. William Cooper was the other guarantor, a baker of Turnmill Street.

Wilkins came before the bench once more in 1611, this time as the injured party (case no. 9). A recognizance of 24 November records that Anthony Gouch, gentleman, of Chancery Lane, was indicted for 'comitting a notorious outrage in the house of George Wilkins and for abusing one Bonner at the same time'. The details are consistent with what we already know. Wilkins, keeping his inn or brothel, is involved in a brawl with Gouch, and Bonner joins in on Wilkins's side. We know that Bonner was a friend of Wilkins's from his standing bail for Mawline Sames.

The year 1612 was a bad one for Wilkins. On 26 March two yeomen of Cow Cross stood bail for him 'for that he hath outragiously beaten one Judyth Walton & stamped upon her so that she was Caried home in a Chayre' (case no. 10). Judyth Walton lived in Cow Cross. In June 1614 she was described as the wife of George Walton, and charged with disturbing the peace.[1] Three months later, described as a spinster, she was complained to be a common bawd. She had also been involved in fights with other women. The generous Geoffrey Eames went bail for her, together with a Roger Eames.[2]

Three months after this attack, on 19 June 1612, Wilkins gave his deposition on behalf of Stephen Belott. At about this time he was again

in trouble with the law. At the Sessions held on 2 July Wilkins was handed in bail to two yeomen of Cow Cross (case no. 11). The bond and the charge were recorded in the Register under the heading 'put downe from victualinge'. The main body of the entry reads:

pro mala gestura sua erga Martinum ffetherbye headborowe de Charterhouse lane & quod imposterim non Custodiet Tabernam & ad comparendum ad proximam sessionem interim pro bono gestu[3]

for an extreame outrage committed upon the saide Constable his watche at xii A clocke in ye nighte

The removal of his licence to keep a tavern, or whatever other punishment the court awarded, may have had a sobering influence on Wilkins. At all events, he seems to have kept within the law for the next two years at least. During this time he came to court, but only as the injured party. In January 1613, Richard Gregorye, a tailor of Cow Cross, was fined for assaulting George Wilkins and his wife (case no. 12). This is the only evidence in the records that Wilkins was married. On 23 July of the same year Wilkins bound himself to give evidence against James Baxter and John Walter, two butchers of Smithfield Bar (case no. 13). Their offence is not on record, but we know that they were 'charged uppon suspicion of fellony by George Wilkins'. In this bond Wilkins is for the first time described as a 'gentleman'. This change of status may have been a result of the ban on keeping a tavern. Wilkins could no longer be truthfully described as a victualler, at least not in the eyes of the law, nor as a yeoman perhaps, for the same reason. This explanation derives some support from the fact that he is not called victualler or yeoman

[1] *Middlesex Sessions Records*, New Series, I, 454; Sessions Register 2/71.

[2] *Ibid.*, New Series, II, 85. Sessions Roll 534/139, 144, 145; Sessions Register 2/109, 110.

[3] 'For his bad behaviour towards Martin Fetherbye, headborough of Charterhouse Lane, and in future not to keep a tavern, and to appear at the next sessions and meanwhile to behave well.' Sessions Register 1/528.

on his two other court appearances at this time. On 8 June 1614, he went bail for Elizabeth, wife of Thomas Fryer, who was a cook from Turnmill Street (case no. 14). Wilkins's status is not mentioned, nor is the offence. He was called a gentleman when he came to court on 3 December for abusing Mr John Sherley, a constable of Clerkenwell (case no. 15). The offence was probably not a serious one, for he was discharged at the request of the constable.

There is now a gap of two years before Wilkins's next appearance in court, in September 1616. It is certain that by then he was victualling again, and the records revert to calling him a victualler and yeoman. He played a central and somewhat unhappy part in two cases which were tried at the Sessions of 5 and 6 September. Both contained elements of farce as well as misfortune. In one (case no. 16) Wilkins was 'charged to have taken a cloke and a hatt from the person of John Parker feloniously', after assaulting him in the highway at Cow Cross. For once the indictment itself has survived. It tells us that the cloak was worth thirty shillings and the 'blacke felt hatt' three shillings and four pence. Wilkins admitted the offence and was fined two shillings. This suggests that his crime was hardly a grave one and that John Parker was in no great danger, despite the words of the indictment: 'in magno timore et periculo vitae posuit' ('he put him in great fear and peril of his life').

The other case (no. 17) arose out of real loss suffered by Wilkins himself. On 28 August he undertook to testify against several persons accused of riot. Their names were John Woolfe, Jasper Staples, Edward Reynoldes, William Jones, John Griffin, and Richard Greeneham. Greeneham, in the words appended to his bond, 'is accused that he in the company of divers others unruly and disorderly persons did make a very notable ryott at Cowcross & pulled downe a great parte of the dwellinge house of George Wilkins'. It was a violent end to Wilkins's four years of comparative peace. Greeneham was a yeoman from Long Lane and was evidently the chief rioter. His fate is not known and he is mentioned nowhere else in the records. The rest were 'delivered from gaol by proclamation', a form of words used when charges were not preferred. Positive identification of the rioters is difficult. John Griffin and Edward Reynoldes are probably the men of that name who crop up again and again accused of various petty crimes. William Jones may have been another often-mentioned malefactor, but the name is so common that no conclusions can be drawn. The case affords further evidence that Wilkins kept a brothel. Theatres and brothels were the buildings most likely to be pulled down. To 'deface Turnbull' and 'ruin the Cockpit' was a custom of the apprentices on Shrove Tuesdays.[1]

There only remains the last case in which Wilkins took part. At the end of April or the beginning of May 1618, an indictment for theft was brought against a certain Ann Badham, and against Wilkins for being an accessory after the fact. Ann was the wife of John Badham, of Cow Cross. They are mentioned several times in the records, usually as prosecutors. John Badham was called a labourer in this case, but he was normally a felt-maker. At about this time he had to answer a charge of keeping a bawdy house. The John Griffin who may have pulled down Wilkins's house was a friend of the Badhams. According to the indictment (which I have translated from the Latin and much shortened), 'Ann Badham, on 25 April, 16 James I, at Cow Cross feloniously assaulted one John Webbe, and secretly and without being noticed by him took, stole and carried off fifty-five shillings and four pence halfpenny

[1] Apprentices often came before the Middlesex bench for such attacks. See also *The Works of Thomas Middleton*, ed. A. H. Bullen (London, 1886), VII, 209–10 (*The Inner Temple Masque*, lines 171–5).

which was in the pocket of the aforesaid John Webbe'. Immediately below is added, also in Latin, an even more verbose version of the following: 'And that one George Wilkins, lately of Cow Cross, a labourer, after the felony committed in this way by the said Ann Badham, on 26 April, knowing that Ann Badham had committed the felony aforesaid, feloniously received, harboured, and comforted the same Anne at Cow Cross against the King's peace and dignity.' This case, in fact, is a repetition of the Mawline Sames case.

Above each part of the indictment is written the latin word 'extra'. This means that Wilkins and Ann were not in custody, but at large, perhaps illegally. At the next Sessions of Gaol Delivery, on 20 May, the same note was written above their names in the Register; neither of them seems to have attended the Sessions. If my reading of the records is right, Ann Badham must have broken bail. For on 27 April three guarantors had bound themselves for £10 each as surety for her attendance at the next Sessions. Her husband was one, and John Griffin another. In June no Sessions were held at Newgate. In the records of the July Sessions, neither of the accused is mentioned. But during the Sessions of 6 August Wilkins was handed in bail of £20 to Richard Barnes, a cutler, and John Bogey, a goldsmith. He was bound to answer the charge of being an accessory at the next Sessions. Ann Badham was recorded still 'at large'. But even at the next Sessions on 3 September Wilkins did not face trial. The case was again put off, and a fresh recognizance was recorded in the register. Richard Barnes was again a guarantor; a yeoman called Robert Ladkins was the other. Ann Badham was still free, and her evidence may have been needed in order to prosecute Wilkins. At the Sessions of 2 October Wilkins has his final entry. It stands at the head of the list, and the space above it on the page is blank. Above the familiar description of Wilkins as a yeoman

of Cow Cross indicted as accessory to Ann Badham, the clerk wrote in ornate letters 'Ball. ss.' – 'Bail. Sessions' – and then, with flourishes of the quill which convey the satisfaction of finality: 'Exon q̄ Mortuus. est.' ('Exoneratus quod mortuus est: he is discharged from his recognizances because he is dead'). He died, therefore, sometime between 3 September and 2 October 1618. It is beautifully appropriate that his epitaph should be written in the records of the court where he was so well-known.

In the light of so much information, we should naturally expect to find points of contact between Wilkins's life and his published work. Such is in fact the case. The elements that we now know to have been important in his life – inn-keeping, whores, stealing, and the law – all have an important place in his writings. A tavern is the scene of much of *The Miseries of Inforst Marriage*, the only play which claims to be solely by Wilkins. Lawyers are satirised in *Law-Trickes*, on which Wilkins probably collaborated with the acknowledged author, John Day.[1] Our new knowledge of Wilkins's life adds meaning to lines like these from *Pericles*:

2nd Fisherman. heere's a Fish hanges in the Net, Like a poore mans right in the law: t'will hardly come out. (II, i, 122–3)[2]

or to the even more vivid simile in *Miseries*:

Butler . . . Whats this world lyke to? Faith iust like an Inne-keepers Chamber-pot, receiues all waters, good and bad, It had need of much scouring. (ll. 1,358–60)

Wilkins's personal experience seems in evidence here, as it does in the following:

[1] See pp. 138, n. 1 above, and *The Works of John Day*, ed. A. H. Bullen (London, 1963), p. xv of the Introduction, by R. Jeffs.
[2] The references are to the Praetorius facsimile of the First Quarto of *Pericles* (London, 1886) and to the Malone Society reprint of *Miseries*, prepared by G. H. Blayney (Oxford, 1964).

Ilford. Be mild in a Tauerne, tis treason to the red
Lettyce, enemy to their signe post, and slaue to humor:

> Prethee, lets be mad,
> Then fill our heads with wine, till every pate be
> > drunke,
> Then pisse i' the street, Iussell all you meet, and
> > with a Punke,
> As thou wilt do now and then

(*Miseries*, ll. 1,079–84)

There are many such passages. Although
they now have a biographical interest, they are
unlikely to add to our knowledge of Wilkins.
But there are other correspondences between
Wilkins's writings and his life which are more
important, because they reveal the unique
individual that he was. Consider what we know
about his life. Between the ages of twenty-
eight and thirty-two, roughly, he was a prolific and varied writer, the companion of some
of the chief dramatists of the day. Despite some
success, he felt that his talent was not given its
due, and resented it. All his work was obsessed
with sin, misery and pain. Then, in about 1608,
his prolific output stopped. So far as we know,
he wrote nothing in the last eight or more years
of his life. On the contrary, he seems to have
led a dissolute life which would have made
literary work difficult, even if it had not been
an emotional substitute for that work, as it
probably was. At this time he was given to
violence, especially against women; he was
implicated in thefts and harboured whores who
had stolen. The conclusion is irresistible that he
destroyed his talent in riotous living, and it
seems even more so when we read his plays.
For it is surely more than mere coincidence
that Wilkins should have created certainly one,
and probably two central characters whose
early promise is ruined in taverns and brothels.
The only difference from his own life is that
their stories turn out happily in the end.

In *Miseries*, the central character is William
Scarborrow. His guardian forces him to break
his betrothal to Clare, who dies as a result, and

marry another, much against his will. Scarborrow is so grieved by Clare's death and so
ashamed of his broken faith that he quite
deliberately sets out to degrade himself.

Scarborrow.
All ryot now, since that my soules so blacke.

(l. 999)

In the ensuing tavern scenes the process of his
self-destruction is shown in detail. It may be
objected that *Miseries* was published in 1607,
and that Wilkins would not be likely to pro-
phesy his own future ruin. But a remarkable
feature of the character of Scarborrow is that
he *does* foresee his own ruin, and, although
he wants to prevent it, is powerless to do so. In
Scarborrow Wilkins showed that he was all too
aware of his own nature and of the influences
which did in fact ruin his life. His state of mind
is precisely described in the following speech:

Scarborrow.
Thus like a Feuer that doth shake a man
From strength to weaknesse, I consume my selfe:
I know this company, theyr custome vilde,
Hated, abhord of good-men, yet like a childe
By reasons rule instructed how to know
Euill from good, I to the worser go.
Why doe you suffer this, you vpper powers,
That I should surfet in the sinne I tast,
have sence to feele my mischiefe, yet make wast
of heauen and earth (ll. 1,118–27)

This has the vigour and simplicity of truth;
Wilkins is experiencing what he describes. The
play's motto is *Qui Alios (seipsum) docet*: 'the
man who teaches others also teaches himself'.
Here too Wilkins shows his awareness that he
needs help. We find a very similar situation to
Scarborrow's in the Wilkins sections of *Law-
Trickes*. The scholarly young hero, Polymetes,
for no obvious reason suddenly adopts
deliberately, as Scarborrow did, a life of riot.
His dissipation turns into a kind of madness
before the inevitable happy ending. And again
in *Pericles* itself we find that the hero suffers

a process of increasing disintegration – one more reason for seeing Wilkins as the play's originator.

Wilkins, I believe, was melancholic almost to the point of madness. His melancholy, or self-hatred, expressed itself in a self-destructive course which he abhorred but could not stop. But to ruin himself was not enough; his misery also found vent in violence against others, as it often does. And in this too there is an extraordinary consistency between his life and his plays. It may even be that by putting his violence into words he was better able to control it in his actions. His aggression follows a clear pattern. In only one of the eighteen cases recorded (no. 16) is it suggested that a man was physically harmed by Wilkins, and that case is doubtful; but in three cases he is said to have attacked women, twice with obvious brutality *and in the same way*. Once he kicked a pregnant woman in the belly (no. 4); he beat another woman and stamped upon her so that she had to be carried home (no. 10). It is surely significant that the kicking of women, a very distinctive action, is twice recorded in Wilkins's life and is mentioned in two of his plays. In *Law-Trickes*, Iulio, 'A noble youthfull Gallant', speaks of 'this kicking age'.[1] The phrase is used of horses, but also seems to have a wider reference. Not long after, the same gallant, speaking of a girl with whom he has been flirting, says to Polymetes:

ile put all my love into one quart of Maligo, & your melancholly humor into another, and he that hath done last, shall for penance give her a kicke a the lips, and a pipe of Tobacco be my witnesse, that's all the love I beare her.   (ll. 431–6)

Kicking is mentioned again sixty lines later. In *Miseries* there is another young gallant, an unpleasant character called Sir Francis Ilford. He has married a girl for her money. When he finds that she has none, he demands her jewels.

Ilford. . . . Nay Sfut, giue em me, or Ile kicke else.
    (l. 2185)

The act of kicking implies contempt. Wilkins's obsession with it suggests that he felt a repugnance for women which would be consistent with his keeping a brothel and using the whores to steal for him. It is interesting that in both the examples quoted kicking is threatened, but not enacted, as it might have been. The destructive impulse is to that extent restrained. In *The Painfull Aduentures*, however, Pericles strikes his daughter Marina on the face, and it seems probable that a similar act of violence was at some time included in act v, scene i, of the play. Such an action would be characteristic of Wilkins, and is further evidence that he originally wrote a complete version of *Pericles*.

© ROGER PRIOR 1972

APPENDIX

(Cases 1–11 are calendared in the mimeographed *Calendar to Middlesex Records*.)

Case 1   Vol. iv, p. 26. Sessions Roll 485/134; Sessions Register 1/247.

2   Vol. iv, p. 71. Sessions Roll 488/90; Sessions Register 1/267.

3   Vol. v, p. 86. Sessions Roll 492/128; Sessions Register 1/300.

4   Vol. vi, p. 143. Sessions Roll 499/78; Sessions Register 1/345, 353, 354.

5   Vol. viii, p. 86. Sessions Roll 506/215; Sessions Register 1/436.

6   Vol. viii, p. 105. Sessions Roll 507/1, 30; Sessions Register 1/424.
    G.D. Register 1/177 *dorso*.

7   Vol. viii, p. 111. Sessions Roll 507/50; G.D. Register 1/177 *dorso*.

8   Vol. viii, p. 123. Sessions Register 1/438.

9   Vol. ix, p. 16. Sessions Roll 508a/72; Sessions Register 1/451.

10   Vol. ix, p. 165. Sessions Roll 512/61; Sessions Register 1/505.

11   Vol. x, pp. 39–40. Sessions Register 1/528.

[1] References are to the Malone Society reprint of *Law-Trickes* by J. Crow (Oxford, 1950). The mentions of kicking are at lines 333, 431–6, 493, 500.

(Cases 12–17 are calendared in the *Middlesex Sessions Records*, New Series.)

12   Vol. I, p. 7. Sessions Register 1/576; Process Record Book 1/17 *dorso*.

13   Vol. I, p. 177. Sessions Roll 523/132, 247, 249; G.D. Register 1/228 *dorso*.

14   Vol. I, p. 454. Sessions Register 2/72, 80.

15   Vol. II, p. 170. Sessions Register 2/132.

16   Vol. III, p. 301. Sessions Roll 553/86, 93, 133; Sessions Register 2/346; G.D. Register 2/93.

17   Vol. III, p. 293. Sessions Roll 553/54, 69, 176; Sessions Register 2/342, 349; G.D. Register 2/91.

18   Not calendared. Sessions Roll 565/150; G.D. Register 2/149 *dorso*, 158 *dorso*, 162, 165 *dorso*.

Details of identification can be tabulated by cases as follows:

George Wilkins (alone): 9, 12.

George Wilkins, of Cow Cross, yeoman: 1, 2, 4, 8, 10, 18 (also 'laborer').
    of Cow Cross, victualler: 6, 16 (twice 'yeoman'), 17.
    of Cow Cross, gentleman: 13, 15.
    of Turnmill Street: 14.
    of Turnmill Street, yeoman: 11.
    of St James's, Clerkenwell, victualler: 5.

George Wilkeson, of St Sepulchre's, victualler: 3.

George Wilkinson, of Cow Cross, victualler: 7.

A NEUROTIC PORTIA

MURRAY BIGGS

One of our most skilful actresses – Stratford's Portia of 1971 – has suggested informally that Shakespeare wrote comedies, tragedies, histories, and *The Merchant of Venice*. For her the play's 'problem' is that it has no attractive characters – not even Portia. (How, then, can it be so popular?)

What a far cry from the sunny sounds of another person of the theatre, writing in 1930:

The Merchant of Venice is the simplest of plays, so long as we do not bedevil it with sophistries . . . Logic may land us anywhere. . .It is as smoothly and completely successful, its means being as well fitted to its end, as anything Shakespeare wrote.[1]

The Merchant is surely more of a problem play than Granville-Barker allowed. It is, as Auden calls it, one of Shakespeare's Plays Unpleasant. We have no easy way, for example, round the problem of Shylock. But it is doubtful if the marriage of Portia and Bassanio was the problem for Shakespeare that it becomes in this Stratford production by Terry Hands.

Portia is generally regarded as one of Shakespeare's most attractive and admirable women. Jessica says of her, though not at Stratford:

Why, if two gods should play some heavenly match,
And on the wager lay two earthly women,
And Portia one, there must be something else
Pawned with the other; for the poor rude world
Hath not her fellow.   (III, v, 74–8)

Yet the Stratford actress does not admire her. Why? Because, I suspect, her Portia is required to put her marriage to a test of excessive, even dangerous, gravity. It is a subtly perverted reading of Shakespeare's text. She must take, in fact, a melodramatic view of her husband's loyalty, despite his recently passing with flying colours the marriage test bequeathed by her father: he has chosen the morally right casket. It is characteristic of this production to solve the problem(s) of the play by turning it into melodrama, thereby creating problems of its own. The line about fatherly sins, for example (III, v, 1 ff.), is applied not to Shylock but to father Gobbo, and so – a touch too clever for most of the audience – Launcelot is made to go blind, as well as mad. The miserly knife is so whetted and waxed and strenuously directed at the mercantile chest, that 'Baltha-zar's' saving grace is not only anti-climactic but even more implausible than usual. But when it comes to the rings, Portia looms positively masochistic. She asks for trouble, and gets it.

Mr Hands's production argues that she is provoked by Bassanio's divided loyalty. Certainly Bassanio's friendship with Antonio might set a problem for his marriage. The text scarcely suggests that it does. Indeed Shakespeare makes Portia's request for the ring an afterthought (she has already taken her leave) inspired simply by Bassanio's typically fulsome insistence on giving something. More than that, Antonio has not only financed his friend's courtship, when he cannot afford it and – as Bassanio anxiously knows – at mortal danger to himself; he has personally encouraged it:

[1] Harley Granville-Barker, *Prefaces to Shakespeare* (Princeton, 1946), I, 336.

Slubber not business for my sake, Bassanio,
But stay the very riping of the time;
And for the Jew's bond which he hath of me,
Let it not enter in your mind of love:
Be merry; and employ your chiefest thoughts
To courtship, and such fair ostents of love
As shall conveniently become you there.

(II, viii, 39–45)

This reported speech sounds more like self-denial than self-indulgence, like action on the leaden casket's advice to 'give and hazard all he hath'; but it gets a lightweight upstage reading at Stratford beside the sonorous innuendo of Solanio's comment on it:

I think he [Antonio] only loves the world for him.
[Bassanio]

In fact Antonio, whose kindness is proverbial (II, viii, 35; III, ii, 292) for all his scorn of Shylock, voluntarily releases the person closest to him – his kinsman, moreover – with a far less selfish love than Shylock clings to his daughter even after she has torn herself from him.

The National Theatre's version of this play, directed by Jonathan Miller, gets all it can (legitimately, in my view) out of Bassanio's bachelor friendship. It does not, however, allow Portia to become neurotic about it. At Stratford she is made – by wide-angled staging – reluctant to receive Bassanio's male friends to her home, at III, ii, 220. Later in the scene she enquires with exaggerated emphasis of his 'dear friend' Antonio (291). Later in the play she addresses her line 'I will become as liberal as you' (V, i, 226) not to Bassanio but, once again, to Antonio, with nasty import. In III, iv – with a Leontes-like suspicion of two good friends – she goes into a trance speaking the lines (omitting those in brackets):

in companions
(That do converse and waste the time together,
Whose souls do bear an equal yoke of love,)
There must be needs a like proportion

Of lineaments, of manners, and of spirit;
Which makes me think that this Antonio,
Being the bosom lover of my lord,
Must needs be like my lord. If it be so,
How little is the cost I have bestowed
In purchasing the semblance of my soul
From out the state of hellish cruelty!

(III, iv, 11–21)

With which she rushes off to court not so much to defend her husband's friend and her own second soul-mate, as to defend her husband from him. This tack makes nonsense of the fact that, according to Shakespeare, Bassanio has returned to Venice at his wife's insistence. It is worth quoting the passage in full.

Portia.
Is it your dear friend that is thus in trouble?
Bassanio.
The dearest friend to me, the kindest man,
The best-conditioned and unwearied spirit
In doing courtesies, and one in whom
The ancient Roman honour more appears
Than any that draws breath in Italy.
Portia.
What sum owes he the Jew?
Bassanio
For me, three thousand ducats.
Portia.   What, no more?
Pay him six thousand, and deface the bond.
Double six thousand, and then treble that,
Before a friend of this description
Shall lose a hair through Bassanio's fault.
First go with me to church and call me wife,
And then away to Venice to your friend!
For never shall you lie by Portia's side
With an unquiet soul. You shall have gold
To pay the petty debt twenty times over.
When it is paid, bring your true friend along.
My maid Nerissa and myself meantime
Will live as maids and widows. Come away,
For you shall hence upon your wedding-day.
Bid your friends welcome, show a merry cheer;
Since you are dear bought, I will love you dear.
But let me hear the letter of your friend.
Bassanio. 'Sweet Bassanio, my ships have all miscarried, my creditors grow cruel, my estate is very low, my bond to the Jew is forfeit. And since in paying it, it is impossible I should live, all debts are cleared

between you and I if I might but see you at my death. Notwithstanding, use your pleasure. If your love do not persuade you to come, let not my letter.'

Portia.

O love, dispatch all business and be gone.

Bassanio.

Since I have your good leave to go away,
I will make haste, but till I come again
No bed shall e'er be guilty of my stay,
Nor rest be interposer 'twixt us twain.

(III, ii, 291–326)

Once in court, however, the Stratford Portia stops Antonio from giving Bassanio's hand even the scripted farewell shake. She broods darkly over Antonio's farewell speech to him, ignoring its compliment to her – 'Commend me to your honourable wife' (IV, i, 270); and the actor playing Antonio is made to release so much passion on 'love' (274) that words fail him there, four lines earlier than Shakespeare directed. In the new version, this passionate declaration of love directly inspires Bassanio's reply. Understandably beside himself, he offers his marriage in exchange not – as a matter of fact – for Antonio's love but for his life:

Antonio, I am married to a wife
Which is as dear to me as life itself;
But life itself, my wife, and all the world,
Are not with me esteemed above thy life.
I would lose all, ay sacrifice them all
Here to this devil, to deliver you. (IV, i, 279–84)

It is at moments like this that one turns to Granville-Barker's opening paragraph: '*The Merchant of Venice* is a fairy-tale. There is no more reality in Shylock's bond and the Lord of Belmont's will than in Jack and the Bean-stalk.'[1] Or to his contemporary Middleton Murry: '*The Merchant of Venice* is not a realistic drama; and its characters simply cannot be judged by realistic moral standards.'[2] For the choice before Bassanio is incredible, and if Portia takes it seriously the play becomes absurd. A serious view should in any case lead her, heavenly-unselfish as she is, to follow the generous instinct of her husband and renounce her conjugal rights, *if* so doing will save a human life. (The marriage may in time be restored, the other only in Shakespeare's miracle-plays.) Bassanio himself has in her hearing twice offered more than his marriage – his own life in fact – to save Antonio's, since that was mortgaged on his behalf. But the text shows clearly enough that Portia takes a good-humoured view of Bassanio's nobly impulsive gesture. She enjoys the usual comic irony of her disguise:

Your wife would give you little thanks for that,
If she were by, to hear you make the offer.

(IV, i, 285–6)

Granville-Barker talks unerringly of the 'quite casual humour' of these lines. The Stratford Portia is obliged to hover over her husband and deliver them like the Angel of Death. But if their tone were not already sure, Shakespeare reduces it to a broader comic level by at once apeing the joke through Gratiano and Nerissa. Even the powerful Hands cannot stop his audience laughing there, if not before: we pull with the text against his actors.

The trial over, a suitably grateful Bassanio and Antonio press 'Balthazar' to accept some reward. She, perversely, asks for Bassanio's wedding-ring. It is her one fall from heavenly grace, and it is – admittedly – in the Shakespeare. It is a joke on the way to being sick, like Launcelot's played on his father, and Shylock's 'merry bond'. Bassanio behaves impeccably. He tells the exact truth of why the ring is the one thing he cannot part with:

Good sir, this ring was given me by my wife;
And, when she put it on, she made me vow
That I should neither sell nor give nor lose it.

(IV, i , 438–40)

[1] *Ibid.*, I, 335.
[2] J. Middleton Murry, *Shakespeare* (London, 1936), pp. 193–4.

A gamesome, even a jealous wife should be satisfied now. But Portia does not leave it there, does not leave well alone. Her behaviour is perhaps a function of that very 'excess' of love against which she had warned herself before (III, ii, 112). It is indeed

> like the mending of highways
> In summer, where the ways are fair enough.
>
> (v, i, 263–4)

She wants to make her assurance of Bassanio's loyalty double sure. In the same way, reunited in Belmont, she taunts him with the charge of infidelity – 'I'll die for't but some woman had the ring!' (v, i, 208) – and provokes the re-iterated response her soul craves:

> No, by my honour, madam! By my soul
> No woman had it . . .

Her need is almost insatiable to hear that he loves her, again and again.

We can imagine these emotional reactions of Portia's in terms of her long confinement. The ring-game is a *jeu d'esprit* born of unbearable emotional relief. At the moment of Bassanio's right choice of casket she had said to herself:

> How all the other passions fleet to air:
> As doubtful thoughts, and rash-embraced despair,
> And shudd'ring fear, and green-eyed jealousy.
> O love, be moderate, allay thy ecstasy,
> In measure rain thy joy, scant this excess,
> I feel too much thy blessing, make it less
> For fear I surfeit.   (III, ii, 108–14)

This is interesting as an index of the negative emotions latent in Portia; but what is important is that she does not sustain them, that they *do* fleet to air once released with the turning of a key. Her simultaneous achievement of three basic desires – the satisfaction of her father's will, the marriage she has pined for, and the rescue of her husband's best friend – makes this the happiest day of her life. Similarly, at their happiest moment, Lorenzo and Jessica poke delicate fun at the very love-troths that have brought them together:

> *Jessica.*   In such a night
> Did young Lorenzo swear he loved her well,
> Stealing her soul with many vows of faith,
> And ne'er a true one.
> *Lorenzo.*   In such a night
> Did pretty Jessica, like a little shrew,
> Slander her love, and he forgave it her.
>
> (v, i, 17–22)

So too, by all accounts, ran the course of love-vows between Gratiano and Nerissa (III, ii, 204–7; v, i, 147–56).

It is in sheer high spirits, then, that Portia insists on the ring, saying (reasonably enough, of a wife as noble as Portia is reputed to be!):

> And if your wife be not a mad-woman,
> And know how well I have deserved this ring,
> She would not hold out enemy for ever
> For giving it to me.   (IV, i, 442–5)

Still Bassanio refuses, and she leaves him in mock-disgust. (The Stratford actress overlays a typical Shakespearian comic irony – 'I pray you know me when we meet again' (IV, i, 416) – with jarring severity.) At once the naturally generous merchant upbraids Bassanio in the name of common gratitude:

> My Lord Bassanio, let him have the ring.
> Let his deservings, and my love withal,
> Be valued 'gainst your wife's commandement.
>
> (IV, i, 446–8)

Once again, the full resources of this Antonio's great voice are summoned to make 'my love' trounce 'his deservings', and give maximum scorn to 'your wife's commandement'. But Shakespeare's Antonio is not here saying 'prefer me to your wife'. His 'love' stands nothing to gain by the transaction of the ring. He is rather suggesting that in these quite extraordinary circumstances an absent wife's command must be waived. He might have added, as the disguised wife has just done, that if she were here she would rescind it herself. Bassanio in the discovery-scene reiterates these themes:

> I was beset with shame and courtesy;
> My honour would not let ingratitude
> So much besmear it. Pardon me, good lady;
> For, by these blessed candles of the night,
> Had you been there, I think, you would have
>   begged
> The ring of me to give the worthy doctor.
>   (v, i, 217–22)

Which is in fact just what she did.

So, on appropriate consideration, Bassanio does the generous thing and sends the ring after his saviour. In so doing, he fulfils the spirit both of the motto on the winning casket of lead – 'Who chooseth me must give and hazard all he hath' – and of Portia's own speech on mercy. In the very special situation now confronting him, he is justified. (His gesture is later repeated at the lower level of Gratiano-Nerissa.) The messenger explains to Portia:

> My Lord Bassanio, upon more advice,
> Hath sent you here this ring, and doth entreat
> Your company at dinner.   (iv, ii, 6–8)

Shakespeare's Portia replies, 'That cannot be': meaning, presumably, 'I cannot dine'. Changing 'That' to 'It', her modern counterpart has to say 'It cannot *be*' (Stratford italics) and mean 'I can't *believe* he's let go of the ring'. Portia is not to know that the 'more advice' is Antonio's. (In Shakespeare, too, 'advise' is often reflexive: as in this play, at i, i, 142; ii, i, 42; v, i, 234.) But even if she suspects, it should not disturb her. The 1971 Portia is so disturbed that, as soon as she's alone (somewhat earlier than in Shakespeare), she actually sobs. She has brought tears on herself by turning her own honeymoon from sportive to sour. But the problem is all in her nerves. Bassanio is *in fact* as loyal as ever, and she knows it. He may have no head for money, but emotionally he's the stabler partner. Adept to a fault at legal reasoning, she makes unreasonable demands of him. That Shakespeare intended her merely to enjoy these demands as a joke, secure in the knowledge that she can trust her husband, is suggested in lines that find no place at Stratford:

> We shall have old swearing
> That they did give the rings away to men;
> But we'll outface them, and outswear them too.
>   (iv, ii, 15–17)

Portia's teasing mood here returns with Nerissa to the girlish delights of their first scene together, and of their later prankish scheme to impersonate young men: another passage excised from the Stratford text, in which Portia becomes like one of her own unwelcome suitors who

hears merry tales and smiles not; I fear he will prove the weeping philosopher when he grows old, being so full of unmannerly sadness in his youth. (i, ii, 45–8)

Similarly, when near the end of the play she tells Bassanio that his voiding the ring symbolizes the void in his heart – 'Even so void is your false heart of *truth*' (v, i, 189) – she cannot mean it. The Stratford Portia means it more than anything else she says, except what should be equally light-hearted, that typically Elizabethan jest about his duplicity:

> In both my eyes he doubly sees himself,
> In each eye one. Swear by your double self,
> And there's an oath of credit.   (v, i, 244–6)

Nor should we rate higher than play or superstition Portia's saying at their engagement that his parting with the ring, *whatever the circumstances*, must necessarily 'presage the ruin of your love' (iii, ii, 173). The tone of Portia's final 'rebuke' of her husband must be governed by its imitation at the obviously comic level of Gratiano and Nerissa. This time Gratiano's 'inconstancy' is exposed first, and the brightness of Shakespeare's treatment of it must reflect on the ensuing 'quarrel' between the supposedly higher lovers. Moreover, Portia is content with a witty parody of her husband's protestations (v, i, 193–202). She goes on from here to restate, the other way round from IV, i, 442–5, the sensible attitude to the ring:

> What man is there so much unreasonable,
> If you had pleased to have defended it
> With any terms of zeal, wanted the modesty
> To urge the thing held as a ceremony?
>
> (v, i, 203–6)

In other words: no one in his right mind would press another for his wedding-ring. Quite right. What's more, Bassanio *had* defended it, with many terms of zeal, as she well knows. But now she makes Antonio promise that his protégé 'will never more break faith *advise*dly', v, i, 253 (a superfluous precaution, since such inhuman conditions are scarcely conceivable once, let alone again); and she reminds her husband that the ring stands for the 'ceremony' of their marriage.

It is, as we should say, a symbol: like an oath, which the trial has shown us should not be absolute irrespective of all other conditions. Portia herself generalises:

> Nothing is good, I see, without respect (of
> circumstances).
>
> . . . .
>
> How many things by season seasoned are
> To their right praise and true perfection!
>
> (v, i, 99, 107–8)

Not even justice is absolute, for, as she has taught us, mercy 'seasons' it (IV, i, 194). Of course symbols have their importance, not least those of marriage. But to save life is more important than to save a symbol or an oath (unless one agrees with Isabella in *Measure for Measure*). In an age when symbols are often wilfully confused with facts – art with life – and sometimes raised above them, an age in which symbols obscure what they are symbols of, it is not surprising that Mr Hands's production of *The Merchant of Venice* should claim that a symbol of Bassanio's hypothetical disloyalty matters more than the fact of his loyalty. (He does not give the ring to Antonio, or a mistress. It is a wholly unselfish gift.) The very virtuosity of these actors and their director, with his deft scissors, may persuade an uninitiated audience that Shakespeare's play is wholly darker than it is.[1] For the author of this play about possessions and obsessions – which teaches us to hazard under heaven all we hold most dear, to lose that we may find – the point seems to have been that even Portia had to learn not to be too possessive: especially of *things*. And if those things are made of gold – ducats, caskets, rings, or whatever else in the rich worlds of Venice and Belmont – so much the more to be let go. 'Human relationships', writes C. L. Barber, 'are stronger than their outward signs.'[2] Shylock had to lose *his* engagement-ring, had to learn to live without it, though he 'would not have *given* it for a wilderness of monkeys' (III, i, 112). Bassanio, wisely, makes no symbolic circumscription of his wife. There is no ring that *she* must wear, and value

---

[1] This is not a plea for some nebulous purism in the production of Shakespeare. Again and again in recent years, the Stratford company has illuminated central, if less obvious, areas of its texts. One need think no further back than Peter Brook's *Midsummer Night's Dream*, or Mr Hands's own *Pericles*. His 1970 *Richard III*, however, already showed signs of eccentricity. The whole play was pulled over to one side of it. It gained in the process a simplification of impact which modern audiences, already converted to theatre (not least by Stratford itself), no longer need to be convinced that Shakespeare is good. Middleton Murry reminds us, in his chapter on *The Merchant*, that we cannot make an 'intellectually coherent whole' of the play without distortion and loss. The mistake lies in thinking that we need to. In any case, a subtle but cumulative shifting of Shakespeare's text is more misleading than frank adaptation, like John Barton's of some of the history-plays.

[2] C. L. Barber, *Shakespeare's Festive Comedy* (Cleveland, 1963), p. 187.

above *her* best friend's life. She becomes, with Bassanio's choice of casket, Shakespeare's most thoroughly Liberated Woman. Can she, then, ungratefully deny her knight-errant his discretion? A Portia so divine as Shakespeare makes her would not *seriously* reduce her marriage to hoops of gold. She must rather trust the spirit of love itself (which first guided her husband to her), and secretly approve – not regret – his acknowledgement of a debt of spirit wholly compatible with, even required by, his love of her.

New College, Oxford
June 1971

OF AN AGE AND FOR ALL TIME:
SHAKESPEARE AT STRATFORD

RICHARD DAVID

A complete survey of six major productions is hardly possible in a short article. What therefore I shall try to do is to pick out some leading ideas and broad comparisons which these productions, when considered together, have suggested and which may have wider implications. But I ought first to establish just what is my own standpoint in viewing a production of Shakespeare and what are the criteria that I find applicable in its appreciation. Our opinions of these performances may well differ and it is as well to know in advance whether such differences arise because of the variations of individual judgement or because we start from quite different premises.

I will, then, briefly set out my criteria under two main heads. My first axiom is, I am glad to think, a totally obvious and accepted one, though this certainly was not so even fifteen years ago. It is that Shakespeare wrote for the theatre, and except in the theatre his work cannot be fully appreciated but must remain as it were two-dimensional, lacking the visual pointing, the human resonance, and the general heightening of attention that only live performance can create. I am satisfied, moreover, that Shakespeare was a highly professional and experienced writer for the theatre, who knew just what effects he wanted to achieve in stage terms and how to achieve them. Indeed, it is salutary to remember how very closely his plays were bound up with a particular theatre and a particular company. They were expressly written for what can be described as a permanent repertory company. It can be called

permanent in that its composition (except for the boys who played the women's parts, until their voices broke) changed surprisingly little during Shakespeare's working life. As for repertory, a company that puts on perhaps five different plays a week, several of them new, throughout a season that might be anything from fourteen to forty-five weeks, certainly deserves that name; and any repertory actor can tell us how much professionalism and adaptability and sheer guts would be required to carry through such a programme. Shakespeare, as he wrote, could visualise exactly how his roles would 'go' on his familiar partners. He wrote *for* the company, for particular actors; and in this season we can see a prime example of how closely the role might be moulded to the actor if we contrast Dogberry in *Much Ado*, perhaps the last part to be played by William Kemp before he left the company for free-lance work, and Feste in *Twelfth Night*, played by Kemp's successor Robert Armin, a clown of a very different style. More of these two later. One must not put too much stress on this. Though Shakespeare wrote primarily for *his* actors playing in their own familiar theatre he must, as a practical theatre man, have been all too well aware that the plays would have to be adaptable for touring stands, command performances in unsuitable buildings, and revivals with changed casts – even if, as a poet, he did not (and I imagine that he did) have at least some eye on the wider audiences of posterity.

For my second axiom I will misquote Ben Jonson and say that one of the difficulties of producing Shakespeare is that he is *both* of an age *and* for all time. If he were not for all time, if his plays were not 'about' something in which we are still deeply interested 350 years after his death, Shakespearian productions would be little more than historical reconstructions and museum displays, and I think that we can agree that they are not that. Yet his plays are rooted not only in the theatre of his age, but in its habits of life, its ideas, and its language, which condition the way in which they are constructed and the way in which they make their effect. And quite often the meanings of the conventions, procedures, words that Shakespeare adopts cannot be appreciated by an uninstructed audience today and may even be taken in a sense opposite to that intended. There can, then, be no 'straight' production of a Shakespeare play. The actors and the director have the delicate task of balancing historical against modern and of translating old into new if Shakespeare's still valid meanings are to appear.

From all this I conclude, first, that the director must be allowed a pretty free hand. He is presenting a thing designed for one set of circumstances, in quite other circumstances. The materials in which he works – theatre, actors, and audience – are not at all the same as those in which the dramatist worked. I say again that there is no ideal or set performance of a Shakespeare play. One production may indeed be nearer to Shakespeare the Elizabethan, and so more remote from us; another may be nearer to us and so further from what the first audience saw and heard. We must assess each in the light of what the director was trying to do and of how far he has succeeded in representing Shakespeare in terms that we can understand. Really the only restriction that we should put on the director's liberty of interpretation is to insist that he should not go against the grain of Shakespeare's intentions,

should not seek, in his whole presentation of the play or in any detail, to bring out implications or effects which Shakespeare demonstrably did not have in mind and which may annul or even contradict those that he did have in mind. The same goes for the actors. Because part of the essential stuff of a play *is* the actor, his physical appearance and natural qualities, he must use himself and his peculiar characteristics to the full, and we must allow for this. There is no one way of playing Hamlet, but as many ways as there are good actors, and all may be equally 'right'. But it is also true that some ways are wrong because they go counter to what the dramatist was clearly trying to do.

Now to the plays. I begin with *The Duchess of Malfi* because as the one non-Shakespearian play of the season it may the more clearly illustrate some of the points that I have been making. For Webster might be expected to be more of the age and less for all time than Shakespeare, and so harder to translate for a modern audience. This indeed is so. The hate and cruelty, in all its psychopathic ingenuity, which are such a main theme of the play, can no doubt be matched in our own times; but it is surely hard to find a modern parallel to the insensate aristocratic pride that sets all this phantasmagoria in train because a sister has married beneath her. The director's first decision must therefore be whether to attempt to present the action realistically, or as a sort of ritual, effective and portentous in itself but not to be taken at its face value, having its connection with real life as it were at one remove. In favour of realism is the fact that this is indeed a true story, though of an age very remote from our own; in favour of ritual is the fact that as compared with Shakespeare Webster was a very consciously literary and bookish writer – perhaps the very reason why he so regularly took the plots of his plays from what the French call 'actualities' was a feeling that the cuttings from his commonplace book would (forgive the play on words) only take root at all if planted in the soil of real life.

Between realism and ritual Clifford Williams's direction inclined much more, I thought, to realism. To illustrate the difficulties that this entails I will begin with a banal example, which has, however, larger implications. You will remember the scene in which a doctor attempts to treat the lycanthropic Ferdinand and is overpowered by his patient. I do not see how a modern director can make anything but farce of this, because the doctor's jargon and the treatment he prescribes are to us ludicrous. Yet if we remember that Jacobeans did actually control their madmen with chains and beating we can perceive that to them the scene (though of course Webster is satirising the self-satisfied doctor) could have a certain horrid reality which would enhance Ferdinand's fearsomeness instead of (as farce must do) diminishing it. It is a pity that it should be diminished but the scene is not crucial. The masque of madmen who visit the Duchess's prison *is* crucial. Here bathos can, I think, be avoided, but was not avoided in this production. The madmen were not farcical, but they were frivolous. It is true that their words are comic and would have been so to a Jacobean audience; but though the Jacobeans visited madhouses for a laugh, to be entertained, they also went for the pleasure of having their flesh creep. A point about madmen is that their words are often irrelevant to anything else about them. Here the director took the words too much as a cue for business which became as lightweight as the words. No doubt it is tiresome and even scary to have a madman fumbling at your skirts, but the menace is not really very great, especially when the madman has a keeper standing over him with a whip. These madmen must be menacing; not for what they say (that is clearly impossible), nor for what they do, but for what they are, strange yet united, an alien race. The Duchess should be as one extradited from normal humanity and

deposited, alone, among savages or Martians. The ironic effect is that the Duchess, from whose standpoint basically we view the action and who therefore personifies normality for us, is for this moment turned into the one abnormal person – in a mad world. The feeling is not dissimilar from that of the hovel scene in *Lear* and should be no harder to achieve. Unless it is achieved a main centre and focus of the play is lost. Perhaps the clue lies in the phrase I used earlier – the 'masque of madmen'. We need not assume that Webster was directly influenced by one of the several court masques that introduce an anti-masque of madmen or 'frantics' as a sort of horrific decoration; but it is reasonable to suppose that Webster's madmen were conceived in the same vein and with something of the same purpose.

Elsewhere indeed the director, helped by a powerfully shaped and shaping set, showed himself no bad hand at formalised effects. The opening dumbshow of the family of Aragon was useful and striking (though the corresponding tailpiece, highlighting the sole surviving member of the family, was not pointed enough and did not come off). The miming of the principal characters as Antonio describes them to his friend was well managed. The pattern for these introduced set-pieces, the central dumbshow of the banishing of the Duchess from Ancona, was splendidly forceful too, though I should have preferred the two pilgrims, who interpret it to the audience, to have been less cosily chatty and more distanced. They are, certainly, on the audience's side of the play, looking in; but the discrepancy between them and the dumbshow struck me as greater than Webster could have intended. They should be more chorus and less clown. The strangling of the Duchess was nicely poised between realism and ritual. The echo scene was exquisitely done; how extraordinary that so essentially corny a trick should in the resonance of theatrical performance turn to magic!

Any indecision on the part of the director as to the pitch and level of a play must gravely handicap the actors. I found Michael Williams's Ferdinand the most successful in sustaining the kind of effect that I would think essential. Voice, stance, mannerisms combined to create a Renaissance prince as fabulous as a cockatrice yet wholly credible. Good for him, too, and for the director that the fact, usually slurred over, that Ferdinand and the Duchess are twins, was so well brought out. The Cardinal had a good deal of edge, but I confess I wanted more. We need to see, under the Cardinal's cap, the kind of stony *condottiere* face that glares from Verrocchio's equestrian statue in Venice. Geoffrey Hutchings succeeded in the difficult task of bringing out the violent contradictions of motive that fight within Bosola, while at the same time making a whole man of him. But I thought that he should have been several rungs higher on the social ladder. A marshal of horse is not a groom. This was no doubt part of the director's general demotion of the aristocracy, which affected the Duchess too. As was to be expected of Judi Dench, her performance was beautifully unforced, affecting, human. Too human, perhaps. The scene in which the Duchess woos Antonio, like that in which they banter before Ferdinand catches her alone, was most moving in its directness and naturalness. The trouble is that the relationship between the Duchess and Antonio can never be one of simple equality as between husband and wife, for their inequality is at the heart of the play. Her declaration of love must really hit Antonio – and the audience – as something hitherto inconceivable. It is not enough that she should be a gentlewoman; he is a gentleman, she a grandee. And I cannot accept that she should say to Bosola 'I am Duchess of Malfi still' in the tone of 'But surely you know *me*'. We must hear something of her twin's voice in that declaration, something of Lear's 'Ay, every inch a king'. But of course it is terribly difficult to

hear these famous quotations with an unbiased ear. We shall meet another example in the comedies, to which I now turn.

The staging of any one of Shakespeare's mature comedies poses the same sort of problem, of balancing realism with artifice, as does *The Duchess*; but I hope it is not too glib a distinction to say that whereas Webster takes a true story and makes a legend of it Shakespeare uses legends to express real life. In his production of *The Merchant of Venice* Terry Hands leant much more to artifice than to realism. In *Much Ado* Ronald Eyre attempted to reconcile the two by setting the play in a historical period but one in which artificiality was the mode. Only John Barton seemed to me, in *Twelfth Night*, to strike the perfect balance.

I must confess that I hated the sets and costumes for *The Merchant*. I hope that the success of last year's superb *Midsummer Night's Dream* has not created a fashion for playing comedies in a gymnasium. This was, of course, a gymnasium with decorations, but I found them cheap and nasty: for example, the fairy lights that descended from the flies each time to create Belmont. May be Belmont should be presented as a sort of child's dream; but not, please, the kind that is offered by Oxford Street at Christmas shopping time. The costumes, too, put me off: the sack dresses and skivvy wigs for Portia and Nerissa; for the men the broad-brimmed hats, straight coats, and boots that suggested an Italian image of puritan New England (Verdi's *Ballo in Maschera*) rather than an English image of the Venetian Republic. It may be that with their hint of Carnaby Street they were designed to create for the young that combination of romantic and everyday that characterises the play, and a grandfather should not complain that they did not work for him. The properties, too: I liked the idea of the *game* of Merchant Adventurers that first introduces us to Antonio and his business acquaintances; the three caskets, with their different operations, provided an ingenious and significant variety, though Shakespeare has given us this more pointedly in the contrasted reactions of the three suitors; Shylock's pop-up house was neat and serviceable. The objection to all these properties, and most of all to the clumsy partitions that cramped the trial scene, was that they cluttered and cut up the stage. Perhaps the director meant to press upon us images of strong-rooms and of treasure-chests; but the merchant-image that in fact pervades the text of this most airy play is that of voyages, far oceans, and the winds of heaven.

Yet if one could pierce through all the rather distracting paraphernalia the structure of the play as here presented could be seen to be foursquare and sound. The personages of the drama had depth and were in scale with each other. Antonio, by a subtle variation of mood and tempo for which the director must share the credit with Tony Church, has never been less of a dummy. The Jew was properly outlandish but never out of scale, just as Gratiano was allowed to play fortissimo but only the notes as written. Both aspects of Portia, the sophisticated and the simply true, were strongly in evidence; and if the sparkish side of Bassanio was perhaps played down, he well matched Portia with truth for truth. As a result the relationships between all the characters were unusually solid. The arias that mark the focal points of the play – 'Hath not a Jew eyes?', 'You see me Lord Bassanio', 'The quality of mercy' – were in tune and sensitively phrased. Some of the director's touches, it is true, worried me a little. The song 'Tell me where is Fancy bred' grew to a babel of sound that created a sense of nightmare hallucination for the moment of Bassanio's choice, ceasing abruptly as the spell is broken and simple reality returns: a good point, but over-elaborately made. The sudden jolt as Portia's word halts Shylock's knife on the very point of incision was terrific; only I did not catch the word itself and could not immediately recall what it should be. It is, in fact, not 'Stop!' but 'Tarry awhile', and this surely indicates that Shakespeare intended a much more lingering suspense, with Shylock subjected in reverse to the same sort of slow torture that he has inflicted on Antonio. Finally I must add a sweet–sour epilogue on Gobbo.

Gobbo's first appearance, and his altercation with conscience and the fiend, I do not think I have ever seen better done. Usually it is much too deliberately acted out. Peter Geddis with his glib zany patter did it, as Andrew Aguecheek might say, more natural. Was it this that decided the director to make him a natural indeed? I imagine that the reasoning may have gone like this: court jesters were, historically, often what we should call harmless lunatics; Gobbo, with his 'voices', is obviously a schizophrenic; it would be a nice touch to send him right round the bend in the last act. The reasoning is unsound for Gobbo is not a court jester but the other kind of 'clown', an unlettered but shrewd rustic, and he shares with Launce, Costard, Bottom and Dogberry one or both of Kemp's special turns, of mistaking words and of telling a story in dialogue. It is as absurd to diagnose Gobbo a schizophrenic as to say that Launce, because he makes his shoe personate his mother, is a shoe-fetishist with incest-fantasies. In itself it may do little harm; but the scene in which Gobbo finally went off his head was that of Lorenzo, Jessica and the moonlight. Jessica, plausibly enough, was disturbed by the condition of her old playmate; and disturbance of any kind is unforgivable in this scene of utter relaxation which knits up the ravelled sleeve of the trial scene and provides a prophylactic against too much edge (and it was splendidly sharp in this production) in the ring quarrel that follows.

Much Ado is a more difficult play to make gell than is *The Merchant*. In the latter all the story elements from which reality is to be distilled have the same degree of fancifulness. In *Much Ado* the materials are disparate: the Ruritanian melodrama of Hero's jilting, the farce of the Watch, and two human beings. I think that we should all agree with Charles I that the human beings come first; and recent directors of the play have therefore striven to find a setting – small-town Sicily, revolutionary Mexico – in which human beings might plausibly find themselves involved in operatic goings-on. Ronald Eyre chose Ruritania, or rather the charade side of nineteenth-century high life, with its fancy-dress military, its clubman camaraderie, its exaggerations of feminine costume, its conservatories, cigars and parasols, out of which Anthony Hope's fantasy of Ruritania grew. Up to a point it worked, and the unity of the play was much assisted by having, in Roger Rees, a strong Claudio for whom one retained some sympathy and respect, in Alison Fiske a spirited Hero who actually answered back, and in Richard Pasco a powerful Don John whose description of Hero as 'A very forward March chick' revealed enough spite and envy to fuel a hundred such plots. But, but, but – can Beatrice and Benedick be presented as Victorians without putting over them a veneer of manners that dulls their natural sharpness? I think that Shaw was wrong in ascribing the rawness of their wit to Shakespeare's provincialism rather than to the whole age in which he lived. Certainly to smooth it down removes much of their special quality. Shakespeare's play is not *The Importance of Being Earnest*, still less *Arms and the Man*.

Within the watered-down convention Derek Godfrey and Elizabeth Spriggs were entertaining and sprightly and 'kept the table in a roar', or at least in a coo. Elizabeth Spriggs did more. The storm of passion and outrage with which she overwhelms Benedick at the end of the church scene was very exciting, all the more perhaps because she had previously cheated our expectation by throwing away the line 'Kill Claudio', another of those famous quotations which it is so dangerous to take as touchstones. Powerful, too, was her self-reproach after overhearing Hero and Ursula criticise her pride. This speech was heightened by the device of making Beatrice conceal herself behind Hero's giant garden-umbrella whose removal suddenly presents her exposed and isolated, a director's gimmick that was amply justified. I thought that making Benedick a bird-watcher (in the ornithological sense) in order to provide him with a hide was more far-fetched. To sum up: elegant, entertaining, sophisticated, but a little lacking in punch.

If anyone can rescue Dogberry it should be Peter Woodthorpe. Of course one laughed; but the best moment was unscripted – the beautifully expressive little movement with which Dogberry showed his instinctive but totally ineffectual sympathy with Claudio in his moment of truth. I have a sneaking feeling not only that with the centuries the Dogberry joke has worn pretty thin but also that Shakespeare too was tired of it when he came to design the umpteenth variation on old Kemp's routine.

Of the three comedies I have least to say about *Twelfth Night*, both because it was not a new production this year (though there were some changes of cast) and because I was in general so moved and delighted by it that individual cavils were submerged. Such as these were, let me get them out of the way. There were some director's inventions that I thought hindered rather than helped, for example the filling out of the midnight carousal with reconstructions *in extenso* of the songs of which the characters only give us snatches. This piece of pedantry substituted a recital by the Elizabethan Glee Society for a row that is supposed to make the welkin ring and draw three souls out of one weaver, thickened the texture of the scene, and destroyed its balance. In the box-tree scene, too, there was imbalance.

It is perhaps a mistake to have the interrupters at the side so that one's eye switches from Malvolio to them and back again. Better to place them behind him upstage, popping up like (rather remote) jack-in-a-boxes. Their frustration must make sudden explosive interruptions without breaking the flow of the scene, which is Malvolio's, or distracting attention from him. Nor do I think it is sensible, though it does not do much harm, to make Maria a puritan maypole when everything in the text indicates a jolly little bundle. In passing I will say that I do not at all object to a Scots Sir Andrew. I suppose it was the name that first suggested the nationality, but it goes well with his general pawkiness. It may not be Shakespeare but it is very much with the grain.

To set against minor cavils there were many examples of John Barton's gift for (to use a musical term) phrasing a scene or indeed a whole play, and for invention that positively assists us to see the matter in the light in which Shakespeare sought to place it. The scenes between Olivia and Viola were splendid instances of the first: the building up of pressure with variations of intensity which are nevertheless all designed to place the climax where it should come. Another example was the swirl and squawk of Viola's final entry out of which the denouement grows, to be consummated in the sudden freeze of motion and sound as lost sister confronts lost brother with all the other characters forgotten save the enigmatic Feste framed in the background between them. For invention, I will quote only Viola's first appearance of all, through a narrow perspectival entrance at the back of the stage, in mist and spray and attended by shadowy figures who are sailors but might be sea-gods; and the sound of the sea reverberating through key-moments in the play – Viola's half-revelations to the love-sick Duke, her final reunion with Sebastian – to remind us of that sense of the changes and chances of life that is surely intrinsic in the mood of the play as in its basic situations.

Viola seems to me the ideal part for Judi Dench. She can seem genuinely boyish without for a moment ceasing to be womanly. The whole colour and quality of this production derived, under the director's hand, from her radiant performance and from the Feste of Emrys James. To that I can give no higher praise than to say that just so must the part have been played by Robert Armin, whose 'slipper tongue' and inward humour must have made Will Kemp's art seem rather old hat. I should like to know whether it was actor or director who was responsible for the extraordinary antic mockery with which the clown sang 'Come away Death'. I thought it a stroke of genius.

The two Histories, *Richard II* and *Henry V*, were Theatregoround productions, designed for touring and translated to the Royal Shakespeare Theatre rather than initially conceived in its terms, but the translation, especially perhaps of *Henry V*, came off well. It was instructive to be shown something of the conditions under which Shakespeare's company must actually have worked – for example, the extensive doubling of parts that must have been adopted by even a medium-sized company when presenting these multi-charactered pieces. It was instructive, too, to see *Henry V* taken almost in rehearsal style, the actor merely capping his workaday all-purpose clothes with mitre or casque to personify specific roles. The cue for this was of course the Chorus's apology for the actor's makeshifts and the impossibility of their doing justice to a great human event. The device, so far from proving a distraction or belittling the theme, did indeed seem to add a sort of extra dimension to it. And because the playing space itself was designedly restricted, as it were to a small spotlight area, outside which the players' stock-in-trade, the props with which they were to create their illusion, were shadowily displayed, it was possible to transfer the whole production to a larger stage with little modification of its centre and only, no doubt, some filling out of the background. In *Richard II*, on the other hand, I felt that at times the action suffered from having been planned with an eye to more cramped conditions.

The problem in both plays – as indeed I suppose in all drama – is again a matter of balance, though it is not quite the same problem as we have met in the other productions of this season, nor is it identical in the two plays. In *Henry V* the question is how to balance the romantic and critical aspects of the play; in *Richard II* how to balance the two protagonists. That there are and have always been two sides to *Henry V* is surely obvious, for in it the pro-war and the anti-war feeling are both perfectly explicit, though their expression is widely and diversely distributed. Only the churchmen and Pistol have views that are unqualified, and neither of these can be said to be looking at the matter in a purely philosophical or disinterested light. Shakespeare being Shakespeare has all the arguments and forces no one of them upon us. In the event, although the programme had half prepared us for a send-up of Glorious King Harry, the production was a very straight one. True, everything was done to make the King very much one with the commoners. He shares the soldiers' soup and offers a ladle-full of it to the French herald in place of the usual purse of gold; with the rest he grovels to escape Macmorris' comic bomb (a legitimate gag, I thought); his usually stately image of 'greyhounds straining in the slips' is a joke, greeted with roars of laughter by his anything but stately troops. I was not sure whether it was to take him down another peg, or more historical pedantry, or just for (successful) comic effect that his Katherine was so very much a child bride. Certainly the exclamation 'Your majesty!' with which the French court

breaks in upon their nursery romp was highly ironic. Polly James's gamine princess was one of two unorthodox bits of casting, the other, equally effective in its way, being Peter Woodthorpe's Dauphin who, without losing any of the comedy, showed that a figure of fun, if a prince, can also be a figure of fear.

My one serious quarrel was with the business at the beginning of the King's speech on ceremony. This is the centre of the play. In it pro-war and anti-war, public and private, heroic and critical, are laid side by side, though there is no formal resolution. It requires the greatest concentration and focusing of attention. Yet at the very outset, just as we are attuning ourselves to it, we are twice disturbed – by the King's leaning over to splash his face with water from a hanging bucket, and by the tolling of a bell. Was this realism? Was some deeper symbolism intended? I do not know; but I found it an intrusion.

The deposition scene in *Richard II* contains the key image of deposer and deposed as buckets in a well, one rising as the other falls. It is vital to the play that the buckets should weigh equally, that the choice before York and the rest should not be an easy one between plain right and plain wrong, but an equipoise of half-right and half-right, of ideal justice and practical expediency. The balance is hard to achieve in an age when the divine right of kings means nothing. Shakespeare could afford to bring out all the weaknesses in Richard because one huge strength, his God-given authority, was taken for granted. If it is not, the balance is destroyed, or can only be restored by a proportional scaling down of Bolingbroke, so that a pitiable poseur is matched by a brutal schemer. In this production the scaling down went too far. The real authority, and the power to inspire devotion in others, which Shakespeare's Richard can show even without the benefit of divinity, was whittled away. The play does not in fact begin with the Queen, and royal dalliance, but with

Richard's initially quite masterful handling of the Mowbray–Bolingbroke quarrel. It is wrong that his own followers should display not anxiety but real boredom at the extravagances of the King's despair, impossible that Bolingbroke should softly clap his rhetoric about heaven's aid. It is faking the odds to have the Queen range herself with Gaunt in his death-bed rebuke. If it would be false to make thunder crown the King's appeals to heaven, it is equally false to make it signal each loss of power that he suffers. Finally, it exaggerates the degradation and dejection of the prisoner of Pomfret to have him actually in chains. Nevertheless at this depressed level there was a real balance and a real conflict. The confrontations between Richard Pasco's agonised Richard and Morgan Sheppard's dryly ruthless Bolingbroke were strong, above all in the deposition scene in which Bolingbroke's remaining casually seated as he puts out his hand to the crown that Richard offers him, and his standing up from his throne to bleakly overtop Richard as he croons over the looking glass, were strokes of power (but the glass really must be smashed!).

Though the King was denied his divinity, much was made of ceremony. The formalities of the lists were, rightly, presented in full. The audience was effectively treated as a vast concourse of spectators at such public scenes as the tourney, the arraignment of Bushy and Green, and the deposition. Odd that in the light of such obvious mastery of effect the King's descent into the base court was so clumsily handled.

Both Histories were fairly heavily cut, Richard in lines here and there, Henry in larger gobbets such as the first Pistol scene and much of the conspiracy. It was discreetly done, but I was not so happy about some of the conflations (for example the rolling of Bagot and Exton into one) and transpositions. The transference of Bushy's pensive analysis of the Queen's first forebodings to the later garden scene removes a note of doom from the earlier scene, where, immediately after Richard's departure for Ireland, it is much more significant. The adjustment of the Agincourt scenes to make the order to kill the prisoners conditional rather than absolute and to enlarge the King's grief at the killing of the boys is to indulge sentimentality. I was pleased that the tragi-farce of Aumerle's treachery was played in full; the break is much needed between the deposition and the murder. Since it was *Richard II* and *Henry V* that were being played together I was sorry that the Duke of York was expunged from the latter. The old soldier who begs the leading of the vaward and dies fighting for his king is the Aumerle who plotted to kill that King's father. But perhaps I too am being sentimental.

The single word that I would use to characterise the whole season is 'workmanlike'; and if that seems faint praise, I would say, with a forgivable quibble, that a season in which each of six major productions really works is quite an achievement. If there was complete conviction and unquestionably starry performances (Viola and Feste), only in a play carried over from a previous season, there were other bonuses to be grateful for. The general level of verse-speaking struck me as unusually high; and before that patronising and prissy phrase sets every actor's teeth on edge, let me hasten to say that I am not talking of elocution but, first, of the actor's realisation that verse is not a decoration but a tool and, second, of his ability to use all the resources of verse, its sound, its phrasing, its pointed syntax, to enhance the power and expressiveness of his own playing. There has been some adroit and admirable teamwork: I think with special delight of Don Pedro, Benedick, Claudio and Leonato in *Much Ado*, and of the French lords in *Henry V*. There were some richly wrought, but not overwrought supporting roles. To those already mentioned I must add Gordon

Gostelow's York in *Richard II*. And this is perhaps the place to pay tribute to Richard Pasco who played four roles, Antonio, Orsino, Don John, and Richard II, none of them easy or grateful, and gave to each in its very different kind an integrity that was very satisfying. But I confess that I end with the suspicion that a main reason why we can call this season satisfactory is that the directors have been playing safe and accepting the easier solutions to the problems set by Shakespeare's dualities. Per-

haps we may encourage them next year to aim higher. There will be disasters, but there might also be greater rewards.[1]

[1] This survey of the season's productions at the Royal Shakespeare Theatre, Stratford-upon-Avon, was given as a lecture to the Theatre Summer School in August 1971.

© RICHARD DAVID 1972

THE YEAR'S CONTRIBUTIONS TO
SHAKESPEARIAN STUDY

1. CRITICAL STUDIES

reviewed by NORMAN SANDERS

Many of the critical approaches to Shakespeare used during the past forty years or so have appeared to offer methods of perceiving the plays' central issues, but have been in fact means of isolating some single aspect of their complexity. In his 1969 Academy lecture, Alfred Harbage[1] looks with wit and good sense at one class of these: the efforts aimed at giving Shakespeare a modern complexion of one sort or another. He realises that most modernisers produce their often spectacular results by ignoring the fact that 'action in a Shakespearian play has . . . more meanings without the words than with them'. And by following up the implications of his idea that 'words are a limiting factor: they restrict our interpretations of an action in the direction of . . . the author's intention', he is able to clip the wings of Kott's reputation, to estimate the degree to which one may speak valuably of a Christian Shakespeare, to indicate fairly the strengths and weaknesses of Soviet criticism, and to contemplate judiciously the possibility of an Absurdist Bard. Clearly Harbage's own sympathy is with the silent critics all over the world who read the plays regularly and apply the only valid test for determining whether a work of art is being justly seen, in its own age or later, which is 'to observe how much of its data is being taken into account'.

A book which would probably be applauded by Harbage is J. R. Brown's *Shakespeare's Dramatic Style*,[2] which aims to teach the reader how to read Shakespeare's text creatively by

exploring and sifting the theatrical possibilities of selected passages and scenes from five plays. All of his observations are well worth reading and show an admirable willingness to follow where a particular play leads rather than impose some rigid critical method upon it. Thus the Prologue to *Romeo and Juliet* is approached via the subtle appreciation of metrical changes, and Juliet's lines at IV, i, 77–88 by an emphasis on the way image content and rhythm reflect the emotional, physical, and sexual pressures felt by a distraught girl. The analysis of the mock marriage scene in *As You Like It* is determined by the various levels of the dramatic texture created by such things as the direction of speeches, the implications of Rosalind's disguise, and the psychological depths behind each character's word use and actions; whereas the murder scene in *Julius Caesar* is shown to be both controlled and wide open to varying interpretations owing to the inherent ambiguity in character creation, styles of speech, theatrical arrangement, and the opportunities offered to the actors. However, among the many good sections, one stands out as being in a class of criticism almost different in kind from the rest: that on the opening scene of *Twelfth Night*, which comes close to defining the very origins of Shakespeare's magical art in this play.

Theatrically aware criticism of a theatrical rather than academic origin, namely actors'

[1] 'Shakespeare Without Words', *Proceedings of the British Academy*, LV (1969), 129–44.
[2] Heinemann, 1970.

171

views of the four great tragedies, is dealt with by Carol J. Carlisle,[1] whose laudable aim is to 'make available in convenient form a body of significant commentaries, hitherto widely scattered and in many instances inaccessible'. When faced with the mass of material at her disposal, Carlisle clearly had to decide between writing a short, lively, highly selective, easy-to-read book or producing a thorough, less readable, useful reference work. Fortunately for us, she chose to do the latter. In her introductory chapter she draws together some of the general features of actors' criticism: e.g. its sharing with academic criticism the taste biases of its age, its practicality, its special insights into character and form, its proneness to alteration, and its cavalier approach to the question of textual accuracy. The sections that follow on the four plays are full of interest. The actors' varying responses to the Witches as hags or fates, the awareness of Barker and Knowles of the play's dramatic structure, and an excellent summary by Carlisle of the possible views of Lady Macbeth stand out in the chapter on *Macbeth*. With *King Lear* actors have clearly felt less at ease, with surprisingly many of their number being struck by its unactable features; however, there is a general acknowledgement of the stature and difficulty of the leading role, as well as a curious unconcern with the play's overall tragic vision. As one might expect with *Hamlet*, the stage has followed closely academic critical attitudes, with only Poel being in the vanguard of a movement; but it is the theatre's obsession with and insights into the Nunnery Scene that stimulate Carlisle to produce the best-written section of the book. It is *Othello* that produces the most thought-provoking views. Why, for example, is this the tragedy that has inspired actors to concentrate on technical criticism rather than character analysis? And why have English actors largely shied away from the emotional content of the main role? Why have the twentieth-century's

clinical approaches to Iago affected theatrical practice so unprofitably? The concluding chapter adds little to the rest of the book and can safely be ignored.

Some new thought on the religious attitudes behind all the History plays may be found in Henry A. Kelly's new book, *Divine Providence in the England of Shakespeare's Histories*.[2] From a fresh reading of the chronicles, he distinguishes a Lancaster myth, which regarded Richard II's overthrow as providentially arranged; a York myth, which considered Henry VI's loss of power the providential restoration of the throne to Edward IV, Richard's lawful heir; and a Tudor myth, which accepted Henry VII as the closest surviving Lancastrian heir and, with his destruction of the wicked Yorkist Richard III, the divinely favoured bringer of peace to England. He argues that the later chroniclers, like Hall, Vergil, and Holinshed, were interested not so much in justifying the legitimacy of the current dynasty as in drawing lessons from the past for their own times; and further, that the 'concept of divine wrath extending for generations over a whole people for a crime committed in the remote past presupposes the kind of avenging God completely foreign to the piety of historiographers of Mediaeval and Renaissance England'.

Kelly sees Shakespeare's great contribution in the two tetralogies as being his unscrambling of the partisan layers of belief blended by the historiographers and his redistribution of them among their appropriate spokesmen. In this way the dramatist eliminates all the purportedly objective judgements of his sources and presents such judgements as those of the persons and parties voicing them. Each play thus creates its own moral ethos and mythos, and offers its

[1] *Shakespeare from the Greenroom. Actors' Criticisms of Four Major Tragedies* (University of North Carolina Press, 1969).
[2] Harvard University Press, 1970.

own hypotheses to demonstrate the springs of human and cosmic action in a world of bygone events whose inner causes are essentially irretrievable. However, while one can agree with Kelly's general conclusions, there are points in his accounts of the various plays with which one may take issue. For example, his assertion that the Lancastrians are not being punished for their usurpation of the crown in the *Henry IV* plays and that Shakespeare implies divine support for the King himself (if for anyone) surely tends to overlook the dramatic and poetic movements of the two plays. Also the interpretation of those passages in *Richard II* concerned with the prophecy of future strife is open to objection. In general, what weaknesses there are in Kelly's argument result from his tendency to treat the plays as historical 'materials' rather than dramatic wholes.

Taking a less academic approach to the same plays, Michael Burn[1] pleasantly fits the plays, as fervent warnings for the nation, into the political events of seventeenth-century England, by making good use of the historical facts and careers that Shakespeare did not draw on as dramatic raw material; but he makes far too much of Malvolio as a politically prophetic figure of Puritan success.

The politico-doctrinal approach illustrated by Kelly's and Burn's work is regarded by A. R. Humphreys[2] with some dismay, as for him 'men, felt in their humanity, and struggling "with that vast mutability which is event", are the historian's theme; it is for the dramatist to interpret this theme as dialogue impelled by dynamic rhythm'. In an excellent Academy lecture, he discusses the way the histories impressionistically incorporate the space, time and life which exist around and beyond their immediate dramatic concerns, because 'English history, for Shakespeare, is a spreading tree rooted in locality'.

In most Western criticism, Jack Cade emerges as an almost undiluted villain, so it is refreshing to have a slightly different view from Heiner Müller,[3] who sees an ambiguity in his portrayal resulting from the conflict between Shakespeare's rejection of civil war as dangerous to the state and his natural sympathy with the plight of the masses. The rather more fundamental conflict between the poet and the dramatist is apparently unavoidable for most critics of *Richard II*. Robert A. Draffen[4] traces a personal change of critical view from tragedy of poet-king to play as study of ὕβρις; but Terence Hawkes[5] finds that 'the play enacts the style its words exhibit', with the central idea of opposition being literally made manifest by the language of antagonism, ranting, and deafness. The prevalent imagery of sun and water in the play are seen by Kathryn M. Harris,[6] in a good article, to be an integral part of the breaking up of a political order, which has itself been wielded against the health of the kingdom. Linking the style of the play with that of the Sonnets, Michel Grivelet[7] discusses the way the poems are 'irradiated with an imaginative energy drawn from the drama of Richard' and are thus 'not impervious to the

[1] 'Why No Henry VII? (With a Postscript on Malvolio's Revenge)', *Manner and Meaning in Shakespeare. Stratford Papers 1965–67*, ed. B. A. W. Jackson (McMaster University Library Press; Irish University Press, 1969), pp. 208–31.

[2] 'Shakespeare's Histories and the "Emotion of the Multitude"', *Proceedings of the British Academy*, LIV (1968), 263–87.

[3] 'Die Gestaltung des Volkes in Shakespeares Historiendramen, untersucht am Beispiel *Heinrichs VI*', *Shakespeare Jahrbuch*, CVI (1970), 127–75.

[4] '"Without Taking Sides Against Poetry": *Richard II*', *English*, XX (1971), 39–44.

[5] 'The Word Against the Word: The Rôle of Language in *Richard II*', *Language and Style*, II (1969), 296–322.

[6] 'Sun and Water Imagery in *Richard II*', *Shakespeare Quarterly*, XXI (1970), 157–66.

[7] 'Shakespeare's "War with Time": The Sonnets and *Richard II*', *Shakespeare Survey 23* (Cambridge University Press, 1970), pp. 69–78.

spiritual awakening which he experiences when his soul opens at last to music'. One article attempts to shift the usual critical emphasis away from Richard. In it, W. J. MacIsaac[1] works from a view of Aumerle as the third cousin, surrogate king, scapegoat, and parallel to Bolingbroke to present the usurper's action in a much more favourable light than usual; however, he does so by ignoring the fact that the Aumerle–York–Duchess scenes are far too weakly written for them to bear the thematic weight he gives them.

The *Henry IV* plays are the subject of two excellent papers well worth everyone's reading. In one of them, M. C. Bradbrook[2] sees the link between the two parts as lying in the idea of 'adaptability, the imaginative ability to create a part and play it'; but her essay is most valuable for the fertile allusiveness in the discussions of the interplay of character and the melting of mood into mood in Part 1, and the sharper separation of man and office in Part 2. In the second paper, D. J. Palmer[3] examines the plays' treatment of the nature of human growth and, in the light of the Biblical allusions that abound in both sections, suggests that Time is redeemed as youth matures and assumes the burdens that age can no longer carry. Also related to the theme of Time in the first part is E. Rubenstein's[4] isolation of the patterns of financial liability as guides to the audience's response to the moral natures of the different characters. It is the second part that is rather surprisingly singled out by John Pettigrew[5] as the 'more profound, mature and searching', apparently by assuming that the nearer a play gets to the tone of *Troilus and Cressida* and the darker elements of the great tragedies, the better it is likely to be. The commentary on three special episodes in these plays is further swelled by Alan D. Isler,[6] who links the 'heroic sherris' with the tropos *sapientia et fortitudo*; by Stephen G. Bolger,[7] who suggests that Hal's phrase 'in Barbary'

should be glossed as the mnemonic name for the first figure of the syllogism in the logic of the schools; and by Alice B. Scoufos,[8] who in a long-winded essay, argues that a series of diplomatic robberies engineered by Lord Cobham in the 1560s lies behind the satire of the Gad's Hill episode.

The flexibility of Shakespeare's skill in presenting his monarchs is nicely illustrated by Waldo F. McNeir[9] and G. P. V. Akrigg.[10] The former traces Richard III's characterisation through his dazzling histrionic displays; while Akrigg illustrates the dramatist's use of prologue, tableau, report, and vivid speech in *Henry V* to create an epic hero. It is rather a pity that Akrigg appears to have ignored some of the recent accounts of the play's tensions and subtleties to arrive at his conclusion of the play's ultimate failure. The odd history-play out, *King John*, receives its annual side glance: this year in connection with Dürrenmatt's adaptation, which Rudolf Stamm[11] ably shows to have at best only a dialectical relationship with the original.

While *Antony and Cleopatra* has not assumed

[1] 'The Three Cousins in *Richard II*', *Shakespeare Quarterly*, XXII (1971), 137–46.

[2] 'King Henry IV', *Manner and Meaning in Shakespeare*, pp. 168–85.

[3] 'Casting off the Old Man: History and St Paul in *Henry IV*', *Critical Quarterly*, XII (1970), 267–83.

[4] 'Henry IV, Part 1: The Metaphor of Liability', *Studies in English Literature*, X (1970), 287–96.

[5] 'The Mood of *Henry IV, Part 2*', *Manner and Meaning in Shakespeare*, pp. 145–67.

[6] 'Falstaff's Heroic Sherris', *Shakespeare Quarterly*, XXII (1971), 186–8.

[7] 'A Logical Note on "Barbary"', *ibid.*, pp. 79–80.

[8] 'Gad's Hill and the Structure of Comic Satire', *Shakespeare Studies*, V (1971), 25–52.

[9] 'The Masks of Richard the Third', *Studies in English Literature*, XI (1971), 167–86.

[10] 'Henry V: The Epic Hero as Dramatic Protagonist', *Manner and Meaning in Shakespeare*, pp. 186–207.

[11] 'King John – König Johann. Vom Historienspiel zur politischen Moralität', *Deutsche Shakespeare-Gesellschaft West Jahrbuch* (1970), pp. 30–48.

the special relevance for our own age that *King Lear*, *Measure for Measure*, or *Troilus and Cressida* appear to have done, a good deal of the recent work on the play seems to me genuinely to further our understanding of it. By far the most substantial study this year is J. Leeds Barroll's[1] monograph, in which he studies the art by which Antony's character is created. Barroll argues that critics have been misled in their stress on the conflict in the hero between allegiance to martial Rome and attraction to luxurious Egypt. Rather he takes Antony's apostleship of soldierly reputation to be only one aspect of a basic physicality, which lies behind all of his actions and attitudes. Antony's responses to this self is traced at length by Barroll in small stage incidents, his personal responsibility for the failure at Actium, his reactions to others and his expectations from them, the Thidias episode, the death scene, and the way Cleopatra possesses a transubstantial identity with Antony's concept of himself as ideal. Altogether a fascinating article, marred only by a lengthy discussion of the textual difficulties presented by Proculeius's role which has no place in a work of this kind. Ranging rather more widely, if less deeply, is Sidney R. Homan's[2] discussion of the attitudes implicit in the praise and blame expressed on the subjects of art, imagination, and theatre, which (none too clearly to this reviewer) appear to add up to a complex dramatic statement in which aesthetics and themes are one. The way this play encourages the reader to think in mythological terms is demonstrated in two excellent articles by Harold Fisch[3] and Robert G. Hunter.[4] The first shows how the protagonists blend with the Mars/Venus, Bacchus/Venus, Isis/Osiris/Set, and Adam/Eve mythological patterns, so that

time and place extend so as to enclose the theme of universal history as it unfolds itself in power upon the vast amphitheatre of the world. The closed myth-world of tragedy is exploded, for the theme of world

history has taken its place. And in this new epic context the mimic apotheosis of the two lovers shrinks to a little measure.

In the latter piece, Hunter traces the blending of Cleopatra with Io in the lines describing her flight at Actium. Rather more conventional is Marilyn Williamson's[5] underprepared discussion of the relationship between the political and erotic elements in the play.

The pivotal position of *Julius Caesar* between the histories and the tragedies is the basis of most of the work done on the play this year. Arnold Edinborough,[6] in a pleasantly written paper, gives the play a key place in Shakespeare's transition from a political dramatist of early orthodoxy to a later one of searing vision; while John W. Velz[7] analyses how the structure, based on a sequence of rises to prominence and declines, gives the play its internal coherence yet enables it to enlarge its scope to convey the sweep of Roman history from Pharsalus to Actium. The conflicts between the characters' personalities and the decisions they make are viewed as the primary concern of the play by D. J. Palmer,[8] who ably uses the common stock of Elizabethan psychology, and interestingly posits a Shakespeare writing under the influence of *Nosce Teipsum*; whereas

---

[1] 'Shakespeare and the Art of Character: A Study of Anthony', *Shakespeare Studies*, V (1971), 159–235.

[2] 'Divided Response and the Imagination in *Antony and Cleopatra*', *Philological Quarterly*, XLIX (1970), 460–8.

[3] '*Antony and Cleopatra*: The Limits of Mythology', *Shakespeare Survey 23* (Cambridge University Press, 1970), pp. 59–68.

[4] 'Cleopatra and the "Oestre Junonicque"', *Shakespeare Studies*, V (1971), 236–9.

[5] 'The Political Context in *Antony and Cleopatra*', *Shakespeare Quarterly*, XXI (1970), 241–52.

[6] '*Julius Caesar*', *Manner and Meaning in Shakespeare*, pp. 129–44.

[7] 'Undular Structure in *Julius Caesar*', *Modern Language Review*, LXVI (1971), 21–30.

[8] 'Tragic Error in *Julius Caesar*', *Shakespeare Quarterly*, XXI (1970), 399–409.

R. Henze[1] locates the Romans' basic tensions in the human desire to have power over others and the need to surrender to something greater than oneself. However, it is the eponymous hero himself, who, for R. E. Spakowski,[2] lifts the play, through his similarity to Christ (*sic*), into the divine realm.

The two other Classical plays received some attention during the year, with Joseph E. Kramer[3] relieving Shakespeare of any responsibility for III, iii of *Titus Andronicus*, on the grounds of its bathetic conceits, textual remoteness, and dramatic ineptness; and Timon's mingled beneficence and misanthropy being attributed by Stephen A. Reid[4] to the infant's unintegrated attitude to the gratification and frustration offered by his mother's breasts. One of the most interesting essays to appear for some time on the earlier play is Andrew V. Ettin's[5] contention that Shakespeare, in exploring the conflicts, contradictions, and insufficiencies in Ovidian and literal rhetorical metamorphoses, was testing the implicit values of Roman literature and culture for the writers of his own time.

The perennial individual difficulties of the Problem Plays continue to perplex more than the nature of the whole group. *Troilus and Cressida* would seem to be detaching itself as a special case, with the interest in recent years focused on its provenance. Jarold W. Ramsey[6] reviews the whole question and while adding very little to Kimborough's work, he usefully presents the case for the play's not being an Inns of Court product, but an aesthetic and philosophical experiment designed by Shakespeare for his own company and theatre. The play's much stressed sexuality is further documented in Beryl Rowland's[7] explication of the grinding/copulation allusions in Pandarus's exchange with Troilus in I, i, which, she suggests, implies a qualification of Troilus's ideals.

With *Measure for Measure* it is the bed-trick, the Duke, Isabella, the marriage contracts, and the moral ambiguity which attract most attention. The Duke of dark corners, according to Hal Gelb,[8] is shown by Lucio to have some failings, which produces a moral and aesthetic unease in the audience with a play that fulfils our comic expectations in form rather than substance; while G. L. Geckle[9] offers us a sainted Isabella, who teaches the Duke as much as she learns from him. Both these characters are taken by Anselm Schlösser[10] to be ambiguously conceived in order to satirise both men's ability to shirk responsibility and the tyranny and duplicity of absolute monarchy. Some qualifications to Schanzer's influential article on the marriage contracts are suggested by J. Birje-Patil,[11] who claims that Shakespeare is dramatising the confusion in the unclearly defined marriage code rather than the legal strands that make up the confusion.

Rehabilitation of two of the problem characters from *All's Well That Ends Well* is undertaken by Carl Dennis,[12] who explains the nature

---

[1] 'Power and Spirit in *Julius Caesar*', *University Review*, XXXVI (1970), 307–14.
[2] 'Deification and Myth-Making in the Play *Julius Caesar*', *ibid.*, pp. 135–40.
[3] '*Titus Andronicus:* The "Fly-Killing" Incident', *Shakespeare Studies*, V (1971), 9–19.
[4] '"I am Misanthropos" – A Psychoanalytic Reading of Shakespeare's *Timon of Athens*', *Psychoanalytic Review*, LVI (1969), 442–52.
[5] 'Shakespeare's First Roman Tragedy', *English Literary History*, XXXVII (1970), 325–41.
[6] 'The Provenance of *Troilus and Cressida*', *Shakespeare Quarterly*, XXI (1970), 223–40.
[7] 'A Cake-Making Image in *Troilus and Cressida*', *ibid.*, pp. 191–4.
[8] 'Duke Vincentio and the Illusion of Comedy or All's Not Well That Ends Well', *Shakespeare Quarterly*, XXII (1971), 25–34.
[9] 'Shakespeare's Isabella', *ibid.*, pp. 163–8.
[10] 'Implizierte Satire in *Mass für Mass*', *Shakespeare Jahrbuch*, CVI (1970), 100–26.
[11] 'Marriage Contracts in *Measure for Measure*', *Shakespeare Studies*, V (1971), 106–11.
[12] '*All's Well That Ends Well* and the Meaning of Agape', *Philological Quarterly*, L (1971), 75–84.

of Bertram by taking the play to be an investigation of *agape* and Helena to be yet another Shakespearian Christ figure; and by J. D. Huston,[1] who stresses the vital energy of Parolles and the way his negative and positive qualities serve to strengthen the theme of youthful vigour incorporated into society by being channelled into the ordered forms of traditional social institutions. A useful context for this play as well as for *Measure for Measure* is provided by William R. Bowden's[2] survey of the theatrical variations of the bed-trick between 1603 and 1642.

Of the Romances, it is *Pericles* that offers the greatest variety of problems, with the contrasting tones of the two parts being an apparently insuperable barrier to any general critical acceptance of the play's total effect. Two writers link the play in different ways with the early comedies. James O. Wood[3] follows the usual division, assigning the first two acts to early in Shakespeare's career and the last three to his maturity on the evidence provided by the handling of various running images common to both sections. A much more convincing article is that by W. B. Thorne,[4] who examines in perceptive detail how the various oppositions arising from the idea of life's continuum give a larger perspective than is found in those early comedies which take their dramatic impulse from a similar vision of Nature. One important episode in this vision – the death of Antiochus – is shown by Michael Gearin-Tosh[5] to have been brought together from various sources for the purpose of the play.

The Winter's Tale's foundations of Time, Pastoral, tragi-comic experience, masque, and spectacle are dealt with in four very fine articles. G. F. Waller[6] usefully draws together the peculiar demands dramatic romance makes on its audience, and proceeds to demonstrate how the things which represent man's triumph over Time are a product of the Romance mode,

even though they can never serve to redeem the loss of Time itself. The tragi-comic elements and their resultant tensions in the play are shown to pervade the sheep-shearing scene, which, P. M. Weinstein claims,[7] does not so much bridge the gap between innocent youth and guilty adulthood as supply an indispensable passionate loyalty in all its value and limitation. On the same topic is Joan Hartwig's[8] first-rate essay on how exactly the tragi-comic vision operates on the audience, particularly in the final scene. The rather more specialised, but equally good, analysis of Richard Studing[9] judges what is achieved by the masque-like characteristics of many episodes in complementing visually the main dramatic movement of the play.

The Tempest's definition of the good life attracts a large amount of interesting comment. Prospero's pessimistic, classical, Christian doctrines are contrasted with the optimistic, romantic, secular utopianism of Gonzalo by M. Seiden;[10] and some parallels drawn between them by Harry Berger,[11] who also, with Klaus

---

[1] 'The Function of Parolles', *Shakespeare Quarterly*, XXI (1970), 431–8.

[2] 'The Bed Trick, 1603–1642: Its Mechanics, Ethics, and Effects', *Shakespeare Studies*, V (1971), 112–23.

[3] 'The Running Image in *Pericles*', *ibid.*, pp. 240–52.

[4] '*Pericles* and the "Incest-Fertility" Opposition', *Shakespeare Quarterly*, XXII (1971), 43–56.

[5] '*Pericles*: The Death of Antiochus', *Notes and Queries*, XVIII (1971), 149–50.

[6] 'Romance and Shakespeare's Philosophy of Time in *The Winter's Tale*', *Southern Review*, IV (1970), 130–8.

[7] 'An Interpretation of Pastoral in *The Winter's Tale*', *Shakespeare Quarterly*, XXII (1971), 97–109.

[8] 'The Tragicomic Perspective of *The Winter's Tale*', *English Literary History*, XXXVII (1970), 12–36.

[9] 'Spectacle and Masque in *The Winter's Tale*', *English Miscellany*, XXI (1970), 55–80.

[10] 'Utopianism in *The Tempest*', *Modern Language Quarterly*, XXXI (1970), 3–21.

[11] 'Miraculous Harp: A Reading of Shakespeare's *Tempest*', *Shakespeare Studies*, V (1971), 253–83.

Bartenschlager,[1] analyses Prospero's dual relationship with the worlds of art and humanity. It is in Prospero's complex character too that T. Bareham[2] finds most of his evidence for his view of the play's surface movement as a controlled fable of redemption and grace with a subterranean current of potential evil. Two important passages are given detailed scrutiny: the opening scene's utilisation of realistic and romance conventions to declare the theme of iconoclastic challenge to Degree, by Guy Back;[3] and the masque scene's original form, as it is reconstructed by Irwin Smith[4] in an article which is required reading for any future editor of the play. Lester E. Barber[5] briefly attempts to dissuade us from making any strong connection between Caliban and Ariel and the sullen and clever slaves of the New Comedy. Although Carol Gesner's[6] study of Shakespeare's use of themes and plots from the Greek Romances is not strictly the province of this section of the review, her evidence for viewing *Cymbeline* as Heliodoran romance does have distinct critical implications, some of which she works out on pages 80–115.

The Comedies are the subject of a book by Larry S. Champion,[7] who argues that Shakespeare's approach to comedy was consistent throughout his career; and provokes a fresh consideration of his artistry through an 'investigation of the comic perspective of the plays – in part, at least, the nature of the characterization and the devices by which the characters are rendered humorous'. He sees Shakespeare's structural difficulties as lying in the fact that as 'his conception of character expanded, so also did his problem of maintaining the proper perspective for the spectator'. Champion detects three basic levels of comic characterization: (1) the puppet at the mercy of action; (2) the socially displaced character who gains self-knowledge; (3) the character who faces evil and reality and achieves a basic alteration of values.

The early works 'of action' are discussed in terms of such things as Shakespeare's experiments with caricature, loosely related parallel action in low characters, broad physical action, etc.; with only *A Midsummer Night's Dream* (which is viewed primarily as a 'refashioning' of *The Knight's Tale* rather than the interweaving of disparate plot strands) being wholly successful. Among the comedies 'of identity', *Much Ado About Nothing* is largely underrated; but *Twelfth Night* is seen as perfect in its 'creation of characters who, while playing a significant narrative role, also serve as comic pointers by providing information for the spectator and by functioning as the primary device for character exposure'. The problem comedies emerge in Champion's scheme as carefully structured intermediate steps between the success of *Twelfth Night* and the profound comic artistry of *The Winter's Tale* and *The Tempest*, in which Shakespeare 'has maintained the spectator's detachment, or withheld the spectator's emotional commitment, thus producing an art form which on occasion resembles tragedy in terms of narrative but is quite distinct from it in terms of the relationship between the character and the spectator'. Altogether a book well worth reading.

Three other articles also deal with special aspects of comic characterisation. In a general

---

[1] 'Shakespeares *The Tempest*: Die ideale Traum und Prosperos Magie', *Deutsche Shakespeare-Gesellschaft West Jahrbuch* (1970), pp. 170–87.

[2] '*The Tempest*: The Substantial Pageant Unfaded', *Durham University Journal*, LXIII (1971), 213–22.

[3] 'Dramatic Convention in the First Scene of *The Tempest*', *Essays in Criticism*, XXI (1971), 74–85.

[4] 'Ariel and the Masque in *The Tempest*', *Shakespeare Quarterly*, XXI (1970), 213–22.

[5] '*The Tempest* and New Comedy', *ibid.*, pp. 207–11.

[6] *Shakespeare and the Greek Romance: A Study of Origins* (University Press of Kentucky, 1970).

[7] *The Evolution of Shakespeare's Comedy: A Study in Dramatic Perspective* (Harvard University Press, 1970).

way, Lásló Kéry[1] shows how the complexities and contradictions of the comic creations account for their homogeneity; and more technically, Robert Weimann[2] uses *The Two Gentlemen of Verona* to demonstrate the interplay between character, audience, and actor. Chris R. Hassel[3] takes on the bigger task of explaining just how the audience joins the comic characters in their attainment of a more comprehensive perspective, based upon the admission of their own imperfectibility.

Work on the early comedies has concentrated on the idea of theatre and symbols, with Richard Henze[4] noting how both the play and Induction of *The Taming of the Shrew* constitute a dramatic exploration of the nature of role playing in comedy and in life, and Herbert R. Courson[5] showing that *Love's Labour's Lost* and the play of the Nine Worthies share the same theme of a false world being overtaken by truth. In another article, Henze[6] discusses the function of the gold chain in *A Comedy of Errors* as a symbol of the cohesion of society; while Neil Taylor[7] charts how the moon provides an appropriate spiritual and chronological time scheme for *A Midsummer Night's Dream*. The character of Shylock naturally bestrides most of the work published on *The Merchant of Venice* and stimulates critical attitudes as extreme as his own, ranging from Hyam Maccoby's[8] insistence that the play is anti-semitic, through M. J. C. Echeruo's[9] contention that Shakespeare was severely limited by the framework of racial ideas the contemporary audience brought into the theatre, and on to J. R. Cooper's[10] reduction of Shylock to only one element in the complex of Venetian values which are set against those of Belmont. It is the power of Shylock also that forced Shakespeare, in J. E. Siemon's[11] view, to resort to a ritualistic restatement of his themes in act v. Only L. W. Hyman[12] refuses to be oppressed by the Jew's presence, for he believes that the main action of the play is centred on the

struggle between Portia and Antonio for Bassanio's love.

The critical problem presented by *Twelfth Night* is occasioned less by a single character than by its tone, which Charles T. Prouty[13] rather unsuccessfully tries to define, and the miraculous balance of its parts. Some of the latter receive intelligent comment in S. Musgrove's[14] explication of Feste's *double entendres* at I, v, 1–30, which bring him into direct contact with the love theme; in Roger Warren's[15] welcome rehabilitation of Orsino as a true lover, by reference to the sea imagery in Sonnet 56; in D. R. Preston's[16] interesting insights into actors' problems with the minor characters; and

[1] 'Einige Bermerkungen zuder Komplexität der komischen Gestalten bei Shakespeare', *Shakespeare Jahrbuch*, CVI (1970), 76–84.

[2] 'Das "Lachen mit dem Publikum". *Die beiden Veroneser* und die volkstümliche Komödientradition', *ibid.*, pp. 85–99.

[3] 'Shakespeare's Comic Epilogues: Invitations to Festive Communion', *Deutsche Shakespeare-Gesellschaft West Jahrbuch* (1970), pp. 160–9.

[4] 'Role Playing in *The Taming of the Shrew*', *Southern Humanities Review*, IV (1970), 231–40.

[5] '*Love's Labour's Lost* and the Comic Truth', *Papers on Language and Literature*, VI (1970), 316–22.

[6] '*The Comedy of Errors*, A Freely Binding Chain', *Shakespeare Quarterly*, XXII (1971), 35–42.

[7] '"Find Out Moone-shine, Find Out Moone-shine"', *Notes and Queries*, XVIII (1971), 134–6.

[8] 'The Figure of Shylock', *Midstream*, XVI (1970), 56–69.

[9] 'Shylock and the "Conditioned Imagination"', *Shakespeare Quarterly*, XXII (1971), 3–16.

[10] 'Shylock's Humanity', *Shakespeare Quarterly*, XXI (1970), 117–24.

[11] 'The Merchant of Venice: Act V as Ritual Reiteration', *Studies in Philology*, LXVII (1970), 201–9.

[12] 'The Rival Lovers in *The Merchant of Venice*', *Shakespeare Quarterly*, XXI (1970), 109–16.

[13] '*Twelfth Night*', *Manner and Meaning in Shakespeare*, pp. 110–28.

[14] 'Feste's Dishonesty: An Interpretation of *Twelfth Night*, I.v.1–30', *Shakespeare Quarterly*, XXI (1970), 194–6.

[15] 'Orsino and Sonnet 56', *Notes and Queries*, XVIII (1971), 146–7.

[16] 'The Minor Characters in *Twelfth Night*', *Shakespeare Quarterly*, XXI (1970), 167–76.

in F. H. Mares's[1] charmingly phrased remarks on the range of emotional response made possible by Viola's transvestism.

The varying influences of character on character are one part of the strength of both *As You Like It* and *Much Ado About Nothing*. A heavily psychological approach to the topic is used by M. D. Faber,[2] who sees Jaques displacing his own retaliatory aggression on the Duke Senior by identifying himself with the wounded deer, and by Ralph Berry,[3] in his definition of the debates in Arden as struggles for mastery by the participants, whose relationships are keynoted by subdued or overt hostility. The moral textures of these two plays are approached by Richard Henze[4] in his contrasting of the right deceptions that lead to marriage and the deceit that breeds conflict in *Much Ado About Nothing*; and by Robert B. Pierce,[5] who fruitfully compares the purely decorative moralism of *Rosalynde* with the critical moral sense displayed in *As You Like It*.

The nature of Shakespeare's tragic vision is part of the subject of George C. Herndl's *The High Design: English Renaissance Tragedy and the Natural Law*,[6] which usefully surveys medieval attitudes to the Natural Law and concludes that it was neither disembodied reason nor inexorable physical fact – rather it was reason understood as dictating for men what it discerns as the demands of his whole nature and thus is capable of illumination by the imaginative exploration of human experience. Herndl finds, from his examination of the tragedies, that they display a profound revelation that the nature of the world is good, that the moral laws to which men are subject are dictated by the constitution of things as we know them, that the heroes survive with integrity to govern their inner and ultimately significant fates, and that suffering yields a reconciling assurance by the meaningful form within which it is set. Except on *King Lear*, the

book does not contain any striking critical insights, but it does a good job of seeing Shakespeare's tragic plays in the context of the later Jacobean works. One dominant element is dealt with by Helen Gardner.[7] In her usual clear-sighted way, she makes the best brief statement about the tragedies' Christian content, showing how they express the mysteries 'that arise out of Christian conceptions, and out of Christian formulations, and that some of their most characteristic features are related to Christian religious feeling and Christian apprehensions'.

Macbeth is seen to be a very baroque piece indeed by J. Bauduin[8] in its themes, world, macabre elements, attitude to man and the universe, form and dialectic; but William B. Hunter[9] detects in its arrangement for offstage deaths Shakespeare's attempt to appeal to the neo-classically trained James I. There is also some interesting comment on the various allegorical levels of the Birnam Wood scene by John P. Cutts;[10] on the images of the 'lease of life' by Matti Rissanen;[11] on the way the opening scene contains the whole thematic

[1] 'Viola and Other Transvestist Heroines in Shakespeare's Comedies', *Manner and Meaning in Shakespeare*, pp. 96–109.

[2] 'On Jaques: Psychoanalytic Remarks', *University Review*, XXXVI (1969), 89–95, 179–82.

[3] 'No Exit from Arden', *Modern Language Review*, LXVI (1971), 11–20.

[4] 'Deception in *Much Ado About Nothing*', *Studies in English Literature*, XI (1971), 187–202.

[5] 'The Moral Languages of *Rosalynde* and *As You Like It*', *Studies in Philology*, LXVIII (1971), 167–76.

[6] University Press of Kentucky, 1970.

[7] 'Shakespearian Tragedy', *Religion and Literature* (Faber and Faber, 1971), pp. 61–89.

[8] 'Les Eléments baroques dans *Macbeth* et leur utilisation', *Études Anglaises*, XXIV (1971), 1–21.

[9] 'A Decorous *Macbeth*', *English Language Notes*, VIII (1971), 169–73.

[10] '"Till Birnam Forest Come to Dunsinane"', *Shakespeare Quarterly*, XXI (1970), 497–9.

[11] '"Nature's Copy", "Great Bond", and "Lease of Nature" in *Macbeth*', *Neuphilologische Mitteilungen*, LXX (1969), 714–23.

structure by Barbara L. Parker;[1] and on the unsolicited encouragement toward royal aspiration Macbeth receives from Ross and Duncan by Edwin Thumboo.[2]

The explication of puzzling details rather than any large critical attempt to grasp the play's vision characterise the year's contributions on *King Lear*; except for Morris Weitz's[3] stimulating essay comparing the play with Camus's *L'Etranger*, which argues that at the play's philosophical centre is man's worth in a morally indifferent universe in which man is forced to mint his own values. The opening scene receives some attention from J. R. Dove and P. Gamble,[4] who take the 'darker purpose' to be Lear's decision to give Cordelia the most opulent third of the kingdom as a bait for her to remain with him; while Simon O. Lesser[5] stresses the natural human responses at the scene's base. The visual effects are examined in H. A. Hargreaves's[6] demonstration of the way verbal utterances are often contradicted by what we see on the stage; and one particular effect – that produced by the Edgar-Oswald duel – is explicated by A. L. Soens[7] in the light of contemporary English and Italian swordsmanship. The phrase 'the good years' is further documented by J. C. Maxwell,[8] who has found its meaning associated with 'devil' in 1568; and by William E. Brady,[9] who connects it closely with Pharaoh's dream. Hilda M. Hulme[10] makes a convincingly new explication of the Fool's enigmatic speech at I, iv, 65–88.

The contradictory impressions that the characters in *Othello* appear to give are seen by Elias Schwatz[11] to stem from the naturalistic and stylised modes that Shakespeare deliberately used to allow the play to move on the natural and quasi-theological levels simultaneously. But for K. W. Evans[12] it is in the hero's racial background that the significance of the tragic climax resides; while Anthony Low[13] locates the essence of the tragedy in Iago's ability to detect and use the flaws in the nobility of Othello and Cassio. Sidney R. Homan,[14] in an unusual essay, gives the Ancient a new dimension, as he traces in him all the negative qualities Renaissance critics found in poets and playwrights. Two details receive some good comment: the handkerchief as proof and symbol in a good article by Peter G. Mudford,[15] and the Turkish invasion, which is shown by Michael Taylor[16] to be a reflection in miniature of the process by which the hero is destroyed. T. Sipahigil[17] tells us that Othello's name was known prior to the play's writing;

[1] '*Macbeth:* The Great Illusion', *Sewanee Review*, LXXVIII (1970), 476–87.

[2] 'Macbeth and the Generous Duncan', *Shakespeare Quarterly*, XXII (1971), 181–6.

[3] 'The Coinage of Man: *King Lear* and Camus's *L'Etranger*', *Modern Language Review*, LXVI (1971), 31–9.

[4] '"Our Darker Purpose": The Division Scene in *Lear*', *Neuphilologische Mitteilungen*, LXX (1969), 306–18.

[5] 'Act One, Scene One, of *Lear*', *College English*, XXXII (1970), 155–71.

[6] 'Visual Contradiction in *King Lear*', *Shakespeare Quarterly*, XXI (1970), 491–5.

[7] 'Cudgels and Rapiers: The Staging of the Edgar-Oswald Fight in *Lear*', *Shakespeare Studies*, V (1971), 149–58.

[8] '"Goodyear"', *Notes and Queries*, XVIII (1971), 149.

[9] 'King Lear's Definition of "The Good Years"', *Shakespeare Quarterly*, XXI (1970), 495–7.

[10] 'On the Detail of Proverb Idiom, *King Lear* II, iv, 65–88', *English Studies*, LI (1970), 529–37.

[11] 'Stylistic Impurity and the Meaning of *Othello*', *Studies in English Literature*, X (1970), 297–314.

[12] 'The Racial Factor in *Othello*', *Shakespeare Studies*, V (1971), 124–40.

[13] 'Othello and Cassio: "Unfortunate in Infirmity"', *Archiv für das Studium der Neueren Sprachen und Literaturen*, CCVI (1970), 428–33.

[14] 'Iago's Aesthetics: *Othello* and Shakespeare's Portrait of an Artist', *Shakespeare Studies*, V (1971), 141–8.

[15] '*Othello* and the "Tragedy of Situation"', *English*, XX (1971), 1–6.

[16] 'A Note on *Othello*, I, iii, 1–47', *English Language Notes*, VIII (1970), 99–102.

[17] 'Othello's Name, Once Again', *Notes and Queries*, XVIII (1971), 147–8.

Robert F. Fleissner[1] defends the 'Indian' over the 'Judean' reading; and Lodowick Hartley[2] discusses the staging of the handkerchief scene.

Shakespeare's earlier love tragedy is the subject of a good article by Susan Snyder,[3] who suggests that, although *Romeo and Juliet* has a dramatic unity, it is essentially comic before Mercutio's death, after which it becomes a tragedy of helplessness. Romeo's particular helplessness is traced by R. C. Johnson[4] to his limited knowledge, in connection with which Benvolio, Tybalt, Paris, and Mercutio act as his foils. The whole play is compared not very fruitfully with Edward Bond's *Saved* by Urs H. Mehlin;[5] and Nurse's 'ropery' is well glossed by Richard Levin.[6]

In recent criticism, the Prince of Denmark has ceased to get in the way of our seeing his play to the extent he was wont. Charles K. Cannon,[7] Michael Taylor,[8] and T. McAlindon[9] all discuss rewardingly the ways in which *Hamlet* enacts its own meaning; with Cannon stressing the stage presentation as a metaphor for the situation of every human being who is predestined to act in a certain way while remaining responsible, McAlindon examining verbal and theatrical features which produce indecorum in the action and the audience's response, and Taylor emphasising how the resolution is not caught up in the dominant mood of doubt and confusion. Even in those articles that focus on the hero, it is his relationship with death rather than his own psyche that is foremost. Harry Morris[10] claims the whole play to be modelled on the *memento mori* lyric, with Hamlet's overwhelming concern being for the plight of his soul; V. Hutton[11] sees the hero's learning to fear death a sign of the maturity that enables him finally to reject the world; Alan C. Dessen[12] takes the poisoned sword to be an appropriate symbol for a death-tainted hero; and John T. Flynn,[13] using Hamlet's inner need to identify with

another human being, sees acceptance of death as the result of an effective final commitment.

Among the other characters in the tragedy, Claudius is given high marks by Morris H. Partee[14] for his kingship, but is seen, by Michael C. Andrews[15] to be damned symbolically with the poisoned chalice. Ophelia emerges, from an essay by J. E. Seaman,[16] as an innocent rose of May comprehensively destroyed by the disproportion of the unweeded garden; and although apparently we must not make too much out of her being a Fishmonger's offspring

[1] 'The Three Base Indians in *Othello*', *Shakespeare Quarterly*, XXII (1971), 80–2.

[2] 'Dropping the Handkerchief: Pronoun Reference and Stage Direction in *Othello*, III, iii', *English Language Notes*, VIII (1971), 173–6.

[3] '*Romeo and Juliet*, Comedy into Tragedy', *Essays in Criticism*, XX (1970), 391–402.

[4] 'Four Young Men: *Romeo and Juliet*', *University Review*, XXXVI (1969), 141–7.

[5] 'Die Behandlung von Liebe und Aggression in Shakespeares *Romeo and Juliet* und in Edward Bonds *Saved*', *Deutsche Shakespeare-Gesellschaft West Jahrbuch* (1970), pp. 132–59.

[6] 'Grumio's "Rope-Tricks" and the Nurse's "Ropery"', *Shakespeare Quarterly*, XXII (1971), 82–6.

[7] '"As in a Theater": *Hamlet* in the Light of Calvin's Doctrine of Predestination', *Studies in English Literature*, XI (1971), 203–22.

[8] 'The Conflict in Hamlet', *Shakespeare Quarterly*, XXII (1971), 147–62.

[9] 'Indecorum in *Hamlet*', *Shakespeare Studies*, V (1971), 70–96.

[10] '*Hamlet* as a *Memento Mori* Poem', *Publications of the Modern Language Association of America*, LXXXV (1970), 1,035–40.

[11] 'Hamlet's Fear of Death', *University Review*, XXXVII (1970), 11–18.

[12] 'Hamlet's Poisoned Sword: A Study in Dramatic Imagery', *Shakespeare Studies*, V (1971), 53–69.

[13] 'The Problem of the Prince', *Identification and Individuality* (Beckman Press, New York, 1970), pp. 52–60.

[14] 'Claudius and the Political Background of *Hamlet*', *English Miscellany*, XXI (1970), 35–54.

[15] 'The Double-Death of Claudius in *Hamlet*', *Renaissance Papers 1970*, pp. 21–8.

[16] 'The "Rose of May" in the "Unweeded Garden"', *Études Anglaises*, XXII (1969), 337–45.

(according to M. A. Shaaber),[1] we can make a closer connection between her and Jephtha's daughter, on the evidence presented by James G. McManaway.[2] Two factual notes are contributed by Roy W. Battenhouse,[3] who claims the 'old mole' to mean a devil; and by James A. Kilbey,[4] who ably argues that the 'odds' of Osric's speech on the fencing match is not a betting term but an indication of the difference in the number of hits by each fencer proposed for the conditions of the wager. The whole play is taken to be adequately representative of Shakespeare work in contrast to the immense variety of Lope and Calderon by Alvaro Custodio.[5]

Since the dark lady–homosexual peer approach to the Sonnets has been largely dropped in recent years, articles on the poems have tended to get either more technical or more detailed. One segment of Alastair Fowler's[6] latest numerological venture is devoted to the poems. He rejects any necessity for reordering the sequence and concentrates on the irregular sonnets (XCIX, CXXVI, CXIV) to see the pattern they form. Each of these is so located that it is denoted by a triangular number within the greater triangle 153, which fact links the arrangement of the whole sequence to the entire set of Psalms, which were thought of as having a three-fold division. While one stands in awe at the ingenuity of such a scheme, it does cross at least this reviewer's mind that the way Fowler allows Sonnet CXXXVI to self-refer to its own exclusion, in order to get the necessary number of 153, might be an example of the scholar's rather than the poet's sleight of hand. Even more specialised is Herbert Donow's[7] computer-derived analysis. The 2,155 lines of the sequence are arranged in groups according to the number and kinds of words in each line; all this being done in the belief that metrical patterns are partially indicated by the presence, location, and distribution of high-frequency monosyllables in a line which has a fixed number of syllables. On rather simpler ground, Martin B. Friedman[8] points out the way the bowling/archery imagery of Sonnet XX is appropriately used in a poem concerned with friendship and rivalry; and R. Koskimies[9] claims that Platonism (particularly *The Symposium*) has a decisive role in the genesis of the poems.

Willard Farnham[10] once again turns our attention to some of the elements in Shakespeare's works which have their roots in the Middle Ages, by commenting, with his usual scholarly expertise, on the grotesque characters in the plays. In his opening chapter, he makes good use of such things as the illuminations of Romanesque and medieval MSS., the cyclical dramas, and the Interludes to trace how the spirit of comedy makes its way into matters of high seriousness and how it is built upon strong antitheses within itself, even while conflicting aesthetically with the spiritual high of which it thus becomes a part. Falstaff, with his monstrous-cum-witty-human nature, is Farnham's first example of the way in which Shakespeare

[1] 'Polonius as Fishmonger', *Shakespeare Quarterly*, XXII (1971), 179–81.
[2] 'Ophelia and Jephtha's Daughter', *Shakespeare Quarterly*, XXI (1970), 198–200.
[3] 'The "Old Mole" of *Hamlet*, I, v, 162', *Notes and Queries*, XVIII (1971), 145–6.
[4] 'The Fencing Match in *Hamlet* and the Wager Upon Its Outcome', *ibid.*, pp. 142–5.
[5] *Lope-Calderon y Shakespeare: Comparacion de dos Estilos Dramaticos* (Ediciones Teatro Clasico de Mexico, 1969).
[6] *Triumphal Forms: Structural Patterns in Elizabethan Poetry* (Cambridge University Press, 1970), pp. 183–97.
[7] 'Linear Word Count as a Function of Rhythm: An Analysis of Shakespeare's Sonnets', *Hephaistos*, I (1970), 1–24.
[8] 'Shakespeare's "Master Mistris": Image and Tone in Sonnet 20', *Shakespeare Quarterly*, XXII (1971), 189–91.
[9] 'The Question of Platonism in Shakespeare's Sonnets', *Neuphilologische Mitteilungen*, LXXI (1970), 260–9.
[10] *The Shakespearean Grotesque: Its Genesis and Transformations* (Oxford University Press, 1970).

uses the grotesque as a foil to glorify the high endeavours of men and at the same time allows it to offer mere humanity a relief from them; though he also uses Launce and Bottom to good effect in displaying how the qualifications of our response to the romantic love code operates in a way similar to the fat knight's manipulations in the cosmic drama of history. However, it is when Farnham turns to consider the relationship between the grotesque-foolish and the serious-wise in *Hamlet*, *Lear*, and the mature comedies, that the book becomes more than a specialised study, and emerges as a profound examination of the techniques of Shakespeare's serio-comic art and its unique vision – a vision which was to utilise the expanding comic grotesqueness of a Thersites and an Iago, and ultimately the hybrid physical form of Caliban in all its enigmatic doubleness of nature. These are the chapters which no student of Shakespeare can afford to ignore and to which no brief summary can do justice.

Animal lore and its symbolic possibilities figure large in a fascinating iconographic piece by Anthony J. Lewis,[1] who links the destructive forces of night with the dog, lion, and wolf in *Richard III*, *Macbeth*, and *Troilus and Cressida*. Also connected with the visual impact inherent in the plays is a group of articles, which deal with the various techniques employed by Shakespeare to illustrate or expand his verbal effects. Eileen Cohen[2] carefully works out the points of contact between the dramatist's attitudes to the weakening hold of ceremony and ritual and the breakdown of order in the major history plays. Dieter Mehl[3] supports many of Cohen's points with his demonstration of how important it is to remember the Elizabethan audience's interest in heraldry and emblematics, when attempting to reconstruct the total impact of the plays. Two scholars, Barbara Mowat[4] and Jorg Hasler,[5] demonstrate how dialogue allows Shakespeare to control physical action and gesture and their effects on the audience; and

Charles B. Lower[6] is hard on many modern editors, in his plea for both the understanding and display in texts of exactly 'who hears what'.

It is the word that is supreme, however, in another group of closely related articles, growing mainly out of the last Stratford-upon-Avon Conference. The philological learning of three of these is enough to fill the average literary scholar with awful uncertainty. G. V. Smithers[7] chills as he expertly classifies the different uses of '–ed' words in Shakespeare's vocabulary, and then for good measure, throws in a warning about the inadequacies of *OED*'s meanings for such words. Bridget Cusack's[8] examination of the dramatist's manipulation of the shifting linguistic conditions of his time warns us of the subtleties not immediately apparent in many of the commentaries we use. And Vivian Salmon's[9] display of the artistic necessity behind many of Shakespeare's neologisms makes me wonder whether we have ta'en too little care of this branch of Shakespeare study.

[1] 'The Dog, Lion, and Wolf in Shakespeare's Descriptions of Night', *Modern Language Review*, LXVI (1971), 1–10.

[2] 'The Visible Solemnity: Ceremony and Order in Shakespeare and Hooker', *Texas Studies in Literature and Language*, XII (1970), 181–96.

[3] 'Schaubild und Sprachfigur in Shakespeares Drama', *Deutsche Shakespeare-Gesellschaft West Jahrbuch* (1970), pp. 7–29.

[4] 'The Beckoning Ghost: Stage-Gesture in Shakespeare', *Renaissance Papers 1970*, pp. 41–54.

[5] 'Bühnenanweisungen und Spiegeltechnik bei Shakespeare und im modernen Drama', *Deutsche Shakespeare-Gesellschaft West Jahrbuch* (1970), pp. 99–117.

[6] 'Separate Stage Groupings: Instances with Editorial Gain', *Renaissance Papers 1970*, pp. 55–72.

[7] 'Guide-Lines for Interpreting the Uses of the Suffix "-ed" in Shakespeare's English', *Shakespeare Survey 23* (Cambridge University Press, 1970), pp. 27–38.

[8] 'Shakespeare and the Tune of the Time', *ibid.*, pp. 1–12.

[9] 'Some Functions of Shakespearian Word-Formation', *ibid.*, pp. 13–26.

On more familiar ground, K. Hudson's[1] commonsense remarks on Elizabethan idiom are valuably supported by real-life examples; Arthur C. Sprague[2] points to some clues we are given about the styles of speech of some characters and the attitudes we should have towards them; J. W. Draper[3] focuses on the functions of final lines; and George R. Hibbard[4] effortlessly shows his mastery of the *lecture expliquée*, as he studies the use of language for dramatic ends in five passages linked by their association of night with criminality. Yet despite all our deductions about Shakespeare's poetic art, the only concrete evidence the plays offer about his attitude to the whole subject are the amateur and professional poets who appear in them and the various characters' remarks on poetry. It is this body of knowledge that Kenneth Muir[5] gathers together to show how far Shakespeare was from being self-admiring about his role in life. A far less substantial, if more influential class of characters, namely the ghosts, are examined by John Jump,[6] who argues that Shakespeare knew well and used for his own ends his audience's hopelessly mixed reactions to the supernatural.

Two important nineteenth-century critics have received some attention in R. A. Foakes's[7] interim report on the brochures containing Collier's longhand transcriptions of his short-hand notes taken at Coleridge's lectures, which would appear to be a better guide to what was said than the text of the published *Seven Lectures*; and in John I. Ades's[8] defence of Lamb's position on the actability of the plays. For those students who distrust commentary on criticism, there have become available three more items in the sumptuously produced Eighteenth Century Shakespeare series: Whately's[9] prophetic remarks on the direction that Shakespeare criticism was to take for close on 150 years, Kemble's[10] far less important, though historically interesting, reply on *Macbeth* and *Richard III*, and the well-received but lightweight counter to Voltaire by Mrs Montagu.[11] Jerome Meckier[12] writes of a more recent (and undervalued) critic in an essay on the spiritual affinities between Shakespeare and Aldous Huxley.

For our own time, several modern critics attempt definitions of where we are going. John R. Brown[13] provides a most useful survey for school teachers of the principal Shakespeare studies in recent years and suggests that there is a general movement away from the location of the plays' 'meanings' and toward a more total 'involvement'; while L. C. Knights[14] reasserts his convictions about the place of literary study in life, by passing informed and experienced comments on methods of teaching the plays to the young. Perhaps most interesting of all for students of the place of Shakespeare in the modern world is the recent *Jahrbuch*

---

[1] 'Shakespeare's Use of Colloquial Language', *ibid.*, pp. 39–48.

[2] 'Meaning and Manner in Shakespeare's Plays', *Manner and Meaning in Shakespeare*, pp. 21–8.

[3] 'Closing Lines of Shakespeare's Plays', *Neuphilologische Mitteilungen*, LXX (1969), 706–14.

[4] 'Words, Action, and Artistic Economy', *Shakespeare Survey 23* (Cambridge University Press, 1970), pp. 49–58.

[5] 'Shakespeare's Poets', *ibid.*, pp. 91–100.

[6] 'Shakespeare's Ghosts', *Critical Quarterly*, XII (1970), 339–51.

[7] 'The Text of Coleridge's 1811–12 Shakespeare Lectures', *Shakespeare Survey 23* (Cambridge University Press, 1970), pp. 101–12.

[8] 'Charles Lamb, Shakespeare, and Early Nineteenth-Century Theater', *Publications of the Modern Language Association of America*, LXXXV (1970), 514–26.

[9] *Remarks on Some of the Characters of Shakespere* (Eighteenth Century Shakespeare No. 17. Frank Cass, 1970).

[10] *Macbeth and King Richard the Third: An Essay, in Answer to Remarks on Some of the Characters of Shakespeare* (No. 19).

[11] *An Essay on the Writings and Genius of Shakespeare* (No. 12).

[12] 'Shakespeare and Aldous Huxley', *Shakespeare Quarterly*, XXII (1971), 111–28.

[13] 'Shakespeare Study Today', *Manner and Meaning in Shakespeare*, pp. 51–64.

[14] 'The Teaching of Shakespeare', *ibid.*, pp. 1–20.

colloquium. The principal contribution is by Armin-Gerd Kuckhoff,[1] who claims that the preservation of the heritage of humanism in the plays is possible only in Marxist and Socialist societies, which have a full understanding of the role of the plebeian classes in the works and hence of the true substance of the characters as a potential for the future. Three other scholars take up points in Kuckhoff's case, with Rolf Rohmer[2] discussing the 'anticipation' in the Mechanicals' scenes in *A Midsummer Night's Dream*, Georg Seehase[3] preferring the optimism of historical continuation to Kott's Absurdist view, and Ursula Wertheim[4] comparing Shakespeare's handling of the common people with that of Schiller and Goethe.

One of the most fascinating articles to appear in the year is Alex Aronson's[5] discussion of how Shakespeare lifted the theme of distorted vision from the personal to universal level. And one of the pleasantest written books is Roland M. Frye's[6] aid to the general reader. In place of the usual play-by-play analysis, it offers means of approaching the works via the techniques of analysis of the types of plays and their special features, structural variations, styles, and characterisation. The opening section on the life and work is about as good an example as one could wish for of detailed knowledge of the essential facts digested and ordered into an easy narrative; and it is readability, clarity, and stimulation that characterise the remainder of the book, which is marred only by the occasional tendency to view Shakespeare as ever 'developing'. One small point on a curious new phase in modern publishing: I perceive that Frye's is another of those books that use quotations and lineation taken from the 'forthcoming Riverside Edition of Shakespeare'. It must be something of a comfort to Blakemore Evans and Houghton Mifflin to see the edition on its way to becoming a standard reference work *before* it has been published.

[1] 'Erbe – Gegenwart – Prognose', *Shakespeare Jahrbuch*, CVI (1970), 29–62.
[2] *Ibid.*, pp. 63–8.   [3] *Ibid.*, pp. 68–72.
[4] *Ibid.*, pp. 72–5.
[5] 'Shakespeare and the Ocular Proof', *Shakespeare Quarterly*, XXI (1970), 411–30.
[6] *Shakespeare: The Art of the Dramatist* (Houghton Mifflin, 1970).

2. SHAKESPEARE'S LIFE, TIMES, AND STAGE

reviewed by NIGEL ALEXANDER

The celebrations which marked the 400th anniversary of the birth of Shakespeare at Stratford first gave Professor Schoenbaum the idea of 'a little book narrating the quest for knowledge of Shakespeare the man; a book describing the different, sometimes opposing ideas of him that people over the centuries had entertained'. The little book which he has now produced runs to over 850 pages.[1] It fulfills his original intention by giving an account, by turns fascinating, alarming and pathetic, of all those who have attempted to discover, or been tempted to invent, facts about the life of William Shakespeare. It exceeds that intention since it is not merely a history of opposed views and a study of the opponents who held them – it is a brilliant piece of modern historical scholarship which will endure as long as the study which it chronicles. No one who sets out to consider the life of Shakespeare can afford to ignore this book since it provides the scholar with the opportunity of reading down to his own starting point.

[1] S. Schoenbaum, *Shakespeare's Lives* (The Clarendon Press, 1970).

Professor Schoenbaum begins his study with a description of the materials which must be used by anyone attempting to construct a biography of Shakespeare. He does more, however, than record their existence. He describes how and when the major documents, the marriage-licence bond, the Belott–Mountjoy deposition, the will, came to be discovered. The time and circumstance of such discovery – together with the ambiguities and matters open to interpretation which are natural in such records – allow him to trace the monstrous birth of extravagant theories and erring speculations which, having achieved the status of myth, still haunt our scholarship. This labour has, of course, been attempted by many of the scholars who are the subject of this book. This meticulous study of the tradition, however, reveals the enduring importance of such men as Edmund Malone, E. K. Chambers and J. S. Smart. The commentary on their work complements their labours.

More entertaining than the history of the slow correction of error is the account of its deliberate manufacture. The strange story of the great forgers, William Henry Ireland and John Payne Collier, serves to remind the critic that 'life is full of improbabilities which fiction does not admit of'. The documents created by their fantasy cannot equal the story of their own triumphal careers and subsequent exposure. The way in which Ireland felt himself obliged to secure his ownership of his own forgeries by inventing a William Henry Ireland who was not only a close associate of Shakespeare's but had also saved the poet's life, so that the dramatist naturally left him all his manuscripts and papers, is a revealing commentary on his obsession.

Wit and judgement have here combined to give us a startling work of social history which is also a scholarly education for anyone who is interested in the life of William Shakespeare. In *Notes and Queries* Professor Schoenbaum

reports on 'Another Collier Forgery',[1] a paper which Collier read to the Society of Antiquaries including references to a letter from 'Richard Cockes' which talks about venison and suggests that there was 'perhaps' a deer-park at Charlecote. Collier is also, in large measure, the subject of R. A. Foakes's introduction to his new edition of the lectures on Shakespeare given by Samuel Taylor Coleridge in 1811–12.[2] Coleridge himself did not publish the lectures and they did not appear until 1856 when John Payne Collier was responsible for the text. They have long been accepted as being the work of Coleridge rather than Collier. Professor Foakes, however, has compared the printed text with Collier's original longhand diary and transcripts of the lectures possessed by the Folger Shakespeare Library. This comparison reveals that Collier 'continually rewrote and added a great deal of material of his own'. The long-hand transcriptions made by Collier are now, therefore, printed for the first time since they 'offer the best text available'. It is clear that anyone who wishes to discuss Coleridge's views on Shakespeare can no longer be satisfied with the edition of 1856 but must compare it with this careful edition of the transcripts.

Forgery is also the subject of Harriet C. Frazier's study of Theobald's *The Double Falsehood*.[3] Here, cogently and convincingly, she argues that Theobald's purported revised version of the lost *Cardenio* is a deliberate forgery. More speculative is Hanspeter Born's treatment of the authorship question in *The Rare Wit and the Rude Groom*[4] which argues

[1] *Notes and Queries*, XVIII (1971), 155–6.
[2] *Coleridge on Shakespeare: The Text of the lectures of 1811–12* (Routledge and Kegan Paul, 1971).
[3] 'Speculation on the motives of a forger: Theobald's *The Double Falsehood*', *Neuphilologische Mitteilungen*, LXXI (1970), 287–96.
[4] *The Rare Wit and the Rude Groom: The Authorship of A Knack to Know a Knave in relation to Greene, Nashe & Shakespeare* (Bern: Francke Verlag, n.d.).

that *A Knack to Know a Knave* was written by Robert Greene with assistance from Nashe and revised by Shakespeare. The notoriously difficult deployment of internal evidence is, perhaps, more convincing in Andrew Gurr's case for 'Shakespeare's first poem: Sonnet 145'.[1] It seems possible that a poem which plays on 'hate' and on throwing 'hate away' was meant to be read by a lady whose surname was Hathaway.

More certain ground for source study is provided by Marco Mincoff. 'The Source of *Titus Andronicus*'[2] considers R. M. Sargent's view that the source is preserved by the chapbook discovered in the Folger library containing a prose history and a ballad of *Titus Andronicus*. Mincoff then demonstrates that there is nothing to show a direct connection between the play and the history, all the points of contact come through the ballad. The ballad, however, is based on the play alone and the 'source' looks more than doubtful.

Shakespeare's Treatment of his Sources in the Comedies[3] is clearly designed by D. C. Biswas for use by his students. It is evident that this account of the sources coupled with an analysis of the plays will be of considerable assistance to them though the occasional omission of major studies such as Robert C. Melzi's 'From Lelia to Viola' (*Renaissance Drama*, IX, 1966) might be rectified in subsequent editions.

Richard Horwich establishes a connection between '*Hamlet* and *Eastward Ho!*'[4] arguing that *Eastward Ho!* both imitates and parodies *Hamlet* and that this is important both for the emotional force and the ironic tone of the play. It is perhaps relevant to note here David George's extremely important survey of 'Thomas Middleton's Sources'[5] since a comparison of the way in which the various dramatists handled their sources is a most instructive exercise for critic and commentator. James O. Wood[6] contributes an interesting piece of information in 'A Touch of Melanchthon in

Shakespeare' pointing out that the awakening of Pericles probably comes from George Paradin's *Heroical Devises* (1591) and that the unacknowledged author of Paradin's story is Philip Melanchthon.

In 'Elizabeth's Entertainment at Elvetham: War Policy in Pagentry'[7] Harry H. Boyle identifies the Earl of Hertford and Lord Admiral Charles Howard as those who co-operated to present the pageant. Thomas Watson and Nicholas Breton were the authors with George Buc a third collaborator and organiser. The pageant itself is allegorically designed to commend Howard's policy to Elizabeth. Royal policy of a rather different kind is studied in John Taylor's discussion of 'Richard II's views on Kingship'[8] since Richard's views on kingship were as vital for his reign as they are for the play.

The emblematic presentation of complex ideas is discussed in 'Two Notes upon Emblems and the English Renaissance Drama' by S. Shuman,[9] which considers the emblem in Henry Peacham's *Minerva Brittana* (1612) of a hand reaching out of a cloud and bouncing a tennis ball on a geometric court. He also argues for the influence of the drama on the emblem books and traces a connection between *Love's Labour's Lost* and Thomas Combe's *The Theatre of Fine Devices* (1614).

An iconography of more physical matters is provided by Gordon Williams in his study of 'An Elizabethan Disease',[10] an examination of references to syphilis in English Renaissance

---

[1] *Essays in Criticism*, XXI (1971), 221–6.
[2] *Notes and Queries*, XVIII (1971), 131–4.
[3] Jadavpur University Press, 1971.
[4] *Studies in English Literature*, XI (1971), 221–33.
[5] David George, 'Thomas Middleton's Sources: A Survey', *Notes and Queries*, XVIII (1971), 17–24.
[6] *Notes and Queries*, XVIII (1971), 150.
[7] *Studies in Philology*, LXVIII (1971), 146–66.
[8] *Proceedings of the Leeds Philosophical and Literary Society*, XIV (1970), 189–205.
[9] *Notes and Queries*, XVIII (1971), 28–9.
[10] *Trivium*, VI (1971), 43–58.

drama. In the popular imagination it appears that gout was not merely a euphemism for pox – its symptoms were frequently connected with the onset of syphilis and references to gout should therefore be considered somewhat curiously by the commentator.

Ideas and Forms in English Literature is a series edited by Professor John Lawlor for Routledge and Kegan Paul. Two new volumes have been published this year which are of great interest to the student of Renaissance drama. *Voices of Melancholy* by Bridget Gellert Lyons[1] is a study which has been eagerly awaited by those familiar with her earlier articles. It does not disappoint expectation. Acknowledging the work of Erwin Panofsky, Fritz Saxl, and Lawrence Babb she concentrates on 'the literary possibilities that melancholy provided, and that made it the basis of great dramatic, lyric and prose works of the period'. Chapters on the expository books and the literary uses of melancholy are therefore followed by a detailed consideration of melancholy in Marston's work, in *Hamlet*, and of the way in which Burton uses it as a method of giving a unified literary structure to *The Anatomy of Melancholy*. This approach proves valuable in dealing with the difficult and disturbing plays of Marston since it permits the plays to be examined with an unusual degree of seriousness. The dramatist is seen as striving to find an appropriate form for the expression of the malcontent's voice or consciousness. It was exactly that appropriate form that Shakespeare discovered in *Hamlet* and the chapter on this play is easily the best and most convincing account of Hamlet's melancholy in existence. The subject is far from exhausted and it is to be hoped that the author will expand her treatment of some matters – such as the use made of melancholy by Webster – at a later date.

Professor Eugene M. Waith has set himself a most difficult and complex task. *Ideas of Greatness*[2] is a study of heroic drama in England up to the time of Dryden and Otway. We must be grateful for the attempt but the subject is too vast for this treatment to be entirely satisfactory. The chapters on the early period properly draw attention to the great influence of chivalric romance but there is hardly space or time to do justice to the importance of *The Arcadia* or *The Faerie Queene* and the necessary effort of condensation commits the author to a narrower view of the 'heroic' than that presented by the plays he examines. If one is grateful for an illuminating account of *Henry V* whose terms are also relevant to *Antony* and *Coriolanus* it is disturbing to have their satiric elements virtually ignored since the satire changes the view of heroism implied by these plays. In similar fashion it might be objected that it is unfair to Dryden to treat him as simply the author of the 'heroic' plays since the 'mock-heroic' masterpieces succeeded in the task which the drama could not then perform – the re-definition of the concept of heroism for a new age. As might be expected, the central section on George Chapman is one of the most rewarding in the book and one can only hope that Professor Waith will one day give us the full study of that dramatist that he is so eminently qualified to write.

Stanley Wells examines the effect of the form on the ideas expressed through it in *Literature and Drama*,[3] a volume in the *Concepts of Literature* series edited by William Righter. Dr Wells advances with steely determination upon the central positions of the great critical and philosophical entanglement which surrounds and defends the purpose of playing. The analogy with music is crucial to his argument: 'Each time a piece of music is played it is, at least slightly, a different piece. The same is true of a

[1] Routledge and Kegan Paul, 1971.
[2] *Ideas of Greatness: Heroic Drama in England* (Routledge & Kegan Paul, 1971).
[3] *Literature and Drama with special reference to Shakespeare and his contemporaries* (Routledge and Kegan Paul, 1970).

play. Each production of it that we see makes it a different play.' The use of 'slightly' shows, I imagine, Dr Wells's awareness of the risk he runs of committing himself to the tautology that every performance is a different performance – whether that performance is 'the play' depends upon the way we choose to use these words. Everyone will not, I imagine, be entirely happy with the formulation contained in this first chapter. The chapter on the printing of plays which follows is a masterly summary of the difficulties and problems which also suggests some ways in which the dramatists might be better served by the printer. The most interesting part of the book is the large number of excellently described examples of stage practice or possibility contained in the last two chapters. The handling of Jonson's masque, *Pleasure Reconciled to Virtue*, or the defence of Marlowe's stagecraft in *The Jew of Malta*, are, in their clarity and analytical power, an example of the proper approach to the difficult problems of literature and drama.

Contemporary arguments about the nature of poetry and drama are studied by Russell Fraser in *The War Against Poetry*.[1] The reaction against poetry and stage plays was 'not simply an English but a European phenomenon'. The opposition appears to be 'Puritan' and to base its arguments on the grounds of religion. It is, however, also a symptom of a remarkable shift in sensibility. 'Modern science enters Oxford in the train of the New Model Army. The immense prestige it wins in the seventeenth century is, however, not contingent on political change but coeval with it. Neither is a cause but an effect.' The impact of new ideas upon a tradition is also the subject of *Tradierte Bauformen und lyrische Struktur* by Volker Deubel[2] which contains an interesting view of the relationship between John Donne and Elizabethan poetry.

Students and historians of the English Renaissance theatre have been particularly for-tunate in recent years as new research is slowly forcing change and development in some well worn ideas and concepts of Elizabethan staging. It is particularly pleasant, therefore, to have a book which provides an accurate and up-to-date summary of the present state of knowledge. Andrew Gurr does not claim to have produced a work of original scholarly research but *The Shakespearean Stage 1574–1642*[3] will be welcomed by students and teachers in schools, colleges and universities. The professional theatre historian may dispute some of the judgements but the book successfully provides the basic information which makes such disputation profitable and instructive to the student. Recent work, however, has already increased our information. T. J. King's *Shakespearean Staging 1599–1642*[4] offers 'a systematic survey of theatrical requirements for 276 plays first performed between the autumn of 1599, when Shakespeare's company probably first acted at the Globe, and 2nd September 1642, when the theatres were closed by order of Parliament'. Professor King begins with a consideration of 'Entrances and Large Properties', a survey of 87 plays which can be acted in any hall or playhouse with minimal equipment. He proceeds to an examination of those plays which require an acting area above the main playing area, those which require doors or a hanging to cover an accessory stage space where 'actors can hide, or where actors, large properties, or both can be "discovered"', and those which require an area below the stage. This survey is then followed by a close study of *Twelfth Night* and some suggestions as to how it might have been staged during Candlemas Feast 1601/2 at the Middle Temple. This demonstrates that the play is well suited for performance in front of an unlocalised screen

[1] Princeton University Press, 1970.
[2] Stuttgart: Kohlhammer, 1971.
[3] Cambridge University Press, 1970.
[4] Harvard University Press, 1971.

with two doorways. This kind of study is essential to our understanding of the staging of the plays and the distinction between plays printed from prompt-copies and other texts deserves the closest possible attention. The book provides essential material for a great advance in our knowledge and appreciation of the theatre.

The difference that a consideration of theatrical conditions may make to our critical understanding is excellently demonstrated in the second volume of papers given at the International Conference on Elizabethan Theatre at Waterloo.[1] *The Elizabethan Theatre II* contains a number of important papers but perhaps R. A. Foakes's paper on 'Tragedy at the Children's Theatres after 1600: A Challenge to the Adult Stage' has the most far-reaching critical implications. His thesis is that 'the revival of the children's theatres in 1599/1600 soon made a great impact on the London theatre as a whole, and challenged the adult stages strongly enough to force them to take over and use in their own way styles and techniques of drama first exploited in the plays put on by the boys; that in order to maintain their challenge to the older and more solidly established adult theatres, the children and their dramatists were driven, especially at first, to bold experiment; and that, during the decade following their revival, the children's theatres and the dramatists who wrote for them formed a major influence in determining the course English drama was to take'. The great strength of this thesis is the necessary revaluation of the work of John Marston and his influence on his fellow dramatists. It makes sense of a number of awkward and hitherto irreconcilable facts and ought to influence in significant fashion the course of English Renaissance studies. D. F. Rowan, in 'A Neglected Jones/Webb Theatre Project, Part II' continues his examination of the theatre drawings found in Worcester College, Oxford and previously reported on in

New Theatre Magazine, IX (1969), 6–15 and, more briefly, in *Shakespeare Survey 23*, 1970. It is evident that these drawings are documents of the highest importance and their interpretation, however difficult, is a matter of vital concern to all scholars. 'Shakespeare and Jonson: Fact and Myth' is an urbane consideration by S. Schoenbaum of the relationships between the two dramatists which disposes of a great deal of nonsense in short space and invites us to consider 'two excellent playwrights who sometimes laboured for the same company, and who took a lively interest in one another's work'. Trevor Lennam studies 'The Children of Paul's, 1551–1582', J. A. Lavin questions the entire basis of some current approaches to the study of theatre history, Lise-Lone Marker examines 'Nature and Decorum in the Theory of Elizabethan Acting', and Bernard Beckerman discusses 'A Shakespeare Experiment: The Dramaturgy of *Measure for Measure*'. There is also an important discussion of D. F. McKenzie's bibliographical views by Peter Davison. There are few academic conferences whose proceedings make so distinguished and scholarly a volume.

D. F. McKenzie contributes an interesting account of the building erected as a playhouse by Queens' College, Cambridge, in 'A Cambridge Playhouse of 1638'.[2] Two unusual studies of Elizabethan Inn Playhouses appear in *Shakespeare Quarterly*[3] and *Theatre Notebook*[4] by O. L. Brownstein. He has used the *Register of the Masters of Defence* (Sloane MS. 2530) to identify inn playhouses since it records the places used by the fencers for their prize

[1] David Galloway (ed.), *The Elizabethan Theatre II* (Macmillan, 1970).
[2] *Renaissance Drama*, New Series III (1970), 263–72.
[3] O. L. Brownstein, 'A Record of London Inn-Playhouses 1565–1580' *Shakespeare Quarterly*, XXII (1971), 17–24.
[4] 'The Saracen's Head Islington: A Pre-Elizabethan Inn Playhouse', *Theatre Notebook*, XXV (1971), 68–72

and exhibition bouts. On this evidence he argues that the origin of the inn playhouses must be put back a decade or more. Another earlier date is suggested by Michael Shapiro in '*Le Prince D'Amour* and the resumption of Playing at Paul's'[1]. He uses evidence from the Middle Temple Entertainment at Christmas 1597/8 to suggest that Paul's was open again by the winter of 1597.

A fascinating account of an earlier kind of theatre, the game place at Walsham le Willows in Suffolk, is given by Kenneth M. Dodd in 'Another Elizabethan Theatre in the Round'.[2]

The structure of the plays rather than the playhouses is Richard Levin's subject in *The Multiple Plot in the English Renaissance Drama*.[3] As a structural study the book is an attempt to provide as searching an examination of Elizabethan multiple plot plays as Bertrand Evans produced in *Shakespeare's Comedies*. It is a notable attempt which contains many individual analyses of great interest, particularly in the matter of clown sub-plots, though its final effect (perhaps by the very nature of its subject) is suggestive rather than definitive.

Theatre history has been well served by two important volumes. Daniel J. Watermeier has edited the letters exchanged between Edwin Booth and William Winter[4] which illuminate theatrical conditions in the nineteenth century as well as Booth's own approach to Shakespeare. Changing concepts of dramatic character is the central subject of *Dramatic Character in the English Romantic Age*[5] by Joseph W. Donohue Jr. It 'seeks a correlation between the characteristic style of an individual actor and those tendencies connected with it which serve to identify the significance his acting held for his age'.

The Third Folio of *Henry IV* which Halliwell–Phillipps cut up and pasted into his scrapbooks, which are now in the Shakespeare Memorial Library at Stratford, has been identified by Gunnar Sorelius as the missing Smock Alley Prompt Books of *1* and *2 Henry IV*.[6] Hilton Kelliher notes a performance of *The Merry Wives of Windsor* before the nominal Elector Palatine in 1639.[7]

Paul Sawyer considers 'The Popularity of Shakespeare's Plays at Lincoln's Inn Fields Theatre 1714–1717'[8] and concludes that they were not as popular as the work of other dramatists. Irene Dash[9] draws attention to the fact that the prompt-copy of Garrick's *Florizel and Perdita* in the Folger library contains two songs which are nowhere attributed to Garrick and which might be considered the work of Colman. In 'Garrick, Colman and *King Lear*: A Reconsideration'[10] A. J. Harris argues that George Colman's work of 1768 precedes any restoration by Garrick of Shakespeare's text to the stage. He should, therefore, be considered partly responsible for this significant shift in theatrical practice. David Roston examines another landmark in performance in 'F. R. Benson's Early Productions of Shakespeare's Roman Plays at Stratford'.[11]

Literary English Since Shakespeare,[12] edited by George Watson, contains a number of essays on the literary use of English since the sixteenth century. It is extremely useful to have such essential articles as A. C. Bradley, 'Monosyllabic Lines and Words'; Otto Jespersen,

[1] *Notes and Queries*, XVIII (1971), 14–16.
[2] *Shakespeare Quarterly*, XXI (1970), 125–56.
[3] Chicago University Press, 1971.
[4] *Between Actor and Critic: Selected Letters of Edwin Booth and William Winter* (Princeton University Press, 1971).
[5] Princeton University Press, 1970.
[6] 'The Smock Alley Prompt Books of *1* and *2 Henry IV*', *Shakespeare Quarterly*, XXII (1971), 111–27.
[7] 'The *Merry Wives* in 1639', *Notes and Queries*, XVIII (1971), 141–2.
[8] *Notes and Queries*, XVIII (1971), 151–2.
[9] 'Garrick or Colman?', *Notes and Queries*, XVIII (1971), 152–5.
[10] *Shakespeare Quarterly*, XXII (1971), 57–66.
[11] *Theatre Notebook*, XXV (1971), 46–54.
[12] Oxford University Press, 1970.

'Shakespeare and the Language of Poetry'; Morris W. Croll, 'The Baroque Style in Prose' in one volumes as well as the more recent contributions by George Watson on the Metaphysicals and Jonas A. Barish on Jonson's prose style.

English Renaissance Studies in German 1945–67 by Hans Walter Gabler[1] is a checklist of German, Austrian and Swiss academic theses, monographs, and book publications on English language and literature c. 1500–1650 which has been supplied with English title versions and an index in English. This is an invaluable reference work for the student of Shakespeare – more specialised bibliographies of this kind would make the scholar's perpetual pursuit of information an easier task than it is at present.

[1] Heidelberg: Quelle and Meyer, 1971.

© NIGEL ALEXANDER 1972

3. TEXTUAL STUDIES

reviewed by RICHARD PROUDFOOT

On the upper slopes of Shakespearian textual studies, where the air is thin and advances are measured in proudly gained inches, Professor Kristian Smidt and Professor J. K. Walton are already familiar figures. Both have returned this year to the scene of previous struggles, the question of the copy for the Folio *Richard III*.[1] As before, they propose different solutions, although Smidt's support for the sixth Quarto, 1622, as providing the printed basis for the F text is attended with more qualifications than he once admitted, while Walton's championship of the third Quarto, 1602, has become, if anything, more absolute, so that he now speaks of its use as copy for F not as hypothetical but as an established fact.

Their two books are of very different scope and character. Smidt's short monograph restates and reassesses the evidence bearing on the nature of the Q text of *Richard III* and on the identification of the particular Quarto used as copy for F. Walton's aim is more ambitious: by examining the whole body of Folio plays printed from Quarto copy, whether or not the Quartos were annotated, he sets out to create a new context for the discussion of those few plays in F about which no consensus of opinion yet exists as to whether they were printed from Q copy or from independent manuscripts, or as to the identity of the particular Quarto edition used for copy.

The first section of Smidt's book qualifies his earlier attack[2] on the view (orthodox since D. L. Patrick published *The Textual History of 'Richard III'* in 1936) that the deficiencies of the Q text are to be attributed to a memorial stage in its transmission. The effect of Patrick's theory was to increase editorial confidence in F: the reopening of the question of Q involves the opinion that its variants from F are often of sufficient merit to prompt attempts to show that they could emanate from the pen of Shakespeare himself rather than that of a reporting actor. Where Smidt was once prepared to reject outright the hypothesis of memorial transmission of Q, he is now persuaded that 'Q is to some extent a reported text suffering from memorial corruption'. He is also convinced, however, that Q agrees with F in a number of peculiarities which argue that 'to some extent and in some way the text of Q1 has come down

[1] K. Smidt, *Memorial Transmission and Quarto Copy in 'Richard III': A Reassessment* (Oslo; New York, 1970); J. K. Walton, *The Quarto Copy for the First Folio of Shakespeare* (Dublin, 1971).

[2] In *Iniurious Impostors and 'Richard III'* (Norwegian University Press, 1964).

by unbroken written transmission'. In an attempt to reconcile these apparently incompatible positions he postulates the compilation of a memorial text by a company touring in the provinces (which is a familiar position) and then goes on to posit revision of this report by 'collation with a sound manuscript' by 'someone in the company' who then sold it to Andrew Wise for publication. The weak link in this argument is the nature of the evidence cited on pages 28–37 as suggesting a manuscript link in transmission between Q1 and F, not only because many of the details are in themselves trivial or dubious, but because other explanations can be offered for their presence in both texts. Q1 could perhaps, as A. S. Cairncross proposed,[1] have been used to supply some leaves in composite printed copy for F, or the collator of Q3 or Q6 with the manuscript used to clean up the text for F could have referred to a copy of Q1 in case of doubt. None of these suggestions can carry much conviction, but they may serve as a caution against each other and as a reminder that the total body of Q1/F agreement is so small as to be within the bounds of coincidence.

In his treatment of the vexed question of the copy for F, Smidt is again aware of apparent contradictions in the evidence and is led by them to elaborate his earlier hypothesis of manuscript copy transcribed from authorial fair copy but checked against the Quartos in the process of transcription. This suggestion has about it an air of cutting the Gordian knot, as well as of wilfully disregarding good evidence, cited in earlier chapters, for a direct bibliographical link between F and the Quartos. It is hard to believe in a scribe who had Shakespeare's fair copy in front of him and who still went out of his way to incorporate in his transcript not only Q3's erroneous repetition of *as* at III, i, 123, but also the thirteen or so common errors usually cited as evidence for the derivation of F from Q6. If his conclusions carry little con-

viction, it is because Smidt has faced up to what he finds truly puzzling in *Richard III*, and because he has come to feel dissatisfaction with his own position in *Iniurious Impostors and 'Richard III'*. Although his intention may have been to lend support to the new optimism about the Q text of *Richard III*,[2] Smidt's new study, if anything, restores confidence in the orthodox hypotheses of memorial transmission for Q and of annotated Q copy for F.

Unlike Smidt, Walton is not often inclined to reassess his own earlier positions, and readers of his past contributions to the controversies to which he now returns will find many familiar positions defended with familiar evidence and unflagging conviction. The four sections of his book deal in turn with the general textual problem in Shakespeare; the identity of the Quarto used as copy for the Folio text of *Richard III*, *King Lear* and *Richard II*; the nature of the copy for other Folio plays, in particular *2 Henry IV*, *Hamlet* and *Othello*; and finally the extent and reliability of the collation of all corrected Quartos used as copy for the Folio. In general, Walton is concerned to detect the errors of logic of other Shakespearian textual scholars: in particular, he wishes to establish that the copy for F *2 Henry IV*, *Hamlet* and *Othello* was manuscript rather than annotated Quarto, and that F *Richard III* was set exclusively from a copy of Q3 annotated throughout, though with strangely variable efficiency, by a single collator.

The opening section of the book sets out to cleanse the editing of Shakespeare from the obscuring film of bibliographical expertise, by arguing that the transmission of texts can only be established on the basis of a qualitative analysis of the introduction of errors. In Walton's view, much that has been offered as

[1] 'The Quartos and the Folio Text of *Richard III*', *Review of English Studies*, n.s., VIII (1957), 225–33.

[2] See E. A. J. Honigmann, 'The Text of *Richard III*', *Theatre Research*, VII (1965), 48–55.

bibliographical evidence for the descent of editions is neither bibliographical nor evidential, because 'we cannot study the history of a text as we would, say, the history of a fossil. A literary document, considered as a material object, is not transmitted: its readings are transmitted. In other words, the physical aspect of the relationship of texts is not of the essence of their relationship when we are thinking in terms of the descent of one from another' (p. 28). Turning to the broader field of the development of textual criticism since Lachmann, he draws particular attention to the problem of contaminated textual transmission, whose effect of confusing any attempt at genealogical reconstruction of the history of a text he holds to have been largely ignored or misunderstood by editors of Shakespeare. Three questions which have been affected by this misunderstanding are 'which derivative quarto of an ancestral series served as copy for a F text when we can be sure that quarto copy must have been used', 'whether certain F texts were printed from a corrected quarto or from a manuscript' and 'how efficient was the collation of the quarto copy for those F texts which represent a contaminated tradition – that is, which were set from quarto copy altered with reference to a manuscript'. He proposes that the analysis of substantive errors provides the only valid evidence for the solution of these problems: the rest of his book is devoted to such analysis and to commentary on it.

Part two is the hardest section to follow, largely because the question at the middle of it is the vexed one of Q copy for F *Richard III*, on which Walton's views have provoked much controversy, recapitulated here. It centres on a statistical demonstration, based on the introduction of indifferent variants into Quartos of eleven plays printed after the Folio, that it is possible to discount the common variants linking Q6 and F *Richard III* as coincidental, thereby destroying the case for Q6 copy for the F text. The argument depends upon the coincidence in F and in Quartos which could not possibly have been used as copy for it of 'indifferent' variants and on the ratio of these variants to (*a*) the total number of 'indifferent variants' introduced into each Quarto; and (*b*) the total number of such variations between the Quarto and Folio texts of the play in question. These ratios (listed on pages 121–2) are presented as evidence that Q6 *Richard III*, Q5 *Richard II* and Q2 *King Lear* were not used as copy for F. This demonstration is impressively presented, but it depends on a distinction between 'indifferent' variants and definite errors which is often harder to maintain in particular instances than Walton will allow. Four readings from *Richard III* may make the point. In Walton's opinion, Q3 and F are linked by twenty-two readings, among them the 'definite errors' '*as as* you call me', III, i, 123, and 'But in your daughters wombe, *I burie* them', IV, iv, 423. When we turn to Q6, however, the coincidences with F at III, v, 66, *ease* Q6, *case* F (*cause* Q1–5) and at IV, iv, 564, *newes* (*tidings* Q1–5), can be dismissed as 'indifferent' variants. Fredson Bowers has given good reasons,[1] to which Walton does not here refer, why these Q6/F readings should be regarded as common definite errors rather than as indifferent variants. Walton's readiness elsewhere to use other scholars' assessments of which variants are erroneous and which merely indifferent makes his failure to do so here, where his conclusion is at stake, doubly damaging to his own argument. The satisfactory explanation of these two Q6/F agreements might be required as a necessary criterion for any account of the copy for F *Richard III* to win acceptance. In fact, despite Walton's repeated assertion that the use of annotated Q3 only as copy for F is an established fact, the view that F *Richard III* is in some way derivative from Q6 continues to be held by such

[1] *Shakespeare Quarterly*, X (1959), 541–4.

experienced students of Shakespeare's text as G. Blakemore Evans.[1]

Walton turns next to the Folio plays where scholarly opinion has differed about the nature of the copy, some arguing for annotated Quarto, others for manuscript. It is here that most is at stake for editors, whose assessment both of common and of variant Q/F readings will be largely influenced by their theory of transmission. Walton takes issue with Alice Walker's position[2] about F *2 Henry IV*, *Hamlet* and *Othello*, all of which, in her opinion, were printed from annotated Quarto copy. Walton follows M. A. Shaaber[3] and Harold Jenkins[4] in preferring manuscript copy for *2 Henry IV* and *Hamlet* respectively: to them he would also add *Othello*. He finds it incongruous that Miss Walker could argue for annotated Q copy for these plays, while failing to find in the F texts distinctive evidence, in the shape of error, of their derivation either from the Quartos in question or from manuscript alterations of them, since 'we have to assume ... that by chance not one but two distinctive stages in transmission left no sign of their existence in the respective F texts, despite the fact that they were the stages immediately preceding F itself' (pp. 132–3). In the absence of such evidence, Miss Walker turned to errors and anomalies in accidentals common to a Quarto and Folio text as evidence of derivation. This evidence is dismissed as merely quantitative by Walton, who proposes that qualitative analysis of substantive errors common to the Q and F texts of these plays indicates that 'if one of them is not in any way the ancestor of the other, [the errors] are such as might have had their source in the original or to which the original might have given rise' (p. 139). On the evidence of H and D in *Sir Thomas More*, the likely types of error in those originals are tabulated and a much higher incidence of error is postulated in the Shakespearian originals of *2 Henry IV*, *Hamlet* and *Othello* 'than the

number of errors common to the respective quarto and Folio texts'. Walton then sets out to demonstrate that of the graphic and non-graphic errors in the quartos, F preserves more of the graphic errors, those that can be traced to a manuscript original, than of others that can be assigned to different agencies, and that, furthermore, the proportion of graphic to non-graphic error in F 'is very close to the proportion of graphic to non-graphic error in *More* D, while it differs greatly from the proportion... in the respective quarto texts' (p. 140). A control is provided by F texts known on other evidence to have been printed from Q copy, *Richard III*, *King Lear* and *Troilus and Cressida*, where the proportion of graphic to non-graphic error in F resembles that in Q. This demonstration seems impressive, but the evidence it is based on again raises doubts. The evidence from the control group of plays includes not only common Q/F errors but F errors attributable to failed attempts to print corrections to Q (a category of error said not to exist in F *2 Henry IV*, *Hamlet* and *Othello*). This makes the comparative ratios of different types of error less compelling, as it reduces the comparability of the figures for the two groups of plays. Apart from the circularity of argument involved in this procedure, the identification and classification of errors inevitably leaves room for difference of opinion. For instance, *Lear*, I, ii, 22–3, is treated as if *to'th'* F (*tooth* Q) were certainly a substantive error, without reference to the suggestion of E. A. J. Honigmann that the error is of punctuation only, that *to* means

[1] In *A New Companion to Shakespeare Studies*, ed. K. Muir and S. Schoenbaum (Cambridge University Press, 1971), pp. 231–2.

[2] In *Textual Problems of the First Folio* (Cambridge University Press, 1953).

[3] *2 Henry IV*, New Variorum (Philadelphia, 1940), pp. 507–15.

[4] 'The Relation between the Second Quarto and Folio Text of *Hamlet*', *Studies in Bibliography*, VII (1955), 69–83.

too and that it should be followed by a period.[1]
At *Troilus*, III, iii, 178, *goe* for *giue* is treated as
non-graphic although it could easily have
arisen from a minim error inducing the misreading of *u* as open-topped *o*. Where the total
amount of evidence is so small such reservations
are important.

Walton adds two telling points to his argument for manuscript copy for F *Othello*. Miss
Walker's clinching argument for Q copy
depended on the distribution of preterite
endings in *–t*, and in *–d*, *'d* or *–ed*, in the two
texts. Positing a Shakespearian original with a
high incidence of old-fashioned *–t* endings, she
presented the fact that such endings are less
frequent in F than in Q, but occur only where
Q also has them, as evidence for progressive
modernisation through Q and its derivative, F.
Walton points out that no evidence exists for
any modernisation in Q and that consequently
the facts are equally consistent with the assumption of transmission in manuscript, Q preserv-
ing Shakespeare's own distribution of *t* and *d*
forms at a date later than *More*, while F reflects
the modernising tendency of Jaggard's compositors A and B. Here he may well be right,
unless it can be shown that Okes's compositors
also habitually modernised *–t* endings, and if
he is, what Greg accepted as the crucial evidence for Q copy for F *Othello* is deprived of its
force. His second point concerns the most
remarkable press variant in F *Othello*, the mis-
placing of a line at the head of vv3a. The misplaced line was set at the head of this new page
by B immediately after he had finished setting
either vv4ᵛb or vv4b. Oddly, the misplaced
line, 'and hell gnaw his bones', could be read
as following on at either of these points in the
text: vv4ᵛb ends with Othello's words 'Thy
Husband knew it all' and the catchword is
'*Æmil.*'; vv4b ends with Desdemona's 'Then
Heauen haue mercy on mee'. Such a misreading could most easily have occurred if the
line stood at the head of a new leaf of copy, but

in Q it falls eight lines from the top of a page.
Had B glanced at the wrong leaf of manuscript
copy among several laid out before him to
make the marking of cast-off clearly apparent,
he could have made the error quite inadver-
tently, altering the punctuation after *bones* to a
comma to make it run into the (correctly set)
next line. The misplaced line is printed fifty
lines before its correct place in the text, which
may again recommend the view that it stood
at the head of a page of manuscript (*More* D
averages forty-nine lines per page).

In his earlier publications, Walton has
attempted to explain the two extended passages
in F *Richard III* which reprint Q3 with very
little alteration as originating in the variable
efficiency of the collator of the copy of Q3
with the manuscript used to correct it for the
printing of F. Reviewers pointed out that his
explanation assumed knowledge of the behaviour of collators beyond the evidence
presented.[2] Section four presents the full
evidence for the efficiency of the collators of
Quartos used as F copy. *Richard II*, where the
evidence is clear, provides a control for the
analysis of the much more complex cases of
Richard III and *King Lear*. In *Richard II*, as in
Troilus, the collator's efficiency diminished,
after a strong start, throughout acts II to IV, to
increase again in act v. The same pattern is not
repeated in *Richard III* and *Lear*, but both
show equally marked variation. Though the
collator's efficiency lapsed in acts III and IV of
Lear, he seems to have continued to make a
special effort to correct Lear's own speeches in
those acts. *Richard III* is different: minor
variations in efficiency throughout the play are
indeed such as are found elsewhere, but from
III, i, 1 to 166 and from v, iii, 48 to the end of the
play correction is light and sporadic and usually

---

[1] *The Stability of Shakespeare's Text* (Arnold,
1965), pp. 164–5.
[2] E.g., I. B. Cauthen, *Journal of English and Germanic Philology*, LV (1956), 505.

involves stage directions and lines adjacent to them (a practice paralleled in *Richard II* and elsewhere). Walton's conjectures about the collator's temptation to shirk bits of his toughest job – this was the longest play collated and the one which required the heaviest correction – could perhaps account for his neglect of the end of the play, but hardly for the passage in act III. The problem is not why he should have stopped taking pains at the end of act II but why he should have started again in the middle of a scene. One possibility, not raised by Walton, is that he was working to time and had roughly divided the play into two sections (perhaps corresponding to two working days) the first shorter than the second to let him run in. The passage in act III could then be seen as falling at the end of his first stint (the second beginning with F2ᵛ) and as having shared the fate of the end of the play because of the pressure of time at the end of the first day's work. But such conjectures are less convincing and less important than the strong case constructed on clear evidence for the variable performance of the collator or collators of Quartos used as copy for F: here Walton has answered his critics.

The question of the lost copy for printed editions is bound to remain among the disputed and conjectural areas of Shakespearian textual studies. Walton's strength is his refusal to take orthodox hypotheses on trust if he finds them logically dissatisfying. He is also aware of some pitfalls in textual studies: there is still room for his insistence on the need to distinguish bibliographical fact from bibliographical fantasy. Unfortunately, his desire to maintain simple and firm conclusions leads him into a repetitive and rhetorical assertiveness which often weakens his case and he is too ready to engage in polemic and the reiterate destructive criticism of scholars, from P. A. Daniel to Bowers and Miss Walker, whose work, however mistaken he may find its methods or conclusions, has laid some of the foundations for his own.

The New Arden Shakespeare takes one more step towards completion with the appearance of *The Merry Wives of Windsor*, edited by H. J. Oliver, who has already contributed *Timon of Athens* to the series.[1] His text relies, as it must, on the Folio and he is less ready than most editors to admit readings from the reported Quarto text of 1602. He prefers *Herne* F to *Horne* Q as the name of the ghostly hunter of Windsor Forest, and he resists the wholesale introduction of oaths from Q, on the grounds that, even if their exclusion from F resulted from the Act of Abuses of 1606, the Q report is unlikely to be accurate in its record either of their occurrence or of their wording. This principle is pushed too far when F *Heaven* is accepted in place of Q *God* at II, ii, 297 and particularly at III, iv, 57, where the repetition of *heaven* in the following line reinforces the view that F *Heaven* is designed to tone down the Q expression. Elsewhere, the exclusion of two Q phrases traditionally accepted by editors is perhaps questionable: Nym's 'and there's the humour of it' at II, i, 133, may be, as Oliver argues, a memorial contamination of Q derived from *Henry V* and if so it should be removed from edited texts, but the plotting against Falstaff in IV, iv, is rendered almost unintelligible to no discernible end by the rejection of Theobald's line, derived from Q, 'Disguis'd like *Herne*, with huge Horns on his Head'. Conservatism extends to the rejection of more of Theobald's suggestions, *lunes* at IV, ii, 15, *tire* at IV, iv, 72 and *Quickly* at IV, iv, 82 among them, of which only the last need be regretted. The mispronunciations of Evans and Caius are indicated by orthography only where F gives warrant, which may be truer to Shakespeare's intention than the systematic frittering introduced by other recent editors of the play.[2] At I, iv, 41, *une boitine verde* is probably the best of

[1] Methuen, 1971.
[2] E.g., F. T. Bowers in *The Complete Pelican Shakespeare* (Baltimore, 1969).

the existing suggestions for F's *vnboyteene verd;*: oddly, *une boite, une verde* seems not to have been proposed, although the next words spoken by Caius, *a Box, a greene-a-box*, would then be explained as a literal translation for the benefit of Mrs Quickly.

The introduction devotes much space to the nature and relation of the Q and F texts and to the questions of the date and occasion of composition. Oliver shares Greg's view of Q as a reported text and conjectures that the reporters may have included the actors of Pistol and Nym as well as the Host, 'since there are conflations of their parts in *The Merry Wives* with their parts in *2 Henry IV* and *Henry V*'. He accepts Leslie Hotson's date of April 1597 for the composition of the play but differs from most earlier supporters of this dating by arguing that *The Merry Wives* was written 'at the same time as' *2 Henry IV*, rather than after it. Some slight confusion is apparent at this point in his argument, as he then proposes that the composition of *2 Henry IV* was completed only late in 1598, although both M. A. Shaaber and A. R. Humphreys in their editions of that play have been ready to accept a date before April 1597. One troublesome result of arguing for the priority of *The Merry Wives* is that it becomes necessary to see Shallow and Pistol in that play as the first appearances of those characters, although they are so much more fully integrated into the structure of *2 Henry IV* as to make it almost incredible that they were not invented for it in the first instance. Less difficulty attaches to the appearance of Nym, although the use of the title 'corporal' in *The Merry Wives* was until recently held to indicate that he too was already a familiar figure to the audience, which implied dating the comedy after *Henry V*, that is, late in 1599.

The brief critical introduction wisely avoids an inflated estimate of a modest play, referring to stage history for evidence of its success, but is content to discuss characters and imagery in isolation from any consideration of the structure or overall effect of the play. Oliver begs one major critical question when he speaks of Falstaff's 'incomparable idiom': the half-dozen brief quotations with which he supports this opinion almost exhaust the material available in defence of the language of Falstaff in *The Merry Wives* against Hazlitt's criticism that his 'wit and eloquence have left him'. Once more the dating of the comedy before *2 Henry IV* seems open to question.

Further discussion of the concording of Shakespeare may wait until the completion of the Oxford Concordances in 1972: eighteen new volumes published in 1970–1 complete the comedies and histories and include the first five tragedies.[1] Meanwhile the remaining four volumes of M. Spevack's modern-spelling concordance have been published, volume VI announcing a further projected volume to contain stage directions and substantive variants rejected by the edited basic text, which has not yet reached publication itself.[2] An elaborate concordance to Hand D's addition to *Sir Thomas More* has been prepared by T. Clayton,[3] unfortunately without a fresh examination of the manuscript itself, which is described as though it were still bound as a volume and as if folio 9b, which has the speech prefix *all* repeated near the top, were blank (as editors have wrongly stated or implied). The

[1] T. H. Howard-Hill (ed.), The Oxford Shakespeare Concordances: *Love's Labour's Lost, Much Ado about Nothing, A Midsummer Night's Dream, King John, Henry VI*, parts 1 and 2 (Oxford University Press, 1970): *Henry VI*, part 3, *Henry IV*, parts 1 and 2, *Henry V, Henry VIII, Richard II, Richard III, Othello, King Lear, Macbeth, Timon of Athens, Julius Caesar* (Oxford University Press, 1971).

[2] M. Spevack (ed.), *A Complete and Systematic Concordance to the Works of Shakespeare*: III, *Tragedies*; IV–VI, *Complete Works* (Hildesheim, 1968–70).

[3] T. Clayton, *The 'Shakespearean' Addition in the Booke of Sir Thomas Moore: Some Aids to Scholarly and Critical Shakespearean Studies*. Shakespeare Studies Monograph Series, ed. J. Leeds Barroll, 1 (Dubuque, Iowa, 1969).

textual apparatus of this concordance also attributes too much textual authority to reprints of the addition which are dependent on earlier reprints rather than representing new work on the original, which wastes space and makes the textual situation look more complex than it is.

T. H. Howard-Hill's *Shakespearean Bibliography and Textual Criticism: A Bibliography*, would be more accurately entitled *Shakespearean Bibliographies and Textual Criticism*.[1] It supplements existing bibliographies and will be of especial value to editors who wish to trace publications relating to the texts of individual works, but its exclusions, which incongruously extend to separate editions of the plays, must reduce its general usefulness as much of the most significant recent work is to be found precisely in the introductions to such editions. Other problems are posed by its method and arrangement. The reader must refer to the compiler's *Bibliography of English Literary Bibliographies*[2] for a clear indication of the earlier date limit of 1890 and must wait for the publication of a third volume for all 'works which discuss Shakespeare's printers and publishers' unless they deal with 'the printing and publication of particular Shakespearean works'. It is hard to see on what principle P. Alexander's *Studies in Shakespeare* (1964), which is a collection of British Academy Shakespeare Lectures, and the *Collected Papers* of Sir Walter Greg are listed under *General Bibliographies*.

Giles E. Dawson adds to understanding of the forgeries of J. P. Collier with a palaeographic study of the handwriting of his annotations in the 'Perkins' Folio.[3] The acquisition, by the Princeton University Library, of eleven Shakespeare Quartos, including the first Quarto of *Love's Labour's Lost*, 1598, is recorded by G. E. Bentley.[4] The correct placing of four lines in *Romeo and Juliet* which are duplicated in Q2, at the end of II, ii and at the beginning of II, iii, is considered by Barry J. Gaines,[5] who argues that the lines belong to Friar Lawrence and to II, iii, but that the misplaced version in Romeo's speech at the end of II, ii represents Shakespeare's revision of them 'ambiguously placed in the foul papers in such a manner that it appeared to the compositor to be part of Romeo's speech'. Halliwell-Phillipps is cleared of having regarded the Quarto text of *The Merry Wives* as representing an early draft of the play by Jeanne Addison Roberts,[6] who points out that both Greg and W. Bracy failed to notice his change of view in his 1854 introduction to the play, where he speaks of it as rather 'an unfair and fragmentary copy of the perfect drama'; she also corrects Greg on the subject of errors in Q likely to have arisen from mishearing. Two passages in *Lear* are the subject of notes. At I, i, 74, a conflation of Q and F, to read 'That the most precious sphere of sense professes' is proposed by S. C. V. Stetner and O. B. Goodman, with arguments urging the thematic relevance of 'sphere' and 'professes'.[7] John C. Meagher has a new solution for the crux at I, iv, 106, where he would emend Q to read 'Ladie oth' th' brach', a reading which 'by balancing *Oath* against *Truth*, fulfills the rhetorical antithesis obviously intended in the Fool's line'.[8] Michael J. Warren defends the Quarto at *Pericles*, II, Chorus, 19, proposing that *for though* 'represents a form of Gower's "forthi" in the sense of "accordingly"'.[9]

[1] Oxford University Press, 1971.
[2] Oxford University Press, 1969.
[3] *Studies in Bibliography*, XXIV (1971), 1–26.
[4] *Princeton University Library Chronicle*, XXX (1969), 69–76.
[5] *Shakespeare Quarterly*, XXI (1970), 196–8.
[6] *Notes and Queries*, XVIII (1971), 139–41.
[7] *English Studies*, 51 (1970), 331–6.
[8] *English Language Notes*, VI (1969), 251–2.
[9] *Shakespeare Quarterly*, XXII (1971), 90–2.

© RICHARD PROUDFOOT 1972

INDEX

INDEX

INDEX

INDEX